DISCOVERING
SYDNEY
AND SURROUNDS

200 kilometres around Sydney

38th EDITION 2005

Gregory's Discovering Sydney and Surrounds
Published in Australia by Gregory's Publishing Company
(A division of Universal Publishers Pty Ltd)
ABN 83 000 087132

Marketed and distributed by:
Universal Publishers Pty Ltd
New South Wales: 1 Waterloo Road, Macquarie Park 2113
Ph: (02) 9857 3700 Fax: (02) 9888 9850
Queensland: 1 Manning Street, South Brisbane 4101
Ph: (07) 3844 1051 Fax: (07) 3844 4637
South Australia: Freecall: 1800 021 987

Victoria: 585 Burwood Road, Hawthorn 3122
Ph: (03) 9818 4455 Fax: (03) 9818 6123
Western Australia: 38a Walters Drive,
Osborne Park 6017
Ph: (08) 9244 2488 Fax: (08) 9244 2554
International distribution
Ph: +61 2 9857 3700 Fax: +61 2 9888 9850

The Publisher would be pleased to receive additional or updated material, or suggestions for future editions. Please address these to the Publishing Manager at Universal Publishers Pty Ltd.
If you would like to use any of the maps in this book please contact the CMS Manager at Universal Publishers Pty Ltd.

First published as *100 Miles 'round Sydney* in 1934
36th edition published as *200 kilometres around Sydney* in 1996
38th edition *Discovering Sydney and Surrounds* published 2005

ISSN 1832-1046
ISBN 0 7319 1777 4
Gregory's Discovering Sydney and Surrounds

Cartography, research and writing, photographic research, project management and editing by:
the staff of **Universal Publishers Pty Ltd**

Printed by: Sirivatana Interprint Public Co., Ltd.

Cover photographs: Tourism New South Wales except front cover top centre (Hunter Valley Gardens) and back cover top right (Lithgow Visitor Centre)

PlanBookTravel (http://www.planbooktravel.com) contributed the following to this edition: project management, research and writing, photographic research, copy editing, cartography and indexing, cover design and internal design and DTP.

Contents

Rawdon Vale
Barrington
Gloucester
Burrell Creek
Purfleet
Old Bar
HWY
Krambach
Hallidays Point
Stratford
Waukivory
Nabiac
1
Chichester
Craven
Bunyah
Tuncurry
Forster
Cape Hawke
Salisbury
Coolongolook
Wallis Lake
Stroud Road
Wootton
Allynbrook
Markwell
Charlotte Head
Gresford
East Gresford
Dungog
Stroud
Bulahdelah
Bungwahl
Booral
Seal Rocks
Myall Lakes
Clarence Town
Paterson
PACIFIC
Seaham
Broughton Islands
Karuah
Tea Gardens
Hawks Nest
Maitland
Medowie
Nelson Bay
Raymond Terrace
122
Hexham
TASMAN
Newcastle
Charlestown
Toronto
Belmont
Swansea
111
Doyalson
Budgewoi
Toukley
SEA
N
0
25
50
75
Kilometres
COPYRIGHT © UNIVERSAL PUBLISHERS PTY LTD

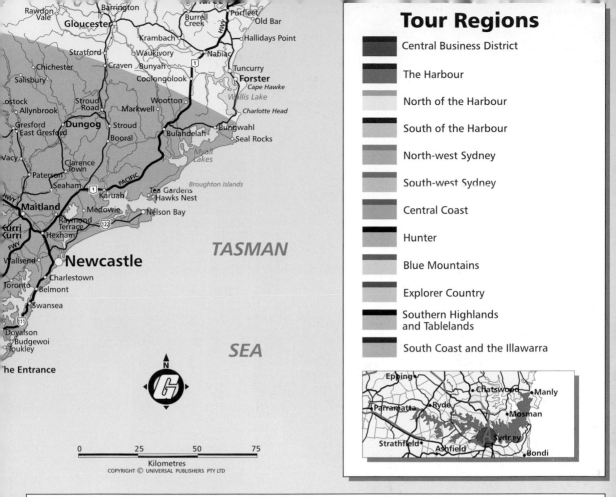

Tour Regions

- Central Business District
- The Harbour
- North of the Harbour
- South of the Harbour
- North-west Sydney
- South-west Sydney
- Central Coast
- Hunter
- Blue Mountains
- Explorer Country
- Southern Highlands and Tablelands
- South Coast and the Illawarra

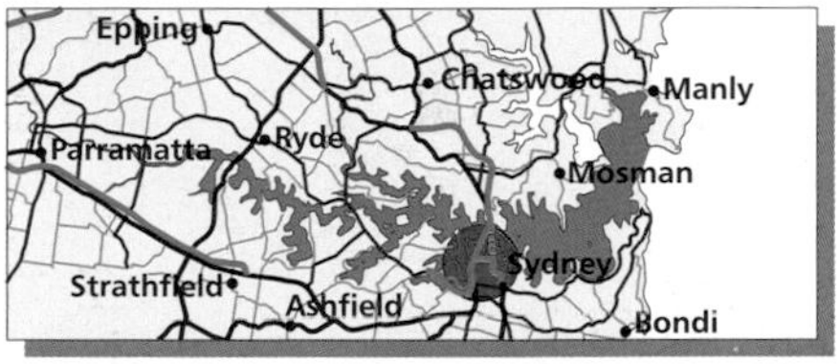

Epping
Chatswood
Manly
Parramatta
Ryde
Mosman
Sydney
Strathfield
Ashfield
Bondi

Explanation of Map Symbols

Region Maps

- Dual Carriageway
- Through Route
- Major Road
- Minor Road
- Railway

Tour/District Maps

- Dual Carriageway
- Through Route
- Major Road
- Minor Road
- Railway
- Walking Track

Street Maps

- CAHILL EXPWY .... Dual Carriageway
- GEORGE ST .... Through Route
- HICKSON RD .... Major Road
- HUNTER ST .... Minor Road
- Railway
- Walking Track

- Airport/Airfield
- Camping Ground
- Caravan Park
- Cave
- Golf Course
- Hospital
- Tourist Information
- Lighthouse
- Lookout 360°, 180°
- (3) Metroad Route Marker
- (31) National Route Marker
- One Way Traffic
- Parking
- Patrolled Beach
- Picnic Area
- Point of Interest
- (20) State Route Marker
- Toilets
- Winery
- Mall/Plaza
- National Park, State Forest, State Recreation Area

Radio stations

702ABC: AM 702
2SM: AM 1269
2DAY: FM 104.1
2UE: AM 954
2GB: AM 873

Tourist information

City Host Kiosks
Circular Quay; Sydney Square

**The Council of the
City of Sydney**
City Info (What's On)
Mon–Fri 9am–5pm
Ph: 1300 657 733
www.cityofsydney.nsw.gov.au

Sydney Transport
Infoline 131 500

Sydney Visitor Centres
106 George St, Sydney 2000
33 Wheat Road
(Palm Grove behind IMAX)
Darling Harbour 2000
9.30am–5.30pm daily
Ph: (02) 9240 8788
www.sydneyvisitorcentre.com

Tourism New South Wales
Information line 132 077
Mon–Fri 8am–6pm
www.visitnsw.com.au

CitySearch
www.sydney.citysearch.com.au

LEFT: SYDNEY'S CENTRAL
BUSINESS DISTRICT

the central business district

SYDNEY IS ONE OF THE SPECIAL cities of the world, a heady combination of cosmopolitan energy, relaxing climate and superb natural assets. This is confirmed by the millions of enthusiastic visitors who arrive each year, and by Sydneysiders themselves. The city skyline, etched behind the glittering harbour, and flanked by the Opera House and the Harbour Bridge, is an image that never fails to impress.

Sydney is the city that symbolises Australia to the rest of the world, and is the point where most overseas visitors enter the country. This focus is even more intense since Sydney hosted the 2000 Olympic Games. Over four million visitors arrive from abroad each year. and this figure continues to grow. Even before the Olympic games, Sydney was consistently voted a top world destination by major travel publications; nearly half of all international visitors to Australia spend their time in Sydney and NSW. The city also attracts many visitors from other parts of Australia.

Sydney's central business district, known to residents simply as 'the city', stretches from Sydney Cove, the site of the country's first European settlement, south to Central Railway Station, the main train terminus. The best way to explore the city is on foot and by public transport.

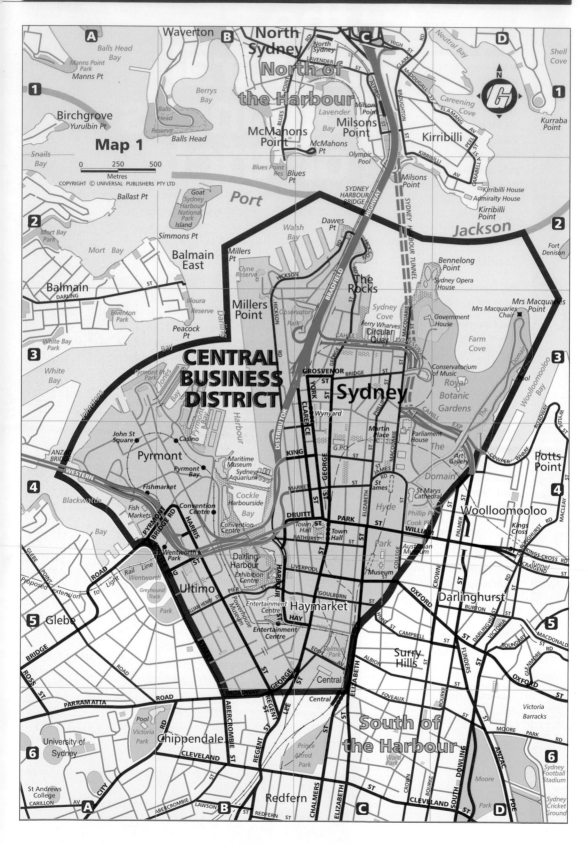

Natural features

The city stands on a bed of Hawkesbury sandstone; and many of Sydney's magnificent historic buildings are built from this sandstone.

To the west of Sydney Cove, the historic district of The Rocks clings to its craggy hill, overshadowed by the Sydney Harbour Bridge. Further west, on the waterfront, lies the Darling Harbour entertainment and convention complex. The central business district (CBD) spreads south from Sydney Cove along a low ridge. Kings Cross occupies the next ridge to the east, with Woolloomooloo and the sweep of the Domain and the Botanic Gardens stretching down to the harbour.

A coal seam lies beneath Sydney Harbour and for many years it was mined from a pithead at Balmain. The Tank Stream, the freshwater creek around which the colony initially developed, still runs under the streets of the city and into the harbour at Circular Quay.

History

Aboriginal people lived here for at least 60 000 years before the arrival of

CELEBRATIONS AT THE ROCKS

Europeans. The Eora people of the Dharruk group lived in the region around Sydney Harbour; in some areas their rock paintings and shell middens remain.

Captain James Cook reached Australia in 1770, and landed at Botany Bay. He and his crew spent several weeks exploring and charting the east coast before claiming possession of the land in the name of King George III of England.

The colony in America was no longer available for the transportation of convicts, so the British government created a penal colony in NSW as a solution to Britain's critically overcrowded jails.

The First Fleet reached Australia's east coast in January 1788, and Captain Arthur Phillip established the first European settlement at Sydney Cove.

Convict transportation ended in 1840 but free settlers continued to arrive in their thousands. The population of NSW had reached 54 000 by 1851, boosted by the success of the wool and wheat trades; it continued to increase with the gold rushes and the mining booms. Today, Sydney remains Australia's largest city, with a population of around 4 million from diverse cultural backgrounds.

Getting there

Via airport links

On the shores of Botany Bay, 20min from the centre of the city, the airport is serviced by shuttle buses, trains and taxis. Regular bus services connect the international and domestic terminals; and several shuttle bus services link the airport to various points around the city and beyond, including **Sydney Airporter**, Ph: (02) 9666 9988. www.kst.com.au The **Airport Link** is a daily rail service operating to and from the Domestic and International terminals and all City Circle stations. Trains run approximately every 10min and take 10–15min to reach the city; 5am–midnight. Airport stations are located below the terminals. Ph:(02) 8337 8417. www.airportlink.com.au

SCULPTURE WALK

The **Sydney Sculpture Walk** is a major City of Sydney initiative. Currently, there are 10 contemporary artworks which were specially commissioned from Australian and international artists. The sculpture walk forms a circuit throughout the city, the Royal Botanic Gardens and the Domain. Ph: 1300 651 301

HISTORIC HOUSES

The Historic Houses Trust's **Ticket Through Time** is valid for three months, giving unlimited entry into 11 diverse museums around Sydney, including the Museum of Sydney, Hyde Park Barracks (pictured) and Elizabeth Farm. Ph: 1300 653 777, (02) 9692 8366. www.hht.net.au

METRO MONORAIL

CENTRAL RAILWAY STN, AND METRO LIGHT RAIL

By public transport

Avoid taking a car into the city; it is usually easier to catch public transport, or a taxi. Sydney's public transport is clean, convenient and recommended. The city is well served by buses, trains, ferries, light rail, the monorail and taxis.

Rail

CityRail trains are a convenient way to travel, with regular services using an extensive network throughout the city of Sydney and suburban areas. The main city terminus is Central Stn. All suburban trains lead into the City Circle, the collection of largely underground railway stations (Museum, St James, Circular Quay, Wynyard, Town Hall and Martin Place) that run beneath the CBD and link to Central. Services throughout NSW and interstate, including daily services to Queensland and Victoria, are operated by Countrylink. One of the great train journeys of the world, the Indian Pacific, leaves twice weekly from Central Stn, crossing the continent from Sydney to Perth, WA. Countrylink Infoline 132 232. CityRail. www.cityrail.nsw.gov.au

Bus and ferry

Major bus terminuses in the city are at Circular Quay, Wynyard Park and the western side of the Queen Victoria Building. From such points, buses travel throughout Sydney and suburbs. Sydney Transport Infoline 131 500. www.sydneybuses.nsw.gov.au

Ferries depart from Circular Quay (p.22) for the eastern suburbs, the North Shore as far as Manly, and various suburbs up the river to Parramatta.

The State Transit Authority, which controls Sydney's buses and ferries, offers a variety of discounts for visitors. Options include the economical DayPass which allows access to all bus and ferry

IN A HURRY
Colourful Aussie idiom recalls Sydney's old trams with the wonderful expression: 'Shoot through like a Bondi tram'.

Disabled access

For disabled people getting around Sydney, a variety of info sources are available. Sydney city's website, www.cityofsydney.nsw.gov.au, and Spinal Cord Injuries Australia 'Ask SCInfo' line can provide details about accommodation, equipment and services, Ph: (02) 9661 8855/Freecall 1800 819 775, www.spinalcordinjuries.com.au. Other organisations with extensive databases include NICAN, focusing on recreation, tourism, sport and the arts, Ph: (02) 6285 3713/Freecall 1800 806 769, and IDEAS, for accommodation, general services, leisure activities, venues, equipment and supplies, Ph: (02) 6947 3377/Freecall 1800 029 904

services. A Bus, Train and Ferry Infoline operates on 131 500, 6am–10pm daily, www.131500.com.au

Metro Monorail

The Monorail loop links the city with Darling Harbour, runs at regular intervals and stops at the Harbourside shopping complex, Sydney Convention Centre and Haymarket (stations close to major carparks), World Square, Galeries Victoria and City Centre. The Monorail operates Mon–Fri 7am–10pm, Sat–Sun 7am–midnight Ph: (02) 9285 5600. www.metromonorail.com.au

Metro Light Rail

This is the city's most recent transport innovation. The Light Rail starts at Central Stn and ends at Lilyfield, stopping along the way at Chinatown, Darling Harbour, Pyrmont Bay, Star City Casino, Sydney Fish Market and Wentworth Park, providing access to a number of attractions. A Day Pass is available for unlimited trips in any one day. Supervoucher Plus 1- and 3-day passes offer unlimited travel on Metro Monorail and Metro Light Rail plus discounts on other Sydney attractions. Passengers can also purchase a TramLink ticket, which is a combined CityRail and Metro Light Rail ticket, available at any CityRail stn. Ph: (02) 9285 5600. www.metrolightrail.com.au

Taxis

Sydney taxis are plentiful and efficiently organised. City hotels will call taxis for their guests, and of course taxi companies are listed in the phone book. Taxi ranks are located at both airport terminals and at key locations through-out the city, or passing cabs can be hailed.

By road

Road traffic can be very slow in Sydney, particularly during peak times, and street parking in the city is limited. Parking meters require coins. Parking stations are available but those in the centre of the city are generally expensive. Slightly cheaper parking is available on the CBD

fringe, at such places as the Domain Parking Station to the east, Goulburn St Parking Station to the south, and near Darling Harbour. For information on day-to-day traffic conditions, contact the Roads and Traffic Authority at the Sydney Traffic Control Centre on 132 701

Getting around
Sydney Explorer

The red Sydney Explorer bus travels a 35km circuit taking in Circular Quay, the Sydney Opera House, Chinatown, Darling Harbour, The Rocks and many points along the way. Operating daily, 8.40am–7.10pm, travellers can spend a day hopping on and off the bus for further exploration on foot. Buses run every 20min; tickets can be bought at any one of the 26 stops.

Cruises

More than 200 passenger-carrying vessels ply the waters of Sydney Harbour and more than one million people are carried on Sydney's many different cruises each year (p.37).

Tours and guided walks

A wide variety of tours operate in and around Sydney. Possibilities range from roaring around on a Harley Davidson to scenic flights over the harbour and up the coast. Tourist info centres are the best sources for details.

Guided tours can provide in-depth local info. **Sydney Guided Tours** (Ph: (02) 9660 7157) have been operating for over 15 years and cater for all tastes

CYCLING

A series of nine **Sydney Cycleways** maps are available from the RTA, covering bike routes all over Sydney. Freecall: 1800 060 607.

SYDNEY FERRY

THE STRAND ARCADE

The Strand is just one of the many interesting buildings that can be seen on Sydney Architecture Walks. Photo: Courtesy Tourism New South Wales

and specialities. **The Rocks Walking Tours** offers a lively 90 minute specialist guided tour around The Rocks, leaving from 23 Playfair Street, Rocks Square Ph: (02) 9247 6678. A spooky alternative is **The Rocks Ghost Tours**. Day and night tours are offered and patrons must be 18yr or older. Tours must be booked on Ph: (02) 9247 7910, at the Sydney Visitors Centre, or with ATS on Ph: (02) 9211 3192. www.ghosttours.com.au

Sydney Architecture Walks (SAW), offered by Historic Houses Trust and conducted by young architects, takes in the more unusual aspects of Sydney's urban landscape. There are several two-hour guided tours leaving from the **Museum of Sydney**. For details and bookings Ph: (02) 9518 6866. www.sydneyarchitecture.org

Scenic flights

For the ultimate overview of Sydney, it is best to get up into the air. Scenic flights by plane and helicopter are provided by a number of companies flying out of the airports at Bankstown and Mascot and the Parramatta Heliport at Granville. The intrepid sightseer can even opt for the thrill of aerobatic flights. Call the Sydney Visitor Centre for info or check the Sydney Yellow Pages under 'Aircraft Charter and Rental Services'.

NEW YEAR'S EVE ON SYDNEY HARBOUR

Festivals and events

Sydney Festival

After Sydney's New Year's Eve celebrations, January kicks off with a feast of artistic activity: theatre, concerts, exhibitions, free street events, and the crowd favourite, spectacular free concerts in the Domain.

Australia Day Celebrations

Jan 26 marks the anniversary of the arrival of the First Fleet into Sydney Cove in 1788. Sydney holds a huge party which lasts all day. Highlights include the ferry race and the tall ships on the harbour, the NRMA Motorfest which takes over the area around Hyde Park, and fireworks in the evening at Darling Harbour.

Chinese New Year

This event is based on the lunar cycle, so the timing changes each year, falling somewhere between late Jan–early Mar. The public celebrations occur around Dixon St in Chinatown, and Darling Harbour. Popular events include dragonboat racing, sedan chair racing, the Dixon St floral market and lunchtime performances at Martin Place. Ph: (02) 1300 657 733

Anzac Day March

Every year on 25th Apr, the date of the WWI landing at Gallipoli in 1915, this march through the city commemorates the servicemen and women who went to war for Australia. It is preceded by a dawn service at the Cenotaph in Martin Place and the laying of wreaths.

National Trust Heritage Festival

This Festival in Apr is the largest state celebration of heritage in all its varied forms, cultural, built and natural. The Trust promotes and compiles a program of up to 300 events across the state, involving up to 150 organisations including corporate, local and state government, community groups and private concerns. Events include walks, lectures, seminars, historic house open days, fetes, dance, music, poetry, exhibitions and more. Ph: (02) 9258 0123

OUTDOOR DINING IN THE ROCKS

AT THE START OF THE CITY TO SURF

City to Surf

Early on a Sun in Aug, around 60 000 people gather on Park St, Hyde Park. At 10am, the gun starts the annual *Sun-Herald* City to Surf Fun Run, a challenging 14km course which leads from the city down to the surf at Bondi. Ph: (02) 9282 2833. www.sunherald.com.au/city2surf

Sydney in Spring

This is a joint initiative of the City of Sydney and the city's retailers. It comprises a unique program of displays and events — a Sept showcase of flowers, fashion, food and fragrance. Ph: (02) 9265 9007

Carnivale

This festival, Sept–Oct, is the largest multicultural arts festival in the country. It's a celebration of cultural diversity in NSW, and is spread around Sydney and the state. Carnivale events range across the artistic and cultural spectrum, including performing arts, music, literature, visual arts and cross-cultural activities.

Main localities

The city of Sydney divides naturally into three distinct areas: the City centre, Darling Harbour and nearby, and Sydney Cove and The Rocks.

City centre

Sydney's CBD is a bustling, vibrant city centre offering a wide range of services and attractions to visitors and locals.

Sydney Tower at Westfield Centrepoint Map 2 D3

Rising to a height of 305m on top of the **Centrepoint** shopping centre, **Sydney Tower**, in Market St, has the tallest observation deck in the southern hemisphere. From the Podium Level, double-decker elevators whisk visitors to

Eating out in the city

The standard of food and dining in Sydney is generally high, and at any given point in the city area, the means for satisfying hunger and thirst are never far away. The city presents a vast smorgasbord of eating possibilities: take-away outlets, fast food, trendy cafes, family eateries, pubs, hotels and world-class restaurants; every taste and budget is catered for.

The Sydney Morning Herald Good Food Guide lists the best of the best around Sydney. *Cheapeats* guide is for those who have a budget but still like to eat well. For a cosmopolitan slant, the *SBS Eating Guide* explores the international flavours of Sydney, listing restaurants by their culture of origin. These guides are updated regularly and are available in most bookshops and some newsagencies.

The website eatability.com Sydney Food Guide provides info which allows the user to search under different categories such as cuisine, name and/or location. Users can also search for the best restaurants as voted by restaurant customers online. Information such as the dishes offered by a restaurant, their signature dish, if they are licensed and wheelchair accessible.

TOP EATERY

The Summit, Sydney's first revolving restaurant, has been revamped. The recent makeover and food revolution accompany spectacular 360° views of the city. This upmarket restaurant offers something for everyone and is located on the 47th floor of Australia Sq Tower, cnr George and Hunter Sts, Sydney.
Ph: (02) 9247 9777

an observation deck with two revolving restaurants, and where on a clear day, the sweeping 360° view stretches from the mountains to the sea. **Skytour: The Great Australian Expedition** offers a virtual tour around Australia. Open Sun–Fri, 9am–9.45pm; Sat, 9am–10.45pm. For bookings Ph: (02) 9223 0933. www.sydneyskytour.com.au Restaurant bookings, (02) 8223 3800.

Art Gallery of NSW Map 1 D4

The Art Gallery of NSW, in the Domain, opposite the Royal Botanic Gardens, was established in 1874 and houses some of the finest works of art in the country including **Aboriginal**, **European**, **Asian**, **Australian**, **contemporary** and **photographic**. Behind its Greek Revival front, visitors will find the original building and several modern additions offering effective exhibition space with some spectacular views.

Major Australian and international art exhibitions are held at the gallery, as well as exhibitions of entries to the annual Archibald, Wynne and Sulman prizes. An excellent introduction to Australia's indigenous culture is the **Yiribana Aboriginal and Torres Strait Islander Gallery**, the largest gallery in the world with a permanent exhibition of Aboriginal art.

Visitors can enjoy the gallery's guided tours, films, lectures, outdoor sculpture garden, well-stocked shop, cafe and restaurant. Open Thur–Tues, 10am–5pm, Wed 10am–9pm (**Art After Hours**) Ph: (02) 9225 1744 or for recorded info (02) 9225 1790. www.artgallery.nsw.gov.au and www.artafterhours.com.au

Australia Sq Map 1 C3

A timeless building designed by world-acclaimed **architect Harry Seidler**, Australia Sq is situated in the heart of the CBD. This much sought-after address is a popular gathering place offering pleasant, sunny and spacious places to sit, particularly at lunchtime, while observing the general bustle of the city.

Australian Museum Map 1 C4

On the cnr of College and William Sts is the Australian Museum, one of the top natural history museums in the world. Founded in 1827, it is **Australia's oldest museum**. The permanent exhibitions — including 'Indigenous Australians', 'More than Dinosaurs', 'Planet of Minerals', 'Skeletons', and Australian birds and insects — provide visitors with a video and audio journey across Australia. Changing exhibitions on a

ART GALLERY OF NSW

SKELETON EXHIBIT, AUSTRALIAN MUSEUM

wide range of subjects are also featured. There are two cafes, an extensive museum bookshop, an info and resource centre and Kids' Island, an interactive play area for the under fives. Open daily, 9.30am–5pm. Ph: (02) 9320 6000. www.amonline.net.au

Great Synagogue Map 1 C4

On Elizabeth St facing Hyde Park (entry 166 Castlereagh St) is the Great Synagogue. Consecrated in 1878, it is the place of worship for Australia's longest established Jewish congregation. Tours every Tues and Thurs at noon. Ph: (02) 9267 2477

Macquarie St Map 1 C4

Named after Lachlan Macquarie, the 5th Governor of NSW, Macquarie St is one of Sydney's most historic and attractive streets.

At the lower end of Macquarie St in the Royal Botanic Gardens is **Government House**, the former residence of the Governor of NSW. The grand Gothic Revival structure was built between 1837 and 1845 and now houses a collection of 19th and 20th century furnishings and decoration. Open for guided tours Fri–Sun, 10am–3pm, gardens open daily 10.30am–4pm. Ph: (02) 9931 5222

Set back from Macquarie St, opposite Bridge St, is the **Conservatorium of**

Music. Looking rather like a castle, it was originally designed as stables and servant quarters for the then unbuilt Government House. Its architect, convict Francis Greenway, went on to design some of the early colony's most beautiful buildings. At the time, though, the structure was criticised by the colonial authorities back in England for being too elaborate, with Governor Macquarie accused of wasting money. Controversy was rekindled in 1998 when building extensions revealed an old convict road. This historic site is now preserved as an internal display within the new building. The Conservatorium regularly holds free concerts by both students and staff. Ph: (02) 9351 1263 for concert enquiries.

Across Macquarie St from the Conservatorium of Music is the former **Chief Secretary's Department**, now integrated into the **Hotel Inter-Continental Sydney**. Where the State's affairs were once managed are now bars, restaurants and meeting rooms.

Further south on Macquarie St is the **State Library of NSW**. The **Mitchell Library**, in the NW wing of the building, holds a unique collection of Australiana, established with a bequest from David Scott Mitchell. A newer building, entered from Macquarie St, houses the high-tech **State Reference Library**.

HISTORY HOUSE

History House at 133 Macquarie St houses the Royal Australian Historical Society who welcome visitors to browse through the library, use the research facilities or even join the society. Ph: (02) 9247 8001

SYDNEY TOWN HALL

A comprehensive public program of special exhibitions, displays, lectures and film screenings is provided, as well as a glass-domed restaurant and a bookshop. The Mitchell Library is open weekdays 9am–9pm, Sat 11am–5pm. The State Reference Library is open 9am–9pm weekdays and 11am–5pm weekends and selected public holidays. Ph: (02) 9273 1414, www.sl.nsw.gov.au

The stretch of Macquarie St next to the Library has great historical significance. In 1810 Governor Macquarie contracted for a hospital, built and paid for by the proceeds of the right to import and trade in rum. The three 2-storey Georgian style sandstone buildings were constructed end-to-end along Macquarie St and became known as the Rum Hospital. Opened in 1816, the buildings served the colony in a variety of ways.

The northern building, adjacent to the Library, was used by the Executive and Legislative Councils. Its facade has been incorporated in today's parliamentary complex. **Parliament House** is open for inspection from 9am–4.30pm, Mon–Fri, with formal tours of the **Legislative Assembly** and the **Legislative Council** at 10am, 11am and 2pm on non-sitting days. Public areas of the building can be inspected during business hours. Ph: (02) 9230 2111, www.parliament.nsw.gov.au

Next to Parliament House is **Sydney Hospital** and **Sydney Eye Hospital**, on the site of the original central building of the Rum Hospital. The site contains some beautifully restored features, including the Worrall Lecture Theatre, the Chapel of St Luke, an impressive entrance hall, grand staircase and the James Brough Fountain. Apart from the 1894 buildings, there are numerous remnants of Sydney Hospital's long history. The oldest building on the site is the **Nightingale Wing**, built in 1869 to accommodate Australia's 1st pro-fessional nurses, sent to Australia by the revolutionary Florence Nightingale. Standing on the Macquarie St frontage outside the Hospital is one of Sydney's best known statues, **Il Porcellino**, a bronze replica of a Florentine statue, which was donated to the city. If the pig's nose looks shiny, it's because of the legend: rub it for good luck.

The most southern of the original Rum Hospital buildings is **The Mint**, Parliament House's 'twin'. In 1853, it became the first branch of the Royal Mint outside the UK and operated in that capacity until 1927, when the mint in Perth took over. The building is now owned by the Historic Houses Trust.

The **Hyde Park Barracks** is a beautifully restored Georgian building next to the Mint at the southern end of Macquarie St. Also designed by the convict architect Francis Greenway, it was built as barracks to accommodate 600 convicts. Today it features per-manent exhibits recalling Australia's convict and social history and special exhibitions on Australian themes. Lunch is available in the cafe. Open daily, 9.30am–5pm. Ph: (02) 9223 8922, lunch bookings Ph: (02) 9223 1155.

Across Macquarie St is **Queen's Sq**, where a statue of Queen Victoria sits outside the modern **High Court** building. The 2nd oldest court building in Australia, the old NSW Supreme Court building (built 1819–28) is here, as well as another Francis Greenway building,

CONCERTS

St James' Church offers a unique musical experience with a series of concerts, on Wed 1.15–2.45pm. Performances include chamber music and organ music recitals. Ph: (02) 9232 3022. www.stjameschurch sydney.org.au

the elegant **St James' Church**, originally designed as a court house.

Martin Place Map 1 C4

Sydney's first pedestrian mall, **Martin Place** runs between George and Macquarie Sts. It is where the traditional lighting of the Christmas tree takes place and the scene of lively concerts in the amphitheatre which delight lunchtime audiences. The luxurious **Westin Sydney** is a blend of a modern 31-storey hotel with the former **General Post Office**, clocktower included. The grand old GPO was built between1874 and 1891. In the hotel's basement there is a section of the historic Tank Stream, once Sydney's only fresh water supply. Outside the former GPO is the **Cenotaph**, which commemorates Australians who died in war. Nearby, in Angel Place, is the **City Recital Hall**, a superb, international standard, purpose-built music venue. Ph: (02) 8256 2222. www.cityrecitalhall.com

St Marys Cathedral Map 1 C4

At the northern end of College St is St Marys Cathedral. The original structure was completed in 1837 but burnt down in a spectacular fire 27yr

later. The present St Marys was erected gradually from 1868, and completed (without spires) in 1928. Sydney's **Catholic cathedral** is an imposing gothic revival building, measuring some 106m in length. Only recently (1999–2000) were twin 30m spires added to the cathedral as was intended in the original design. Every Sun at noon, a tour takes place in the cathedral as well as such fascinating areas as the crypt, with its splendid mosaic tile floor. Ph: (02) 9220 0400

Sydney Sq Map 2 D3

On one side of Sydney Sq is the **Sydney Town Hall**, built between 1866 and 1888, another example of Sydney's fine Victorian heritage. The main hall is used for concerts and recitals and has been extensively restored. The ground floor is usually open to the public during business hours. Ph: (02) 9265 9333. A more comprehensive tour is available through Centrepoint Touring, Ph: (02) 9231 4629

Across Sydney Sq is **St Andrews Anglican Cathedral**, built in 1868. Guided tours of the cathedral are available by appointment. The organ has been restored and free recitals are held every Fri, except public holidays, at 1.10pm. Other musical offerings for which dates must be checked, include Monday recitals 1.10pm, Band concerts Wed 12.30pm, and Thursday recitals 12noon. Ph: (02) 9265 1661. www.cathedral.sydney.anglican.asn.au

Darling Harbour and nearby

Once a bustling centre for Sydney's maritime industry, by the middle of the 20th century the **Darling Harbour** area had become a run-down industrial zone. It was redeveloped for Australia's Bicentennial celebrations and combines open public space with shopping, eating, entertainment, convention and accom- modation venues. Darling Harbour attracts some 14 million visitors, both local and overseas, each year.

Many of these also visit nearby attractions such as Chinatown, the Sydney Fish Market and the Powerhouse Museum.

DARLING HARBOUR

Though visitors wouldn't know it now, **Darling Harbour** saw the beginnings of Australia's industrial age when Sydney's first steam mill opened there in 1815.

MARTIN PLACE AMPHITHEATRE

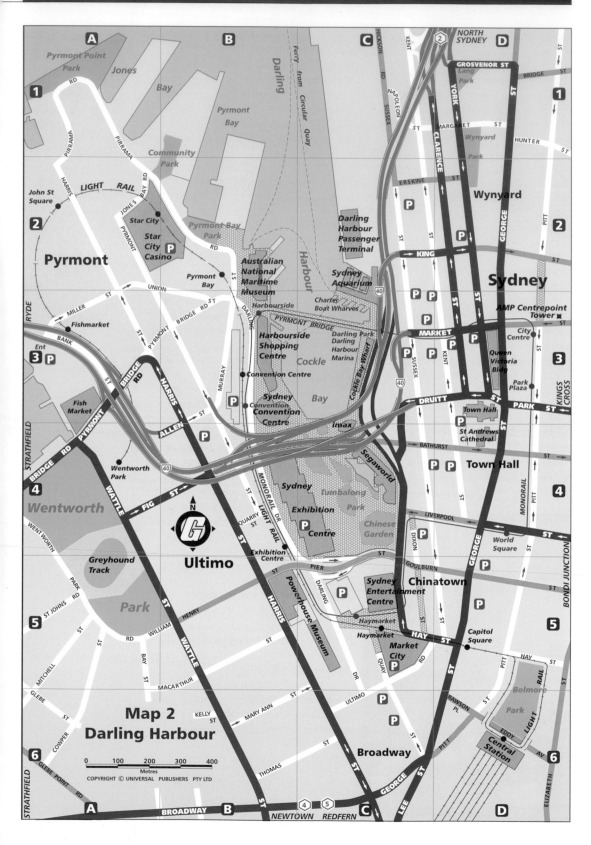

Map 2
Darling Harbour

0   100   200   300   400
Metres
COPYRIGHT © UNIVERSAL PUBLISHERS PTY LTD

DINING OUT IN CHINATOWN

TOP YUM CHA RESTAURANTS
★ Silver Spring, 477 Pitt St, Haymarket
★ Marigold, 683 George St, Sydney
★ Golden Harbour, Dixon St, Haymarket
★ Regal, 347–353 Sussex St, Sydney
★ Kam Fook Sharks Fin, 9 Hay St, Haymarket

Chinatown Map 2 C5

Sydney has had a significant Chinese population since the time of the gold rushes. For many years, Sydney's Chinese community centred around Chinatown, running along Dixon St, Haymarket. Within walking distance of Darling Harbour and the CBD, Dixon St is a pedestrian mall bracketed by tall Chinese gates and distinctive lanterns, lined with restaurants serving all manner of Chinese cuisine. A favourite for a quick, cheap meal are the food halls at several locations along Dixon St, where food from all over Asia is sold from an array of stalls and often cooked on the spot. Chinatown is always full of life, night and day, with many clothing and accessory stores, supermarkets, Chinese cinemas and a Buddhist temple.

At the southern end of Dixon St, at 9–13 Hay St, is **Market City,** a huge complex of factory outlets, specialty stores, cinemas, restaurants and an international food court. Ph: (02) 9212 1388. www.marketcity.com.au. On the ground floor is **Paddys Market**, a Sydney institution for bargain shopping and fresh produce, open Fri–Sun and public holidays. Ph: (02) 9325 6294

On Thomas St, behind Market City, the **Burlington Centre Supermarket** is the place to go for more unusual Asian produce.

Yum cha — a Chinese tradition

A must during a jaunt through bustling Chinatown, yum cha is a popular late breakfast or lunch for families, friends and business people. A feature of yum cha, which literally means 'to drink tea', is an endless cup of refreshing Chinese tea. The meal consists of dim sum, snack-sized delicacies such as steamed prawn dumplings, tasty fried beancurd, succulent roast duck and steamed seasonal vegetables, to name a few. Trolleys stacked high with bamboo steamers are wheeled past crowded tables. When offered dim sum, accept or refuse as is your wont. Each selection is added to a bill (prices are usually very reasonable). Take your time — it is said there are thousands of types of dim sum — and when you have finished, lay your chopsticks flat on the bowl or table. It's bad luck to leave them standing up in the bowl like incense sticks — and it's rude!

SYDNEY AQUARIUM, DARLING HARBOUR

Wharf 7 Maritime Heritage Centre there are guided tours of the National Maritime Collection in storage, and berthed alongside the centre is the tall ship *James Craig*. Ph: (02) 9298 3777. www.anmm.gov.au

The **Sydney Convention and Exhibition Centre** holds large public exhibitions, conventions and conferences. The five exhibition halls cover some 25 000m^2 and the public areas of the Convention Centre include an outstanding selection of Australian art.

A popular attraction of Darling Harbour is the **Sydney Aquarium**, where over 160m of underwater tunnels offer superb viewing of one of the world's greatest aquatic collections. The collection includes 11 000 Australian aquatic animals including crocodiles and endangered grey nurse sharks, a natural seal sanctuary and the largest Great Barrier Reef exhibit in the world. Open daily, 9am–10pm. Ph: (02) 8251 7800. The Aquarium's interactive website is fun and informative. www.sydneyaquarium.com.au

The **Outback Centre**, located next to the Chinese Gardens, has Sydney's largest collection of Aboriginal arts, crafts, clothing, music and books. A 30min live didjeridoo performance — **Sounds of the Outback** — accompanied by a spectacular visual journey of

Darling Harbour Map 2

This massive harbourside complex covers some 60ha, with major attractions, numerous shops, restaurants, bars and water features. The network of parks includes outdoor entertainment areas such as **Tumbalong Park** where bands and other performers regularly appear. For details, call the Darling Harbour Info Line (charges apply) Ph: 1902 260 568

There are several carparks at Darling Harbour, and other transport options are available. The complex is an easy walk from the city across the historic **Pyrmont Bridge**, or visitors can take the Metro Monorail. The Metro Light Rail services this area well. A State Transit City Shuttle bus runs from Circular Quay to Darling Harbour every 10min, 6.10am–midnight during peak hours and 15 min off peak. Ferries run from Wharf 5 at Circular Quay.

The **Harbourside Shopping Centre** has around 100 specialty shops and 30 international food outlets as well as a variety of restaurants, cafes and bars. Open daily 10am–9pm. Ph: (02) 9281 3999

A fascinating exhibition of Australia's seagoing heritage is on display at the **Australian National Maritime Museum**, from the smallest to the largest vessel, including the former RAN big-gun destroyer HMAS *Vampire* and the submarine HMAS *Onslow*. The museum brings history alive with a variety of events including live theatre and music, and heritage outings. At the museum's

AUSTRALIAN NATIONAL MARITIME MUSEUM

Australia's outback is offered daily at 1pm, 3pm and 5pm. Also here is **Australia's Outback Gallery**, which showcases some of the most exciting Aboriginal art in Australia sourced from communities as far apart as the Kimberleys and Arnhem Land. Ph: (02) 9283 7477. www.outbackcentre.com.au

Situated on the waterfront, the **LG IMAX Theatre** has the world's biggest cinema screen. The images are 10 times larger than in conventional cinemas, and several different films, in 2D and 3D, are shown each day from 10am–10pm. Ph: (02) 9281 3300. www.imax.com.au

At 80 Pyrmont St is **Star City**, Sydney's 1st **casino**, providing gaming, entertain-ment and quality hotel accommodation. All the main casino games are on offer, as well as restaurants, bars, a nightclub, theatres, gym, pool, spas and a retail area. The casino provides parking, shuttle buses to and from the city, a Metro Light Rail station and a ferry wharf opposite the main entrance. Ph: (02) 9777 9000. www.starcity.com.au

The Darling Harbour **Super Ticket** includes a 1hr Matilda Cruises harbour cruise, entry into the Sydney Aquarium, a meal at the Aqua Bar & Grill, entry to the Imax Theatre, and a ride on the Monorail. The ticket also entitles the holder to discounts at other attractions. Tickets can be purchased from the Sydney Aquarium, Imax Theatre or Matilda Cruises Ph: (02) 9262 2300. www.darlingharbour.com

Powerhouse Museum Map 2 B5

The old **Ultimo Power Station** at 500 Harris St, Ultimo, once supplied power for Sydney's trams. It has now been transformed into one of the world's great museums — a hands-on, user-friendly expanse of exhibits detailing science, technology, social history and design. Permanent displays cover such diverse subjects as the 1st locomotive to run in NSW, a NASA space station, a 1920s suburban kitchen, aircraft, Aboriginal culture, fashion, musical instruments and a great deal more. A constantly changing program offers exhibitions,

films and entertainment. Facilities include a well-stocked shop and courtyard cafe. Open daily, 10am–5pm. Ph: (02) 9217 0111. www.powerhousemuseum.com

Sydney Fish Market Map 2 A3

Located at **Blackwattle Bay, Pyrmont**, the Sydney Fish Market is very much an authentic working market and the largest of its kind in the southern hemisphere, offering over 100 species of fish to Sydney's culturally diverse community.

The fishing fleets arrive with their cargoes early in the morning, and the seafood Dutch auction clock (starting with the highest price and descending) starts at 5.30am. About 65 tonnes of fresh seafood are sold every day. Visitors can reach the market by bus, ferry, Metro Light Rail or on foot — a 15min walk from the city. The market carpark charges a small fee.

Shops at the market open 7am–4pm. Sydney's six top seafood retailers have outlets here. There are cafes, a sushi and oyster bar, a deli, bakery, greengrocer, bottle shop and net and tackle shop; everything you need for a picnic, BBQ, dinner party or fishing trip. Also located at the market, the **Sydney Seafood School** holds a variety of

ALL ABOARD!
Visitors of all ages are fascinated by this historic locomotive at the Powerhouse Museum.

STAR CITY CASINO

CITY EXHIBITION SPACE

This display at **Customs House** features a huge scale model of Sydney City's urban landscape. The exhibition will also include a multimedia harbour model, maps, and audiovisual displays.

seafood cooking classes including some that are hosted by guest chefs. 'Behind the scenes' tours are conducted, which includes coffee and a visit to the auction areas. For info, call the Fish Line (02) 9004 1122, or Sydney Seafood School classes (02) 9004 1111. www.sydneyfishmarket.com.au

Sydney Cove and The Rocks
Circular Quay Map 3 C3

Public and private ferry services for the harbour and the Parramatta River, as well as major cruise operators, all use Circular Quay. During the week, it is crowded with busy commuters;

on weekends, camera-wielding tourists pack the waterfront, mingling with buskers and other street entertainers.

Cafes and takeaway food bars line the Quay, adding to its vibrant buzz.

In Alfred St, directly across from Circular Quay, is **Customs House**. First built in 1845, it has since undergone extensive renovations and additions which allowed it to continue operating at this location until 1990. The building has again undergone major refurbishments, transforming it into a dynamic public space for a wide variety of activities. Ph: (02) 9247 1797

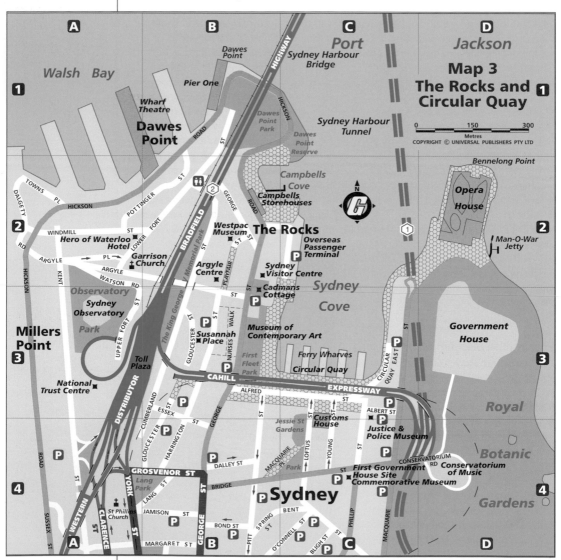

CUSTOMS HOUSE

Nearby, at the cnr of Albert and Phillip Sts is the **Justice and Police Museum**. Integrating the **Water Police Court** (1856), the **Water Police Station** (1858) and the **Police Court** (1885), the buildings have been restored as a police and legal museum. The Magistrate's Court provides a glimpse of law and order in the past, a museum highlights Australia's most infamous crimes and regular exhibitions are held. The entrance is from Albert St. Open weekends and daily in Jan, 10am–5pm. Ph: (02) 9252 1144

The **Museum of Sydney**, on the corner of Phillip and Bridge Sts, stands on the site of the first Government House, which was built in 1788 for Governor Arthur Phillip. This was the home and administrative centre of NSW for nine Governors until its demolition in 1846. It lay forgotten beneath the developing city until the 1980s when its foundations were exposed during the construction of a new office tower. Building was halted and the Government stepped in to ensure this significant part of Sydney's history was not lost again.

The planned office building was then redesigned to include a public area for the viewing of the exposed foundations and a museum to focus on pre-1788 Aboriginal culture and early European settlement. The foundations can be viewed in First Government House Place,

near the evocative *Edge of the Trees* public sculpture.

Inside the museum is an interactive presentation that brings Sydney's colonial past to life. A giant video wall spans the height of the museum, Collectors Chests feature archaeological finds, while ghost-like narrators tell stories of old-time Sydney. Special exhibitions are also featured, about Sydney past and present. Open daily 9.30am–5pm. Ph: (02) 9251 5988. www.hht.net.au

Millers Point Map 3 A3

Through the Argyle Cut from The Rocks is the quiet residential area of Millers Point. Climb Watson St behind the bus terminus to **Observatory Park** for panoramic views across the harbour.

Originally, Observatory Hill was the highest point overlooking the harbour, an ideal spot for the **Sydney Observatory** built in 1858. Now part of the Powerhouse Museum, the Observatory features an exhibition, **By the Light of the Southern Stars**, which includes hand-on exhibits. There are daytime tours and celestial viewings as well as the evening program, which includes a short talk and tour of the building, films or videos, a 3-D Space Theatre session and a viewing through the state-of-the-art 40cm mirror telescope of the night sky.

Space Theatre sessions Mon–Fri 2.30pm and 3.30pm; weekends and school

LITERARY SYDNEY

The **Writers Walk**, a series of brass plaques set into the paving around Circular Quay, chronicles the impressions of Sydney as penned by famous writers such as DH Lawrence, Charles Darwin, Germaine Greer and Peter Carey.

SYDNEY OBSERVATORY

PIER ONE AND THE HARBOUR BRIDGE

DANCE ICON

Graham Murphy, founder (in 1976) of the Sydney Dance Co, is still its artistic director, and a choreographer of international renown.

holidays 11am, noon, 2pm, 3.30pm, bookings essential. Daytime tours are 10am–5 pm daily. Bookings essential for evening tours, Ph: (02) 9217 0485, or www.phm.gov.au; for general information www.sydneyobservatory.com.au

Also on Observatory Hill is the **National Trust Centre**. Housed in a building originally erected in 1815 as a military hospital, from 1850 it served as Fort St High School before becoming the headquarters of the National Trust in NSW. The centre includes a National Trust gallery shop and cafe. Open 11am–5pm on weekdays and 12pm–5pm on weekends and public holidays. Ph: (02) 9258 0123. www.nationaltrust.org.au

Also in the Centre is the **SH Ervin Gallery**, showing changing art exhibitions on Australian themes. (02) 9258 0135

At the base of Observatory Hill is **Argyle Place**, with its elegant Georgian and Victorian terrace houses. To the east is the Holy Trinity Church, which is more commonly known as the **Garrison Church**, built in 1840 by convict labour.

The **Colonial House Museum** at 53 Lower Fort St is a 4-storey terrace house. Six rooms, furnished in Victorian style, present the house and its occupants as it would have been a century ago. Open daily, 10am–5pm. Ph: (02) 9247 6008

Several of the old piers along Walsh Bay have been turned to community use. **Pier One** was one of the first to be converted and there is now a hotel, a brasserie and restaurants. The **Wharf Theatre**, home to the Sydney Theatre Company (STC), operates from Pier 4. STC produces a year-round program of theatre and events, with performances at its Pier 4 home base, the new 850-seat Sydney Theatre at Walsh Bay and the Opera House. Box office enquiries, Ph: (02) 9250 1777. In the same building, the Wharf Restaurant offers dining with a superb view. Ph: (02) 9250 1761. www.sydneytheatre.com.au

Several other arts organisations are also housed at Pier 4. **Sydney Dance Company** presents two major seasons in Sydney each year. As well the **Sydney Dance Company Dance Studios** hold open dance classes daily, catering for different styles and levels of skill. Ph: (02) 9221 4811. www.sydneydance.com.au.

The **Bangarra Dance Theatre** is a unique company which fuses traditional Aboriginal and Islander history with contemporary dance influences. Ph: (02) 9251 5333. www.bangarra.com.au Each year the **Sydney Philharmonia Choirs** (4) perform a series of major concerts at the Sydney Opera House and the City Recital Hall at Angel Place as well as as acting as chorus for the Sydney Symphony Orchestra. Ph: (02) 9251 2024. www.sydneyphilharmonia.com.au

The Rocks Map 3 B2

Covering some 23ha, The Rocks evokes the sights and atmosphere of Sydney's **colonial heritage**. The rocky terrain meant the area was developed later than others around Sydney Cove, but from the 1820s onwards, as the colony began to prosper, commercial, maritime and defence buildings were built here.

For much of its history, The Rocks was a boisterous, unruly place, very heavily dependent on the maritime trade for its livelihood.

In 1900, an epidemic of bubonic plague broke out and many of the oldest houses were demolished to control the disease. Victorian terraces were subsequently built. When construction of the Sydney Harbour Bridge began in 1926, much of the land towards Millers Point was resumed. In the past few decades, as a result of the work of the Sydney Cove Redevelopment Authority, The Rocks has seen a remarkable transformation and is now a major attraction.

A good starting point is the **Sydney Visitor Centre**. Located in a former sailors' home at 106 George St, this is Sydney's main walk-in info source with details of all the attractions and events within Sydney and NSW. The Centre also provides an interesting insight into the past: upstairs is a history exhibition. Open 9.30am–5.30pm daily. Ph: (02) 9240 8788, Freecall 1800 067 676. www.sydneyvisitorcentre.com or www.therocks.com

Specialist shopping abounds in The Rocks. **The Argyle Department Store**, located on the corner of Argyle and Playfair Sts, is a group of former bond stores and warehouses. Nearby are further shopping arcades including **The Rocks Centre** and **Clocktower Sq**. Other shops are spread along George, Harrington and Playfair Sts. On weekends, **The Rocks Market** closes off lower George St from Hickson Rd to under the Harbour Bridge. The market has over 150 colourful stalls, and live music and free entertainment in The Rocks Sq. Open Sat–Sun 10am–5pm Ph: (02) 9240 8717. www.rocksmarket.com.au

Halfway up Argyle St is the **Argyle Cut**, one of the most ambitious engineering projects of early Sydney. In 1843 convicts started hacking a deep roadway through the sandstone ridge of The Rocks to connect the storehouses of Sydney Cove with Cockle Bay. It was such a huge task that the convicts were replaced by council labourers who used explosives to cut through, and the project was eventually completed in 1859.

Restored early examples of Sydney buildings include **Campbell's Warehouses**, along Hickson Rd at Campbells Cove. Owned by Robert Campbell, a successful colonial merchant, they date from the 1820s and today house some of the district's most popular restaurants.

At **28–30 Harrington St** are houses built for Thomas Ryan in the mid-1820s and now used as shops. **Susannah Place** at 58–64 Gloucester St, an 1840s terrace and four brick houses including a corner store, is an outstanding 'living museum'. Ph: (02) 9241 1893

Cadmans Cottage, built in 1816 for John Cadman, Superintendent of Government Boats, is the oldest surviving house in Sydney's city area. It is now an information centre for the National Parks and Wildlife Service of NSW, specifically for **Sydney Harbour National Park**, and is reached by steps at 100 George St. Ph: (02) 9247 5033

Next door to Cadmans Cottage, the **Museum of Contemporary Art** (MCA) is in the grand art deco former headquarters of the Maritime Services Board on the western edge of Circular Quay. The gallery holds frequent special exhibitions as well as showcasing its

THE ROCKS PUB TOUR

The Rocks Pub Tour is a fun way to meet the locals as well as finding out about the history of The Rocks and some of its colourful characters not to mention a few of its less savoury ones. Discover how the green bans of the 1970s saved so much of the area from being demolished. Bookings Sydney Visitor Centre (02) 9240 8788. www.therockspubtour. com

THE ROCKS MARKET

Historic pubs

The Rocks boasts several old watering holes, including the Fortune of War at 137 George St which claims the longest continuous liquor licence in Sydney (a hotel of the same name was operating on the site by 1839 although the present building dates from 1922). Also of interest are the Orient Hotel at 89 George St, which dates from 1843–44; the Art Nouveau Mercantile Hotel at 25 George St; and the wedge-shaped Australian Hotel at the corner of Gloucester and Cumberland Sts. Through the Argyle Cut at Millers Point, the Lord Nelson Hotel on Argyle Place is popular, while The Hero of Waterloo in Lower Fort St has changed little since the 19th century. Along with great atmosphere, a number of pubs in The Rocks offer good pub food and live jazz.

impressive permanent holdings. It has a shop with a vast collection of art books and designer-made items, while the MCA Cafe on Circular Quay has become one of Sydney's most fashionable dining and socialising spots. Ph: (02) 9252 4033. www.mca.com.au.

Sydney Opera House Map 3 D2

An extraordinary building perched on a spectacular harbour, the **Sydney Opera House** is an internationally recognised symbol not only of Sydney, but of Australia itself.

In 1955, Danish architect Jørn Utzon's design won an international competition and building began in 1959. Almost immediately, the project was plunged

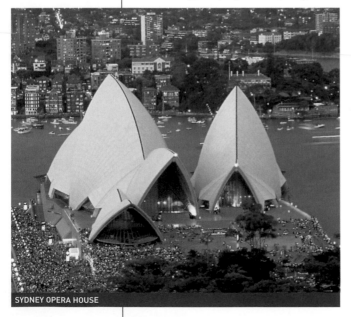

SYDNEY OPERA HOUSE

into controversy. Australian engineers, builders and the public service had difficulty interpreting Utzon's out-standingly clear vision of the finished building. Utzon resigned in 1966 although the relationship has subsequently been mended. In 1998, the then Sydney Mayor, Frank Sartor, presented Jørn Utzon with the key to the city as acknowledg-ment of his major contribution to Sydney's heritage.

The construction was originally estimated to cost $7 million; on completion, this had skyrocketed to over $100 million. An Opera House lottery was established to finance the extra cost. The Sydney Opera House was opened by Queen Elizabeth II in 1973 and paid off by 1975. Although the exterior of the building retains much of Utzon's original vision, the interior was changed radically, resulting in a long-held mis-conception that Utzon had failed to adequately plan the interiors. Recent research reveals the original design would have worked perfectly.

As well as a range of theatre, ballet, opera and musical productions, the Sydney Opera House is open for **tours daily**, departing every half hour 9am–5pm, leaving from the Guided Tours Office on the Lower Concourse Level. Two-hour backstage tours, including breakfast, are run according to demand, bookings essential, Ph: (02) 950 7777. Refreshments can be enjoyed in the bars, food outlets, cafes and restaurants including fine-dining at the spectacular **Guillaume at Bennelong,**

Ph: (02) 9241 1999. On Sundays and public holidays, weather permitting, the Tarpeian Market sets up on the Opera House forecourt, selling arts and crafts. Ticket bookings Ph: (02) 9250 7777, general enquiries Ph: (02) 9250 7111. www.sydneyoperahouse.com

Parks and gardens

Chinese Garden of Friendship Map 2 C4

The people of Guandong Province in China presented the **Chinese Garden of Friendship** to the people of Sydney as a Bicentennial gift. It is the largest garden of its type outside mainland China, with a classic design incorporating graceful pavilions, winding pathways, lakes and ponds. The garden, in the SW corner of Darling Harbour, is open 9.30am–5pm daily, depending on weather and time of year Ph: (02) 9281 6863. www.cityofsydney.nsw.gov.au

Cook and Phillip Park Map 1 C4

Between St Marys Cathedral and the Australian Museum, **Cook and Phillip Park** is a city recreational area, with open space, trees, terraces, fountains, gardens and artworks. The park provides a leisurely environment as well as sporting facilities. These include an olympic pool, gym and children's playground.

The Domain Map 1 D4

Running along Mrs Macquaries Rd, bordering the Royal Botanic Gardens (p.28), and stretching to St Marys Cathedral (p.17), the Domain was set aside as a public park early in the colony's history. The green expanse is perfect for rallies and the huge open-air concerts held during the Sydney Festival (p.12) each year.

At the end of Mrs Macquaries Pt overlooking the harbour is **Mrs Macquaries Chair**, cut into the sandstone cliff face by convict labour. It is said to have been a favourite resting place of Mrs Macquarie on her long walks from Government House. On the Woolloomooloo side of Mrs Macquaries Rd is the refurbished **Andrew 'Boy' Charlton Pool**, a favourite city swimming venue in a spectacular location perched above the harbour. The open-air pool and a cafe are open from Oct to Apr.

Hyde Park Map 1 C4

The leafy open space of Hyde Park extends from **Queens Sq** at the top of Macquarie St to **Liverpool St**. Hyde Park was a public recreation area before it was officially named during the governorship of Lachlan Macquarie. In 1810 it hosted Australia's first official race meeting and continued as a race-course until the late 1820s when it

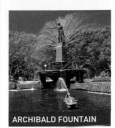
ARCHIBALD FOUNTAIN

CHINESE GARDEN OF FRIENDSHIP

SOAP BOX ORATORS
On Sundays, under the trees near the Art Gallery, the Domain soap box speakers have their say and are willing to discuss (or argue) their point with bystanders.

LUNCHING AT HYDE PARK

became a cricket ground. Today, Hyde Park provides a haven for the busy city. At the Queens Sq end is the extravagant **Archibald Fountain**, erected in 1932 to commemorate the association of France and Australia during WWI. At the Liverpool St end is the **Anzac War Memorial**, a huge Art Deco structure with an impressive atmosphere of quiet respect. Downstairs is an exhibition with photographs and memorabilia from the wars in which Australia has participated.

The Royal Botanic Gardens Map 1 D3

Wrapped around Farm Cove between the **Opera House** and **Mrs Macquaries Chair**, the **Royal Botanic Gardens** is a 30ha oasis of calm on the edge of the city. The area was set aside for the cultivation of vegetables for the First Fleet and then laid out as gardens in 1810. Today, it is a wonderful place for strolling, picnicking, get-togethers, lazing, theatrical performances and even weddings.

The Gardens are landscaped with plantings of exotic and Australian trees, shrubs and flowers, special environment areas, ponds, waterbirds and statuary.

The **Sydney Tropical Centre**, with its two imposing glasshouses, contains tropical plants from around the world and an exhibition on tropical rainforest conservation. Open daily, 10am–4pm.

A vast range of herbs used for a variety of purposes are grown in the **Herb Garden**. The **Sydney Fernery** shadehouse showcases lush ferns from around the world. Plants of Asia are on display in the **HSBC Oriental Garden**. The **Rare and Threatened Plants Garden**, features the world's endangered plants and rare species including the recently discovered Wollemi Pine (see p.226).

The Gardens also include the **National Herbarium of NSW** with its **Botanical Information and Plant Identification Service**. The **Visitors Centre and Gardens Shop** contains one of Sydney's leading horticultural and botanical bookshops, as well as stocking a wide range of souvenirs, cards and gifts. Open 9.30am–4.30pm daily. Ph: (02) 9231 8125

Access to the Royal Botanic Gardens is via the Opera House near the Man o' War Jetty, Macquarie St, Mrs Macquaries Rd near the Art Gallery, or Shakespeare Pl in front of the Mitchell Library. Open daily, 7am, closing times range 5–8pm depending on the time of year. Ph: (02) 9231 8111. www.rbgsyd.nsw.gov.au

BOTANIC GARDENS WALKS

Free guided walks leave the Visitors Centre most days at 10.30am. Or catch the Trackless Train for a scenic tour with an informative commentary. Passengers can get on and off at various points in the Gardens.

BOTANIC GARDENS RESTAURANT

This eatery offers a unique and delicious surprise in one of the world's most beautiful gardens, within walking distance of the city. Lunch 12–3pm daily, brunch weekend from 9.30am. Ph: (02) 9241 2419

THE SYDNEY FERNERY, ROYAL BOTANIC GARDENS

THE STRAND ARCADE

Recreational activities

There is a seemingly endless list of things to do in the city; filmgoing, shopping and theatre are among the favourites. A range of free newspapers offering numerous recreation and entertainment options is distributed around the city. These include: *Drum Media, Nine to Five*, *The Hub, On the Street, Beat Magazine, Star Observer* and *3D World*. Friday's *Sydney Morning Herald* includes the *Metro* section, a guide to current and up-coming arts and entertainment events.

Film

Sydney has a healthy film scene, with a wide variety of movies showing at any time. They range from blockbusters and commercial releases to the most recent arthouse and foreign films, as well as reruns of old favourites and classics. The main commercial artery is along George St, where all the major chains — Hoyts, Village and Greater Union — have multiplex cinemas. Greater Union's Pitt Centre on Pitt St runs artier commercial new releases. The Dendy Opera Quays at East Circular Quay and the Dendy on King St Newtown (outside

city centre) show a more independent and arthouse program.

Also outside the city centre Hoyts is on Broadway and Fox Studios is in Moore Park. Some other independent cinemas include the Verona and Academy Twin on Oxford St, Paddington; the Valhalla on Glebe Point Rd, Glebe; Randwick Ritz, Randwick; and on the north shore, the Cremorne Orpheum on Military Rd, Cremorne; and Roseville Cinema, Pacific Hwy, Roseville. For more information, see the website www.sydney.citysearch.com.au

IMAX at Darling Harbour shows 2-D and 3-D films on a huge screen (see p.21). The big movie chains run cinema complexes in the suburbs. Details in the daily papers and on the Internet.

The magnificent **State Theatre** in Market St is one of the last examples of the grand picture palaces of Hollywood's heyday. It opened in 1928 and is now a venue for live theatre, concerts and the annual **Sydney Film Festival**, a two-week affair showing films from around the world. Self-guided tours of the State Theatre or guided school or group bookings are available Mon–Fri, 11.30am–3.00pm — it is essential to

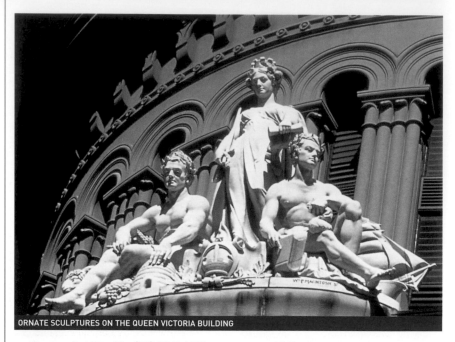

ORNATE SCULPTURES ON THE QUEEN VICTORIA BUILDING

PADDY'S MARKET
Map 1 C5

Paddy's has been Sydney's flea market for 150 years. It claims to be Australia's largest market and sells everything imaginable. Currently Paddy's operates in two locations, the Market City complex (pictured), at **Haymarket** next to Chinatown, opens Thur–Sun, public holidays 9am–5pm. See p.102 for details on the **Flemington** location. Infoline 1300 361 589. www.paddysmarket. com.au

confirm availability, Ph: (02) 9373 6660. www.statetheatre.com.au

Shopping

Sydney city offers shopping of a world-class standard, from designer labels to great bargains. The shopping precinct centres on Elizabeth, Castlereagh, Pitt and George Sts. Traditional department stores are located in this area, as well as large shopping arcades such as Centrepoint, Skygarden, the Imperial, Piccadilly and Strand Arcades and the Mid City Centre. For details see www.sydneycity.nsw.gov.au

Pitt St Mall is a city shopping focus, a central pedestrian zone lined with shops and arcades. Underground passages and overhead walkways provide all-weather links. It's possible these days to walk from the George St cinema precinct to the MLC Centre on a rainy day without getting wet.

The department store David Jones is a Sydney shopping institution. There are two stores, one on Elizabeth St and one on Market St, where the upgraded Food Hall's culinary delights are legendary.

Joining Pitt St Mall and George St, the Strand Arcade is an elegant example of Sydney's Victorian history. Originally opened in 1892, it was extensively

restored following a fire in the early 1980s. The Strand houses antiques, gifts, jewellery and many top designers. www.strandarcade.com.au

Shops featuring the work of well-known European designers including Armani, Gucci, Louis Vuitton, Ferragamo and Cartier are clustered around the MLC Centre and along Castlereagh St.

The glamorous Chifley Plaza on Hunter St houses 1st class shopping on three levels such as MaxMara and Marina Rinaldi, as well as classy restaurants.

Occupying an entire city block adjacent to the Sydney Town Hall, the Queen Victoria Building (QVB) opened in 1898. Originally housing a concert hall with an assortment of other businesses, the QVB is a grand, elaborate building with an imposing dome and beautiful stained-glass windows. It has five levels of shops, cafes and restaurants, with underground access to Town Hall Railway Stn and Myer. Guided tours of the QVB run daily leaving from the Information desk. Bookings and enquiries Ph: (02) 9264 9209. www.qvb.com.au

Gowings has been a shopping institution in Sydney since 1868. The main store is on the corner of George and Market Sts, with two other outlets at Wynyard further down George St and on

Fun for the young

★ Andrew 'Boy' Charlton Pool (p.27)
★ Australian Museum with Kids' Island for the under fives (p.14)
★ Hyde Park Barracks (p.16)
★ IMAX Theatre (p.21)
★ Justice and Police Museum (p.23)
★ Australian National Maritime Museum (p.20)
★ Powerhouse Museum (p.21)
★ Sydney Aquarium (p.20)
★ Sydney Observatory (p.23)
★ Sydney Tower at Westfield Centrepoint (p.13)

Oxford St. Although officially Gowings are men's outfitters, they provide a wide range of quality clothing and goods for everyone, accompanied by some good old-fashioned service. www.gowings.com.au

With the explosion of inner city apartments, supermarket shopping is now available in town: Woolworths Metro on the corner of George and Park Sts near Town Hall Stn, and Coles X-Press on the second floor of the Wynyard Stn arcade, underneath the bus terminal.

On Broadway, down the road from Central Stn, is The Broadway shopping centre, a huge development with 120 specialty shops, supermarket chains such as Coles and K-Mart, cinemas and parking.

The Rocks (p.24) and Darling Harbour (p.20) also provide good shopping opportunities. For further info about shopping in Sydney or a free shopping map, contact Sydney City Marketing, Ph: (02) 9265 9653

Theatre

Sydney has a rich theatrical tradition and theatre lovers can choose between the latest overseas productions and Australian works. The State Theatre in Market St and the Capitol Theatre in Campbell St are historic gems, carefully restored and listed by the National Trust.

The various theatres of the Sydney Opera House (p.26), Her Majesty's Theatre in Quay St and the Theatre Royal in the MLC Centre stage large-scale productions; other venues include the Wharf Theatre and Sydney Theatre both at Walsh Bay (p.24), the Seymour Centre on City Rd, Belvoir St Theatre at Belvoir St, Surry Hills, the SBW Stables Theatre at Kings Cross and home to the Griffin Theatre Company, the Performance Space on Cleveland St, Redfern, and the Footbridge Theatre in Parramatta Rd, Glebe. Tickets from theatres or booking agencies.

The Sydney Entertainment Centre is in Harbour St, situated along the western edge of Chinatown. Holding up to 12 500 people, it is a major venue for international entertainment, pop concerts, major indoor sporting events, even ice shows, as well as specialising in staging corporate events, such as conferences, Ph: (02) 9320 4200. www.sydentcent.com.au

FOR THE CHILDREN

Sydney's Child is a free monthly newspaper focused entirely on children. It has comprehensive listings of activities, events, services and anything else of interest to kids.

STATE THEATRE

Must see, must do

★ Ferry to Watsons Bay (p.37)
★ Harbour Bridge walk (p.41)
★ North Head (p.47)
★ RiverCat to Parramatta (p.38)
★ Sydney Harbour NP (p.46)

Radio stations

Radio National: AM 576
Triple M: FM 104.9
Triple J: FM 105.7
2DAY FM: 104.1
Nova 969: FM 96.9

Tourist information

Tourism New South Wales
Information line 13 2077
Mon–Fri 8am–6pm
www.visitnsw.com.au

City Host Kiosks
Circular Quay; Sydney Square
Manly Visitor Information Centre
The Forecourt, Manly Wharf
Ph: (02) 9977 1088
www.manlytourism.com.au

**Sydney Harbour National Park
Information Centre**
Cadmans Cottage,
The Rocks 2000
Ph: (02) 9247 5033
www.nationalparks.nsw.gov.au

Sydney Visitor Centres
106 George St, Sydney 2000
33 Wheat Road
(Palm Grove behind IMAX)
Darling Harbour 2000
9.30am–5.30pm daily
Ph: (02) 9240 8788
www.sydneyvisitorcentre.com

Waterways Authority
Ph: (02) 9563 8511
Infoline: 131 256
www.waterways.nsw.gov.au

LEFT: SYDNEY HARBOUR

the harbour

THERE IS NO DOUBT THAT
Sydney Harbour is one of the most
breathtaking in the world. Although
very much a working harbour, its
sparkling expanse offers the perfect
escape from big city stress, and the
sprawling waterways with their idyllic
foreshores are an integral part of the
city's identity.

Sydney Harbour impressed its first
European visitors in 1788 with its size
and beauty, and it continues to be a
major focus of attention. Watercraft
constantly ply the harbour. Commuter
ferries, tourist cruises, tall ships,
private yachts, water taxis, motorboats,
jet skis, kayaks, fishing trawlers — there
are so many ways to get out onto the
water. Enormous commercial vessels
and stately cruise ships also regularly
make their way down Port Jackson,
escorted by tug boats, while yacht
races enhance the spectacle with their
billowing spinnakers.

The harbour also represents Sydney's
prime real estate, with some magnificent
properties lining the water's edge.
Fortunately much of the foreshore still
offers public access, with endless
opportunities for enjoyment. Splendid
views, scenic walks, natural bushland,
quiet picnic areas, calm beaches,
laid-back eateries ... Sydney Harbour
has it all.

Natural features

The harbour covers 55km², and although it is only 21km from the Heads to Ryde Bridge, the foreshore measures 240km. The explanation for the many bays and inlets that make up this distance is to be found in the evolution of the harbour. It is a ria (a drowned river valley), and the inlets are the flooded valleys of tributaries. Its remarkable depth is also typical of a ria; about half of it is more than 9m deep even at low tide, and its deepest point, just west of the Harbour Bridge, is over 48m. These charac-teristics make Sydney Harbour an excellent deepwater port, as well as a superb recreational waterway.

The harbour consists of several distinct sections. **North Harbour** is the bay just inside North Head with Manly at its northern end. **Middle Harbour** reaches up into Sydney's North Shore to the Roseville Bridge. **Port Jackson** is the main body of water stretching from Middle Head under the Harbour Bridge to Long Nose Pt at Birchgrove. From here all the way up to Ryde Bridge is part of the **Parramatta River**.

Sydney is built on a bed of sandstone, and the harbour has many cliffs and headlands made of this relatively soft material. Both **North** and **South Heads** are vertical cliffs, as is much of the shoreline in this area.

Between the headlands there are many small sandy beaches as well as numerous bathing beaches in **Middle Harbour** and in the outer part of **Port Jackson**.

History

Australia's first English Governor, Arthur Phillip, described it as 'the finest harbour in the world, in which a thousand ships of the line may ride in the most perfect security'. The harbour was initially the domain of the Eora people of the Dharruk Group, who took advantage of

FURTHER READING

For further info on the harbour's history, the **Mitchell Library** has a number of relevant publications.
Ph: (02) 9273 1414

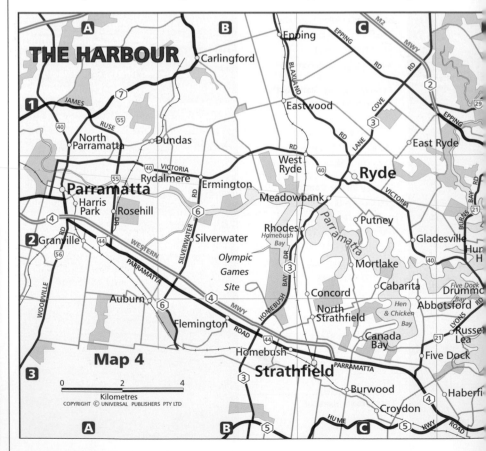

Map 4

the plentiful food sources here. Evidence of their lifestyle remains around the foreshores; good examples can be viewed at Berry Island Reserve (see p.44). The harbour's European history began in January 1788. The First Fleet, under the leadership of Captain Arthur Phillip, found Botany Bay an unsuitable site for settlement and ventured further north to Port Jackson.

They explored a number of bays and coves on both sides of the harbour and, almost 8km from the coast, found a small inlet fed by a clear stream. Phillip named it Sydney Cove after Lord Sydney, Secretary of State, at a simple ceremony on 26 January (now celebrated as Australia Day) 1788.

ANZAC BRIDGE

Getting there

By road

There are four major road crossings of Sydney Harbour: the Harbour Bridge, the Harbour Tunnel, Anzac Bridge and Gladesville Bridge. The **Harbour Bridge** connects the city with North Sydney, and the **Harbour Tunnel** provides a fast link between eastern Sydney and the North Shore. Victoria Rd begins at the

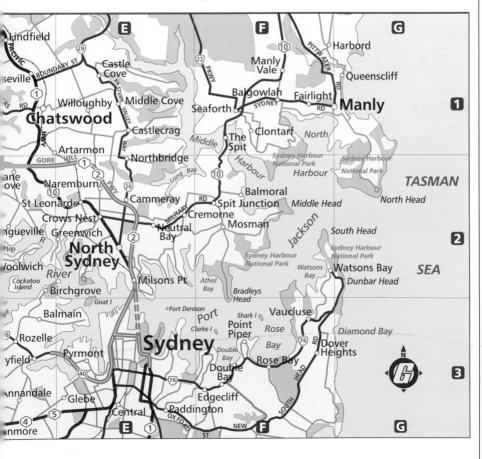

CAUTION

It is not advisable to swim at harbour beaches for three days after heavy rain, and not recommended to swim or fish anywhere upstream from Gladesville Bridge (pictured).

impressive **Anzac Bridge**, linking Glebe Island to Pyrmont, and continues on to cross the harbour at several further points. The major crossing is the **Gladesville Bridge** which runs between Huntleys Pt and Drummoyne.

Between Anzac and Gladesville Bridges is the **Iron Cove Bridge**, linking Rozelle and Drummoyne. Upstream from the Gladesville Bridge, the **Ryde Bridge** crosses the Parramatta River, linking Rhodes and Ryde.

For cyclists, Sydney can be challenging, due partly to the lack of cycleways and partly to the steepness of much of its terrain, yet many riders still pedal the harbourside roads, especially in the west around **Iron Cove** and **Hen and Chicken Bay**. The **Parramatta Valley Cycleway** is also popular. The best place to find out about enjoyable harbour cycling routes is **Bicycle NSW**, who also publish a helpful guide, *Cycling Around Sydney*. Ph: (02) 9283 5200. www.bicyclensw.org.au

By ferry and rail

Circular Quay, right beside the Harbour Bridge in Sydney Cove, is the heart of the harbour. It has its own railway stn, and buses from all over Sydney stop here to meet the ferries that service the waterside suburbs.

It is advisable not to drive right to the Quay as parking is very limited. Leave the car at home or at a parking stn and catch a bus, train or ferry.

The suburban parks and public foreshores are generally most easily reached by ferry or car, although **Taronga Zoo**, **Watsons Bay**, **Balmain** and **Birchgrove** all have bus services that terminate at the harbour. **Milsons Pt** and **Waverton** railway stns also give access to pretty harbourside parks.

Getting around

Harbour ferries

All Sydney Ferries depart from Circular Quay to wharves around the harbour, and each route has something different

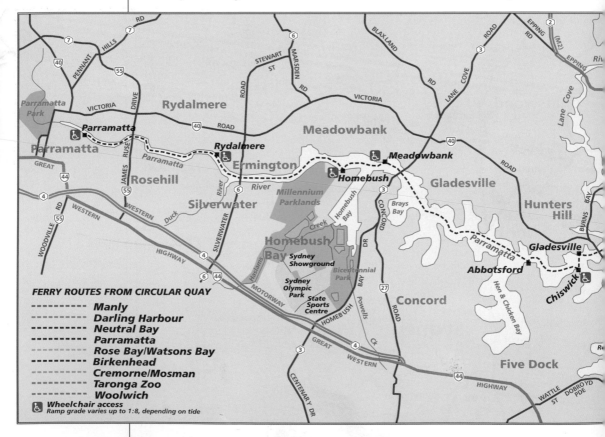

FERRY ROUTES FROM CIRCULAR QUAY

- - - - - - - - - - **Manly**
- - - - - - - - - - **Darling Harbour**
- - - - - - - - - - **Neutral Bay**
- - - - - - - - - - **Parramatta**
- - - - - - - - - - **Rose Bay/Watsons Bay**
- - - - - - - - - - **Birkenhead**
- - - - - - - - - - **Cremorne/Mosman**
- - - - - - - - - - **Taronga Zoo**
- - - - - - - - - - **Woolwich**

♿ **Wheelchair access**
Ramp grade varies up to 1:8, depending on tide

to offer. Ferries go either west under the Harbour Bridge or east toward the Heads and Middle Harbour. Fares for the runs vary and payment is made either at the Quay or, if the trip does not touch there, aboard the ferry. If you are planning to use ferries frequently, it pays to purchase a Ferry TenPass, which does not have an expiry date. Servicing the areas west of the Bridge are the Parramatta RiverCat ferries, the Woolwich/Balmain ferries and the Darling Harbour ferry. Sydney Ferries also has good value combined tickets to the zoo (ZooPass) or Sydney Aquarium (AquariumPass). Check with Sydney Ferries for other good value tickets.

Eastbound ferries include those touching on the North Shore, Neutral Bay, Mosman and Taronga Zoo; and on the southern shore, Rose Bay and Watsons Bay ferries which also call at the Zoo on weekends. Taking the ferry to Manly, right down the middle of the harbour, is an unbeatable Sydney experience. Indicator boards at each of the Circular Quay jetties show the destinations of the ferries and which wharf they depart from. Timetables and routes vary from time to time; for exact timetable and route info, Ph: 131 500. www.sydneyferries.info

Water taxis

Water taxis can be used to access places on the harbour where public transport does not go. They can also be a convenient option, and are great for sightseeing. A number of companies operate on the harbour, including Taxis Afloat, Ph: (02) 9955 3222, Harbour Shuttles, Ph: (02) 9810 5010 and Harbour Taxi Boats, Ph: (02) 9555 1155. See also 'Water Taxis' in the Sydney Yellow Pages.

Harbour cruises

To appreciate the beauty of Sydney from the water, take a cruise — half of all international visitors to NSW do this.

HISTORIC DETAIL

When the surrounding stone wall was originally built in 1844, Circular Quay was known as Semicircular Quay.

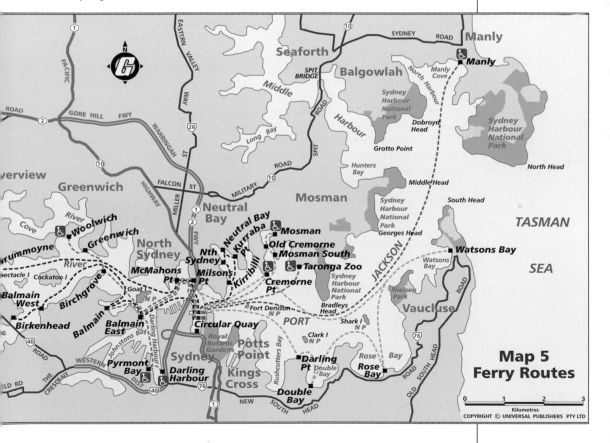

Map 5 Ferry Routes

COPYRIGHT © UNIVERSAL PUBLISHERS PTY LTD

WHALE-WATCHING TOURS ARE NOW VERY POPULAR IN SYDNEY

A number of cruise operators run regularly scheduled departures from Circular Quay and Darling Harbour.

Sydney Ferry Harboursights cruises

Apart from running the regular ferries, Sydney Ferries also offers a daily cruise program departing from Circular Quay. The 1hr **Morning Harbour Cruise** runs east towards Watsons Bay, following the southern harbour shore and returning along the northern shore past Taronga Zoo and Kirribilli House. The longer **Afternoon Harbour Cruise** heads past the Opera House and eastern suburbs towards the Heads before entering the serene greenery of Middle Harbour. Both of these cruises include an informative commentary, and light refreshments are available on board.

From Mon to Sat an **Evening Harbour Lights** cruise sets out to show Sydney dressed in her evening finery of dazzling colours and shimmering reflections, past the illuminated Opera House and Harbour Bridge as well as Garden Island, Fort Denison and Darling Harbour. A commentary is provided and in summer, the cruise catches the sunset.

Although not technically a cruise, the **Parramatta RiverCat** passes many interesting locations including Goat Island and Sydney Olympic Park at Homebush Bay. Passengers can alight at Parramatta (p.100) to visit some of Sydney's oldest buildings, such as Elizabeth Farm and Old Government House, before catching another RiverCat back to the Quay. Ph: 131 500, or enquire at the Ferry Info Office opposite Wharf 4.

Other cruises

Captain Cook Cruises is Sydney Harbour's largest cruise operator. **Coffee cruises** in the morning and afternoon provide a comprehensive view of Port Jackson and the upper reaches of Middle Harbour. The daily **Luncheon Cruise** includes a buffet lunch, and various dinner cruises are also on offer. The 1.25hr **Budget Cruise** passes the major points of interest on the harbour and can be combined with a visit to the Sydney Aquarium. The *Sydney Harbour Explorer* covers five major harbourside attractions: The Rocks, the Opera House, Watsons Bay, Taronga Zoo and Darling Harbour. Passengers may disembark wherever they wish and rejoin the next boat to travel on to another stop. Ph: (02) 9206 1111. www.captaincookcruises.com.au

Vagabond Cruises depart from East Circular Quay and Darling Harbour, offering a variety of trips including a morning and afternoon coffee cruise and a lunch cruise. The **Super Sights** half-day cruise provides morning tea on the way to Taronga Zoo, where passengers disembark for a zoo visit. The next stage is a visit to Oceanworld in Manly, and passengers then join the Luncheon Cruise for lunch. Ph: (02) 9660 0388. www.vagabond.com

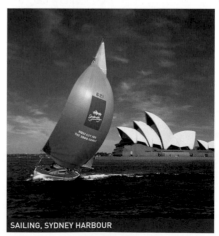

SAILING, SYDNEY HARBOUR

Matilda Cruises run morning and afternoon coffee cruises, and lunch and dinner cruises on large, luxury catamarans with outdoor decks. On the **Rocket Express Sightseeing Cruises**, passengers can board for an hour or spend the whole day getting on and off at different stops including Darling Harbour, Circular Quay, the Opera House, Rose Bay, Watsons Bay, Manly and Taronga Zoo. Departs from King St Wharf 4 and Jetty 6, Circular Quay. Ph: (02) 9264 7377. www.matilda.com.au

Some unusual cruises include the **Sydney Showboats**, which offer authentic paddlesteamer cruises featuring a Moulin Rouge-style show accompanied by a gourmet dinner. Departs King St Wharf 5 at 7.30pm. Ph: (02) 8296 7200. www.sydneyshowboats.com.au.

Magistic Cruises offer a variety of cruises aboard their luxury catamarans including a Premium Lunch Cruise, Dinner Cruise and a Total Harbour Experience. Departs King St Wharf 5, or Jetty 6, Circular Quay. Bookings essential, Ph: (02) 8296 7222. www.magisticcruises.co.au

The **Australian Heritage Fleet** offers several cruises, including a sea voyage under sail every other Sat on the majestic three-masted barque, *James Craig*. Ph: (02) 9298 3888, www.austfleet.com

True Blue Cruises offers an exceptional experience aboard the 16m super cat *True Blue*. During the whale watching season (May to Aug) you can watch and listen to humpback whales— the gentle giants of the sea—at play as they migrate north to the warm waters of the Whitsunday Islands to calve. Humpbacks have fought their way back from the brink of extinction to once again thrive in the southern oceans. Other migrating whales are the southern right whale, minke, killer whale and the rare blue whale. Cruises depart daily 8am (4.5hr) and 12.45pm (3.45hr) — morning and afternoon tea is served on board. Ph: 1800 309 672. www.sydneywhalewatching.com

Sydney's 18-footers

Sydney Harbour really doesn't need any help; but there is one introduced element that highlights its great natural beauty. As Jørn Utzon recognised when he designed the Opera House, the white sails of the yachts and sailing boats only enhance the superlative scenery.

One group of yachts holds special significance for Sydney: the magnificent 18-footers. They were initially designed at the turn of the century in response to the existing large yachts which only the rich could afford. The smaller 18-footer allowed 'the working man' to get out onto the harbour and race — at the time they were the fastest craft on the water. These days, the design has evolved into a much lighter, more streamlined vessel, the fastest mono-hulled sailboat in the world, given the right conditions.

The popularity of the 18-footer has spread world-wide, but Sydney remains its spiritual home; there is no finer sight than their billowing sails on a breezy weekend. Two clubs hold races every weekend, Sept–Apr. The **Sydney Flying Squadron** at Milsons Pt (Ph: (02) 9955 8350) is the birthplace of the 18-footer and races on Sundays. The club also races once a month during winter. The **Australian 18-Footers League** at Double Bay (Ph: (02) 9363 2995) races on Saturdays. Both clubs have spectator vessels from which the public can view the races.

AUSTRALIA DAY FERRY RACES (FERRYTHON)

Scenic flights

For a spectacular overview of the harbour, **Sydney Harbour Seaplanes** run scenic flights from Rose Bay, either over the main Port Jackson area, or over the harbour and up the coast (north) as far as Palm Beach. Ph: 1300 732 752

Helicopters also conduct scenic harbour flights, with a number of companies operating from different airports. For suggestions, contact the Sydney Visitors Centre, or look up 'Aircraft Charter and Rental Services' in the Sydney Yellow Pages.

Festivals and events

Ferrython

Every Australia Day (26 Jan), the **Ferrython** gives some of Sydney's working ferries, commercially sponsored and loaded with cheering supporters, the chance to show their stuff by racing against each other. In the evening there are fireworks, a spectacular sight from the harbour.

Dragon Boat Races

Each year in Feb dragonboat races are held as part of the Chinese New Year Festival at Cockle Bay/Darling Harbour. The colourful decorations adorning the boats, and the speeds achieved by the teams on the water, make this an exciting harbour event.

SYDNEY TO HOBART
YACHT RACE START

Blessing of the Fleet

This traditional Italian community festival takes place in early Oct each year. The Italian-owned fishing fleet gathers at Cockle Bay, Darling Harbour to be blessed by a Catholic priest. Festivities include day-long entertainment.

Sydney to Hobart Yacht Race

Probably the most keenly watched event on Sydney Harbour begins at 11am on Boxing Day (26 Dec) each year. The water is crowded with yachts and pleasure craft, and every vantage point is crammed with spectators for what must surely be the most exciting and spectacular start to a yacht race anywhere in the world. The **Sydney to Hobart Yacht Race** is an often-gruelling 1260km passage down the coast of NSW and across Bass Strait to Hobart, Tasmania.

Sydney's New Years Eve Skyshow

The year ends with a bang, and Sydneysiders come out en masse to watch the fireworks explode over the harbour. Take a blanket, radio and picnic with ample supplies of champagne, secure a spot near the water early, preferably with a good view of the Harbour Bridge, and wait for the best free show of the year to start at 9pm and midnight, simulcast with music on FM radio. Ph: (02) 9247 5033

Features of the harbour

Crossings

Each of the main harbour crossings has distinctive features that make it more than just a means of getting to the other side.

Anzac Bridge Map 4 E3

Anzac Bridge, which replaced the former Glebe Island Bridge, opened in Dec 1995. Delicate and light in appearance, the bridge is one of the longest concrete cable-stayed bridges in the world. With a main span of 345m and a structure length of 805m, this engineering landmark represents the western entrance to Sydney's CBD. Over 110 000 vehicles use the bridge each day.

Pedestrians and cyclists can access the bridge via ramps at both ends and a 3.5m wide corridor on the northern side of the deck.

Gladesville Bridge Map 4 D2

Gladesville Bridge was opened in 1964. This prestressed arch was constructed by the Dept of Main Roads and links Drummoyne and Gladesville via Huntleys Pt. A shared walkway/cycleway is located on the eastern side of the bridge, and offers spectacular views down the harbour to the Sydney Harbour Bridge and beyond.

Harbour Tunnel Map 4 E3

Crossing underneath the harbour just east of the Sydney Harbour Bridge, this engineering feat is 2.3km long and is constructed of concrete and steel. The Tunnel took 4.5yr to build and was completed in Aug 1992. The purpose of the Tunnel is to reduce traffic congestion on the Harbour Bridge and to provide a route from the northern to the eastern and southern suburbs, bypassing Sydney's CBD.

Sydney Harbour Bridge Map 4 E3

A readily identifiable icon for Australia the world over, the distinctive outline of Sydney Harbour Bridge has been a feature of the city since Aug 1930 when the centre of the arch was joined. The Bridge is big and its statistics impressive: it took 9yr to complete, from the turning of the first sod in July 1923 to the opening ceremony in Mar 1932; the arch is 134m high and weighs 39 000 tonnes; 6 million rivets were used to hold it together; clearance for shipping is 49m; and a single coat of paint for the Bridge uses 80 000L.

One of the best ways to appreciate the Bridge is to walk across it. A public walkway runs along the eastern side and a cycleway along the western side. Access to both is from Cumberland St above Argyle Cut in The Rocks, or from steps near Milsons Pt Stn on the northern side.

The Bridge's eastern walkway provides access to the SE **Pylon Lookout**. The view from the top is spectacular and well worth climbing the 200 steps. On the way up, look at the fascinating pictorial history of the Bridge's construction. Open daily, 10am–5pm except Christmas Day. (See also BridgeClimb p. 48). Ph: (02) 9241 2151

Harbour islands

Five historic islands are part of **Sydney Harbour NP** (see p.46) — Clark, Goat, Rodd and Shark Islands, and Fort Denison. Fort Denison and Goat Island can only be visited with tours leaving from Cadmans Cottage. Trips to Shark, Clark and Rodd must be booked with the NPWS and a fee paid at Cadmans Cottage. As numbers on the islands are

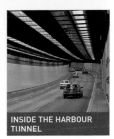

INSIDE THE HARBOUR TUNNEL

SYDNEY HARBOUR FROM THE AIR

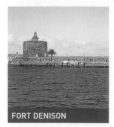

FORT DENISON

limited, it is best to check beforehand that they are not fully booked for a special event. **Cadmans Cottage** at The Rocks is the Sydney Harbour NP Info Centre, open Mon–Fri 9.30am–4.30pm, 10am–4.30pm on weekends. Ph: (02) 9247 5033

Clark Island Map 4 F3

Situated off Darling Pt, **Clark Island** was named after Lieutenant Ralph Clark of the Sydney Cove Marines who began to grow vegetables on the island in 1789. It has a number of secluded picnic spots. Bookings essential. Groups restricted to max 25 people. Access same as Shark Island. Book at Cadmans Cottage. Ph: (02) 9247 5033

Fort Denison Map 4 E3

The unmistakable silhouette of Fort Denison is visible from many vantage points. A perpendicular rock rising nearly 25m from the water, the island was first named Pinchgut; there are a variety of possible reasons. Some say it was because it was used briefly to confine troublesome convicts in the early days of the colony, and that these convicts had very little food. Others claim that Pinchgut is a nautical term for the point at which a channel narrows.

In 1841, work began on converting the islet into a fort to defend Sydney. This was not completed until 1857 when fear of a Russian invasion (spurred by the Crimean War) revived interest in finishing the defences. Records show, however, that the Governor of the time was actually more concerned about the French and the Americans. In the end, no shot was ever fired in anger from the fort.

Tours of Fort Denison are conducted daily, allowing visitors to explore the island and enjoy views of passing ships and the harbour, with a **cafe** providing refreshments. Tours depart from Cadmans Cottage; bookings essential. Ph: (02) 9247 5033

Goat Island Map 4 E3

Goat Island lies just off Balmain. Aboriginal people called it Mel-Mel (the eye) but it was renamed by the early colonists who kept their goats on it. In 1833 convicts cut sandstone from the island for building purposes. Visitors can also see the infamous **Convict Couch**, where convict Charles 'Bony' Anderson, after many escape attempts, was chained for 2yr. Daytime tours are held Wed, Sat, Sun; and Sat evening, leaving from Cadmans Cottage, Ph: (02) 9247 5033

Rodd Island Map 4 D3

Lying within Iron Cove near Drummoyne, Rodd Island has been a public reserve for more than a century and was once used to quarantine pet dogs owned by French actress Sarah Bernhardt. Usage as per Shark and Clark Islands. Book at Cadmans Cottage, Ph: (02) 9247 5033

Shark Island Map 4 F3

Located off Rose Bay, Shark Island used to be an animal quarantine area, but is now a popular picnic spot for larger groups. As with Clark and Rodd Islands, Shark Island is open daily from 9am–5pm in May, Jun and Jul, and 9am–8pm during summer. Access is by private boat or operators such as **Matilda Cruises**, Ph: (02) 9264 7377 and **Taxis Afloat**, Ph: (02) 9955 3222.

Port facilities

Commercial wharves, which once lined Woolloomooloo Bay, Rozelle Bay and Walsh Bay, are now mainly restricted

KIRRIBILLI HOUSE

SHELLY BEACH

to the northern end of Darling Harbour and the western side of Circular Quay. The Sydney Port Corporation's Port Operations Control Centre, an 87m tower on the foreshore at Millers Pt, provides essential navigation services for commercial vessels on Sydney Harbour and Port Botany.

Northern foreshores

East of the Bridge Map 4 E2

East of the Bridge it is possible to glimpse from the water two very attractive buildings overlooking the harbour on Kirribilli Pt, directly across from the Opera House. **Kirribilli House** is the Sydney residence of the Prime Minister and next door, **Admiralty House** is the Sydney residence of the Governor-General. Both are open to the public on rare occasions only.

Further east, past Neutral Bay, is Cremorne Pt, a tranquil peninsula with marvellous views of the city and harbour, bordered by **Cremorne Reserve.** Catch a ferry from Circular Quay to Mosman Wharf; follow the pretty walking track (see Map 6) around Mosman Bay to the tip of Cremorne Pt and enjoy the views; then catch a ferry back from Cremorne Wharf.

Manly Map 4 G1

At North Harbour, Manly has long been a favourite destination for daytrippers. It boasts both harbour and ocean beaches as well as sheltered coves, a lively promenade and such attractions as Oceanworld and giant waterslides at

Waterworks. Another plus is the **Manly Scenic Walkway**, one of Sydney's best walks, from Manly to the Spit Bridge. The track winds past beaches, reserves, forests, harbourside suburbs, Aboriginal sites and lookouts with superb views. The walk is 9.5km long and is medium to difficult. It takes 4hr one way; however, there are seven different sections which may be walked individually or combined for a shorter journey. For more information, contact the park info centre or Manly Council, Ph: 9976 1500. www.nationalparks.nsw.gov.au

Middle Harbour Map 4 F1

This arm of the harbour stretches from **Middle Head** back up into the suburbs, past Spit and Roseville Bridges to

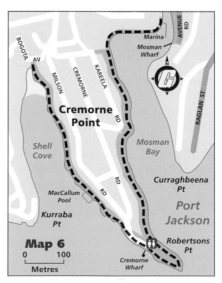

Map 6

MIDDLE HARBOUR

MANLY SCENIC WALKWAY VIEWS

Garigal NP. Although less frequented than the main reaches of Port Jackson, this part of the harbour has its own pleasures: peaceful beaches, quiet foreshore parks and picturesque walks.

The main beaches in Middle Harbour are situated before the Spit Bridge. **Balmoral Beach** is very popular for its safe swimming, and for strolling along the seafront. In summer, **Shakespeare by the Sea** draws crowds to the rotunda in the waterfront park. **The Bathers Pavilion** is a well-established restaurant, with various other venues along **The Esplanade** providing scenic dining. Around the corner from Balmoral is tranquil **Chinamans Beach**, backed by a grassy reserve, a favourite for family picnics. Opposite Spit Bridge, **Clontarf Beach and Reserve** are also ideal for picnics.

Further up Middle Harbour, various parks and reserves line the many bays and headlands. Some offer unspoilt bushwalks along the water, such as the **Harold Reid Foreshore Walk** at Middle Cove, the **Beauty Pt Foreshore Walk** at Beauty Pt and the **Flat Rock Track** in Garigal NP (see p.62). Garigal protects the upper reaches of Middle Harbour which narrows after the Roseville Bridge until it becomes Middle Harbour Creek. The park contains a variety of walks and

facilities. **Davidson picnic area**, underneath Roseville Bridge, is an agreeable location by the water, with picnic areas, swimming baths and walks. For suggestions of leisure activities on Middle Harbour, see p.48.

West of the Bridge Map 4 E2

West of the Bridge, **Balls Head Reserve** has extensive views of the harbour, with full picnic facilities, lookouts and toilets. Access from Waverton Railway Stn or by car from Crows Nest Rd. **Berry Island Reserve**, at the end of Shirley Rd at Wollstonecraft, is also an excellent picnic spot and provides a 750m signposted bushwalk, the **Gadyan Track**, which reveals aspects of the area's Aboriginal heritage. For fantastic views of the Harbour Bridge, **Blues Pt Reserve** at McMahons Pt is a must, with a string of cafes, restaurants and pubs lining **Blues Pt Rd** for post-view indulgence. At **Milsons Pt**, next to **North Sydney Olympic Pool**, is Sydney's most famous face: the **Luna Park** clown. Walk into the magical world of a 1930s amusement park where crazy rides like the tango train or nostalgic favourites such as the beautifully restored antique carousel are available. There are hilarious sideshow games, a history and mechanical music tour and, of course, fairy floss. With a backdrop of smiling faces, street performers and stunning harbour views, Luna Park Sydney is fun for everyone. An on-site car park is provided and regular ferry, train and bus services arrive right at the doorstep.

Parramatta River Map 4

Where the Parramatta and Lane Cove Rivers converge at Long Nose Pt, Birchgrove is where Port Jackson officially ends. However, there are still many parks and reserves along the waterfront with pretty views, facilities for picnics and BBQs and in some cases, bicycle paths. Between the two points at Greenwich and Woolwich, the Lane Cove River heads up to Lane Cove NP (p.64), while the Parramatta River continues west under the Gladesville Bridge, past parks and reserves on both shores.

At Homebush Bay is **Sydney Olympic Park**, which includes aquatic, golf and tennis centres and the Telstra Stadium, the centrepiece of the 2000 Olympic and Paralympic Games. Tours of the stadium are conducted daily between 10.30am and 3.30pm.

The park hosts major sporting and entertainment events; there are cafes, restaurants and picnic areas. A vast expanse of parkland, including Bicentennial Park (p.108), surrounds Olympic Park including mangroves and wetlands offering a variety of activities and attractions such as cycling, walking tracks, playgrounds, lookout towers with sweeping views of the city, birdwatching, guided tours and the Wetlands Explorer

Train. For more info, contact the Visitor Info Centre, Ph: (02) 9714 7888. www.sydneyolympicpark.com.au

Southern foreshores

The Bays Map 4

Watsons Bay is a favourite spot for a weekend excursion by ferry. The legendary **Doyles Seafood Restaurant** is here, and the beer garden of the Doyles Watsons Bay Hotel is always packed on a sunny Sunday afternoon. In front of the ferry wharf, **Robertson Park** is handy for picnics or munching Doyles take-away fish and chips. Around the corner from Village Pt, the peaceful expanse of grass at **Parsley Bay Reserve** is ideal for family outings.

Part of Sydney Harbour NP (see p.46), **Nielsen Park** is a popular recreation spot with shady picnic areas and a foreshore walk. Dressing sheds and showers are provided for swimmers and in the swimming season **Shark Beach** is protected by a sharkproof net. **Nielsen Park Kiosk** serves stylish Italian food in the restaurant and excellent coffee and snacks from the kiosk, www.npk.com.au

The 1.4km **Hermitage Foreshore Scenic Walk** starts here, winding along the waterfront past beaches and bays to Rose Bay. This walk can be combined with a swim, a picnic and visits to historic **Greycliffe House** and **Vaucluse House**. Nielsen Park is open from 5am–10pm. Wheelchair access from Greycliffe Ave, Vaucluse.

The next two bays back towards the city, **Rose Bay** and **Double Bay**, along

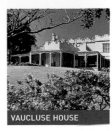
VAUCLUSE HOUSE

DOYLES SEAFOOD RESTAURANT, WATSONS BAY

ENDANGERED SPECIES

When cruising around the harbour, keep an eye out for **little penguins** *(Eudyptula minor)*. Sydney Harbour's small colony of about 60 breeding pairs are the only little penguins known to exist on the NSW mainland. They are protected by NPWS.

with Vaucluse and Bellevue Hill, represent the top end of Sydney's expensive real estate market; these suburbs are where multi-million dollar homes overlook the harbour.

Behind Kings Cross and Potts Pt lie **Elizabeth Bay** and **Rushcutters Bay**, the home of the **Cruising Yacht Club of Australia**, with a good view from Rushcutters Bay Park past the yacht masts.

Garden Island on **Woolloomooloo Bay** is the base for the Sydney Naval Fleet, and Mrs Macquaries Pt forms one side of **Farm Cove**, the scenic harbour foreground of the **Royal Botanic Gardens** (see p.28). Sydney's iconic **Opera House** (see p.26) perches at the end of Bennelong Pt, and across Sydney Cove is **The Rocks** area (see p.24).

West of the Bridge Map 4 E3

West of the Harbour Bridge is **Darling Harbour**, formerly a run-down dock area, and now one of Sydney's top spots, with shopping, parks, exhibition halls, restaurants and major attractions such as the Aquarium, the National Maritime Museum, Chinese Garden of Friendship and IMAX (see p.21).

National Parks

Sydney Harbour NP Map 4

Between 1975 and 1995, much of the harbour's foreshore bushland and open space, as well as five harbour islands, was taken under the protection of the NSW NPWS and proclaimed **Sydney Harbour NP**. The northern harbour foreshores make up a significant portion of the park, which is one of Sydney's greatest natural assets, providing valuable green expanses and recreation opportunities in the heart of the city.

Detailed info on activities and tours available in the park can be obtained by contacting Cadmans Cottage at The Rocks Ph: (02) 9247 5033

South Head is the southern section of the harbour entrance, and part of Sydney Harbour NP. Access is from the NE end of Camp Cove beach, where a level track passes HMAS *Watson* and the popular nudist beach **Lady Jane** (officially Lady Bay). This section of the park includes many historic fortifications and there are magnificent views of the harbour and the Heads. **Camp Cove** is a pleasant beach for a swim and a sandwich from the kiosk, away from the bustle of Watsons Bay. At the western end of the cove, on the hill, **Green Pt Reserve,** with more fantastic views, is perfect for picnics. The **South Head Heritage Trail** is a walking track that features panoramic views of Sydney and leads visitors to some of the city's important historic heritage — Hornby Light, lightkeepers' cottages and gun emplacements.

Facing South Head across the 1500m-wide opening to the harbour is **North**

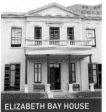

ELIZABETH BAY HOUSE

RUSHCUTTERS BAY

GROTTO PT LIGHTHOUSE

CADMANS COTTAGE

Head, one of the most scenic areas in Sydney. Sheer cliffs and sweeping coast and harbour views are complemented by extensive areas of bushland. Access to North Head is from Darley Rd, Manly, leading to **North Head Scenic Dr**. A small park-use fee applies at North Head. It is a popular place for picnics, with parking bays for lookouts, especially good for watching sunsets over the city. At the end of the Drive, the **Fairfax Walk** is a circuit with impressive views and signs describing the plants and wildlife of the area. Wheelchair accessible.

For many years the **Quarantine Station**, situated on North Head, was Sydney's main defence against infectious diseases. The station opened officially in 1832 and closed in 1984. The station can be explored alone, or the NPWS offers lantern-lit **Ghost Tours** of the historic buildings, including the hospital, mortuary and cemetery followed by a more lighthearted supper, Fri–Sun, Wed 7.30pm and 8pm during daylight saving. Bookings Ph: (02) 9247 5033 (not recommended for children under 12 years). The **Quarantine Station Ghost Tour for Kids**, a popular party activity, takes place 2nd Sat each month; private group bookings can also be made, Ph: (02) 9247 5033.
www.nationalparks.nsw.gov.au

Overlooking North Harbour and the Heads, **Dobroyd Head** supports excellent examples of dry sandstone vegetation. The views, especially from **Arabanoo** and **Crater Lookouts**, are magnificent. Access is via Dobroyd Scenic Dr or Cutler Rd, Clontarf.

Interesting features on Dobroyd Head include **Castle Rock**, with huge rocks and caves, **Grotto Pt**, with its Aboriginal carvings and a picturesque lighthouse, and **Reef Beach**. A spur track leads to this secluded bathing beach.

Middle Head has lots of fascinating old fortifications and a series of interlinking underground tunnels dating from the 1800s. Guided tours to view these are recommended, running on the 2nd and 4th Sun of each month. Contact Cadmans Cottage Ph: (02) 9247 5033. There is no vehicle access to the fortifications. Access to **Obelisk Beach**, a popular little harbour nudist beach, is via a short steep track off Chowder Bay Rd. On the other side of the head at **Cobblers Beach**, clothing is optional.

Ashton Park on Bradleys Head, near Taronga Zoo, is a quiet spot for a stroll along tracks with picturesque harbour views. There are historic fortifications with gun-pits, firing walls and numerous trenches to explore. Encompassing some 45ha, access to the Park is from Bradleys Head Rd or near the zoo ferry wharf. Parking is available in the park and there are facilities for disabled people. On the 1st Sun of each month 1.30pm at Ashton car park near Athol

SYDNEY HARBOUR NATIONAL PARK
Guided Discovery activities in and around the park are led by Discovery Rangers. Find out about the fate of ships such as the *Greycliffe*, *Dunbar* and *Rosa* on the **Shipwrecks at Sunset** walking tour. Learn the history of Sydney's white settlement on the **Goat Island Heritage Tour**. Ph: (02) 92475033. www.nationalparks. nsw.gov.au

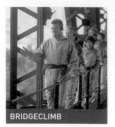

BRIDGECLIMB

Hall, the NPWS run **Bradleys Head Bushfood Tours**, taking a look at the park's natural environment. Discover a little about bush food and bush medicine on this easy 2hr walk. Ph: (02) 9968 4441. www.nationalparks.nsw.gov.au

Recreational activities

Action

This award-winning Sydney adventure offers a heady opportunity to rise above it all. **BridgeClimb** escorts groups to the very top of the Sydney Harbour Bridge to enjoy sensational 360° views and feel the achievement of conquering the world-famous span. High safety standards apply and special clothing and equipment must be worn; climbers aged 12–16 must be accompanied by an adult. The whole experience takes 3hr, covering 1.5km and climbing to 134m above sea level. For dawn, day, twilight and night bookings Ph: (02) 8274 7777. www.bridgeclimb.com

Combining harbour views with an adrenalin rush, **Parasail Sydney Harbour** at Manly tows the intrepid, strapped into a parachute, into the air over 100m above the water. Available Nov–Apr, Ph: (02) 9977 6781. www.parasail.net

Fishing

Sydney Harbour offers some excellent angling opportunities. Over 50 species, including bream, snapper and leatherjacket as well as lobster and prawn, are swimming around just waiting to be caught.

A number of boat launching ramps are situated around the harbour, and recommended fishing spots include **Bantry Bay**, **North Harbour**, **Clifton Gardens** and the **Sow and Pigs Reef** (between Lady Bay and Middle Head at the entrance to Port Jackson). Good fishing can also be pursued from land, around the harbour foreshores in many places such as **Roseville Bridge**, **Spit Bridge**, **Bradleys Head**, **Rose Bay** and **Bottle and Glass Rocks** off Vaucluse Pt.

Regulations apply relating to legal lengths, bag limits and protected species; brochures and info are available from **NSW Fisheries**. Ph: (02) 9438 5046

Fishabout Tours take half-day or day trips out onto the harbour. All tackle, bait and lures are provided and facilities are available on board to consume the day's catch on the spot. Longer weekend or week trips are also on offer. Ph: (02) 9451 5420

PARASAILING AT MANLY

KAYAKING ON THE HARBOUR

On the water

Some of the commercial cruises from Circular Quay venture up Middle Harbour, but there are also options for self-guided exploration on the water. The **Sydney Kayak Centre** at Spit Bridge hires out single and double kayaks hourly or daily. Ph: (02) 9969 4590. For those who like to sail, **Northside Sailing School** (Ph: (02) 9969 3972), also at Spit Bridge, hires out lasers; and hobie cats are available at the **Balmoral Boat Shed** (Ph: (02) 9969 6006) on the Esplanade at Balmoral Beach. They can also provide kayaks, canoes, surf skis and tinnies. The **Balmoral Windsurfing, Sailing and Kayaking School** hires out windsurfers and offers tuition on windsurfers, kayaks and catamarans. Ph: (02) 9960 5344. www.sailingschool.com.au

For thrill seekers **Harbour Jet** offers a variety of jet boat experiences including a jet boat ride followed by a seaplane flight, a Jet and Shark Dive and other combinations. Bookings 1300 88 73 73. www.harbourjet.com.

On the Parramatta River, Abbotsford Pt Boat Hire hire out motorboats, Ph: (02) 9713 8621

Sydney by Sail yacht charters offer hands-on experience with expert instruction during a 90min introductory sail. Tuition in all levels of sailing is provided in the company's **Learn to Sail** programs, and yacht charters are available. The trips leave from the National Maritime Museum at Darling Harbour. Ph: (02) 9280 1110. www.sydneybysail.com

Another great way to get out on the water is to enter one of the regular **twilight sailing races** held by the numerous yacht clubs around Sydney Harbour. Several companies such as Ausail, Eastsail, Simply Sailing and Sunsail offer the opportunity, some even for would-be sailors with no experience, to get out and participate. If this whets the appetite for wind in the sails, longer sailing courses are conducted at the many sailing schools around Sydney. For details, contact **Yachting New South Wales.** Ph: (02) 9660 1266. www.nsw.yachting.org.au

The **Waterways Authority's** website provides much useful information about boating, safety, environmental advice and links to national and overseas boating sites. www.waterways.nsw.gov.au

Fun for the young

★ BridgeClimb (p.48)
★ Ferry to Manly (p.37)
★ Harbour Bridge Pylon (p.41)
★ Learning to sail (p.49)
★ Australian National Maritime Museum, (p.20)
★ Quarantine Station Ghost Tour (p.47)
★ Swimming at Nielsen Park (p.45)

HARBOUR POOLS

A number of pools are scattered along the harbour foreshores, providing enclosed and usually picturesque bathing, including:

★ Redleaf Pool, New South Head Rd, Double Bay
★ Dawn Fraser Pool, Elkington Park, Balmain
★ Balmoral Baths, Balmoral Beach
★ Greenwich Baths, Albert St, Greenwich
★ McCallum Pool, Cremorne (pictured)

Must see, must do

★ Ku-ring-gai Chase NP (p.62)

★ Manly Food and
    Wine Festival (p.54)

★ Palm Beach (p.58)

★ Taronga Zoo (p.65)

★ Waratah Park
    Earth Sanctuary (p.65)

Radio stations

702ABC: AM 702

Mix FM: FM 106.5

ABC Classic FM: FM 92.9

2CH: AM 1170

2MBS-FM: FM 102.5

Tourist information

Hornsby Information Centre

The Hawkesbury Gateway

28–44 George St, Hornsby 2077

Ph: (02) 9847 6584

Kalkari Visitors Centre

Ku-ring-gai Chase Rd,

Mt Colah 2079

Ph: (02) 9457 9853

Manly Visitor Information Centre

The Forecourt, Manly Wharf,

Manly 2095

Ph: (02) 9977 1088

Tourism New South Wales

Ph: 132 077

www.visitnsw.com.au

Sydney Visitor Centres

106 George St,

The Rocks 2000

33 Wheat Rd,

Darling Harbour 2000

Ph: (02) 9240 8788

www.sydneyvisitorcentre.com

LEFT: MANLY BEACH

north of the harbour

FROM THE DRAMATIC CLIFFS OF North Head to Barrenjoey Lighthouse at Broken Bay and through the exclusive suburbs of Killara and Wahroonga, the area north of the harbour offers a host of enticements. Sydneysiders' fascination with boats of all sizes and shapes is clearly evident here, and the northern beaches have spawned some of Australia's greatest surfers.

The region is clearly defined by three distinct boundaries: Sydney Harbour to the south; the Hawkesbury River and Broken Bay to the north; and the Pacific Ocean to the east. To the west, the region stretches to Ryde, Beecroft and the outer edges of Berowra Valley Bushland Park, much of which is still bushy but becoming increasingly developed. The north shore of Sydney Harbour comprises some of the most valuable real estate in Australia, with water view property fetching into the millions of dollars.

Most people in this area are within a 15min drive of major recreational resources. Ku-ring-gai Chase, Lane Cove and Garigal NPs provide the bush, while the beaches extend up the coast from Manly, Sydney's own seaside resort, to the serenity of Palm Beach and the solitary splendour of Barrenjoey Head in the north.

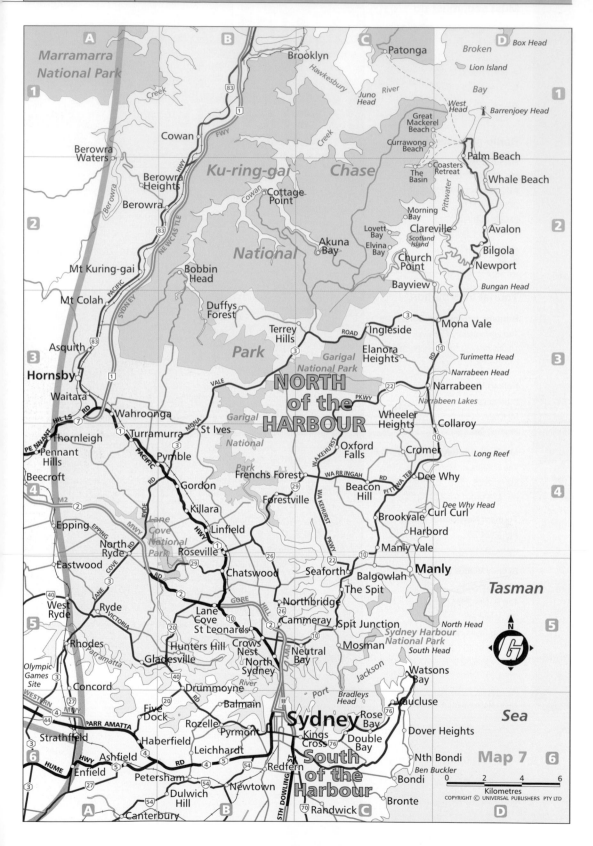

Marramarra
National Park

Brooklyn

Patonga

Broken · Box Head

Lion Island

Hawkesbury River

Juno
Head

Bay

Cowan

Ku-ring-gai

Chase

Great
Mackerel
Beach

West
Head

Barrenjeoy Head

Berowra
Waters

Berowra
Heights

Berowra

Cottage
Point

Currawong
Beach

Palm Beach

Cowan

Coasters
Retreat

The
Basin

Whale Beach

Mt Kuring-gai

National

Akuna
Bay

Lovett
Bay

Elvina
Bay

Morning
Bay

Clareville

Scotland
Island

Pittwater

Avalon

Bilgola

Bobbin
Head

Church
Point

Newport

Mt Colah

Duffys
Forest

Bayview

Bungan Head

Asquith

Park

Terrey
Hills

Ingleside

Mona Vale

ROAD

Garigal
National Park

Elanora
Heights

Turimetta Head

Narrabeen Head

Hornsby

Waitara

NORTH
of the
HARBOUR

Narrabeen

Narrabeen Lakes

Wahroonga

VALE

PKWY

Wheeler
Heights

Collaroy

Turramurra

St Ives

Garigal

National

Oxford
Falls

Cromer

Long Reef

Thornleigh

Pymble

Park

Frenchs Forest

Dee Why

Pennant
Hills

Beecroft

Gordon

Forestville

Beacon
Hill

Dee Why Head

Curl Curl

Epping

Killara

Linfield

Brookvale

Harbord

North
Ryde

Lane
Cove
National
Park

Roseville

Manly Vale

Eastwood

Chatswood

Seaforth

Manly

Tasman

West
Ryde

Ryde

Lane
Cove

St Leonards

Northbridge

Balgowlah

The Spit

North Head

Sydney Harbour
National Park

Rhodes

Hunters Hill

Crows
Nest

Cammeray

Spit Junction

South Head

Gladesville

North
Sydney

Neutral
Bay

Mosman

Olympic
Games
Site

Concord

Drummoyne

Jackson

Watsons
Bay

Port

Bradleys
Head

Sea

Balmain

Five
Dock

Rozelle

Pyrmont

Sydney

Vaucluse

Rose
Bay

Dover Heights

Strathfield

Haberfield

Leichhardt

Kings
Cross

Double
Bay

Map 7

Ashfield

Nth Bondi

Ben Buckler

Enfield

Petersham

Redfern

South
of the
Harbour

Bondi

Bronte

Dulwich
Hill

Newtown

Canterbury

Randwick

0   2   4   6
Kilometres
COPYRIGHT © UNIVERSAL PUBLISHERS PTY LTD

Natural features

Long fingers of water from Sydney Harbour and Broken Bay have cut their way into the northern suburbs, creating deep valleys through which creeks and rivers run. As a result, the topography of the region is varied, with little flat land.

The base rock is Hawkesbury sandstone with occasional cappings of shale. The fine, dark shale soils of Gordon and St Ives were once prized for market gardening, but the pressures of Sydney's urban sprawl have left little arable open land in the area.

The many bushland parks of the northern suburbs are home to a wide variety of natural vegetation. Heath, woodland, forest and mangrove areas are all represented. These large tracts of bushland have meant that many native birds survive in the urban environment. There are also colonies of pygmy and long-tailed possums and a large colony of fruit bats at Gordon. While these creatures are all protected by various state environmental acts, foxes and other introduced vermin pose a serious threat to indigenous wildlife.

History

Sydney's north shore has a history of human habitation stretching back many thousands of years. Remnants of ancient Aboriginal civilisation still remain, such as the rock engravings in various parts of Sydney Harbour and Ku-ring-gai Chase NPs. Some of the largest of these engravings are up to 8m long and depict a variety of cultural and religious figures, including mythical beings such as Daram-ulam, the all-father spirit. These priceless artworks are now fully protected. Detailed info is available from visitor centres in these parks.

The European history of the region is far more recent by comparison. On 21 Jan 1788, a few days before Captain Arthur Phillip established the settlement at what is now Circular Quay, he recorded seeing a number of Aboriginal people, whom he described as being particularly manly in appearance. The site was then named Manly Cove in recognition of this.

Despite this early encounter, white settlement of the north shore occurred much later than the development of the south side and areas up the Parramatta River and inland. It was not until 1810 that the first land grants were recorded at Manly, and another decade before a significant settlement was established.

It was the opening of the Great North Rd that hurried the pace of development in the north. In 1819 John Howe had established an overland route from the north shore to the extensive fertile lands around the Hunter River. But the road was no engineering masterpiece and was so treacherous that it was commonly known as the Drovers Nightmare. In 1826 work began on its replacement, the Great North Rd, completed in 1830. The road simplified and sped up the trip between the north and the Hunter, and

ABORIGINAL HERITAGE

Sydney Aboriginal Discoveries conduct daily tours from Pitt St, Sydney, to North Sydney, Ku-ring-gai NP, Pittwater and the Spit. Ph: (02) 9599 4219

ABORIGINAL ROCK ENGRAVINGS, WEST HEAD, KU-RING-GAI CHASE NP

partly because of the impetus this created, Sydney began to spread northwards.

Perhaps the biggest influencing factor on the development of the north shore was the completion of the Sydney Harbour Bridge in 1932. Previously, the harbour could only be crossed by ferry, restricting the spread of suburbia along railway lines and major roads. The bridge made the north shore easily accessible, and suburbs quickly flourished.

Getting there

By road

The major arteries are the Pacific Hwy and Gore Hill Fwy to the northern suburbs, M2 Mwy to the NW, and Military Rd/Pittwater Rd to the north and northern beaches. Eastern Valley Way, Warringah Rd and Mona Vale Rd also share much of the load in the coastal area where the car dominates. Buses run all the way up the northern peninsula from the CBD to Palm Beach and from Manly Wharf. Dee Why and Manly are accessible by bus from Chatswood. Parking at popular beaches can be a problem in summer.

By rail

An excellent train service operates up the north shore to Hornsby Stn, and on to Berowra, Cowan and Hawkesbury River (at Brooklyn), linking to suburban and regional bus and ferry services.

From midnight until 5am, buses replace the suburban trains.

By ferry

Ferries from Circular Quay service the harbour suburbs daily, with JetCat and regular ferries to Manly. Infoline: 131 500

A ferry service operates regularly during the day from Church Pt on Pittwater, visiting Scotland Island, Lovett Bay and Elvina Bay, Ph: (02) 9999 3492. Many of the ferry departure times are linked to the arrival of buses from Manly Wharf.

The Palm Beach Ferry Service provides water transport at the northern end of Pittwater and Broken Bay, as well as being the only scheduled link between the northern beaches and Patonga on the Central Coast. Ph: (02) 9918 2747

At Berowra Waters, a free vehicular ferry operates 24hr daily, providing an alternative route from the outer northern suburbs to the NW.

Getting around

Sydney's major coach tour companies offer daily 3hr morning **tours** of the northern beaches, and include the Spit Bridge, Manly and north to Dee Why. Ph: (02) 9252 2788 or 131 304

Harley Rides operate Harley Davidson bike trips throughout the Sydney area, including the northern beaches up to Palm Beach. Ph: 1800 800 784 or 0408 618 982

Festivals and events

Australia Day

Australia Day, 26 Jan, is celebrated throughout Sydney's north shore with parades, concerts and citizenship ceremonies. Breakfast on the Beach happens at Dee Why and Newport. Community breakfasts are also held at Berry Reserve, Narrabeen, and Lionel Watts Park, Frenchs Forest. At Pymble's Bicentennial Park the concert features dancers, singers, marching bands and fireworks.

Manly Food and Wine Festival

One of Sydney's largest regular community-based food and wine festival

PITTWATER FERRY SERVICE

BEROWRA WATERS

is held outdoors on Manly's ocean beach front in late May/early Jun. Local restaurateurs operate food stalls offering a wide range of cuisines, and wine-makers from throughout the state are also well represented.

Festival of Wildflowers

In late Aug/early Sept each year, the **Ku-ring-gai Wildflower Garden and Bush Education Centre** located off Mona Vale Rd, St Ives hosts a celebration of Australia-wide wildflowers. Guided tours include bush tucker strolls and habitat homes. Open 9am–4pm Sat and Sun. Ph: (02) 9440 8609

Surf carnivals

Surf carnivals are a major northern beaches attraction during summer. Carnivals are held at all major surf beaches and offer a range of events, from Iron Man to surf boat races. Check with individual surf clubs for their carnival schedules.

Manly Jazz Festival

Manly becomes the focal point for jazz lovers for the Oct long weekend. Attracting the very best local and international jazz performers, the free festival takes place on six outdoor stages. Ticket entry concerts are also part of this festival.

Carols by Candlelight

Community carol singing is held on the **Manly Corso** in Dec, and at the **International College of Tourism and Hotel Management** (previously St Patricks College) at North Head.

MANLY SURF LIFESAVER

THE CORSO, MANLY

Main localities

Although the suburbs north of the harbour can be collectively categorised by their general affluence and abundance of trees and parklands, they remain diverse enough to offer visitors an interesting range of attractions.

Beach suburbs

Manly Map 8 B1

For almost 150 years Manly has held a very special place in the hearts of Sydneysiders. Traditionally this beachside suburb was promoted as '7 miles from Sydney and 1000 miles from care', Manly has long enjoyed its reputation as Sydney's premier seaside resort.

Despite the ease of access by car and bus, catching the ferry is integral to the whole Manly experience for many people. The ferry departs regularly (every 30min) from Circular Quay and the route traverses almost the entire length of Sydney Harbour in the rather sedate **Manly Ferry**, which takes approx 30min to reach Manly and can accommodate more than 1000 passengers.

Located at the ferry terminal, **Manly Wharf** has various restaurants, a food court, boutiques, souvenir shops and a small fun fair.

Opposite is **Oceanworld Manly** with an underwater viewing tunnel, 110m long, enables visitors to observe sharks, giant stingrays, a loggerhead turtle and other wonders of the deep. In addition, Oceanworld has a Dangerous Australian Animals Show, which includes Australia's most venomous creatures. For the thrill of a lifetime, consider the Shark Dive Extreme Program where you can get up close and personal with 3m grey nurse sharks. For information on show times, the **Shark Dive Extreme Program**, or activities such as functions, sleepovers or birthday parties, Ph: (02) 8251 7877 www.oceanworld.com.au.

Manly Waterworks, a funpark with giant waterslides, operates during summer. To check days and times Ph: (02) 9949 1088

Adjacent to Oceanworld on West Esplanade, **Manly Art Gallery and Museum** displays a permanent collection of paintings as well as visiting exhibitions. Open Tues–Sun, 10am–5pm. Ph: (02) 9949 2435

Manly's ocean beach is within easy walking distance of the ferry wharf via **The Corso**, a pedestrian mall lined with small shops, restaurants and cafes and the venue for free outdoor

OCEANWORLD MANLY DISPLAY

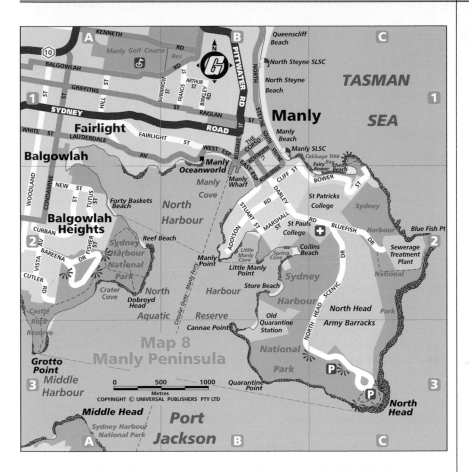

entertainment (including watching the passing parade) especially at weekends. With some 80 restaurants in the Manly area, there is a cuisine to suit all tastes and pockets.

Excellent for swimming, **Manly Beach** is also the focal point for surf carnivals and Iron Man competitions. Rollerblading along the beachfront is a popular pastime. A pleasant stroll along Marine Pde leads to two smaller and more sheltered ocean beaches, **Fairy Bower** and **Shelly Beach**. Safe swimming is also possible in the enclosure next to the ferry terminal in **Manly Cove**.

For lovers of the bush, Manly has much to offer. Most of **North Head**, the huge rocky outcrop that guards the entrance to Sydney Harbour, is part of **Sydney Harbour NP** (see p.46), and boasts fabulous harbour views. The historic **Quarantine Station** is also located here. A State Transit bus (no. 135) runs regularly from Manly Wharf

to North Head. Ph: 131 500. There are several good walks from Manly, as well as a scenic loop drive at the top of Darley Rd. The **Manly to Spit Bridge Walkway** encompasses panoramic views of the entrance to Sydney Harbour along its 10km track. There are numerous entry points, with public transport services available for the return trip. Maps available from Manly Visitor Info Centre. Ph: (02) 9977 1088

Narrabeen Lakes Map 7 C3

This system of lakes behind **Narrabeen Beach** is a good sailing and sailboarding spot, with **Pelican Path** near the mouth of the lakes at Narrabeen a popular fishing locale.

The **Coastal Environment Centre** adjoining the Lakeside Caravan Park at Narrabeen has displays and a comprehensive library describing the Sydney coast, lagoons, wetlands and catchment areas. Part of Pittwater

SAILBOARDING,
NARRABEEN LAKES

Council, the centre offers school holiday activities, including community programs and lectures, environmental art and bird-watching. Self-guided walk brochures are available. Open Mon–Fri, 9am–5pm; Sun, 10am–2pm. Ph: (02) 9970 6905

Palm Beach Map 7 D1

On the northern tip of the narrow peninsula that separates Pittwater from the ocean lies Palm Beach, holiday playground of the captains of commerce and industry.

Beaches lie on both sides of the peninsula, which comprises a golf course and a recreation reserve with a picnic area and play equipment. The sea breezes and relative calm of the Pittwater side make Palm Beach a magnet for keen sailboarders, while surfers enjoy the ocean beach.

At the tip of the peninsula, **Barrenjoey Lighthouse** offers breathtaking views across Pittwater to Lion Island, Brisbane Waters, Ku-ring-gai Chase National Park and the Central Coast. The uneven and at times strenuous uphill walk (see Map 9) starts at the northern end of **Barrenjoey Beach**. The lighthouse, dating from the 1880s, and the adjoining keepers' houses, are built from Sydney sandstone; an engraved plinth describes the various views and a headstone over a grave has a sobering inscription. An alternative

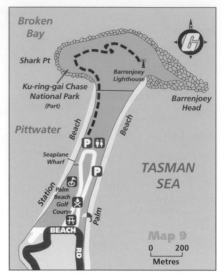

walk takes in giant sand dunes at the base of the Barrenjoey outcrop. Bus services run from Wynard and Manly Wharf up the coast to Palm Beach.

Pittwater Map 7 D2

Pittwater is a protected waterway bordered by Ku-ring-gai Chase NP and the Palm Beach peninsula. On weekends, Pittwater is alive with watercraft of every description and visitors can seek out their own private beach along the northern coastline. Yacht races provide an enchanting spectacle on most evenings in the summer months.

PALM BEACH

Hanging with the Duke

It may seem strange but there was a time when surfing was unknown in Australia. That was certainly the case in 1915 when **Duke Kahanamoku**, an Hawaiian athlete, was invited to Sydney to take part in a swimming championship. While surfing had been popular in Hawaii for many years, Australians had little exposure to this new sport. The Duke decided to change all that; he bought a length of sugar pine and carved a surfboard. Soon he was dazzling crowds at **Freshwater Beach** with his surfing prowess. When he left Sydney, he gave the board to a youngster named Claude West who went on to become a surfing champion in his own right. Duke Kahanamoku's board still hangs in Freshwater Surf Club and a statue honouring him is located near Harbord Diggers Club.

CRAGGY CLIFFS OFF THE NORTHERN BEACHES, WITH PITTWATER IN THE BACKGROUND

Scotland Island lies at the southern end of Pittwater and is serviced by ferry from Church Pt, Ph: (02) 9999 3492. It is mainly residential and most residents have their own small boat. There are no shops on the island, but visitors can picnic at Catherine Park which adjoins Tennis Wharf. Pink Water Taxi provides a 24hr service. Ph: 0428 238 190

Queenscliff to the Peninsula Map 7
A ribbon of fine swimming and walking beaches, craggy headlands, green reserves and gentle lagoons links Manly to Palm Beach and Barrenjoey Lighthouse. These beaches include **Queenscliff, Freshwater, Curl Curl, Dee Why, Collaroy, Narrabeen, Mona**

BARRENJOEY SANDSTONE

Vale, Bungan, Newport, Bilgola, Avalon and **Whale** beaches.

The **Warringah and Pittwater Bicentennial Coastal Walkway**, which stretches along the northern beaches between Manly and Palm Beach, is a series of headlands and lookouts which connect the ends of each beach to form a continuous coastline route.
Ph: (02) 9970 6905 or (02) 9970 1111.
At Beacon Hill, above Dee Why, **Governor Phillip Lookout** provides a superb view of the coast and the Sydney skyline.

Surf Lifesaving Clubs operate on most of the beaches. Swimmers should swim between the flags in the area patrolled by lifesavers; extreme care must be taken when surf conditions are rough. A number of the beaches have tidal pools.

At weekends there are a number of arts and crafts **markets** at different sites around the northern beaches. For info on markets in Manly, contact Manly Visitor Info Centre, Ph: (02) 9977 1088

Inner northern suburbs
Chatswood Map 7 B5
Regarded as the **shopping** mecca of the north shore, Chatswood offers a variety of major department stores, shopping malls, boutiques, cafes and restaurants. Some of the Chinese restaurants equal the best in Chinatown.

Chatswood is centrally located in the heart of the lower north shore, and is easily accessible by train. Victoria Ave, the suburb's main thoroughfare, offers the greatest range of shops.

GLIDERS
Depending on wind conditions, hang gliders, kites and radio-controlled model gliders are often in action at weekends on **Long Reef Pt**, Collaroy

BEST VIEWS

The Alexandra St Wharf in Hunters Hill provides an ideal spot for photography and views of the waterfront mansions.

Historic homes

Although not as long settled as areas such as Parramatta, the suburbs north of the harbour retain their fair share of historic homes. **Carisbrook Historic Homestead and Museum**, 334 Burns Bay Rd, Lane Cove was built in the late 1860s from local sandstone. It has been completely refurbished in the style of the period and is filled with antique furniture; it boasts a heritage garden. Wheelchair accessible. Open Wed, Thur, weekends and public holidays, Ph: (02) 9428 1364. The oldest surviving house in North Sydney is the **Don Bank Museum**. Once known as St Leonards Cottage, this 19th century timber slab cottage, with its remnant Victorian garden, is hidden away between towering office blocks at 6 Napier St. The museum features displays of local history and changing exhibitions. Open Sun, 1pm–4pm, call Stanton Library for other times Ph: (02) 9936 8400.

Crows Nest Map 7 B5

Willoughby Rd in Crows Nest has been landscaped and significantly upgraded into one of Sydney's leading restaurant precincts, with many cafes and restaurants offering alfresco dining.

Crows Nest also has some interesting shopping; for food supplies, don't miss the **Five Star Gourmet Deli**, which sells a huge range of quality goods including Australian bush food.
Ph: (02) 9438 5666

The **Crows Nest Markets** are held on the 3rd Saturday of the month in the grounds of the Crows Nest Centre. Stalls sell a variety of goods including clothing, jewellery, artworks and plants,.

CARISBROOK HISTORIC HOMESTEAD, LANE COVE

Hunters Hill Map 7 B5

Sharing a long harbour peninsula with Woolwich, Hunters Hill remains one of Sydney's best preserved **historic suburbs**. Colonial and Victorian architecture abounds, while strict local council regulations ensure that new buildings must complement the existing historic style. Although many of Hunters Hill's houses began life as simple sandstone worker's cottages, the passage of time has ensured that these once modest dwellings are now highly prized and expensive homes.

At 38 Alexander St, **Vienna Cottage** is a former stone worker's home, now a museum owned by the National Trust. The adjoining land, once an orchard, is a public park suitable for picnics. Open 2nd and 4th Sun of the month, 11am–4pm. Other times by appt. Ph: (02) 9816 2240

Housed in a quaint sandstone-and-wood workman's cottage is **Jaspers Restaurant**. One of Sydney's finest restaurants, it is also located in leafy Alexander St (54). Ph: (02) 9879 3200

Mosman Map 7 C5

One of Sydney's most fashionable suburbs, Mosman has hilly terrain and a harbourside location which offer spectacular water views. While **Military Rd** carries much of the northern beaches traffic, the eastern end of the road has retained some of its village atmosphere and has an excellent range of shops and restaurants. This is the main route to **Taronga Zoo** (p.65).

Nearby **Balmoral Beach** is a safe swimming beach popular with families, with a shark-netted area and baths. Balmoral is home to some of Sydney's leading restaurants including The Watermark and Bathers Pavilion. There are also a number of cafes as well as a popular fish and chips outlet (see p.44). Also within the Balmoral area, **Chinamans Beach** includes a wide grassed area, ideal for picnics. (Swimming at harbour beaches within three days of heavy rain is not advised.)

Luxury cruisers and yachts can be viewed at the marinas at **Balmoral** and **Spit Bridge**. For a scenic walk within the city limits, the path from **Bradleys Head** at Taronga Zoo east to **Chowder Bay** (6km) follows the foreshore of Sydney Harbour within the Sydney Harbour NP, passing quiet beaches and the historic remains of fortifications from Sydney's past. For other harbourside attractions, see 'The Harbour', p.33.

Outer northern suburbs
Berowra Waters Map 7 A2
Take Berowra Waters Rd off the Pacific Hwy 10km north of Hornsby (or via the F3 Fwy from Wahroonga) and follow its winding way down a narrow gorge to Berowra Waters. The village nestles on either side of Berowra Creek and most residences are accessible by boat only. With a marina on either bank, four restaurants and a fish and chip cafe, eating, boating and fishing are the principle activities in this idyllic spot.

Picnickers are catered for on the western bank where a boat ramp is also located. A free vehicle ferry operates 24hr, carrying traffic from Berowra Waters Rd to Bay Rd and on to Arcadia. North shore and northern line trains stop at **Berowra**; Shorelink buses service **Berowra Heights** from the north shore; but due to the narrow road, there is no service for the 4km from Berowra Heights to Berowra Waters. www.shorelink.com.au (See p.66 for boating information.)

A section of the **Great North Walk** passes through Berowra Waters on the eastern side of the creek, where a detailed map provides info on the walking trails in the area.

Brooklyn Map 7 B1
Brooklyn lies near the mouth of the **Hawkesbury River** system and is renowned for its fresh oysters. A haven for yachties and fishermen, the village springs to life on weekends in the warmer months. Named by American workmen employed to build the bridge across Broken Bay, Brooklyn also attracts nature lovers and those just

BALMORAL BEACH

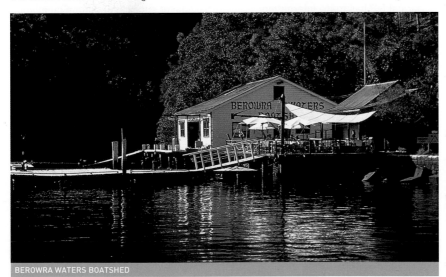
BEROWRA WATERS BOATSHED

BOTTLEBRUSH

looking for a peaceful getaway. Families enjoy the shark-netted swimming pool with nearby BBQs and playground area. Access by road from the Pacific Hwy or the F3 Fwy to the north of Sydney; by train to Hawkesbury River Stn; or by water from Broken Bay.

Ferries depart regularly from Brooklyn Public Wharf to **Dangar Island**, a car-free community of about 200 houses within the waterway, and a great spot for a family picnic. Ph: (02) 9985 7605. (For river cruises, see p.67.)

National Parks

A large part of Sydney's north has been preserved as parkland, the majority of which is contained within three large reserves.

Garigal NP Map 7 C3

Garigal NP snakes its way from **Middle Harbour** north to **St Ives** and protects 2100ha of the harbour's catchment area. Largely surrounded by suburbia and some industry, the park is best known and utilised at the picnic ground at **Davidson picnic area**.

Davidson picnic area is located at **Roseville Bridge** and has picnic tables, electric and wood BBQs (wood provided), shelter sheds, and toilets with provision for the disabled. There is a public boat ramp and a wheelchair accessible pontoon.

Garigal NP has many interesting creeks featuring sandstone waterfalls and rockpools. It abounds in wildlife and features a large number of rare and endangered plant species.

GARIGAL NP

Horseriding is permitted along designated tracks. The park is well used by **boating** enthusiasts and for **fishing**. **Canoeing** is also a popular pursuit on middle harbour. Five **walking track** maps and an info sheet on the historic **Bantry Bay explosives magazine** complex (now disused) are available from Northern Beaches area office. Ph: (02) 9451 3479

Ku-ring-gai Chase NP Map 7 B2

The natural jewel of the region is Ku-ring-gai Chase NP. Founded in 1894, the nation's 2nd oldest NP covers some 15 000ha of superb sandstone bushland, only 24km from Sydney's CBD. It attracts around two million visitors a year.

Steep-sided river valleys give it a spectacular and rugged beauty. The

The Great North Walk

One of the lasting legacies of the Bicentennial year of 1988 is the Great North Walk, a 250km walking track from Sydney to Newcastle. The walk caters for people of all ages and levels of experience. It provides a series of day walks and weekend walks with numerous access points, facilities and connections to public transport. The short walks can be combined into a 14-day trek passing through some of the State's most outstanding natural scenery. The route includes **Sydney Harbour**, **Lake Macquarie** and the **Newcastle** coastline. Discovery kits for each section can be obtained from the NSW Dept of Infrastructure, Planning and Natural Resources Ph: (02) 4929 9817

vegetation is mainly heath and woodland with an amazing variety of animal life. Hundreds of Aboriginal sites dot the park, including rock engraving, cave art and middens.

The name Ku-ring-gai is taken from the language of the Aboriginal people who lived in the region, which was known as Guringai or Kuringai. Within 50yr of European settlement in the area, almost the entire group had been wiped out.

The **Kalkari Visitor Centre** on Ku-ring-gai Chase Rd, Mt Colah, has a theatrette which shows videos on Aboriginal culture and native Australian animals as well as displays of the park's ecology. Guided walks are available around the **Kalkari Discovery Track**. Open daily, 9am–5pm. Kalkari Visitor Centre (02) 9472 9300

On the farthest tip of the park, **West Head Lookout** provides a magnificent panoramic view over the whole of Broken Bay, Palm Beach and most of Pittwater. The network of walking trails from West Head and throughout the park are detailed in pamphlets available at Kalkari Visitor Centre, the park Info Centre at **Bobbin Head**, and at entrance stations.

The recreational area at **Bobbin Head** has been developed over decades into an outstanding facility with a large play area for children, picnic shelters, BBQ areas, a restaurant and cafe. A suspension bridge takes visitors deep into the dense mangroves protecting the waterway.

Picnic and BBQ areas are provided throughout the park, but visitors are advised to bring their own electric or gas BBQ to help preserve the bush. There are also picnic facilities at **Akuna Bay**.

Scenic waterways such as **Coal and Candle Creek** and **Jerusalem Bay** are also part of the park's attractions. There are **boat ramps** at Appletree and Akuna Bays, and boat hire is available from Akuna Bay, Cottage Pt and Bobbin Head.

Hawkesbury River Cruises, MV *Erringhi* operates out of Bobbin Head and offers weekend cruises. Food and wine are accompanied by historical commentary. Bookings essential Ph: (02) 9217 7095

A section of the **Great North Walk** passes through the northern part of the park from near Cowan to Brooklyn.

Ku-ring-gai Chase NP is accessible by road from Terrey Hills and Church Pt (McCarrs Creek Rd), North Turramurra (Bobbin Head Rd) and Mt Colah (Ku-ring-gai Chase Rd). There are walking paths from railway stns north of Hornsby and from Mona Vale and Booralie Rds. Open daily, 9am–5pm. Ph: (02) 9472 9300/9301; the Basin (02) 9974 1011

THE SPHINX

The sphinx in Kur-ing-gai Chase NP was chiselled from a solid block of sandstone by WWI veteran Pte William Shirley in memory of his fallen comrades, during his recuperation at a nearby hospital.

VIEW FROM WEST HEAD

AKUNA BAY

Lane Cove NP Map 7 A4

Sandwiched between the north shore suburbs of Chatswood, Lindfield and North Ryde, Lane Cove NP winds along the **Lane Cove River** and provides a welcome green 'lung' in the midst of suburbia.

There are three **entrances** to the park: one from the west off Lane Cove Rd and two at Fullers Bridge, off Delhi Rd and Lady Game Dr. Visitors may use the fireplaces provided or bring their own portable BBQs. An excellent range of freshly cooked take-away meals is available in the visitor centre precinct.

A **river walk**, which is part of the **Great North Walk**, passes through dense canopied forest and past sandstone overhangs; a wide variety of birdlife, including lorikeets, herons, rosellas, cockatoos, kookaburras and egrets abounds. The walk to **De Burgh's Bridge**, the boundary of the park, takes about 2hr, starting from the entrance at Lady Game Dr.

Four- and five-man rowboats can be hired on the spot Sat noon–5pm, Sun and public holidays 10.30am–5pm. Swimming in the river is not permitted.

In the Jenkins Hill area off Lady Game Dr, **Kukunde Wildlife Shelter** is a centre for the rehabilitation and release of injured native animals. Its strong focus on community education makes it a great place to visit. The Lane Cove NP **Visitor Centre** is open Mon–Fri, 9am–4pm; the park is open daily 9am–6pm (7pm during daylight saving). Ph: (02) 9412 1811. Within the park, **Lane Cove River Tourist Park** offers camping, caravans and cabins, Ph: (02) 9888 9133

Parks and gardens

Ku-ring-gai Wildflower Garden and Bush Education Centre Map 7 B3

Situated on Mona Vale Rd at **St Ives**, this delightful garden has more than 123ha of native plants and bushland. Walks, ranging in length from a few metres to 4km, pass through a variety of habitats. **The Senses Track** is suitable for wheelchairs. Facilities include picnic areas, BBQs and a playground. Open daily, 8am–4pm. Ph: (02) 9440 8609

Stony Range Flora and Fauna Reserve Map 7 C4

At **Dee Why**, this native plant haven is set in original bushland improved with additional plantings of Australian species. The reserve provides a natural buffer between the residential and light industrial areas. There are easy, well-marked tracks to follow and a picnic area with tables and electric BBQs. A feature of the reserve is the Federation Cascades, which attracts a variety of birdlife to the fresh running water. Open daily 8am–sunset. Ph: (02) 9981 3026

Waratah Park Earth Sanctuary
Map 7 B3

This 12ha site at **Duffy's Forest** was used for filming the historic *Skippy* television series. The sanctuary was established to put back the wildlife of the region as it was in 1788. To do this a 2km feral-proof fence has been built around the boundary and ferals removed and species returned to roam free in the sanctuary, including bettongs, potoroos, wallabies, pademelons and many more. Open 4–9pm with an Ausssie BBQ available 6–7pm, to book Ph: 9986 1788. www.esl.com.au

Other attractions

Baha'i House of Worship Map 7 C3

This distinctive landmark north of the harbour sits on its hilltop setting on Mona Vale Rd at **Ingleside**. The Baha'i movement was founded in Persia over 150yr ago and has about 10 000 followers in Australia. An inter-faith service is held every Sun at 11am. There is an info centre and tours are provided. A picnic area is located in the 3ha grounds. Open daily, 9am–5pm. Ph: (02) 9998 9221

Mary MacKillop Place Map 7 B5

The story of the Blessed Mary MacKillop, receives high-tech treatment at Mary MacKillop Place, 7 Mount St, **North Sydney**. The museum recounts the events that led to the nun's beatification and a tour includes a visit to Mary MacKillop's tomb. Open daily 10am–4pm Ph: (02) 8912 4878

Nutcote Map 7 C5

May Gibbs, creator of the famous children's characters Snugglepot and Cuddlepie, was a long-time north shore resident. 'Nutcote', her home at number 5 Wallaringa Ave, **Neutral Bay**, was built in 1925 and was restored to become a museum in 1994. The house contains a large selection of Gibbs memorabilia and has been refurbished in a typical 1930s style, with much of May Gibbs' furniture and work. Nutcote has special function

facilities for children's birthday parties, weddings and the like. Open Wed–Sun, 11am–3pm. Ph: (02) 9953 4453. www.maygibbs.com.au

Taronga Zoo Map 10

At Bradleys Head, **Mosman**, Taronga Zoo enjoys majestic views over the harbour and the city. Long regarded as one of the world's great zoos, Taronga Zoo is constantly evolving and contains Australia's finest collection of native and exotic animals which includes about 380 species and over 2200 specimens. Photo sessions with koalas are offered 11am–3pm at **Koala Encounters**.

Exhibits include the **Gorilla Forest**, the **Orang-utan Rainforest** and the **Cats of Asia**, whose inhabitants include the Asiatic golden cat and the clouded leopard. A rare white tiger and a pair of Sumatran tigers are also on show. Leon and Samarra are the zoo's beautiful snow leopards. Keeper talks at animal feeding times are held throughout the day and there are various daily presentations such as the **Free Flight Bird Show** (3pm), **KidZoo Backyard to Bush** 10.30–11.30am. Visit the zoo's very informative website and see how to

NUTCOTE

BAHA'I HOUSE OF WORSHIP

TARONGA ZOO — A GREAT ZOO WITH A GREAT VIEW

'**Plan Your Day**', an excellent timetable of what is on and where.

Getting to Taronga can be half the fun. It is only a short 12min ferry ride from Circular Quay to the zoo's wharf and a cable car runs from the wharf to the main entrance. Buses also run to the zoo and there is plenty of parking at the main entrance off Bradleys Head Rd, Mosman. Special public transport tickets offer discounts on travel and admission: the all-inclusive ZooPass includes return ferry, Sky Safari/bus and Zoo admission and is available for the trip from Circular Quay.

The zoo is the venue for a wonderful series of open-air, twilight concerts in summer. Open daily, 9am–5pm. Check for later closing times in summer when the zoo lights are lit at dusk. Ph: (02) 9969 2777. www.zoo.nsw.gov.au

Recreational activities

Camping
The only campsite in Ku-ring-gai Chase NP is at **The Basin** on the northern shore of Pittwater. This sheltered site is accessible by a regular ferry service from Palm Beach. The Basin offers safe swimming in a large lagoon, cold showers, and **Beechwood Cottage** may be hired for special events. Bushwalking tracks lead out from the Basin and

further into the park. Bookings essential, Ph: (02) 9974 1011. There are also extensive picnicking facilities for day-trippers. www.nationalparks.nsw.gov.au

Cycling
Although the often hilly terrain that characterises northern harbour suburbs can be a challenge to cyclists, the natural beauty and stunning water views encountered along the way more than compensate for the extra exertion.

For those with limited time, the 10km round trip ride from **Manly Wharf** to **North Head** is ideal. Serious cycle enthusiasts north of the harbour claim that the cycle tracks of **Ku-ring-gai Chase NP** are among the best in Sydney. The Bicycle NSW (BNSW) publication *Cycling Around Sydney* contains comprehensive maps and tips about these particular rides and several others around the city. Ph: (02) 9281 4009. www.bicyclensw.org.au. Also check the RTA's *Sydney Cycle Ways* Freecall: 1800 060 607

On the water
There are many opportunities to go boating on the scenic waterways to the north of the region. Broken Bay and Pittwater are popular spots for rental craft while a number of operators

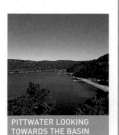

PITTWATER LOOKING TOWARDS THE BASIN

Fun for the young

- ★ Balmoral Beach, Mosman (p.61)
- ★ Bushwalking in the national parks (p.62)
- ★ Canoeing at Narrabeen Lakes (p.57)
- ★ Ferry to Dangar Island (p.62)
- ★ Fishing at Berowra Waters (p.61)
- ★ Ice skating, Macquarie Shopping Centre rink, North Ryde (Map 7 A4)
- ★ Manly Wharf (p.56)
- ★ Oceanworld Manly (p.56)
- ★ Surfing the northern beaches (p.59)
- ★ Taronga Zoo (p.65)

The MV *Macquarie Princess* served for 38yr as a Sydney Harbour ferry. It is now the linchpin of *Macquarie Princess Cruises*, with a wide variety of short and long cruises on offer, including weekend getaway cruises. Bookings essential. Ph: (02) 9680 3909. www.macquarieprincesscruises.com.au

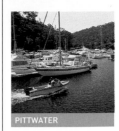
PITTWATER

The **Palm Beach Ferry Service** has a 60km daily cruise on the Hawkesbury River from Palm Beach to Bobbin Head at Ku-ring-gai Chase NP, calling at Patonga. There is a lunch stop at Bobbin Head, before returning to Palm Beach at 3.30pm. There is also a 2hr coffee cruise service on Pittwater for groups. Ph: (02) 9918 2747. www.palmbeachferry.com.au

Pittwater Yacht Charter and Sailing School at 1714 Pittwater Road, Bayview, has a range of yachts for charter with either a skipper or bareboat. Ph: (02) 9997 5344, www.yachtcharter.com.au

Ripples Houseboat Hire, 87 Brooklyn Rd, Brooklyn, provides cruising on the Hawkesbury River in well-appointed houseboats. No licence required. Ph: (02) 9985 7333. www.ripples.com.au

Skipper-a-Clipper, Gibson Marina, Pittwater Rd, Bayview, has a selection of cruisers, yachts and motor catamarans sleeping 4–10. Explore Pittwater and the Hawkesbury River. Boats are fully equipped and no licence is required — instructions given. Ph: (02) 9979 6188. www.skipperaclipper.com.au

run Hawkesbury River cruises. Hire charges are significantly reduced by most companies in the winter months.

Exploring the Hawkesbury River in an aluminium buggy boat, hired from **Berowra Waters Marina**, is an inexpensive way to discover the area. Ph: (02) 9456 2866

Church Pt Charter at Newport offers a large selection of self-drive cruises, yachts and catamarans. Skippers and waitresses are provided or you can drive yourself, no licence required. Ph: (02) 9999 4188. www.churchpointcharter.com.au

Halvorsen Marina at Bobbin Head has skiffs and motor launches for hire 8am–4pm daily Ph: (02) 9457 9011. www.halvorsenmarina.com.au

Hawkesbury River Ferries provide a chance to join Australia's last **riverboat postman** on his daily rounds. The ferry carries all sorts of supplies (including the mail) for the riverside community. The postman departs from the Hawkesbury River Ferry Wharf at Brooklyn at 9.30am weekdays and returns around 1.15pm. The service does not operate on public holidays. This is also the **Dangar Island** ferry service. Bookings preferable, Ph: (02) 9985 7566

THE HAWKESBURY RIVER

PALM BEACH

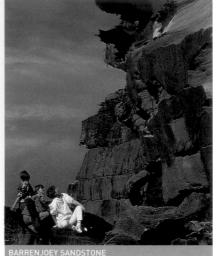

BARRENJOEY SANDSTONE

Suggested tours – Map 10

Scenic tour to Palm Beach

Approximate distance

80km return from Sydney CBD, plus 25km for Akuna Bay side trip.

About the tour

This stretch of beautiful NSW coastline comprises a ribbon of beaches guarded by sandstone headlands from North Head to Barrenjoey Head. The tour provides ample opportunity for swimming, surfing and snorkelling but it can be equally enjoyed during the cooler months.

There are plenty of BBQ and picnic spots, all offering spectacular scenery. A favourite with tourists is the Bilgola Headland Lookout, which provides a wonderful panoramic view of the local beaches and the Central Coast.

A distinct contrast to the beaches is provided at Pittwater, where the bushland meets the waterway.

The tour includes an opportunity for a trip up the Hawkesbury River into Ku-ring-gai Chase NP or a ferry ride to Patonga on the Central Coast.

Lower north shore tour

Approximate distance

45km return from Sydney CBD

About the tour

Sydney's lower north shore has wide appeal for locals and visitors alike, providing cosmopolitan big-city experiences of shopping, dining and entertainment, cheek by jowl with Australia's original surf beach culture at Manly.

National parks and quiet harbour beaches appeal to nature lovers. Oceanworld at Manly has something for everyone, and Taronga Zoo offers everything you'd expect from one of the world's great zoos, as well as some of the most impressive harbour views you are likely to see anywhere in the world.

Many kms of scenic coastal walkways are also popular local attractions. This tour provides many ways to enjoy the area's natural assets, and when you need a break, there's no shortage of charming cafes and restaurants.

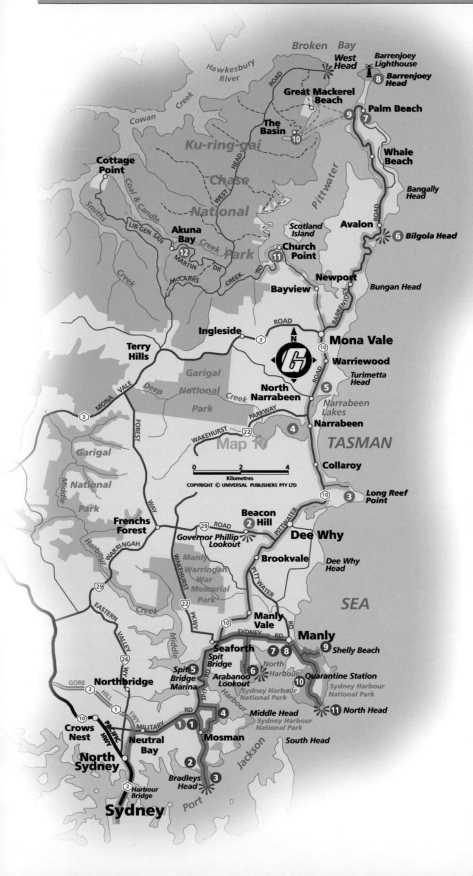

Must see, must do

★ Balmain (p.82)

★ Bondi Beach (p.75)

★ Cronulla (p.76)

★ Kings Cross (p.79)

★ Paddington (p.80)

★ Royal NP (p.86)

★ Watsons Bay (p.81)

Radio stations

Eastside Radio: FM 89.7

Radio Sutherland: FM 87

**Sutherland Shire Community
Radio 2SSR:** FM 99.7

Tourist Radio: FM 88

2KY: AM 1017

Tourist information

Randwick Tourism

Randwick City Tourism Inc

Ph: (02) 9399 0810 and
(02) 9344 7066 (after hours)

**Royal National Park
Visitors Centre**

Farrell Ave, Loftus 2232

Ph: (02) 9542 0648

**Sutherland Shire Tourism
Association Inc**

Cronulla Railway Stn,
Cronulla 2230

Ph: (02) 9544 2144

www.visitoz.com

**Sydney Harbour National Park
Cadmans Cottage**

110 George St,
The Rocks 2000

Ph: (02) 9247 5033

www.nationalparks.nsw.gov.au

**Sydney Visitor Centres
106 George St, Sydney 2000**

33 Wheat Rd,
Darling Harbour 2000

9.30am–5.30pm daily

Ph: (02) 9240 8788

www.sydneyvisitorcentre.com

LEFT: BONDI BEACH

south of the harbour

THIS VIBRANT PART OF THE CITY has a great deal to offer, from trendy inner city suburbs to lively surf beaches and tranquil national parks. A wide social cross-section is represented here, with the wealthy eastern suburbs of Vaucluse and Double Bay, the relaxed beachside ambience of Bondi, Coogee and Cronulla, the fashionable and historic inner suburbs of Paddington, Glebe and Balmain, Sydney's famous bohemian night spot, Kings Cross, and the rich cross-cultural flavours of Newtown, Marrickville and Leichhardt. One of the most pleasant ways to enjoy this plurality is via the taste buds — an incredible range of restaurants, hotels and cafes offer some of Sydney's best eating and drinking.

For a refreshing brush with nature, Royal NP, Sydney Harbour NP and Botany Bay NP offer a winning combination of beauty and history, located within easy reach of the city.

History buffs have plenty to explore in this region, which offers stately old buildings such as Vaucluse House, as well as suburbs like Paddington, with its beautiful old Victorian terrace houses and Balmain with its quaint sandstone cottages. Botany Bay NP, straddling both sides of the entrance to Botany Bay, is rich in Aboriginal and early colonial history.

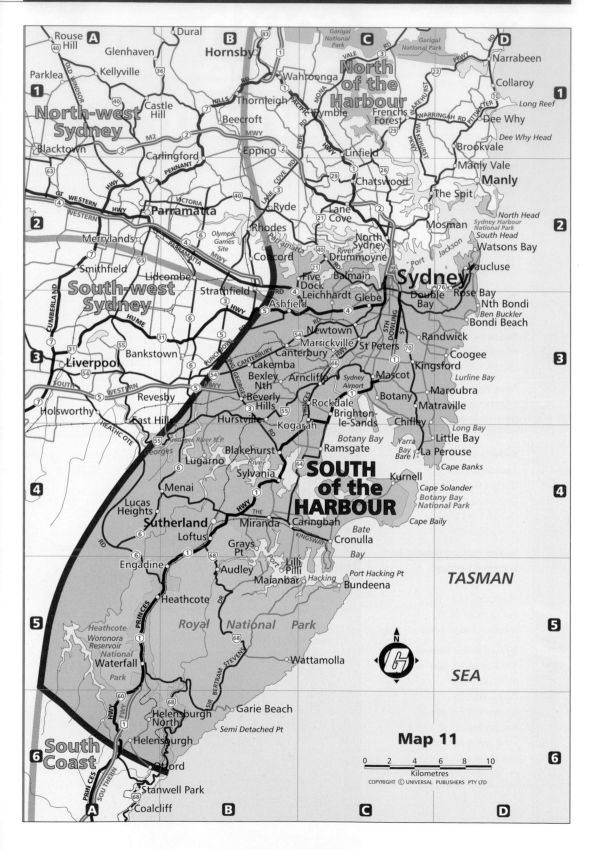

Map 11

Natural features

Southern Sydney is part of the Sydney Plain, consisting of ridges along the coast, dropping away inland to flat, mainly sandy country. Between the headlands formed by the rocky ridges are many beaches, including famous Bondi. South of Botany Bay, a long beach backed by sandhills sweeps around Bate Bay to Cronulla.

Botany Bay, the most northerly of the area's inlets, has a sandy, flat foreshore. Port Hacking, to the south, is a drowned valley more like Sydney Harbour and beyond it the country becomes more rugged. This is true Sydney sandstone country and includes areas of spring-flowering heathlands, eucalypt forest, rainforest and a stunning stretch of coastline with towering sandstone cliffs. This special place is Sydney's Royal NP.

The Georges River drains most of southern Sydney and together with its major tributary, the Woronora River, has many parks, reserves and peaceful bushland suburbs along its shores.

History

Like the rest of Sydney, these southern parts were inhabited by Aboriginal people for around 60 000 years before Europeans arrived. The Gwyeagal people gave Captain Cook's men a mixed reception when they landed in Botany Bay on 29 Apr 1770.

The French explorer Jean-Francois de Galaup, Comte de La Perouse, arrived just a few days after Captain Arthur Phillip inspected Botany Bay in 1788, and stayed on the northern headland for six weeks. His visit is commemorated by the name of the nearby suburb and the La Perouse Museum near the site of his landing.

The inner city and inner western suburbs were the first to be settled in Sydney. They still contain many excellent examples of grand old houses of the early rich, as well as terraces and cottages of the working classes.

Getting there

By road

Bus routes extend from railway stations into the suburbs, with buses also running from the major city stops to many destinations in the area. Bus services connect all the beaches as far south as Maroubra with the city.

Parramatta Rd heads west from Broadway, eventually becoming the Great Western Hwy (Hwy 32) at Parramatta. The Princes Hwy is the main southern arterial road. Hwy 1 follows the route of the Sydney Harbour Tunnel from the northern suburbs and joins the Princes Hwy at

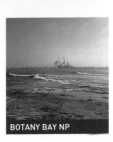
BOTANY BAY NP

RANDWICK CITY'S COASTAL WALKWAY

SYDNEY PASS

For the intrepid traveller a Sydney pass (3, 5 or 7 days) is a convenient all-in-one ticket, which provides unlimited travel on the Bondi and Sydney Explorer buses, Sydney Ferries Harboursights Cruises as well as regular train, bus and ferry services
Ph: 131 500

ICY DIP
The **Bondi Icebergs** are a group of intrepid swimmers who brave the icy winter waters in Bondi Baths.

GAY AND LESBIAN MARDI GRAS

FROM THE ARCHIVES OF SYDNEY TRAMWAY MUSEUM

Kogarah. From Taylor Sq on Oxford St, Flinders St leads to Anzac Pde which runs south to the northern headland of Botany Bay and is a convenient route to the beaches of the eastern suburbs, alternatively, take the Eastern Distributor (ED) and take the Bondi exit.

By rail
Suburban railway lines run from Central Stn along four main lines: the East Hills line to Campbelltown; the Bankstown line; the Parramatta line; and the Illawarra line to Cronulla via Sutherland (this line continues at the Central Stn end as the eastern suburbs line, terminating at Bondi Junction).

By ferry
Ferries run from Circular Quay to Darling Pt, Double Bay, Rose Bay and Watsons Bay, while Bundeena in the Royal NP is accessible by ferry from Cronulla.

Getting around
The blue **Bondi Explorer** bus is a good option for reaching the beaches. It travels through the eastern and SE suburbs including Double Bay, Rose Bay and Watsons Bay, to the beachside suburbs of Bondi, Bronte, Clovelly, Coogee, and back towards the city through Paddington, the Royal Randwick Racecourse, the Sydney Cricket Ground and Football Stadium, Oxford St, Hyde Park and Martin Pl. Travellers can leave and rejoin the buses, which run every 30min, at any time.

Various tour companies offer daily **afternoon coach tours** of the southern beaches. Contact Sydney Visitors Centre for more info.

Tram buffs can catch a vintage tram to Royal NP from the **Sydney Tramway Museum** (p.88).

Festivals and events
Surf carnivals
During the swimming season, life saving clubs hold surf carnivals and displays of life saving skills, both marked by pageantry. For a special experience while in Sydney, check with the Sydney Visitors Centre for dates and venues.

Gay and Lesbian Mardi Gras
Sydney's internationally renowned Gay and Lesbian Mardi Gras runs for four weeks in Feb, with festivities including theatre, film, art, photography, concerts,

cabaret, comedy and sport, culminating in one of the world's most dazzling costume parades. Get there early for a viewing spot on the parade route, as well over half a million people turn up to watch. For info call Mon–Fri 10am–5pm, Ph: (02) 9568 8600

Captain Cook Historic Festival

Every May, **Kurnell** celebrates the arrival of Captain Cook and the European discovery of Australia with live shows, static displays, music, dancing, amusements and fireworks.

City to Surf

A challenging 14km fun run from the city to Bondi (see p.13).

Newtown Festival

The Newtown Festival is a major fair day held on the 2nd Sun in Nov, with markets, competitions and a program of events such as community arts, entertainment and band nights held for up to a month before the fair day. Ph: (02) 9516 4755

Glebe Street Fair

This annual open-air street fair takes place on the 4th Sun of Nov, providing a kilometre of stalls selling all manner of things. Food, wine tastings, a Kids' Fair, music and a grand parade are part of the fun.

Main localities

The southern region of Sydney divides into three distinctive areas, each with its own character and personality: beach suburbs, eastern suburbs and inner western suburbs.

Beach suburbs
Bondi Beach Map 13 D4

Bondi Beach is an Australian icon and has one of the world's most famous beaches, highly regarded for its surf, cosmopolitan atmosphere, restaurants and cafes; thousands of tourists gather here to celebrate Christmas Day and New Year. The **Bondi Pavilion** is an important local cultural centre, hosting exhibitions, regular classes, workshops, music and school holiday programs,

GLEBE STREET FAIR

BONDI BOY

BRIGHTON-LE-SANDS

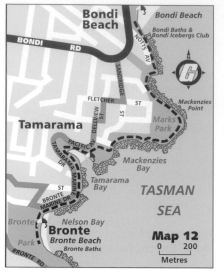

theatre productions and festivals, including the **South American Festival**, the **Pacific Wave Festival** and the wonderful **Festival of the Winds** and much more. The pavilion is an initiative of Waverley Council. For more info see www.waverley.nsw.gov.au.

The **Bondi Walk** (see Map 12), a marked trail with fitness stops, runs from the southern end of Bondi beach to **Coogee** and is a superb coastal track. The route continues to **Maroubra Beach** and in its entirety is known as **Randwick City's Coastal Walkway**. It has wheel-chair access, offers excellent scenery and numerous swimming and eating spots, and places just to rest and relax. For more info Ph: (02) 9344 7006

www.randwickcitytourism.com.au
Coo-ee Aboriginal Art, 31 Lamrock Ave, Bondi Beach is famous for its fine art. Open Tues–Sat, 11am–5pm or by appointment, Ph: (02) 9332 1544

Brighton-Le-Sands Map 11 C3

Brighton-Le-Sands is a delightful spot on **Botany Bay**. A strip of parkland runs along the shore from **Kyeemagh** through Brighton-Le-Sands to **Cook Park** at **Sans Souci**, offering an abundance of picnic sites. Several protected baths are scattered along the beach. **Bay St** and the adjoining section of the **Grand Pde** contain many highly-regarded restaurants.

Coogee and Maroubra Map 11 D3

Coogee is a busy beachside suburb with excellent hotels, restaurants and cafes, particularly concentrated along **Coogee Bay Rd**, including the **Coogee Bay Hotel**, known as a regular live music venue.

At **Maroubra**, the wide beach has a good reputation for surf and is less crowded than other beaches in summer.

Cronulla Map 11 C4

Cronulla is a popular surfside suburb for tourists who prefer a base away from the city centre. There is ample accommodation, and several of the many restaurants offer outdoor seating and water views. **The Esplanade** walkway is one of Sydney's prettiest coastal walks: the beaches and rocky coves all have

Waverley Cemetery

Waverley Cemetery is situated on a dramatic coastline and is dominated by white marble headstones of high Victorian and Edwardian styles. The first 2.5ha was bought in 1875 for £200 and the first burial was made in 1877. Gravestones of famous Australians include those of writers Henry Lawson, Dorothea Mackellar and Henry Kendall, sportsman Victor Trumper, aviation pioneer Lawrence Hargrave and Jules Archibald of Archibald Prize fame.

The cemetery contains the single largest monument to the Irish Uprising outside Ireland, with a 2.1m white marble angel taking the deceased to heaven, built over the graves of Michael and Mary Dwyer. The gates at the cemetery entrance are dedicated to those killed in WWI and WWII. Guided tours of the cemetery are conducted at various times April–Sep.
To check times Ph: (02) 9369 8141. www.waverley.nsw.gov.au/cemetery

CRONULLA BEACHES AND PORT HACKING

great views. It runs from the southern end of **North Cronulla Beach** to **Bass and Flinders Pt**, providing superb views of **Port Hacking**.

Wanda, **Elouera**, **Cronulla** and **North Cronulla** are excellent surf beaches, all patrolled, while the pretty beach at **South Cronulla** has smaller surf. Popular picnic places include **Gunamatta Park**, **Shelley Beach** and **Oak Park**, all with swimming.

Cronulla Cruises operate charter cruises departing from Tonkin St Wharf near Cronulla Stn, Ph: (02) 9544 1400, www.cronullacruises.com.au Houseboats can be hired from **Cronulla Houseboats**, for info Ph: (02) 9523 6919, www.cronullahouseboats.com.au

Cronulla and NP Ferries offer 3hr scenic cruises of Port Hacking and its river as well as regular ferry service from **Cronulla** to **Bundeena** in Royal NP. Take a leisurely stroll on the beach or enjoy the beauty of the crystal clear water. Cruises depart Tonkin St, Gunnamatta Bay, near Cronulla railway Ph: (02) 9523 2990, www. cronullaandnationalparkferrycruises.com

Kurnell Map 11 C4

At **Inscription Pt**, a plaque marks the point of the 1st European landing (by Capt Cook) at Botany Bay. Up until the 1920s, Kurnell was frequented mainly by fishermen because of its close proximity to Botany Bay and the open sea, along with its abundant fish stocks. It has since developed into a large industrial area accommodating the Caltex Oil Refinery while retaining a small, close-knit residential community along the bay.

Tamarama, Bronte and Clovelly Map 13 D4

The tiny beach at **Tamarama** is prone to tidal rips, but this does not discourage those who come here, often to sunbake and be seen rather than swim.

Next door, the beach at **Bronte** is slightly larger, with a sea pool, playground, open space and several open air cafes; great for weekend brunches, although it does get crowded and parking is very restricted.

Clovelly is a sheltered beach perfect for families with young children or for those just wanting to relax. It offers a safe pool for swimming and snorkelling.

Eastern suburbs Darlinghurst Map 13 A3

Next door to Kings Cross, **Darlinghurst** is also renowned for nightlife, restaurants and bars, especially on lively **Oxford St**. This is the main artery of the area, running from Liverpool St at

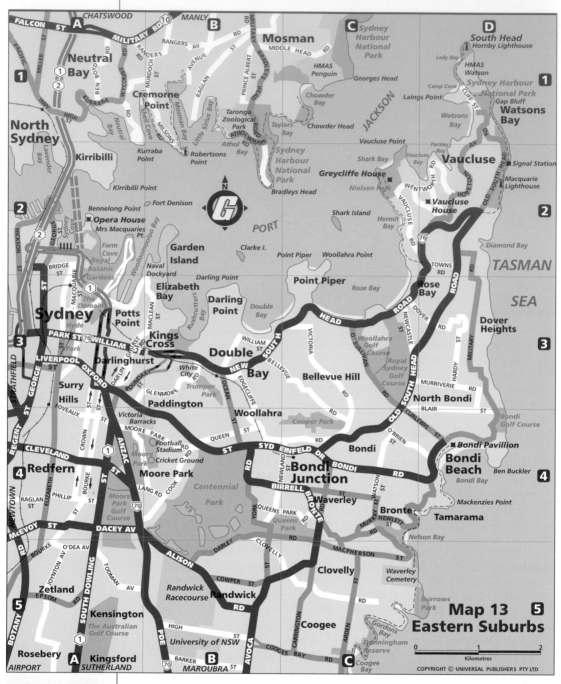

Map 13
Eastern Suburbs

Kilometres

COPYRIGHT © UNIVERSAL PUBLISHERS PTY LTD

ELIZABETH BAY HOUSE

the edge of Hyde Park through Paddington and on to Bondi Junction. Along its length are a tempting array of restaurants, cafes, bars, galleries, boutiques and nightclubs. The area is also known for its artistic community, and as the focus for Sydney's large gay and lesbian community.

On Darlinghurst Rd, the **Sydney Jewish Museum** is well worth a visit. It documents the Holocaust and tells the story of more than 200 years of Jewish settlement in Australia. There are eight exhibition levels. Open Mon–Thurs, Sun, 10am–4pm, Fri 10pm–2pm.
Ph: (02) 9360 7999

KINGS CROSS

TOP FOOD

Some of Sydney's best restaurants at The Cross include **Tharen Restaurant & Bar**, **Venice Beach Restaurant**, and **Ju Ju**. For a stand-up Sydney institution, try the famous late-night pie cart, **Harry's Cafe de Wheels**, at Woolloomooloo Bay.

Elizabeth Bay Map 13 B3

Surely Sydney's loveliest Regency mansion, **Elizabeth Bay House** in Onslow Ave has some of the best harbour views in Sydney. Dating from 1835, it was built for Colonial Secretary Alexander Macleay and his wife Eliza. The main features are a unique elliptical cantilevered staircase and elegant furnishings, carefully recreating the period. Open Tues–Sun, 10am–4.30pm. Ph: (02) 9356 3022, www.hht.net.au

Kings Cross Map13 B3

Just east of the city is Sydney's most **colourful nightlife** spot. In the Victorian era, this was a genteel district, known for its gracefully bohemian atmosphere. The area first started to change in the 1940s, with the influx of sailors based at nearby Garden Island naval base.

Although these days **The Cross** is renowned for its seamy side, with strip shows, sex shops, streetwalkers and illegal drugs, it is as much frequented for its good cafes, restaurants and busy nightclubs. The main strip runs along **Darlinghurst Rd** north of William St, and is full of pulsating neon, souvenir shops and spruikers while the side streets such as **Bayswater Rd** are lined with restaurants and cafes.

After decades of neglect, some of the streets and houses have undergone a revival. **Kellett St** is a striking streetscape of late 19th century terrace houses, with many of the ground floors transformed into attractive restaurants and coffee shops. **Victoria St** is another example, with refurbished terraces, fashionable restaurants, bars and coffee shops where most patrons prefer to sit outside and be seen.

Moore Park, Kensington and Randwick Map 13 B4, A5 & B5

The **Moore Park** Precinct is Australia's premier leisure playground, located only minutes from the CBD. There are regular

PADDINGTON TERRACES

TOP PUB GRUB

Paddington is home to a number of hotels serving outstanding food in a relaxed atmosphere, including the **Four in Hand**, **Grand National** and the **Royal Hotel Sydney**

bus services from key train stations to the park. On event days express shuttle buses from Central Stn are the best way to get to Moore Park. The precinct offers a great opportunity to watch major cricket or football teams at the **Sydney Cricket Ground** (SCG) or Aussie Stadium. These two stadiums are home to cricket, Australian Rules football, rugby union, rugby league and soccer.

Fox Studios, also here, offers cafes, bars, restaurants, cinemas, shops, bungy trampolining and more. The University of NSW dominates nearby Kensington, while adjacent Randwick is best known for the Australian Jockey Club's Royal Randwick Racecourse. Ph: (02) 9663 8400

Paddington Map 13 B3

Paddington has a heritage and social history surpassed in Sydney only by The Rocks. The stylish suburb's most recognisable feature is the beautiful wrought ironwork on the old Victorian terrace houses, best appreciated by wandering the streets behind Oxford St. Local features of particular interest include the fine terraces in Glenmore Rd, a row of workman's terraces in **Comber St** and the area's oldest pub, **The Rose and Crown** (1850). To find out some more about local history go to Woollahra Council's website, www.woollahra.nsw.gov.au

Packed with cafes, restaurants, trendy shops and galleries, the Paddington end of **Oxford St** encourages full-blown shopping excursions, especially on Saturdays when the **Paddington Market** is in full swing in the grounds of the Uniting Church (395 Oxford St) and adjoining school. Open 10am. Buskers, artists and some of Sydney's more colourful characters also congregate here. Ph: (02) 9331 2923, www.paddingtonmarket.com.au

The area is known for its galleries, covering many themes including tribal art at **Galleries Primitif**, 174 Jersey Rd, Ph: (02) 9363 3115; and indigenous works at **Bandigan Aboriginal Arts & Crafts**, 39 Queen St, Woollahra. Open Tues–Fri 10am–6pm and Sat–Sun 11am–4pm Ph: (02) 9328 4194

Victoria Barracks (1841) on Oxford St is an architecturally outstanding military complex, still in use by the army. A flag raising ceremony and a marching band performs here most Thurs at 10am. The display is followed by a guided tour of the barracks and **Army Museum**. Open Thur 10am–2pm also open Sun, 10am–3pm, museum only. Ph: (02) 9339 3000

Rushcutters Bay, Double Bay and Rose Bay Map 13 B3 & C3

Next to Elizabeth Bay and home to the Cruising Yacht Club of Australia,

SEAPLANE AT ROSE BAY

THE BRETT WHITELEY STUDIO

Rushcutters Bay offers excellent harbour views from Rushcutters Bay Park. *The Harbour Walk — Rushcutters Bay to Rose Bay* pamphlet outlines features such as the area's pleasing harbourside parks and gardens, including **McKell Park** at Darling Pt, built around the historic ruined foundations of 'Canonbury' and 'Lansdowne'. Contact Woollahra Council, Ph: (02) 9391 7000. www.woollahra.nsw.gov.au

The social centre of the eastern suburbs, **Double Bay** is a prestigious address with some of Sydney's most expensive real estate. The wealth of the area is reflected in the many boutiques crammed with designer labels, antique shops, art galleries, restaurants and cafes.

Affluent **Rose Bay** has a particularly long waterfrontage with great harbour views. Seaplanes land and take off here.

DOYLES, WATSONS BAY

Surry Hills Map 13 A3

Surry Hills is an old, inner suburb with some elegantly renovated terraces. The main thoroughfare of **Crown St** has a strong fashion pulse, as well as an eclectic choice of restaurants, hotels and cafes. The area around **Foveaux St** is also well-known for its fashion bargains. Around the intersection of **Elizabeth** and **Cleveland Sts** is a concentration of popular Lebanese restaurants, some featuring belly dancing.

The **Brett Whiteley Studio** at 2 Raper St, Surry Hills opened in 1995 as a museum of the life and times of this acclaimed Australian artist. Group bookings essential. Open weekends, 10am–4pm. Ph: (02) 9225 1881. www.brettwhiteley.org

Surry Hills has a number of traditional Australian pubs. A local landmark located at 412 Crown St is **The Dolphin on Crown Hotel** with its refurbished restaurant; **The Forresters Hotel** at 336 Riley St has an excellent restaurant; and the **Strawberry Hills Hotel**, 453 Elizabeth St, Surry Hills, features live up-and-coming bands and great jazz. The food is wholesome and very reasonably priced. Ph: (02) 9698 2997. www.strawberryhillshotel.com.au

Watsons Bay and Vaucluse Map 13 D1 & D2

Watsons Bay is accessible by bus, car or, most pleasantly, ferry from Circular Quay. With its prime position on the

AT BALMAIN MARKET

IN DAWN'S WAKE

The **Dawn Fraser Pool**, where the great swimmer trained, is a Balmain institution located in Elkington Park, also an ideal picnic spot.

●●●●●●●●●

WINNING WAYS

The award-winning **Exchange Hotel** (1885) cnr Beattie and Mullins sts, Balmain has often featured in TV shows.

BIRKENHEAD POINT MARINA

TRY VICTOIRE

Victoire at 285 Darling St, Balmain is a bakery famous for its French sourdough, and has a separate deli selling 100 different cheeses.

harbour, glorious views of the city skyline across the water, and restaurants such as the famous **Doyles**, Watsons Bay is a must during a visit to Sydney (see p.45).

The impressive coastline can be appreciated on the scenic **Coast Walk**. This leads from **Christison Park** to **South Head**, taking in historic **Macquarie Lighthouse** (1883), **Hornby Light** (1858), the **Signal Station** (1842) and its fortifications, and the dramatic 80m cliffs of **The Gap** which mark the boundary of **Sydney Harbour NP** (see p.46). The walk is 5km but can be done in sections. A map is available from Woollahra Council, as are pamphlets on other walks such as *The Harbour Walk — Rose Bay to Watsons Bay*. Ph: (02) 9391 7000. www.woollahra.nsw.gov.au

Vaucluse is arguably Sydney's most exclusive address, its streets lined with imposing residences taking advantage of the harbour views. Much of the suburb is parkland, including Vaucluse Park, Nielsen Park and Parsley Bay. In Vaucluse Park is **Vaucluse House**, a Gothic mansion and one of Sydney's most famous historic houses. Now a museum, the house has lavish entertaining rooms, splendid harbourfront grounds and manicured gardens. A tearoom in the grounds is famous for its Devonshire teas (bookings advisable).
Open Tues–Sun, 10am–4.30pm.
Ph: (02) 9388 7922

Inner western suburbs
Balmain Map 11 C2

A short ferry ride from Circular Quay or Darling Harbour, Balmain was a working class suburb for most of its history but is now a coveted address. Many of the small stone terraces and timber residences have been restored, and **Darling St** hosts a multitude of shops and cafes, always worth a wander.

Any visit to Balmain should include a look at the houses. A stroll along Adolphus St, Vincent St and back up Stephen St is particularly recommended for the 1850s **sandstone cottages**, timber cottages and terraces. There are also views of one of Sydney's outstanding landmarks, the **Anzac Bridge**.

Darling St Wharf displays a location map showing local historic sites, and the **Balmain Watch House** in Darling St sells assorted publications about Balmain, including *Balmain Walks* leaflets. Historical sites and buildings are detailed on three walks: Balmain East, Ewenton and Mort's Dock. Guided walks can also be arranged through the Watch House (1854), is open Sat, 12pm–3pm. Ph: (02) 9818 4954. www.balmainassociation.homestead.com

A local institution, **Balmain Saturday Market** is famous for its quality crafts, as well as antiques, second-hand books, plants, clothing and jewellery. It is held in the grounds of St Andrews

Congregational Church, Darling St, Sat, 8am–4pm. Ph: (02) 9555 1791

Drummoyne Map 11 C2

Birkenhead Pt houses high-rise units, a marina, and a shopping complex specialising in samples and seconds' stores, which attracts keen bargain shoppers.

A number of waterside suburbs in the Drummoyne Council area offer pleasant walks. A pamphlet, *Walks in the Drummoyne Council Area*, describes walks at **Abbotsford**, **Five Dock Bay**, **Hen and Chicken Bay** and **Iron Cove** (which also has a jogging track with 22 fitness stops). The council also provides a *Heritage Walks* pamphlet encompassing a number of historic houses and other points of interest.

Glebe Map 11 C3

Originally part of the Glebe Estate granted to the Anglican Church in the 1800s, Glebe is now a fashionable inner suburb which retains many historic houses.

St John the Evangelist Church in Glebe Pt Rd was designed by well-known architect Edmund Blacket, and in Edward St, the **Chinese Joss House** (1889) is another noteworthy feature.

Glebe has a host of restaurants and coffee shops with a distinctly bohemian flavour, mostly lining **Glebe Pt Rd**. The **Valhalla Cinema** has long been Sydney's home of quality alternative cinema, and occasionally offers live theatre . A large student population from the nearby universities adds to the bohemian atmosphere. At the northern end of Glebe Pt Rd, **Jubilee and Bicentennial Parks** overlook Rozelle Bay. Around the corner back towards the city is Blackwattle Bay Park with great views of the **Anzac Bridge** (p.40).

For those interested in a bit of a flutter, harness and greyhound racing are held at **Harold Park**, Minogue Cr, and **Wentworth Park**, Wentworth Park Rd, both in Glebe.

Glebe Markets, with a vast collection of stalls, are held every Sat in the school grounds, Darley Pl, accessible from

Glebe Pt Rd. Glebe is easily reached from the city by bus, or about a 15min walk from Central Stn.

Leichhardt Map 11 C3

This suburb is Sydney's original Italian area with an ambience all its own. The shops, restaurants and cafes along **Parramatta Rd** and **Norton St** are packed with authentic Italian goods and cuisine. **The Italian Forum** in Norton St offers Italian gelato, coffee, meals, fashion and a great atmosphere. With plenty of cafes open till late, Leichhardt is also a great place to go after a show and is easily reached by any of the bus routes along Parramatta Rd. The Norton St Cinemas is a 4-cinema complex at 99 Norton St, which shows a varied program of international films.

In nearby Annandale at 83 Parramatta Rd, the **Side On Cafe** has a reputation for good jazz. Ph: (02) 9516 3077

Marrickville Map 11 C3

South of Newtown, Marrickville has an interesting combination of cultures and heritage. A good place to find out about the past is the **Local Studies Collection** at the **Archives/History Centre** in Petersham Town Hall, which has 4000 items on history, people, places and events in the Marrickville area, as well as an expanding collection of valuable

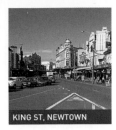

KING ST, NEWTOWN

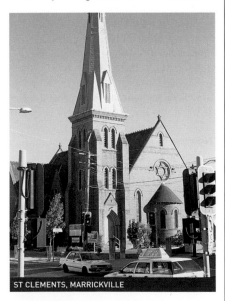

ST CLEMENTS, MARRICKVILLE

BARE ISLAND

local 'Diana' pottery from the 1940s. The centre is open to the public on Tues 10am–1pm, 2–4pm, other times by appointment Ph: (02) 9335 2287.

The Marrickville Town Hall, is worth a visit for its impressive architecture. Marrickville also retains some superb examples of Federation architecture, particularly along David St and Livingstone Rd. On Marrickville Rd, the spire has recently been restored on St Clements Anglican Church which also features a striking pressed metal ceiling.

At the southern end of the suburb, the **Cooks River** is lined with attractive parks providing sporting facilities, walks and a bicycle track.

Eating out in Marrickville is a treat and reflects the diverse communities living here. This has long been a **Greek** enclave, with excellent restaurants and delis, and some **Lebanese**-style cafes. For a taste of **Vietnam**, head for the delicious and affordable pho and laksa at the many Vietnamese restaurants on **Illawarra Rd** (between Marrickville Rd and The Warren).

Newtown Map 11 C3

Early in its history, Newtown became one of Sydney's most important commercial centres, and this heritage is still reflected along **King St**'s bustling **shopping** strip with its wide range of books, clothing, antiques, food and interior decorations. Historically, the suburb has always been home to a diverse mixture of cultures, supplemented by the student population

of neighbouring Sydney University and a vibrant artistic community.

Newtown's appealing character is reflected in the huge variety of international **restaurants** on King St, which attract hordes of visitors looking for a good, cheap meal, as well as in the various pubs and hotels hosting the area's energetic nightlife.

Just off King St, on Church St, is the beautiful Gothic Revival style **St Stephens Anglican Church**, with some fascinating old headstones from the original cemetery, now a park.

Newtown is easily accessed by bus on any of the routes along City Rd and King St.

National Parks
Botany Bay NP Map 15

This park conserves the northern and southern headlands of Botany Bay as well as the historic landing site of Captain James Cook. The southern section is reached by road along Captain Cook Dr or by train to Cronulla and then bus. Highlights include the **Banks-Solander Track** and the **Cape Baily Coast Walk**, with its historic sites and spectacular coastal views. Longer walking tracks provide fabulous views particularly from **Cape Solander**. In spring, a profusion of wildflowers bloom around the park.

Displays at the **Discovery Centre** focus on the coastal landscape, with its wetlands, heathlands and woodlands, from 1770 to the present. Open Mon–Fri, 11am–3pm, weekends 10am–4.30pm.

BOOMERANG LESSONS AT LA PEROUSE

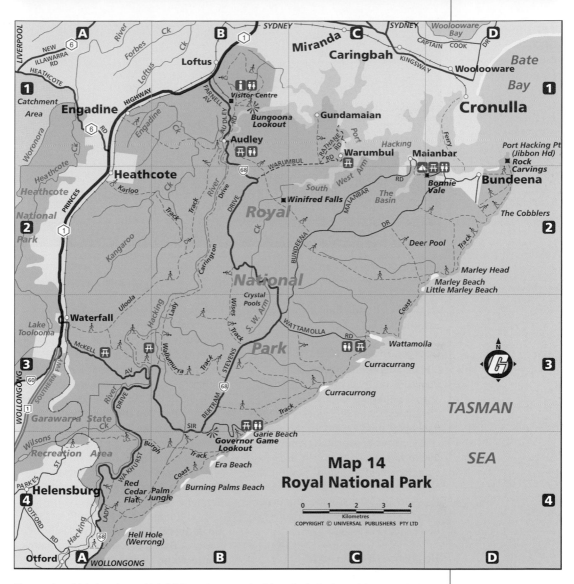

Map 14
Royal National Park

0 1 2 3 4
Kilometres
COPYRIGHT © UNIVERSAL PUBLISHERS PTY LTD

The park, which has beautiful BBQ and picnic areas, is open daily, 7am–8pm. Entrance fees apply. Ph: (02) 9668 9111 for park info and for permission to visit **Towra Pt Nature Reserve**, one of the last coastal wetlands in the Sydney region. It plays an important role in providing a resting place for migratory waterfowl from as far afield as China and Siberia.

Access to the park's northern section is from the end of Anzac Pde, La Perouse. It is also accessible by bus from the city. The **La Perouse Museum** in the **Old Cable Station** commemorates the ill-fated voyage of La Perouse with relics

and a historical display of the wreck site, navigational instruments and rare maps and drawings. Open Wed–Sun, 10am–4pm. Ph: (02) 9311 3379

Also on the headland is the oldest building in the area, **Macquarie Watchtower**, which was built in 1822 to watch for smugglers entering Botany Bay, and **Bare Island**, a fort built in 1885, now connected to the mainland by a 100-year-old bridge. Ph: (02) 9311 3379 for info on the museum and the fort.

The **Cape Banks Walking Track** is a local highlight. Commencing at Congwong Bay, it passes through heathland and historic fortifications and

FLANNEL FLOWERS

GARIE BEACH

skirts along the cliff tops around several golf courses, with extensive views, striking rock platforms, an excellent shipwreck at **Cape Banks** and swimming at **Little Bay**.

Georges River NP Map11 B4

Situated between **Lugarno** and **Picnic Pt**, the national park contains open woodland and eucalypt forest conserving some of Sydney's best river habitat for native animals and plants. BBQs, picnic areas, boat ramps and toilets with disabled access are provided at a number of locations. Several short bushwalks with lovely river views traverse the area. Contact the Discovery Centre Ph: (02) 9668 9111, Visitor Info Centre (02) 9542 0648

Heathcote NP Map 11 A5

Heathcote NP lies to the west of the Princes Hwy between the suburbs of **Heathcote** and **Waterfall**. Consisting of a deeply dissected sandstone landscape carved out by the **Woronora River**, it has rockpools perfect for swimming, particularly **Kingfisher Pool** and **Lake Eckersley**. The park has excellent spring wildflower displays. Ph (02) 9542 0648

Royal NP Map 14

The splendid scenery in this 16 000ha park features soaring coastal cliffs, sandy beaches, heath-covered plateaus and deep river gorges. The variety of plant life ranges from tall open forests and rainforests to swamps and mangroves, representing some of the most diverse vegetation communities in the State.

Royal NP has numerous picnic spots, the most popular at **Audley**, **Wattamolla** and **Garie**. Over 150km of walking tracks cover the park, and track pamphlets and maps are available from the Visitor Info Centre at the **Farnell Ave** entrance. Open daily 8.30am–4.30pm. Ph: (02) 9542 0648

Ranger guided **Discovery walks, talks and tours** are an excellent way to learn more about Australia's first NP. For program details, Ph: (02) 9542 0666

At the park's northern boundary, **Bundeena** is reached by ferry from Cronulla (see p.76). From here, tracks lead to **Bonnie Vale**, **Jibbon Pt** and the **Coast track**. Good surf can usually be found at **Garie**, **Era** and **Burning Palms**. **Wattamolla**, with its lagoon and sheltered beach, is a favourite. At **Audley**, boating is popular and craft may be hired from Audley Boat Shed, Ph: (02) 9545 4967

The Audley **Kiosk** is open Mon–Fri, 9am–sunset and weekends 7.30am–sunset. Licensed cafe meals are available from 10.30am weekends and holidays Ph: (02) 9521 2240. **Lady Carrington Dr** runs from Audley to the southern side of the park. It is ideal for walking and cycling, and is closed to all motor traffic.

Facilities for car camping are provided at **Bonnie Vale**. Bush camping is allowed only in designated areas. Bookings and permits are essential for all camping.

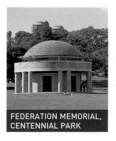

FEDERATION MEMORIAL, CENTENNIAL PARK

Contact the Visitor Info Centre, Ph: (02) 9542 0648. Park entry fee.

Sydney Harbour NP Map 13 D1
This park consists of pockets of bushland adjoining the harbour. South of the harbour, this includes parts of **South Head** and the foreshore from **Nielsen Park** to **Rose Bay** (see p.45).

Parks and gardens
Centennial Park Map 13 B4
A vast green expanse at the top of Oxford St, **Centennial Park** was established to celebrate the centenary of Australia's European founding. Its ponds and wetland remnants are home to many waterbirds, and it is a favourite spot for family picnics. Activities include walking, rollerblading, cycling, and horseriding on the 3km of riding track (Sydney is one of only a few cities in the world where it's possible to ride so close to the city centre). BBQs, a cafe and take-away food are available within the park. Open daily, sunrise–sunset, Ph: (02) 9331 5056. Cycle and rollerblade hire from **Centennial Park Cycles**, Ph: (02) 9398 5027. Horse hire, pony parties, riding lessons and much more from **Moore Park Riding Stables**, Ph: (02) 9360 8747. www.mooreparkstables.com.au; and **Centennial Park Equestrian Centre**, Ph: (02) 9332 2809

Oatley Park Map 11 B4
Oatley Park is an area of natural bushland accessible from Douglas Haig St, Oatley. A popular cycling venue, it offers plenty of BBQ and picnic sites and scenic views of the Georges River. On the waterfront is the river's best kept secret: **Oatley Tidal Baths**, complete with amenities block and historic sandstone BBQ pavilion.

Sydney Park Map 11 C3
Sydney Park has reclaimed 44ha of disused industrial land at **St Peters**. The old brickpit chimneys form a picturesque landmark on the corner of Princes Hwy and Sydney Park Rd, opposite St Peters Stn. The park has an oval with an amenities building and a children's bike track. The highest points of the park are popular for kite flying, while in other areas there are wetland and bushland regeneration projects. People from the local community are involved in tree planting; and the park provides open green space for families and dog lovers. On-site parking.

E G Waterhouse Camellia Garden Map 11 B4
Located off President Ave, **Caringbah** overlooking Yowie Bay, this beautiful garden displays over 1500 camellias, 3000 azaleas and hundreds of Australian native plants in a natural setting, with picnic and BBQ areas and a Japanese teahouse. Open Mon–Fri, 9am–4pm, weekends 9.30am–5pm. Ph: (02) 9540 2018

Sir Joseph Banks Native Plants Reserve
This beautiful reserve contains a number of different gardens with a self-guided walk, waterfalls, ponds and BBQ facilities. Access from Manooka Pl, **Kareela**. Open Mon–Fri 7.30am–3pm, weekends 10am–5pm Ph: (02) 9545 1598

Other attractions
Australian Nuclear Science and Technology Organisation Map 11 A4
Tours of ANSTO and its facilities are available. Bookings essential and photo identification required. Ph: (02) 9717 3111

CAMELLIA

HORSERIDING AT CENTENNIAL PARK

CYCLIST

Bus and Truck Museum Map 11 C3

The Bus and Truck Museum at **Tempe** displays restored and operating public transport and industrial vehicles from Australia's past. Enquire about double-decker bus rides through Newtown. Open Wed, 10am–3pm, Sun 10am–4pm. Ph: (02) 9558 1234

Sydney Airport Tours Map 11 C3

Airside Tarmac Tours conduct tours of **Sydney Airport**, including viewing a jumbo jet from under the wing, watching aircraft take off and land from within the airport, inspection of the massive jet hangars and jet base and more. General public tours operate 10am Sat and selected week days, 10am one Sun per month; groups by appt. Bookings essential. Ph: (02) 8338 8414. www.airsidetarmactours.com

Sydney Tramway Museum Map 11 B4

A fascinating reminder of Sydney's public transport history rests beside the Princes Hwy at **Loftus**, with a large collection of trams. Rides are conducted on a 1.2km track. Open Sun and public holidays, 10am–5pm, Wed, 9.30am–3.30pm. Ph: (02) 9542 3646

The University of Sydney Map 11 C3

The earlier buildings of the University are some of the most striking in Sydney. Commenced in 1850, it was modelled on the universities of Oxford and Cambridge and designed by Edmund Blacket. Tours

of the heritage buildings of the main **Quadrangle** are conducted, including the **Great Hall** with its beautiful stained glass and carved cedar, and the **Clock Tower**. Ph: (02) 9351 2274.

The Nicholson Museum of Antiquities, specialising in archaeological exhibits, is best seen as part of a university tour. Ph: (02) 9351 2812. The Macleay Museum has an interesting collection of zoological specimens, some of the world's oldest Aboriginal bark paintings, special collections of scientific instruments and historic photographs of Sydney. Ph: (02) 9351 2274

Recreational activities

Cycling
Cook's River Cycleway and Walkway

This easy 15km route runs from **Gough Whitlam Park** in **Tempe** to **South Strathfield**. For most of its course it runs through pretty parks and reserves along the river, offering plenty of picnic spots, views and a variety of urban landscapes.

Rockdale Cycleway Map 11 C3

The 12km long **Rockdale Cycleway** begins at Cahill Park, **Arncliffe**, follows wetlands and parks and continues along the fore-shore of Lady Robinsons Beach to **Sans Souci**. Generally a flat and easy ride, with picnic spots along the way, and swimming baths at Brighton, Monterey and Ramsgate. Pamphlet available from Rockdale City Council. Ph: (02) 9562 1666

ROYAL NP

Fun for the young

★ Airside Tarmac Tours of
   Sydney Airport (p.88)
★ Bondi-Waverley Gymnastics,
   1 Dove Lane, Randwick,
   is a gym suitable for children
   up to 13 years old
★ Malabar Riding School, Franklin
   St, Malabar, Ph: (02) 9311 4758
★ Otford Valley Farm (p.89)
★ Rockdale Cycleway (p.88) and
   Cook's River Cycleway (p.88)
★ Rollerblading at Bondi,
   Centennial Park and Cronulla
★ Sutherland Leisure Centre,
   Rawson Ave, Sutherland, offers
   indoor and outdoor pools, beach
   volleyball court, gym and boxing
   circuit room

Horses
Horse racing Map 13 B5
On Alison Rd, Randwick, **Royal Randwick**
is one of Sydney's most famous and
fashionable racecourses.

Otford Farm Trail Rides Map 14 A4
At the southern end of Royal NP, **Otford
Farm** offers trail rides, lessons and kids'
horse riding camps. Ph: (02) 4294 1296.
www.otfordfarm.com.au

Live theatre
Some of Sydney's best known live
theatres are located in this southern
region. Enjoy a meal on Elizabeth or
Cleveland Sts and continue on to **Belvoir
St Theatre**, 25 Belvoir St, Surry Hills,
Ph: (02) 9699 3444. Dine in King St,
Newtown, as there is much to choose
from, and then head for the **Seymour
Theatre Centre**, cnr Cleveland St and
City Rd, Ph: (02) 9351 7940. **The
Footbridge Theatre** is on Parramatta Rd
at Glebe, Ph: (02) 9692 9955

On the water
Botany Bay is ideal for boating, sailing,
fishing and swimming. On its northern
side near **La Perouse** are a number of
reserves fronting onto serene bays, and
sheltered beaches such as **Frenchmans
Bay** (with a boat ramp), **Yarra Bay** and
Congwong Bay.

On the southern side, **Silver Beach** at
Kurnell also offers sheltered swimming
with a convenient boat ramp at **Bonna
Pt. Lady Robinsons Beach** runs all the
way from **Kyeemagh** to **Sans Souci** along
the western edge of the bay. **Bass and
Flinders Cruises** offer trips up the
Georges River as well as on Botany Bay,
Ph: (02) 9583 1199. Further info on
cruises available from Sans Souci Wharf,
Sutherland Shire Tourism Assoc Inc or
Ph: (02) 9544 2144

Both the **Georges** and **Woronora
Rivers** offer lovely scenery and reserves
and are popular for watersports. Canoes,
kayaks and runabouts can be hired from
Star Boatshed, which also has a cafe.
Ph: (02) 9545 2584. **Port Hacking** is a
delightful waterway flanked by Royal
NP and bushland suburbs. **Swallow
Rock Reserve** at **Grays Pt** is a great
picnic spot.

For water activities on Sydney Harbour
see p.49.

SURFER

RACING AT ROYAL RANDWICK

Places of interest (Botany Bay)

❶ Maroubra Beach (p.76)
❷ La Perouse (p.85)
❸ Bare Island (p.85)
❹ Yarra Bay (p.89)
❺ Brighton-le-Sands (p.76)
❻ Dolls Pt
❼ Captain Cook's Landing Place, Historic Site (p.84)
❽ Cronulla (p.76)

Side trip

❾ Cronulla Ferry Wharf
❿ Bundeena (p.77)

Places of interest (Watson's Bay, Vaucluse and Bondi)

❶ Double Bay (p.80)
❷ Hermitage Foreshore Scenic Walk (p.45)
❸ Nielsen Park (p.45)
❹ Vaucluse House (p.45, 82)
❺ Watsons Bay (p.81)
❻ Coast Walk (p.82)
❼ The Gap (p.82)
❽ Macquarie Lighthouse (p.82)
❾ Bondi Beach (p.75)
❿ Bronte (p.77)
⓫ Waverley Cemetery (p.76)
⓬ Coogee (p.76)
⓭ Centennial Park (p.87)

CAPT COOK HISTORIC LANDING SITE

Suggested tours – Map 15

Botany Bay tour

Approximate distance
65km return from Sydney CBD

About the tour

As well as being scenic and relaxing, the coastline and beaches around Botany Bay are steeped in both Aboriginal and early colonial history. The suburb of La Perouse commemorates an early French explorer, as well as being an important cultural site for the local Aboriginal community. Bare Island was once a fort and is a great place to explore or to enjoy a family picnic.

Captain James Cook's landing place at Kurnell has been preserved as an Historic Site, where you can see various monuments and learn about this period of history in a Discovery Centre.

End the tour with a walk along the beautiful Cronulla foreshore, and perhaps take a ferry ride to Bundeena on the edge of the Royal NP.

Watsons Bay, Vaucluse and Bondi tour

Approximate distance
30km return from Sydney CBD

About the tour

After the cosmopolitan glamour of Double Bay, the Hermitage Foreshore Scenic Walk provides a relaxing opportunity to enjoy the harbourside scenery, including rocky coves and quiet beaches. It ends at Nielsen Park, a lovely quiet spot for a picnic and/or a swim. Nearby is the unique and historic Vaucluse House, a must-see for anyone interested in colonial architecture.

Watsons Bay and its surrounding area is also a must on the visitor's list of places to go in Sydney. Enjoy the sunshine in outdoor restaurants and bars. To fully enjoy the superlative views of the harbour, coastline and city skyline, take all or part of the South Head Heritage Trail.

Visit the Gap and the Macquarie Lighthouse before moving on to legendary Bondi Beach, where you are likely to spot a few celebrities. Neighbouring attractions include the historic Waverley Cemetery, set atop a cliff overlooking the sparkling Pacific Ocean. Centennial Park, one of Sydney's oldest parks, offers a leisurely stopover on the way back to the city.

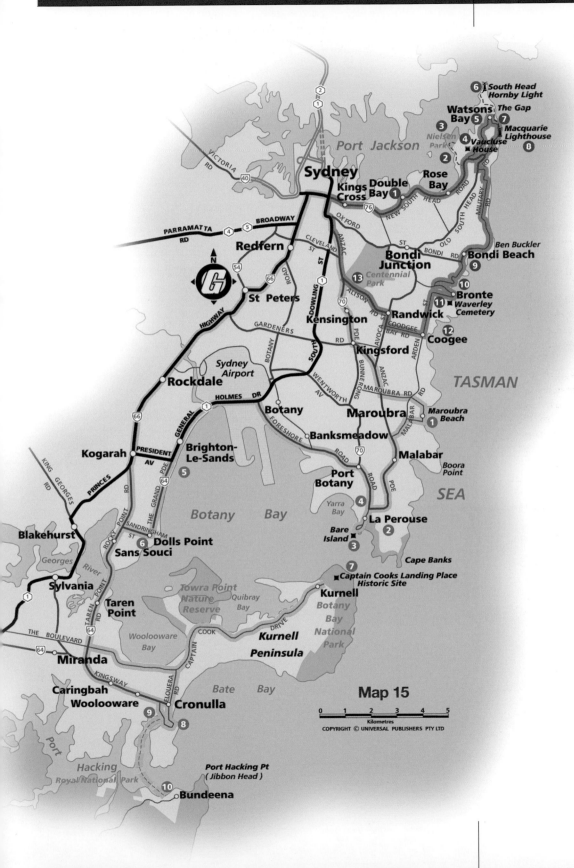

Map 15

6 South Head
Hornby Light

Watsons
Bay 5   The Gap

3   Macquarie
4   Lighthouse

Nielsen   Vaucluse
Park   House

2   8

Port Jackson

Sydney

Kings   Double
Cross   Bay 1

Rose
Bay

VICTORIA RD

40

PARRAMATTA RD   BROADWAY

4   5

Redfern

54

66

St Peters

CLEVELAND

OXFORD ST

ANZAC PDE

Bondi
Junction

BONDI RD

Bondi Beach

Ben Buckler

9

76

NEW SOUTH HEAD RD

OLD SOUTH HEAD RD

MILITARY RD

13   Centennial
Park

70

Kensington

1

Randwick

10   Bronte
11   Waverley
Cemetery

12   Coogee

GARDENERS RD

Sydney
Airport

BOTANY RD

SOUTH

Kingsford

BUNNERONG RD

ANZAC PDE

TASMAN

HOLMES DR

Rockdale

1

WENTWORTH AV

Botany

Maroubra

Maroubra
Beach   1

Banksmeadow

FORESHORE RD

66

GENERAL HOLMES DR

Kogarah

PRESIDENT AV

Brighton-
Le-Sands

5

64

Port
Botany

70

Malabar

Boora
Point

MALABAR RD

SEA

Yarra
Bay

4

La Perouse
2

KING GEORGES RD

PRINCES

SANDRINGHAM ST

Blakehurst

Georges

Dolls Point

6

Sans Souci

Botany   Bay

Bare
Island
3

Cape Banks

Sylvania

1

River

TAREN POINT RD

Taren
Point

Towra Point
Nature
Reserve

Quibray
Bay

7   Captain Cooks Landing Place
Historic Site

Kurnell

Botany
Bay
National
Park

THE BOULEVARD

64

COOK DRIVE

CAPTAIN COOK DRIVE

Kurnell
Peninsula

Miranda

KINGSWAY

Woolooware
Bay

Caringbah
Woolooware

ELOUERA RD

9

Cronulla

8

Bate   Bay

Map 15

0 1 2 3 4 5
Kilometres
COPYRIGHT © UNIVERSAL PUBLISHERS PTY LTD

Port
Hacking

Royal National Park

Port Hacking Pt
(Jibbon Head)

10   Bundeena

Must see, must do

★ Featherdale Wildlife Park,
Doonside (p.109)

★ Hawkesbury houseboat
cruise (p.111)

★ Historic Parramatta (p.100)

★ Parklea Markets (p.110)

Radio stations

2WS: FM 101.7

Mix FM: FM 106.5

2SM GOLD: AM 126

Tourist information

**Hawkesbury Valley Visitor
Information Centre**

Ham Common, Windsor Rd,
Clarendon 2756

Ph: (02) 4588 5895

www.hawkesburyvalley.com

www.hawkesburyweb.com.au

Hills Visitor Information Centre

The Pines,

656 Old Northern Rd, Dural 2158

Ph: (02) 9651 4411

www.sydneyhills.com.au

**Parramatta Visitor
Information Centre**

Parramatta Heritage Centre

346 Church St, Parramatta 2150

Ph: (02) 8839 3311

www.parracity.nsw.gov.au

**Penrith Valley Visitor
Information Centre,**

Panthers World of

Entertainment carpark

Mulgoa Rd, Penrith 2750

Ph: (02) 4732 7671,

1300 736 836

www.penrithvalley.com.au

LEFT: HAWKESBURY GATEWAY

north-west sydney

SYDNEY'S NW IS DOMINATED BY
the mighty Hawkesbury/Nepean river
system. It is the prime source of local
recreational and leisure pursuits, from
family picnics along its banks to boating
and waterskiing. For most of its length
in this region, the Hawkesbury wends
its way through fairly flat country, but
by the time it gets to its northernmost
loop, cliffs of Hawkesbury sandstone
flank its banks.

Closer to Sydney is the area called
the Hills District where a rural charm
still survives and horseriding is a
common pastime.

Between the Hills District and the river,
and between the river and the edge of
the Blue Mountains, much of the land
remains agricultural. The Blue
Mountains NP, Marramarra NP, Cattai
NP and state forests preserve large
tracts of beautiful, unspoilt and
accessible bushland.

While a sense of history has helped
establish NW Sydney as a popular
destination, its thoroughly modern
development will ensure its continued
popularity in the years to come.
Homebush was transformed from
an ordinary suburb to the sophisticated
centre of the 2000 Olympic Games.
The fantastic legacy of the games is
Sydney Olympic Park, which not only
houses NSW's main sporting arenas
and centres, it is also the site of the
Sydney Showground, home of the
city's Royal Easter Show.

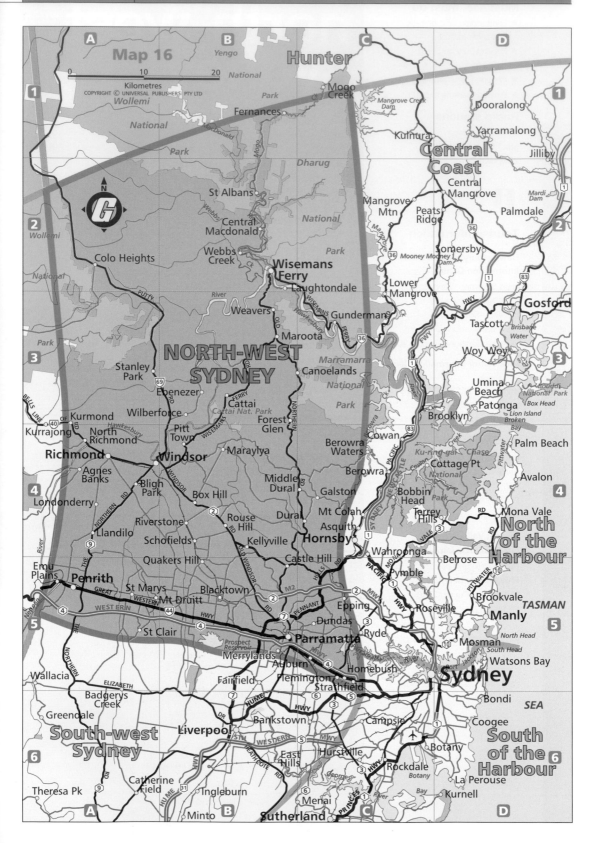

Map 16

Kilometres
COPYRIGHT © UNIVERSAL PUBLISHERS PTY LTD

Natural features

Several million years ago, slow uplifting occurred along what is now the Blue Mountains Escarpment, and the shape of the land was formed. As the Blue Mountains made their way slowly upwards, the Sydney Basin dropped in response. Over time, the rivers carved their way down into the gradually rising land, forming the gorges of the Colo and Hawkesbury Rivers.

The eroded soil was deposited downstream on the flat land of the Sydney Basin, forming the deep alluvial soils of the Hawkesbury floodplain. Flooding still occurs periodically despite some control by the Sydney Water dams to the south.

History

While the earliest white settlers to the NW region undoubtedly faced many hardships, the people of the various Aboriginal nations in the region suffered most. As European settlers flocked to the fertile plains around Parramatta, the original inhabitants were simply removed from their traditional homes.

In Feb 1788, less than a month after arriving, Governor Phillip first travelled up the Parramatta River searching for arable land. By Nov, work had begun on a barracks and provision store to service the farm being established on an area of fertile land he named The Crescent.

The city of Parramatta grew from this site, which is now in Parramatta Park. By 1792, Parramatta was the largest settlement in Australia. Direct access to shipping ensured Sydney's rapid growth, however, and the fledgling city eventually encompassed the city of Parramatta in its suburban sprawl.

Governor Phillip explored the Hawkesbury River in 1789, naming it in honour of an illustrious acquaintance — Baron Hawkesbury, President of the Board of Trade. The first land grant was issued to James Ruse in 1791 to develop an experimental farm and in 1794, the Hawkesbury land grants were made along its banks at Green Hills, later renamed Windsor.

In 1810, Governor Lachlan Macquarie established five of the six Macquarie Towns in the upper Hawkesbury area. They were among the first planned and surveyed settlements in Australia, laid out on high ground to protect inhabitants from floods. Windsor, Richmond, Pitt Town and Wilberforce remain today, although their fortunes have varied enormously. The 5th town, Castlereagh, is now the site of Penrith Lakes and the

EXPERIMENT FARM COTTAGE, HARRIS PARK

THE HAWKESBURY

WIND SCULPTURES

Visible from the RiverCat on the Parramatta River are three wind sculptures in the **George Kendall Riverside Park** at Ermington. They represent the Olympics, the Environment and Recreation.

International Regatta Centre, which was the venue for rowing and canoeing at the 2000 Olympics. The 6th was Liverpool, one of Australia's fastest growing areas.

The river was the original transport route and boats brought stores and passengers as far as Windsor. Shipbuilding flourished as a result. With the completion of the 1st roads, the area became Sydney's main source of food and prospered accordingly.

Getting there

By road

The Western Mwy (M4) and the Great Western Hwy (Hwy 44) run through the southern end of this region and provide comprehensive access. The M2 Mwy provides a quick route from Lane Cove to Seven Hills to join Old Windsor Rd to Windsor. The far north, towards Wisemans Ferry, relies on the Old Northern Rd (Route 36). The rest of the NW is serviced by main roads including Route 40 from Parramatta to Windsor and Richmond, and Route 69 which connects the M5 at Campbelltown with Windsor via Penrith. This road crosses

the river at Windsor and eventually becomes the Putty Rd, leading to the Hunter Valley.

Parramatta can be reached easily from Sydney by either Victoria Rd across Gladesville Bridge, the M4 Mwy or Parramatta Rd.

By rail

The Blue Mountains railway line runs from Central Stn more or less parallel to the road to Parramatta, then on to Penrith and beyond. The Richmond line leaves it at Blacktown and runs out to Windsor and Richmond.

By ferry

The RiverCat ferry service operates from Circular Quay, reaching Parramatta in around 70min, providing great harbour and river views. Stops along the way include Milsons Pt, Drummoyne, Gladesville and Rydalmere.
State Transit Infoline: 131 500

Getting around

Bushsports Adventures runs abseiling courses and organises canyoning, skydiving, mountain biking on a number of trails and canoeing on the Hawkesbury and Nepean rivers.
Ph: (02) 9630 0587.
www.bushsports.com.au

Trike Tours are a great way to get around and see the sights of the Hawkesbury from a different angle. Tours include a trip to Australia's oldest church at Ebenezer, a jaunt up the Kurrajong heights hill on the way to Bilpin for coffee. Ph: 0414 799 122.

Hot Heritage Harley Tours is a fun and an adventurous way to take in the sights and sounds of this lovely area.

Festivals and events

Castle Hill Show

An important forerunner to the Royal Easter Show, the Castle Hill event is held over the 3rd weekend in Mar.
Ph: (02) 9651 4411

Bridge-to-Bridge Water Ski Classic

Held in Nov, the 120km course runs from Dangar Island to Windsor on the

PARRAMATTA RIVERCAT

Hawkesbury River, one of the world's classic water ski races, with speeds reaching 200km/hr. Ph: (02) 9552 4311

Orange Blossom Festival

Held in Sept of each year at various venues throughout the **Hills District**, the festival includes street processions, a garden competition and sports events.

Jazz at the Pines

In **Dural**, Jazz at the Pines is held Feb–May, Sep–Nov, 12.30pm–4pm, 656 Old Northern Rd. Check dates. Ph: (02) 9651 4411

Fruits of the Hawkesbury Festival

In Sep the Macquarie Towns of **Richmond** and **Windsor** celebrate their colourful history and the arrival of spring with a full program of events. Ph: (02) 4560 4434

Hawkesbury Agricultural Show

The annual Hawkesbury Agricultural Show is held held two weeks after Easter. The Showground is on Racecourse Rd, Clarendon opposite the Richmond RAAF Base. Ph: (02) 4577 3591

Hawkesbury Canoe Classic

A weekend of canoe races on the Hawkesbury River is a colourful sight in Nov. Ph: (02) 9666 7786

Riverfest

Regatta Park at **Emu Plains** explodes with the fun of Riverfest in Nov as part of the Penrith City Festival, with spectacular water-based activities, fireworks and lots of music.

Parramatta Foundation Day

On 2nd Nov the city celebrates its founding as Australia's 2nd oldest city. Date of celebrations subject to change, Ph: (02) 8839 3311

Main localities and towns

Hills District/Dural area

Castle Hill Map 16 B5

The town's first claim to fame was as the site of the Battle of Vinegar Hill, a convict

KOALA PARK SANCTUARY

uprising in 1804. One of the uprising's leaders, Phillip Cunningham (p.107), was later hanged at Windsor. Castle Hill became the seat of local government for the area 100 years later.

The **Hills Centre for the Performing Arts** in Carrington Rd is reputed to be Australia's most versatile theatre. It was built using the concept of interconnected performance spaces and can be easily transformed from theatre to cabaret venue. The complex includes a restaurant and bistro. Ph: (02) 8858 2777. www.hillscentre.com.au

The **Mean Fiddler** on the cnr of Commercial and Windsor Rds, Rouse Hill is Australia's number one Irish pub. It offers a bistro, live music and a great atmosphere. Open daily, Ph: (02) 9629 4811

Excelsior Reserve at Castle Hill contains fine examples of sclerophyll forests and a wide variety of fauna such as possums, echidnas, bandicoots, wombats and more than 50 bird species. The reserve follows a section of the Darling Mills Creek. A leaflet on the walks is available from the Hills District Tourist Info Centre. Ph: (02) 9651 4411

SENSORY TRAIL

The **Cumberland State Forest**, off Castle Hill Rd, has a 350m sensory trail for disabled visitors. Braille brochures are available and there is a guide rope for the visually impaired. Wheelchair accessible. Ph: (02) 9871 3377

GALSTON GORGE

Koala Park Sanctuary on Castle Hill Rd at West Pennant Hills has operated since 1927. The 4.5ha of rainforest is a sanctuary for koalas, and offers picnic and BBQ facilities. Koala cuddling and photo sessions take place four times a day at 10.20am, 11.45am, 2pm and 3pm. Open 9am–5pm every day except Christmas. Ph: (02) 9484 3141

Dural Map 16 C4

Best known for its many splendid plant nurseries and peaceful rural atmosphere, Dural lies on the Old Northern Rd on the edge of Sydney's suburban sprawl, about an hour's drive from the city.

The Hills Info Centre is located at **The Pines**, home to five generations of the Roughley family, following its acquisition in 1830 by Joseph Roughley. The house was sold for $1 to the Baulkham Hills Council as a perpetual museum documenting the changing lifestyle of one family over successive generations. View by appt on jazz festival days. Ph: (02) 9651 1038

At 686 Old Northern Rd, the **Golden Ridge Animal Farm** gives city dwellers hands-on experience of rural life. The farm shows visitors how to feed baby animals, milk cows and goats and offers wagon rides. Picnic and BBQ facilities are available. Entrance in Wyoming Rd.

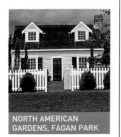

NORTH AMERICAN GARDENS, FAGAN PARK

Wheelchair accessible. Bookings essential. Ph: (02) 9651 1028. www.goldenridgeanimalfarm.com.au

Swane's Nursery, 490 Galston Rd, is one of the landmarks of the area and maintains a busy program of events throughout the year to celebrate the changing seasons. Roses have been grown at the site since 1919 and annual highlights include the Rose Show (Apr), Camellia Show (Jun) and Orchids (July). Open daily, 9am–5pm, the nursery has a coffee shop and allows picnicking on the lawns. Bookings can be made for tours. Ph: (02) 9651 1322

Galston Map 16 C4

Just to the north of Dural lies Galston, with a similar rural ambience of large properties and hobby farms. The village is linked to Sydney's northern suburbs by way of a picturesque winding road through **Galston Gorge**.

The gem of Galston is **Fagan Park**, a 55ha multi-purpose recreation area created on what were once the largest citrus orchards in the southern hemisphere. The pride of place in Fagan Park is **Netherby Cottage**, the original three-bedroom homestead. The 'Gardens of Many Nations', a 10ha Bicentennial project, has within it gardens in the styles of Holland, England, Africa, Japan, China and the Americas. Fagan Park also provides playgrounds, walking trails

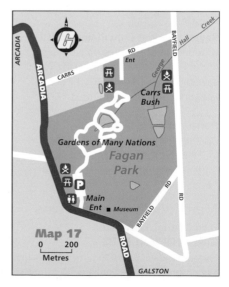

SYDNEY INTERNATIONAL AQUATIC CENTRE

(see Map 17) and picnicking amenities. Wheelchair accessible. The park is home to **Galston Country Music Festival** in Sep. Open daily, 7am–sunset, coin-operated carpark. Ph: (02) 9847 6791

Parramatta area
Homebush 16 C5

Just 5km east of Parramatta, via the M4 Mwy or the Great Western Hwy, is Sydney Olympic Park where the 2000 Olympic Games were held. Former wetlands and heavy industrial areas on the edge of the Parramatta River were transformed into international-standard sporting facilities. Here, the **Sydney Olympic Park Sports Centre** provides a venue for sports like basketball as well as concerts and other events. The centre includes a **Hall of Champions**, a tribute to Australia's sporting heroes. For tours of the Olympic Sports Centre, Ph: (02) 9714 7545

Sydney International Aquatic Centre was purpose-built for the Olympics and offers some of the best swimming and diving facilities in the world. It contains a number of swimming pools, including a competition pool, a utility pool, a training pool and a leisure pool with spas, a rapid river ride, waterslide, bubble beach, toddler pool and sauna. There is a snack bar, lockers, childminding, a gym and fitness club. Tours operate daily at noon, 1pm and 2pm. Ph: (02) 9752 3666

Sydney Olympic Park is also home to the **Sydney Showground**, where Sydney's annual Royal Easter Show was held for the first time in 1998. The showground lies on the eastern side of the Olympic complex and features various pavilions for livestock and produce displays, and a high-tech agricultural exhibition building.

Limited car parking is available, but must be pre-booked for some events. Travelling by train or bus is just as convenient and far cheaper, and an extensive public transport network is available. During the two weeks of the Show, trains run from all major Sydney stns. Those not able to get to a railway stn are well catered for with special 'show buses'. Showlink tickets, which

Cycleways

Transport links have made getting to Sydney's Royal Easter Show easier than ever, even for cyclists. An extensive network of cycleways linking Sydney Olympic Park to local areas has been established, all with distinctive signposting to ensure nobody gets lost along the way. RTA Motor Registries can provide details on cycling to the Show and regional cycleway maps. Freecall: 1800 060 607

HOME OF THE EELS

Parramatta received its existing name in 1791. Taken from the language of the local Aboriginal people, Parramatta means 'the place where the eels lie down'; hence the name Parramatta Eels for the local Rugby League team.

ROXY THEATRE

View all the latest **movies** in the historic Art Deco Roxy Theatre, located at 69 George St, Parramatta. Ph: (02) 9635 8499

combine the cost of both show entry and return transport, are available on all CityRail stns and Show Bus routes. Ph: (02) 9704 1244. www.sydneyshowground.com.au

Parramatta Map 16 B5

Parramatta lays claim to an enviable number of firsts in Australia — the site of Australia's 1st land grant for an experimental farm, 1st orchard, tannery, legal brewery, woollen mill, steam mill, marketplace, observatory and fair. Fortunately, a number of old buildings have been preserved. Some are still used for their original purpose and many have been restored and opened for public inspection.

The *Parramatta History and Heritage* leaflet contains information on Historic Houses walks, buildings and parks within Parramatta. The pamphlet is available from the Parramatta Heritage and Visitor Information Centre, open daily 9am–5pm, Ph: (02) 8839 3311.

A modern complex designed to blend in with the historic stone arch of the nearby Lennox Bridge, **Parramatta Riverside Theatres**, cnr Market and Church Sts, has become the focus for entertainment in the area, with a large and a smaller theatre. Ph: (02) 8839 3398

Lennox Bridge was designed by pioneer bridge builder and architect David Lennox in 1836. It is an elegant stone arch bridge that crosses the river at Church St, replacing an earlier wooden structure. The river end of Church St is now a popular restaurant precinct.

The present **St John's Cathedral** in Church St was completed in 1855.

Many historically significant buildings and memorials are situated in and around **Parramatta Park** (p.109). The most important of these is **Old Government House** (1799) which replaced an earlier building built in 1790. This former vice-regal residence has been fully restored by the National Trust

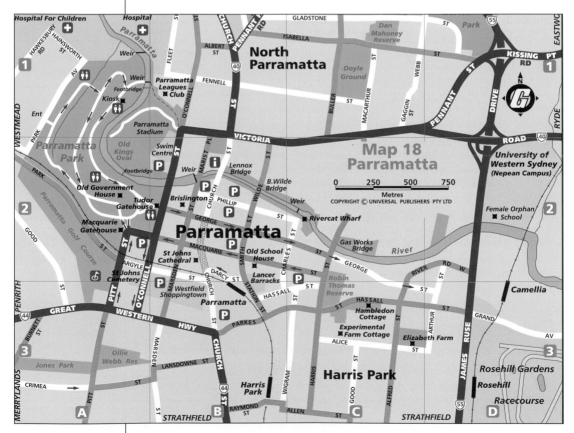

AT OLD GOVERNMENT HOUSE, PARRAMATTA

HISTORIC HEADSTONE

St John's Cemetery in O'Connell St, Parramatta, behind St John's Cathedral (pictured) contains the oldest known headstone in Australia. It belongs to First Fleeter, Henry Edward Dodd, who died in Jan 1791.

and displays the country's finest collection of pre-1855 furniture. Open Mon–Fri, 10am–4pm, weekends and public holidays, 11am–4pm. Ph: (02) 9635 8149

The Macquarie St Gatehouse, cnr Pitt and Macquarie Sts, dates from 1887. It was originally the home of the gatekeeper of the southern gates of Parramatta Park. Open Tues–Fri, 11am–3pm, Sun, noon–4pm.

Brislington (1821) is the oldest house in the inner city of Parramatta. Located next door to Parramatta Hospital on the corner of George and Marsden Sts, it contains a museum of medical and nursing history. Exhibits include operating tables, anaesthetic and sterilisation equipment. Visitors are greeted by guardians dressed in nurses' uniforms as worn at Parramatta Hospital in the 1890s–1930s. Open 2nd and last Thurs of every month, or by appointment Ph: (02) 9843 3106

Set in a glorious 1830s garden, **Elizabeth Farm**, 70 Alice St, Rosehill, contains part of the oldest surviving building in Australia, dating from 1793. It is a fine example of early colonial architecture, built originally as a home for John and Elizabeth Macarthur, pioneer breeders of merino sheep. The garden includes some of the oldest exotic plants in Australia, with the olive trees believed to have been planted by John Macarthur in 1805. Open daily, 10am–5pm. Ph: (02) 9635 9488

Surgeon John Harris built **Experiment Farm Cottage** in 1834 on a tract of land that had originally been granted to James Ruse as a reward for his success-ful farming experiments. The National Trust restored and furnished the cottage in period style. It is located at 9 Ruse St, Harris Park. Open Tues–Fri,

TOP WALK

On the 1st Sun of every month, the Friends of Elizabeth Farm offer a 2hr walk to explore **Elizabeth Macarthur's** home and garden at Rosehill.
Ph: (02) 9635 9488

ELIZABETH FARM

HANDMADE BRICKS, EXPERIMENT FARM

10.30am–3.30pm, weekends and holidays, 11.30am–3.30pm. Ph: (02) 9635 5655

Hambledon Cottage in Hassall St was built in 1824 by John Macarthur as a home for the retired governess of his three daughters. Restored in the style of the mid 19th century, its gardens contain a Spanish cork tree and an olive tree brought out by Macarthur in 1817. Open Wed, Thurs, weekends and public holidays, 11am–4pm. Ph: (02) 9635 6924

Opposite Parramatta Stn is the **Lancers Memorial Museum and Barracks**. The museum is located in **Linden House** (1828), which was originally a School of Industry for girls that was opened by Governor Darling and stood in Macquarie St. The house was dismantled and moved in 1963 to the grounds of the Barracks to serve as a museum for the Royal NSW Lancers. Displays include tanks, saddlery, weapons and trophies. Open Sun, 11am–4pm. The Barracks is an attractive two-storey building completed in 1820 by Governor Macquarie and is the oldest continuously used military barracks in Australia.

Strathfield Map 16 C5

Strathfield's first estate dates from 1867. Today the leafy, green suburb hosts some excellent examples of early architecture including Victorian and Federation styles and workers' cottages. Two pamphlets are available from Strathfield Council: *The Redmire Estate* and *The Crown of Strathfield*. Strathfield contains a number of beautiful parks and reserves, many located along the Cook's River Cycleway/Walkway (see p.88).

Sydney Markets Map 16 C5

Sydney Markets are located at **Flemington**, close to Homebush, and are reached along Parramatta Rd or by train to Flemington Station. Tours visit Sydney's busy fresh produce markets, Mon–Fri 6am. The tour winds through the bustling sections where flowers, fruit and vegetables for Sydney's restaurants and shops are traded. Bookings essential. Ph: (02) 9325 6294. Sydney Fresh Food markets are open Sat 6am–2pm.

Sydney's most famous market, **Paddy's Markets**, has a wide range of food, fashion and gifts on offer. Paddy's Flemington is open Fri 10am–4pm, Sun 9am–4.30pm. (See p.30 for Paddy's Haymarket.) Infoline 1300 361 589. www.paddysmarkets.com.au

HAMBLEDON COTTAGE, PARRAMATTA

NEPEAN BELLE

Sydney Swap and Sell Market, Flemington, is open Sat 6am–2pm. Enter off Parramatta Rd.

Penrith area
Penrith Map 16 A5

A busy regional centre with much appeal for the visitor, Penrith lies at the foot of the Blue Mountains beside the Nepean River. The town is believed to have been named after Penrith in Cumbria, England. Blaxland, Wentworth and Lawson and set out from this area for their amazing epic crossing of the Blue Mountains (1817).

One of the area's best-preserved buildings is **The Arms of Australia Inn**, Great Western Hwy, Emu Plains, where the first liquor licence was issued in 1836. It is now a local history museum and there is a barn housing a range of heritage farm machinery. Open Sun, 1pm–5pm, Wed–Thur 10am–2pm. Ph: (02) 4735 4394.

Another local watering hole worth visiting is the **Peachtree Inn**, Peachtree Rd, Penrith, which is full of memorabilia, as much a museum as a pub. Ph: (02) 4731 3444

Also of interest, at 29 Cassola Pl, Penrith, is **Sun Masamune**, Australia's 1st sake brewery. Open for inspection and tastings weekdays, 2pm–3pm, please book, Ph: (02) 4732 2833

In a beautiful setting on the banks of the Nepean River at 86 River Rd, Emu Plains, the **Penrith Regional Gallery and the Lewers Bequest** comprises three galleries. A permanent collection is housed in the original homestead; changing exhibitions in the regional gallery; and an intimate gallery houses community exhibitions. Open Tues–Sun, 11am–5pm. Ph: (02) 4735 1100

In Castlereagh Rd next to Penrith Railway Stn is the **Museum of Fire and Safety Education Centre**, housing a unique collection of vintage fire engines. Displays show the drama and dangers of fire and firefighting. There is a kiosk (weekdays only), playground and facilities for the disabled. Open Mon–Fri, 9.30am–4.30pm, weekends and public holidays, 10am–3pm. Ph: (02) 4731 3000

The acclaimed **Sydney International Regatta Centre** off Castlereagh Rd, Penrith, has competition and warm-up lakes to suit a wide range of water sport activities, including catch-and-release fishing competitions. The centre is surrounded by 196ha of wetlands, native and landscaped park, and when fully developed (2011) the complex will have 2,000ha of public recreation space with

WHITEWATER RAFTING AT PENRITH STADIUM

Arts Centre at 597 High St, has been described as the finest venue in the Western Sydney area and hosts many of Penrith's cultural events as well as conferences, seminars and exhibitions. Ph: (02) 4721 5423

Built in 1867 as a joint road and railway bridge, **Victoria Bridge** was prefabricated in Great Britain and carries the Great Western Hwy across the Nepean River.

See and experience Aboriginal heritage and culture at the **Muru Mittiga Aboriginal Cultural and Education Centre**, open Mon–Fri, 9am–4pm, weekends 10am–2pm, tours by appt only. 1951 Castlereagh Rd, Cranebrook. Ph: (02) 4729 2377

Experience the thrill of whitewater rafting at **Penrith Whitewater Stadium**. This is the only man-made whitewater river in the southern hemisphere, and was designed to re-create the characteristics of a wild river. Guided and self-guided trips are available. Penrith Whitewater also offers kayaking, beach volleyball, guided venue tours and a cafe. This was the competition venue for the exciting canoe/kayak slalom events during the Sydney 2000 Olympics; national and international competitions are still held here. Whitewater rafting experience is not necessary but restrictions do apply. Bookings essential Ph: (02) 4730 4333

Richmond/Windsor area
Richmond Map 16 A4

A long avenue of London plane trees welcomes the visitor to the historic garden town of Richmond, which owes its name to an Englishman, the Duke of Richmond. Apart from its historical connection, Richmond is perhaps best known as a principal site for the **Royal Australian Air Force**. The RAAF base can only be viewed from the outside, but **Ham Common**, on the opposite side of Windsor Rd, is an excellent vantage point to watch the airforce jets and transport aircraft. The common has BBQs, a shelter, shade and a playground for children as well as a visitors centre. Some of Australia's greatest artists have

seven lakes. The centre provides picnic facilities and a 5km cycle path for public use outside of competition. Open daily, 8am–5pm.

Starting from the jetty off Nepean Ave, the paddlewheeler *Nepean Belle* cruises the Nepean River, going into the gorge and close to the international rowing course at Penrith Lakes. The vessel cruises on Sat nights and Sun lunch, however, it can be used at other times. Coffee, lunch and dinner cruises include commentary and entertainment. Bookings essential. Ph: (02) 4733 1274

Panthers World of Entertainment, home of the Penrith Panthers Rugby League team, is Australia's largest licensed sporting club and resort complex. Located in Mulgoa Rd, Penrith, Panthers is within easy reach of the Blue Mountains and other tourist attractions such as Eastern Creek Raceway (p.111). A regular bus service runs from Panthers to Penrith Railway Stn and Penrith Plaza shopping centre. Club open daily, 9am–6am Ph: (02) 4720 5555. www.panthersworld.com.au

The Joan Sutherland Performing

ST MATTHEW'S CHURCH, WINDSOR

St Albans Map 19

Located 21km north of Wisemans Ferry on the MacDonald River, St Albans can be reached via the Webbs Creek Ferry or Wisemans Ferry. The **Settlers Arms Inn** was built by convict labour and began operation in 1836. It became an overnight stop on the Cobb & Co route from Sydney and Parramatta to Newcastle. The Inn is a good spot for lunch, dinner or an overnight stay. Ph: (02) 4568 2111.

St Albans has many historic buildings including the ruins of **St Josephs Catholic Church** (1843), and St Albans Cemetery which contains the graves of several First Fleeters.

The Fickle Wombat, a restaurant, antiques and gift store in St Albans, also operates as a tourist info centre for the area. Open Wed–Mon, 11am-4pm, for dinner Sat night. Ph: (02) 4568 2078

Wilberforce Map 16 B3

Established as the 4th Macquarie town in 1810, Wilberforce guards the road to the wilderness of Wollemi NP (see p.108) and the back road to the Hunter Valley (see p.155).

St John's Anglican Church (1859) was constructed by Edmund Blacket, who was responsible for a number of fine churches in colonial times.

A large insect collection is on show at the **Butterfly Farm Indy 800 Kart** at Wilberforce on Wilberforce Rd. In addition to butterflies, exhibits at the Butterfly Farm include spiders and scorpions, displays of fossils and Aboriginal artefacts. Facilities include picnic grounds, BBQs, waterski beaches

found inspiration from the Hawkesbury region and local historian John Miller leads a tour, *In the Footsteps of the Masters*, to the sites where famous artists such as Arthur Streeton, Charles Conder and Julian Ashton painted their landscapes. Ph: (02) 4577 6882

St Peter's Church (1841), contains solid cedar pews and gallery and memorials to early pioneering families. The oldest tombstone in the churchyard is dated 1809.

Yarramundi House (1894) at the University of Western Sydney — Hawkesbury was the former home of the principal of the Hawkesbury Agricultural College and is now a restaurant. A jazz day is held on the last Sun of each month. Ph: (02) 4570 1999

GHOST TOUR

John Miller's **Haunting Hawkesbury Ghost Tours** in Windsor recalls tales from the early days of European settlement, taking visitors down into the oldest cellars in Australia.
Ph: (02) 4577 6882

Grave concerns

The graveyard of **St Matthew's Church,** Windsor, is even older than the church itself. Its burial register carries some intriguing though rather gruesome information about the difficulties and dangers of life in the early days of settlement. For example: speared by native, 1 March 1814; died through the bite of a snake, 25 March 1819; died through the wheel of a bullock cart accidentally running over his neck, 8 March 1822; died at Windsor, in consequence of a pistol ball being lodged in his head by a constable in the execution of his duty, 6 July 1823; was wilfully murdered by her husband with an axe inflicting five fractures, died 9 February 1825, aged 29.

PIONEER HEADSTONE, WINDSOR

ST ALBANS VIA WEBBS CREEK FERRY

and swimming pools. The outdoor 800m Indy 800 go-kart track is open Sun–Mon 10am–5pm, Thur–Fri 10am–5pm, Sat 10am–10pm. Ph: (02) 4575 1265 (p.111); Butterfly Farm open daily, 10am–5pm. Ph: (02) 4575 1955 or 4575 1265

At nearby **Ebenezer**, an interesting historic grouping in Coromandel Rd includes the beautifully restored **Ebenezer Uniting Church** (1809) — the oldest existing church in Australia — and its cemetery which contains the graves of hundreds of pioneers. The nearby **Schoolmaster's House** is now a small museum furnished in period style with a shop providing refreshments and gifts. Open daily, 10am–3.30pm.
Ph: (02) 4579 9350

Also at Ebenezer is the **Tizzana Winery** on Tizzana Rd. This delightful winery, with its National Trust classified sandstone building, was originally established in 1887. Open weekends and public holidays, noon–6pm or by appt. Ph: (02) 4579 1150

Windsor Map 16 B4
Another original Macquarie Town, Windsor is on a small bluff overlooking the Hawkesbury River. Many of its early buildings have survived and can be best enjoyed by a walk along Windsor Mall, part of George St. Cafes and restaurants line the mall, which is given over to an

interesting arts and crafts market every Sun, 9am–4pm.

At the top of the main shopping street is T**hompson Sq**, originally known as Bell's Post. The **Macquarie Arms Inn** (1815) is the oldest hotel in Australia still trading in its original building. **The Hawkesbury Historic Museum** is also in Thompson Sq and is housed in another old hotel, **Coffeys Inn**. This local history museum depicts early pioneering life in the area and also dedicates one room to RAAF activities. Open daily, 10am–4pm, Ph: (02) 4577 2310. A *Windsor and Richmond Walks* brochure is available from the Visitor Info Centre, Ph: (02) 4588 5895.
www.hawkesburyvalley.com

Famous convict architect Francis Greenway designed two of Windsor's public buildings: **St Matthews Church** in Moses St (1817) and the **Courthouse** in Court St (1822). The church is open daily, 7am–6pm.

John Tebbutt's Observatories in Palmer St have been restored by his great-grandson, but are currently only available as a function centre or part of the Clydesdale horse-drawn restaurant tour.

At the rear of the Verandah Restaurant and Bar on Windsor Rd, is the **Green Hills Burial Ground** which predates the arrival of Governor Macquarie. It is here

MOBILE DINNER
Clydesdales
Restaurant at Windsor is believed to be the world's only horse-drawn restaurant. The restored 1890s horse-drawn omnibus seats eight and offers fine dining and a leisurely 3hr tour of historic Windsor.
Ph: (02) 4577 4544

that **Phillip Cunningham**, an Irish political prisoner and one of the leaders of the battle of Vinegar Hill in 1804, was buried after being hanged without trial at the government granary.

Wisemans Ferry Map 16 B2

The little settlement of Wisemans Ferry sits in the steep-sided Hawkesbury River valley, and is named after ex-convict Solomon Wiseman who set up the original ferry service. Historic **Wisemans Ferry Inn** was originally Cobhan Hall, Wiseman's home. Open daily for meals and refreshments. Ph: (02) 4566 4301. Wisemans Ferry is a good place to hire a houseboat (p.111).

National Parks

Cattai NP Map 19

Located between the junction of the Hawkesbury River and Cattai Creek, the 424ha Cattai NP provides facilities for leisure activities.

The park conserves the Cattai farm area, originally a land grant to First Fleet surgeon, Thomas Arndell. The original 1821 cottage is furnished in the style of the period, although is not currently open to the public.

In a separate section is **Mitchell Park**, which features rare riverine rainforest, a network of walking tracks, and picnic areas with BBQs near Cattai Creek.

The land at Cattai Farm is flat to gently undulating with shady trees, mown grass with picnic areas and sandy river beaches. Car-based **camping** is possible throughout the year and amenities include shelter sheds beside the river and BBQs. There is also play equipment for children. Bookings essential for campers. Ph: (02) 4572 3100

Marramarra NP Map 16 C3

A NPWS ranger describes Marramarra NP as 'a park for resourceful people who know what they want to do for themselves'. Apart from some toilet blocks, the park has no facilities.

The park's rugged slopes and mangrove communities are inhabited by swamp wallabies, wombats, antechinus and waterbirds, including the white-breasted sea eagle. Keep an eye out for wedgetailed eagles and white-cheeked honeyeaters.

Access is from Bloodwood Rd, Arcadia or Canoelands Rd. There are two rudimentary camping sites and places where canoes can be launched. For further details, contact the Ku-ring-gai Chase NP Visitor Info Centre, Ph: (02) 9472 8949

TIZZANA WINERY

WISEMANS FERRY INN DINING ROOM

A TASTE OF HISTORY
Bowman Cottage tearooms at 370 Windsor St, Richmond dates from 1817 and serves traditional Aussie fare. Open Sun–Fri, 8am–3pm. Ph: (02) 4578 3056

WEDGETAILED EAGLE

Wollemi NP Map 16 A1

The 2nd largest NP in NSW, Wollemi covers some 487 500ha of rugged wilderness terrain adjoining the Blue Mountains, Yengo and Goulburn River NPs. The visual rewards are many: mountain rainforests, sandstone formations, perched swamps and spectacular cliffs at the Colo River catchment (see main entry p.226).

Parks and gardens

Auburn Botanic Gardens Map 16 C5

Beside the Duck River, Auburn Botanic Gardens provide an oasis of greenery in the western suburbs. There are 12 distinct areas including the well-known **Japanese garden**. A walk-through **aviary** was built to celebrate Australia's Bicentenary. Facilities include a kiosk and picnic area. Open daily, 9am–5pm. Ph: (02) 9735 1222

Bicentennial Park Map 19

Part of Sydney Olympic Park, only 30 mins from the centre of Sydney and 15 mins from Parramatta, Bicentennial Park comprises 60ha of natural wetlands and 40ha of rolling parklands. A Bicentennial project, the park is an important recreation and conservation facility that draws visitors from all over Sydney. The focal point of the park is the Trelliage, the high viewing platform for the park and surrounding areas. There are 8km of paths, a waterbird refuge, a salt-marsh area and a system of elevated timber boardwalks, providing access to the mangrove forest. A well-equipped children's playground, cycling track, jogging stations, teahouse, excellent BBQ and picnic facilities make Bicentennial Park an ideal stop on a family outing. Open daily sunrise–sunset, Visitor Centre open weekends and public holidays, 10am–4pm. Ph: (02) 9714 7888

Central Gardens Map 16 B5

In the heart of **Merrylands**, Central Gardens comprise 12ha of natural bushland, complete with ornamental lakes, waterfalls, wildlife sanctuaries, aviary and a boardwalk. Excellent facilities include playgrounds, picnic areas and BBQs. Ph: (02) 9840 9840

Lake Parramatta Reserve Map 16 B5

Alongside the North Parramatta Bypass, Lake Parramatta Reserve is a 65ha area protecting the lake and bushland around the Hunt's Creek Dam. It was the 1st **wildlife reserve** dedicated in NSW and features splendid trees that shade the

GIFTS OF LIFE
The **Silent Hearts Memorial Garden** in Bicentennial Park commemorates those who have died and donated their organs so that others may live.

BICENTENNIAL PARK

GHOST TOUR, OLD GOVERNMENT HOUSE, PARRAMATTA

drives and picnic areas and provide shelter for birds, possums, bandicoots and other wildlife.

The dam forming the lake was the first of its type in Australia and was built for water storage in 1857 by William Randle, who also built Fort Denison in Sydney Harbour. There are wood BBQs and a kiosk. Enter from Lackey St only. Open daily, sunrise–sunset.

Parramatta Park Map 18 A2

This is one of the country's most significant cultural landscapes and as such is protected by a permanent conservation order under the NSW *Heritage Act.*

What is now Parramatta Park was once part of the territory of the Burramatta people, a clan of the Dharruk Group, prior to white occupation. The park contains over 100 archaeological sites—Aboriginal and historic—and monuments and buildings. Enter this vibrant urban park via the elaborate George St Gatehouse. Significant historical sites include Old Government House and the Dairy Precinct, then there is the beauty of the Rumsey Rose Garden with its planting of 500 heritage roses. Cricket ovals, a golf course, swimming pool and playing field are also provided. The park is situated on the banks of the

Parramatta River, and the magnificent settings make this park a perfect venue for festivals, celebrations, picnics and sporting activities. Enquiries and bookings, Parramatta Park Administration Office, Ph: (02) 8833 5000 (p.100–101)

Prospect Reservoir Map 16 B5

Built in 1888, the reservoir at Reservoir Rd, Prospect, has landscaped gardens, picnic and BBQ facilities and cycling, walking and jogging tracks. Open daily. Ph: (02) 9795 4399

Other attractions
Featherdale Wildlife Park Map 19

Located in Kildare Rd, **Doonside**, Featherdale has a large private collection of Australian animals, from koalas and kookaburras to penguins and pelicans. There is a picnic area, kiosk and large souvenir shop. Wheelchairs are available, as are other facilities for the disabled. Open daily, 9am–5pm. Ph: (02) 9622 1644 or (02) 9671 4984 for recorded info.

PARRAMATTA RIVER AT SUNSET

FEATHERDALE WILDLIFE PARK

Hawkesbury Leisure Centres

This centre is at the corner of Church and Drummond Sts, South Windsor. The Hawkesbury Leisure Centre is a two-site facility, incorporating Hawkesbury Oasis, which is an Aquatic and Fitness Centre and Hawkesbury Indoor Stadium which is a six-court Indoor Sports Stadium. There are many features that cater for the whole family, including indoor and outdoor swimming pools, swimming lessons, waterslide, aerobic and aqua-aerobic classes, a fully equipped gymnasium and a variety of indoor sports. A cafe is on site. Open Mon–Fri 6am–9pm, weekends 8am–6pm, Ph: (02) 4587 8900

Sydney Children's Museum (Kidseum) Map 16 B5

This is a wonderful children's museum, which was founded in May 1986 as a private, not-for-profit organisation. It was the first and remains the only independent children's museum in Australia. It is located in Holroyd Garden Park in Walpole St, **Merrylands**, not far from Merrylands Stn. There are also picnic facilities, playground and a safety bike track. The museum offers a variety of hands-on activities, both indoors and outdoors. Open daily including most public holidays, 10am–4pm. Ph: (02) 9897 1414. www.sydneykids.org Nearby is a well-equipped playground.

Parklea Markets Map 19

On 601 Sunnyholt Rd, Parklea, this 2ha covered market is one of the NW's major attractions. Hundreds of stalls offer a vast range of fresh fruit and vegetables, seafood, meats, deli, bakery items, cooked food, plants, flowers, pottery, gifts and clothing at bargain prices. A busy program of entertainment keeps children amused. Open weekends, 8.30am–4.30pm, Ph: (02) 9629 3311

Tobruk Merino Sheep Station Map16 B3

On the Old Northern Rd, **Maroota**, just before Wisemans Ferry, this working sheep station offers shearing demonstrations and sheep dog work

RODEOS

The following venues occasionally hold rodeos. It is best to phone for dates and times.
* Windsor Leagues Club (a Sat in Nov every year), Ph: (02) 4577 6488
* Vineyard Hotel and Gateway Motel at Vineyard (held on the land at the back of the pub), Ph: (02) 9627 1754

BICENTENNIAL PARK

Fun for the young

* ★ Bushwalking in Cattai NP (p.107)
* ★ Fagan Park, Galston (p.98)
* ★ Featherdale Wildlife Park, Doonside (p.109)
* ★ Go-karting at Indy 800 Kart Track (Butterfly Farm), Wilberforce (p.111)
* ★ Golden Ridge Animal Farm, Dural (p98)
* ★ Hawkesbury Leisure Centres, (p.110)
* ★ Sydney Children's Museum (Kidseum), Merrylands (p.110)
* ★ Koala Park Sanctuary, West Pennant Hills (p.98)
* ★ Sydney International Aquatic Centre, Sydney Olympic Park (p.99)
* ★ Penrith Whitewater Stadium (p.104)

trials as well as wilderness walks and genuine Australian country hospitality. The Woolshed dining room serves many Australian specialities, and there is a shop selling country clothes and accessories. Open by appt only. Ph: (02) 4566 8223

Recreational activities

Cycling

Plenty of wide open countryside and a wealth of natural and historical scenery make the NW region an ideal location for cycling enthusiasts.

A ride through the **Parramatta Valley**, starting at Homebush Railway Stn and concluding at Parramatta Railway Stn, takes in **Bicentennial Park**. The RTA's **Sydney Cycleways Series** provides full details as well as rules of the road and tips. Freecall: 1800 060 607

Experienced riders can take the 47km ride through the rural colonial towns of Windsor, Ebenezer and Wilberforce. See RTA Sydney Cycleways Series.

Motorsports

Eastern Creek Raceway hosts a variety of motor racing events. Access is from the Great Western Hwy along Brabham Dr. Next door is **Eastern Creek Carts**, for cart racing. Open daily from 9am, restrictions apply to children. For details, Ph: (02) 9672 7530. **Butterfly Farm Indy 800 Kart Track** is on 446 Wilberforce Rd, Wilberforce. The outdoor 800m go-kart

track features single and dual carts. Open Sun–Mon 10am–5pm, Thur–Fri 10am–5pm, Sat 10am–10pm.Ph: (02) 4575 1265 or 4575 1955 (see p.105).

On the water

Able Hawkesbury Houseboats at Wisemans Ferry has eight sizes of well equipped houseboats for hire; no licence is required. The houseboats have more than a 100km run of the river, west to Windsor and east to Brooklyn. Ph: (02) 4566 4308

Fish the Hawkesbury River for bass, bream and flathead with **Australian Bass Fishing Charters** at Windsor. All fishing tackle and light refreshments supplied. Operates daily, Ph: (02) 4575 1893

TOBRUK MERINO SHEEP STATION, MAROOTA

Places of interest (nature and history)

OLYMPIC PARK, HOMEBUSH BAY

Suggested tours – Map 19

Nature and history tour

Approximate distance
205km return from Sydney CBD

About the tour

This tour samples the twin delights of the NW region: natural beauty and reminders of Australia's past. The tour starts at Koala Park Sanctuary at West Pennant Hills, which provides a chance to see these lovable marsupials up close, and follows a scenic route along Old Northern Road to Wisemans Ferry. Take in St Albans, a charming village in a time warp, or enjoy a picnic lunch by the majestic Hawkesbury River.

Head south via Wisemans Ferry Rd to the Cattai NP, which is ideal for bushwalking, birdwatching, or just taking in the scenery. There's also plenty for plant enthusiasts to get excited about. At Windsor, stop in Thompson Sq to view the historic buildings; then finish up with a visit to Parklea Markets, where you're sure to pick up a few bargains.

Treasures of Sydney's NW tour

Approximate distance
135km return from Sydney CBD

About the tour

This tour highlights the attractions of Sydney's NW. Start out at the amazing Sydney Olympic Park, Homebush Bay, and then relax in some of the 425ha of perfect parklands, which includes Bicentennial Park.

Parramatta offers great shopping and restaurants, and you can also view some fine examples of the earliest days of white settlement here. Then make your way down to Featherdale Wildlife Park in Doonside, where you can get a bird's eye view of some of Australia's unique native animals.

At the foothills of the Blue Mountains, Penrith has a great deal to offer in the way of outdoor activities, and a visit to the area would not be complete without seeing the fascinating Museum of Fire.

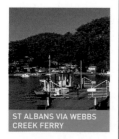

ST ALBANS VIA WEBBS CREEK FERRY

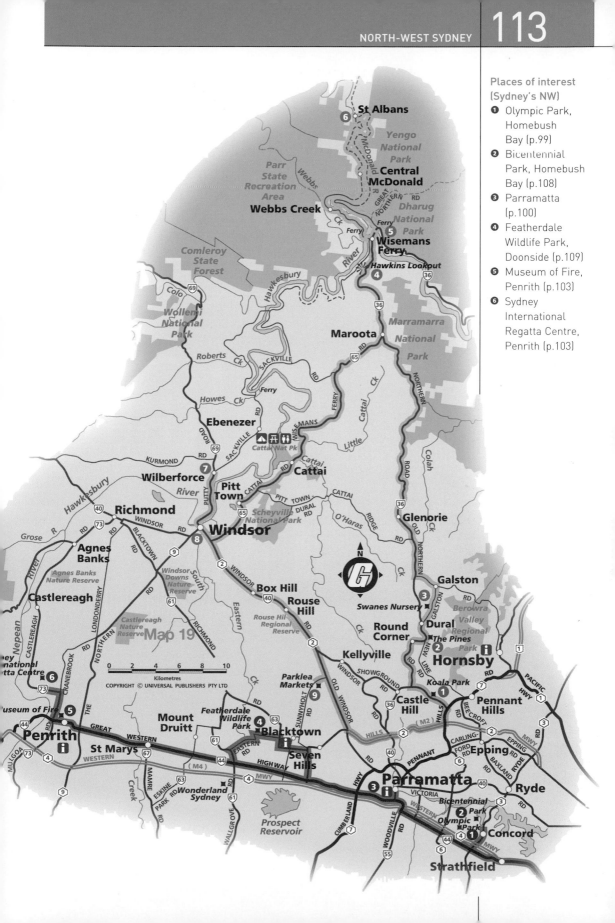

Places of interest
(Sydney's NW)
❶ Olympic Park,
   Homebush
   Bay (p.99)
❷ Bicentennial
   Park, Homebush
   Bay (p.108)
❸ Parramatta
   (p.100)
❹ Featherdale
   Wildlife Park,
   Doonside (p.109)
❺ Museum of Fire,
   Penrith (p.103)
❻ Sydney
   International
   Regatta Centre,
   Penrith (p.103)

Radio stations

**Macarthur Community
Radio:** FM 100.5

2RDJ: FM 88.1

2GL: FM 89.3

Tourist Info Radio: FM 88

Tourist information

**Camden Visitor
Information Centre**

John Oxley Cottage

Camden Valley Way,

Elderslie 2570

Ph: (02) 4658 1370

Fax: (02) 4658 1563

www.camden.nsw.gov.au

**Quondong Visitor
Information Centre**

Quondong House

15 Old Menangle Rd,

Campbelltown 2560

Ph: (02) 4645 4921

Fax: (02) 4645 4920

www.campbelltown.nsw.gov.au

**Visitor Information
Centre Wollondilly**

Old Picton Post Office

Cnr Argyle and Menangle Sts

Picton 2571

Ph: (02) 4677 3962

Fax: (02) 4677 3217

www.stonequarry.com.au

LEFT: HISTORIC CAMELOT HOUSE
AND GARDENS, CAMDEN

south-west sydney and macarthur country

HISTORY, SCENERY AND FAMILY attractions such as Fairfield City Farm and Gledswood are all part of SW Sydney's appeal. In the north, the region's densely settled urban areas hold many delights, from beautiful parks and gardens to cycleways, heritage features and museums. Add to this the international influences in suburbs such as Cabramatta and Fairfield, and the result is an enticing district rich in colours, textures and flavours.

Busy Bankstown Airport carries most of the light aircraft traffic for the entire city, as well as being home to an exciting museum, while bustling Liverpool is at the heart of Sydney's fastest growing area, and is the region's major business and shopping hub.

At the southern end of the region, the cosmopolitan suburban buzz gives way to a more sedate semi-rural atmosphere; and in fact, some of colonial Australia's formative history was played out in rural Macarthur Country. This is particularly evident in the picturesque towns of Camden, Appin and Cobbitty. Campbelltown, the busy centre of Macarthur Country, retains many of its elegant historic buildings, and is renowned for combining history with fun at the Fisher's Ghost Festival.

To the west, the impressive Nepean River runs through the entire region, providing a scenic venue for cruises, watersports and riverside picnics.

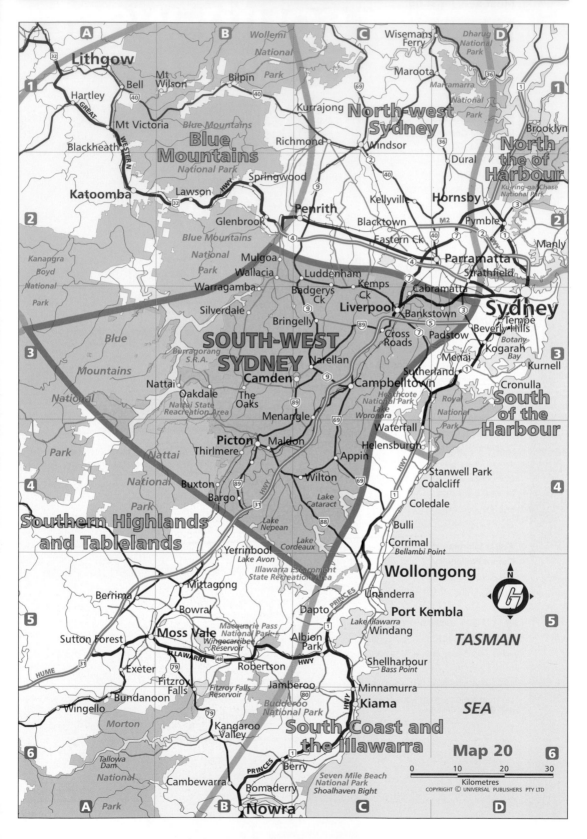

Natural features

With the exception of the sandstone and dry scrub of the Blue Mountains escarpment, Sydney's SW comprises mainly the alluvial plains of the Nepean and Georges River systems. The area is bounded by rugged country to the west and south, much of which serves as Sydney's water supply catchment area. The Nepean River flows through the spectacular Nepean Gorge on the western margin of the region.

It was the fertile soil that led to the early and rapid rural development of the area; Macarthur Country is still a major supplier of fruit and vegetables to Sydney's markets. The relatively flat countryside is also suited for housing the ever-growing population of the city, and large satellite settlements have been established at the fringes.

History

The most significant event in the area's early colonial history was the 1803 grant of 2023ha on the Nepean River to John Macarthur. The work of John and his wife Elizabeth in breeding merino sheep provided the foundation for Australia's wool industry. Camden grew up around Macarthur's estate.

Liverpool, founded in Macarthur Country by Governor Lachlan Macquarie in 1810, and then connected by road to Sydney in 1814, was quick to prosper. In 1820, Macquarie founded Campbelltown which was originally developed as a wheat farming area. On the Appin Rd between Campbelltown and Appin is the monument to Hume and Hovell, whose exploration expedition set out from Appin.

The steady encroachment of Sydney since then has meant enormous growth for the area. However, many rural pockets remain, with local councils and the National Trust endeavouring to maintain the colonial heritage.

Getting there

By road

Road access to the SW and Macarthur region is excellent, with the Hume Hwy (Hwy 31) running through Liverpool to Campbelltown and beyond; Camden Valley Way (Route 89) links Camden to the Hume Hwy. The South Western Mwy (M5) provides a fast route through the Bankstown/Milperra area, linking with Hwy 31 beyond Liverpool, while the Northern Rd (Route 69) connects Camden to Penrith. Elizabeth Dr (Route 50) runs from Liverpool to Wallacia and Warragamba. Buses travel regularly from Campbelltown Railway Stn to the Camden district.

By rail

Trains from Sydney's Central Stn reach Liverpool in 40min and Campbelltown in under an hour. CountryLink trains service towns beyond this point.

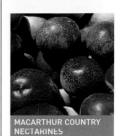

MACARTHUR COUNTRY NECTARINES

THIRLMERE RAILWAY MUSEUM

RARE WHITE WARATAH

Getting around

NSW Wilderness Transit Service offers a tour of Aboriginal, European and Blue Mountains Heritage sites on the **Wollondilly Explorer Bus** The bus departs Tahmoor Railway Stn every Thur morning. Also on offer is the **Yerranderie Ghost Town Tours** available first Tues in the month returning Wed via Wombeyan Caves. A charter service for bushwalkers to Kanangra Walls and Yerranderie is available.
Ph: (02) 4683 2344 or 0428 819 655.

Paddlewheeler *Nepean Belle* (see p.104) offers morning and afternoon tea cruises, luncheon and dinner cruises through the spectacular Nepean Gorge into the foothills of the Blue Mountains NP. Ph: (02) 4733 1274

Festivals and events

Festival of Steam

On the 1st Sun in Mar, **Thirlmere** celebrates the start of 'steam season' at the Railway Museum. Ph: (02) 4681 8001 for a program of family festivities; Ph: (02) 9379 1031, 9am–4pm daily, for info on steam trains departing Sydney. www.nswrtm.org

New Year celebrations

The **Khmer and Lao New Year Festival** is celebrated at the Buddhist Temple in Edensor Park in Apr, Ph: (02) 9823 7338.

These festivals are also celebrated in Cabramatta as well as **Vietnamese New Year** which occurs in Jan/Feb, with lion dancing, firecrackers, and traditional ceremonies, food, dance performances and much more. The three-day festival is held at Warwick Farm Race Course Ph: (02) 9796 8036

Heritage Week

Celebrated in Apr each year, with many special events in the Macarthur region. Heritage buildings are open for inspection and a coach tour visits privately owned colonial mansions.

Holroyd City Fest

This festival is held in the Holroyd area over an eight-day period, usually in Mar or Apr. The program includes entertainment, community events, a parade, festival of song and dance, fun run, teddy bear's picnic, band concert and a fireworks finale. Ph: (02) 9840 9718

Yulefest

Christmas in July is celebrated throughout the region, with many restaurants offering a Yulefest package.

Dingofest

Dingo parades and educational displays form the basis of this festival held at the **Dingo Sanctuary, Bargo** on a weekend in

FESTIVAL FEVER

There are at least 13 multicultural festivals celebrated in SW Sydney including the Chilean Festival and Octoberfest, all celebrated at Fairfield Showground.

VIETNAMESE NEW YEAR LION DANCE

Oct each year (coinciding with the White Waratah Festival). Ph: (02) 4684 1156

White Waratah Festival

The rare white waratah, native to the Wollondilly Shire, blooms in Oct. To celebrate this, a variety of events including train rides, fun fairs, music and a cart derby are held throughout the month. Ph: (02) 4677 3962

Fisher's Ghost Festival

In 1826 Frederick Fisher was murdered and his ghost was seen pointing to the body in a paddock. Campbelltown's Fisher's Ghost Festival celebrates this famous legend for two weeks late Oct to early Nov, with a parade, fireworks, jazz and rock concerts, arts exhibitions and mardi gras. www.fishersghost.com.au

THE GRAND PARADE, FISHERS GHOST FESTIVAL

Main localities and towns

Bankstown/Liverpool area

Bankstown Map 20 D3

The dense urban development in the City of Bankstown is home to a vibrant community which includes a rich multicultural component. Bankstown Council has developed a series of walkways and cycleways throughout the local area and along the **Georges River Foreshore**.

The **Picnic Point to Lambeth Reserve Boardwalk** is one of the most beautiful and scenic sections of the walkway. From Picnic Point Reserve to Lambeth Reserve a combination of boardwalk, swamp decks and bush tracks weave through a variety of natural environments, such as mangrove forests, river and creek foreshores, landscaped parklands and bushland areas. This section of the walkway also links up with open-grassed recreational areas that have picnic and BBQ facilities, toilets, car parking and children's playground equipment. This beautiful section of Bankstown's natural environment provides the perfect setting for a leisurely stroll, taking the dog for a walk or even an energetic bike ride.

There is parking at the Lambeth Reserve entry. The Boardwalk is open sunrise to sunset. For more information on walks, maps and brochures in the Bankstown area Ph: (02) 9707 9400, www.bankstowncity.nsw.gov.au

Liverpool Map 20 C3

Many historic landmarks have been preserved in Liverpool. Info is available from the **Liverpool Regional Museum** which specialises in photographs, textiles, memorabilia and domestic and industrial objects relating to the region's history. It also has touring exhibitions. Open Tues–Sat 10am–4pm, Ph: (02) 9602 0315

While at the museum, buy a ticket to see **Collingwood House**, an historic house and museum nearby. Its hours are the same and tickets are only available at the museum. The house is fully restored and set in beautiful grounds. There are pioneer graves in **Pioneers Memorial Park** at the corner of Campbell St, Macquarie St and Hume Hwy. Other historic sites are described in Liverpool Heritage Walk pamphlet available from Liverpool City Council, 193 Macquarie Mall, Ph: 1300 362 170. www.liverpool.nsw.gov.au

Cabramatta/Fairfield area

Cabramatta Map 20 C3

Since the 1970s, Cabramatta's increasing Vietnamese population has shaped its vibrant Asian character. With over 100

PIONEER GRAVES, PIONEERS MEMORIAL PARK

LUNAR NEW YEAR CELEBRATIONS

FAIRFIELD CITY FARM

restaurants, the suburb offers some of Sydney's freshest and most authentic Asian cooking and produce.

Fairfield City Council commissioned 20 giant painted murals with a food theme to add to this atmosphere. Wander down **John St** to pick an appealing restaurant; admire the array of Asian produce at AA Supermarket in Cabramatta Mall; visit the Buddhist Temple for a moment of meditation and contemplation; enjoy the street decorations. Indulge in some bargain shopping — Cabramatta has more fabric shops than any other part of Sydney. Chinese, Laotian and Vietnamese New Year and the fascinating Moon Festival are all celebrated here. www.fairfieldcity.nsw.gov.au

Fairfield Map 22

Fairfield is one of Sydney's most culturally and ethnically diverse municipalities. The **Fairfield City Museum and Gallery**, cnr Oxford St and Horsley Dr, Smithfield, presents an interesting exhibition of the area's past, including an operating blacksmith display, general store, slab hut and 1880s cottage.

The **Stein Gallery** has changing exhibitions of textiles, social history and the works of local artists. Open Tues–Sat, 9.30am–4.30pm,

Sun 1pm–4pm. Ph: (02) 9609 3993, www.fairfieldcity.nsw.gov.au/museumgallery

Fairfield City Farm, Abbotsbury, is a large working farm. The main paddocks house farm animals and visitors can take part in activities, from pony and tractor rides to fishing in the **Wildlife Dam**. Children can touch and feed baby animals, 'help' milk a cow, watch the Sheep Shearing Show and the sheepdogs rounding up sheep. Electric BBQs and a childrens' playground are available. Also located within the farm is the Sydney 2000 Olympic Games mountain bike track and the **Farmhouse Restaurant**. Open daily, 9am–5pm. Ph: (02) 9823 3222, www.cityfarm.com.au

Macarthur Country
Appin Map 20 C4

Appin is reached from either the Princes or Hume Hwys. The 5th village in the colony, it was named by Governor Macquarie in 1811. Historic **Northampton Dale** is an early Georgian sandstone house, external viewing by appt only. **St Mark the Evangelist Anglican Church** (1843), Church St, and **St Bedes Catholic Church**, King St, both have historic headstones.

Cataract Dam at Baden Powell Dr has picnic areas with electric BBQs, shelters and playgrounds Open daily 10am–5pm. Ph: (02) 4631 1202

Bargo Map 20 B4

The small town of Bargo lies SW of Picton and has two sanctuaries nearby. The **Dingo Sanctuary**, 590 Arina Rd, Bargo (Map 22) offers an opportunity to meet and learn about Australia's native dog. Gas BBQs and picnic tables are available in a natural bush setting. Open Sat–Mon and Thur 10am–3.30pm, Tues, Wed and Fri by appointment. Ph: (02) 4684 1156 www.dingosanctuary.com.au

Wirrimbirra Sanctuary is a National Trust property containing a wildlife refuge, wildflower gardens, bushwalking tracks, a native plant nursery and cafe, picnic and accommodation facilities. Open daily, 8am–5pm. Ph: (02) 4684 1112

Mermaids Pool is a beautiful set of pools on the Bargo River, excellent for swimming. A spectacular walk (see Map 21) takes in the sandstone canyon and the pools. Allow about 1.5hr for the 3.8km return trip.

The **Avon Dam** (completed 1927) on Avon Dam Rd is the largest of the four Nepean dams (see also p.127). The **Nepean Dam**, also on Avon Dam Rd, was completed in 1935. Both offer spectacular scenery and are open daily with picnic and BBQ facilities.

Camden Map 20 B3

Camden has blossomed since the freeway removed all but local traffic from its streets. Parkland fronts the Nepean River on the northern side with three reserves, **Chellaston**, **Belgenny** and **Macarthur**, linked by a cycleway. These are just some of the excellent picnic areas.

The town was founded by John Macarthur in 1830; the *Walking Tour of Camden Township* pamphlet documents 34 historic features. This tour can be done on foot or by car. *A Scenic Drive through Camden Countryside* pamphlet takes in 20 different stops around Camden and Cobbitty. Both are available from the Visitor Info Centre housed in **John Oxley's Cottage**, built in the 1890s as a workman's cottage. Ph: (02) 4658 1370. This is the starting point for the scenic drive. www.camden.nsw.gov.au

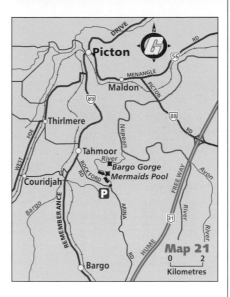

Map 21
0   2
Kilometres

This tour takes in State Heritage registered, **Kirkham's Stables**, erected in 1816 on part of John Oxley's original land grant, and nearby is **Oxley's Anchor**, an inscribed anchor believed to be from one of his ships. Ph: 0428 213 578

The **Stables Wivenhoe** (1834) has been renovated into art and craft workshops. Local art, craft and pottery is for sale as well as herbs and cottage garden plants. There are BBQ and picnic areas. Open Fri–Wed, 9am–4pm. Heritage listed **Wivenhoe House** (1837) is open 1st Sun of the month 10am–3pm,

BELGENNY FARM

TOP PUB

The **Camden Valley Inn** on the Old Hume Hwy at South Camden is a local landmark. Built in the 1930s, the gracious old English-style pub and restaurant are set in prize-winning gardens.

CAMDEN PARK HOUSE

and groups at other times by appt, Ph: (02) 4655 6061

The **Camden Historical Museum,** John St, is open Thur–Sun 11pm–4pm weekends and public holidays. Historic aircraft and a number of engines, cockpits and military vehicles are on display at **Camden Museum of Aviation**, 11 Stewart Ave, Harrington Park (Narellan), has a collection of military aircraft, aero engines and tanks. Open Sun and public holidays, 10.30am–4.30pm, other times by arrangement. Ph: (02) 4648 2419 or 9529 4169

Belgenny Farm on the **Camden Park Estate**, off Elizabeth Macarthur Dr, is Australia's most important group of colonial farm buildings, with the earliest cottage dating from around 1820. The farm itself dates from 1805 and is the home of Australia's wool industry and the pioneering agricultural activities of Elizabeth and John Macarthur. The buildings are remarkably intact. Open for group bookings Mon–Fri 9am–4.30pm (excluding public holidays); there are five special event open days in Jan, May, Jun and Sep, Ph: (02) 4655 9651, www.belgennyfarm.com.au. Also on the estate, **Camden Park House**, the Macarthurs' home, is open for inspection on the last weekend in Sept. Contact Camden Visitor Info Centre.

Camden's weekly stock market **Saleyards** was started in 1870 on the site behind the Plough and Harrow Hotel (now known as the Argyle Inn). Today Camden is the biggest stock selling centre within 100km of

Historic grapes

Few people realise that the Camden area has a long history of association with the wine-making industry. Elizabeth and John Macarthur introduced grape growing to the area in 1817 with experimental plantings at Camden Park. In 1824, the first vintage wine was made and in 1829 the Macarthurs exported 2200L of wine to England. In the 1830s, 34 000 vines were sent to the Barossa Valley to start South Australia's wine industry. The estate also propagated vines for the Hunter Valley and many other parts of Australia.

By 1853, 33 grapevine varieties were available for sale at Camden Park and in 1861, the estate won a gold medal for a range of its wines at the Paris Exhibition. German settlers brought their expertise to the industry and many of them set up their own vineyards. Descendants of these settlers still live in the district.

Sydney, with sales held every Tues and Wed in Edward St.

Camden Aerodrome is home to a number of companies who offer visitors opportunities (some more challenging than others) to get airborne (see p.129).

Campbelltown Map 20 C3

Campbelltown was founded in 1820 and retains many colonial buildings. The visitors centre has two pamphlets with walks in Queen St and its historic buildings.

The **Campbelltown City Art Gallery** at the corner or Camden and Appin Rds, has an excellent collection and hosts major travelling exhibitions. The coffee lounge and terrace overlook a Japanese garden and teahouse. Open Tues–Sat 10am–4pm, Sun, Mon by appt, Ph: (02) 4645 4416

The **Campbelltown Arts and Crafts Society**, Queen St, has local arts and crafts for sale. Open Mon–Fri, 10am–2pm, weekends, 10am–4pm, Ph: (02) 4628 3944. Close to the historic Georgian house **Glenalvon** (open 1st Sat month 9am–1pm) on Lithgow St is the **Richmond Villa Heritage Centre**, which houses the local history museum. Open Sun 1.30–3.30pm and 1st Sat of the month 9am–noon. Ph: (02) 4625 1822

Cobbitty Map 22

North of Camden is the picturesque village of Cobbitty. The first mention of

the name 'Cobbedee' was in Governor Macquarie's diary in 1815. **St Paul's** stone church (1840) and nearby **Heber Chapel** are surrounded by the gravestones of pioneers. There is an antique shop, fine art gallery and folk art studio. Cobbitty's well-known craft market in Cobbitty Public School, Cobbitty Rd is held on the 1st Sat of each month.

Mulgoa Map 20 B2

The picturesque settlement of Mulgoa has an attractive park on Mulgoa Rd with picnic tables, a shelter and wood BBQs . Points of interest include historic homes, **St Thomas' Church** (1838) with its pioneer cemetery and Mt Schoenstatt Shrine, an ivy-clad miniature German Chapel also used as a retreat centre, visitors welcome. **The Rock Lookout**, 8km away and **Rileys Mt Lookout** (a 20min walk from The Rock Lookout), offer glorious views of the Blue Mountains NP and the Nepean Gorge.

The Oaks Map 20 B3

In Edward St, The Oaks, a few km SW of Camden, the **Wollondilly Heritage Centre** is a complex of buildings in landscaped gardens, including a timber and iron furnished cottage. Changing, interactive exhibitions tell the stories of the working lives of the people of Wollondilly and Burragorang Valley and indigenous history. Facilities include local and family history archives, a

TOP SPOTS
While in the Campbelltown area, have a picnic in the bush setting at **Pembroke Park**, Pembroke Rd, Minto or swim at **Simmo's Beach Reserve**, Macquarie Fields.

HISTORIC BUILDINGS CAMPBELLTOWN

COBBITTY CRAFT MARKET

GHOSTLY TRAIL

For a fun Fri or Sat night with a difference, the **Ghost Hunt of Picton** revisits the haunted hideaways of Picton's ghosts. There is a choice of dinner or supper ghost hunts. Children can also have fun on the Kids Ghost Hunt or a Scary Birthday Party. Ph: (02) 4677 2044 www.lizvincenttours. com.au

GEORGE IV HOTEL, PICTON

DAM STATISTICS

Warragamba Dam (Lake Burragorang) holds 2 057 000ML of water and its foreshores measure 354km. The dam wall is 351m long and 142m high and was made using three million tonnes of concrete.

community room with a/v facilities, sheltered gas BBQ, disabled access, large coach/car park and museum shop. Open weekends and public holidays 10am–4pm. Closed 25 Dec to 26 Jan, and Good Friday. Ph: (02) 4657 1796

Picton Map 20 B4

Known as Stonequarry until 1841 when it was renamed Picton, the earliest land grants were made here in 1822. This is a pretty town with art, craft, gift and antique shops and there are many historic buildings—a walking tour brochure is available from the Visitor Info Centre Wollondilly, which can also arrange both historic tours and ghost tours of Picton. Buildings of interest include **Jarvisfield**, an impressive house built in 1864, and the **Imperial Hotel** (1860), built when the railway first came to Picton. Railway buffs will be interested in the **Stonequarry Viaduct**, the first viaduct to be built in NSW outside Sydney, the **station** (1863), the **stationmaster's residence** (1877) and **Redbank Range Tunnel**, NSW's 1st railway tunnel. Ph: (02) 4677 2044

Perhaps Picton's most famous build-ing, the **George IV Hotel** (1839), serves boutique beers brewed on the premises.

The Shed Bar and Grill in Remembrance Dr offers feasting, dancing and singing in the original 1880s woolshed. Ph: (02) 4677 1379

Wallacia Map 20 B2

Wallacia has picnic grounds along the Nepean River with swimming holes and canoes for hire. The beautifully restored **Wallacia Hotel** offers accommodation, spacious dining areas and a beer garden overlooking the golf course. Ph: (02) 4773 8888

Warragamba and Warragamba Dam Map 20 B3

Warragamba village is the gateway to Warragamba Dam, Sydney's major source of domestic water. The village has quaint shops, houses and narrow streets. The dam stands high above a rugged gorge on the Nepean River to form Lake Burragorang, four times the size of Sydney Harbour and an impressive sight from above or from the viewing area.

Facilities include picnic and BBQ areas, children's playgrounds and extensive walking trails suitable for disabled people. Picnic grounds open daily, 10am–4pm. Kiosk open Mon–Fri, 10am–2pm, weekends, 10am–4pm. An info centre with a scale model of the dam is open 10am–4pm. Guided tours depart the dam Mon–Fri, 11am, 2pm and 3pm, weekends between 10.30am and 4pm. Ph: (02) 4720 0349

National Parks and State Recreation Areas

Bents Basin SCA Map 22

Bents Basin State Conservation Area can be accessed from Wolstenholme Ave off Greendale Rd (from Wallacia or Bringelly) or along Bents Basin Rd (from Wallacia).

Visitors can enjoy the scenic **Gulguer Gorge**, rapids and sheer cliffs. Sandy beaches surround Bents Basin, a deep waterhole where the Nepean River exits the gorge. Activities include swimming, canoeing, picnic areas, BBQs and camping (bookings essential) are available, as are toilet facilities with hot and cold showers. Bents Basin is adjacent to the 350ha **Gulguer Nature Reserve** where bushwalkers and campers can enjoy native flora and fauna in a relaxed setting.

THIRLMERE LAKES

The area has tremendous significance for the Aboriginal community, who, it is believed, have enjoyed it for the past 5000–6000 years. Bents Basin open daily, 9am–4.30pm with extended hours on daylight saving weekends.
Ph: (02) 4774 8662

Chipping Norton Lakes and Mirambeena Regional Park Map 20 C3

The restored foreshores of **Chipping Norton Lakes** offer a boat ramp, sailing, walking, bicycle tracks, and picnic and BBQ areas. Access from Epsom or Alfred Rds, Chipping Norton.

Mirambeena RP consists of five parks with a variety of facilities, including boating, playgrounds, BBQs, exercise tracks, cross-country track and the Lansdowne Rd Cycling Circuit.

Nattai NP Map 20 A1

Relatively isolated, Nattai NP forms an important part of the **Warragamba Dam** catchment. East of **Lake Burragorang** between Warragamba Dam and Wombeyan Caves Rd, it offers beautiful scenery and bushwalking. Backpack camping is allowed beyond the 3km exclusion zone around Lake Burragorang. Ph: (02) 4677 0859

Thirlmere Lakes NP Map 22

Just south of the small township of Thirlmere is Thirlmere Lakes NP part of the Greater Blue Mountains World Heritage Area. It protects five unspoiled freshwater lakes set in pleasant wooded country, inhabited by birds and other native wildlife. Swimming and canoeing are popular, as are picnics and

MT ANNAN BOTANIC GARDEN

RARE AND UNUSUAL

The collection at **Mt Annan** contains many rare and endangered plants, some being cultivated for the 1st time. Some 135 rare and endangered species have been recorded as naturally occurring at Mt Annan.

AUSTRALIAN AVIATION
MUSEUM, BANKSTOWN

bushwalking. No camping or powerboats. Ph: (02) 4677 0859

Western Sydney Regional Park Map 22

At **Horsley Park**, this park offers BBQs, picnic areas, an extensive walking track system, cycling paths, horseriding trails and Pimelia Playspace, which is a great play area for children of all ages. The **Olympic Equestrian Centre** is located within the park, which also has several vantage points with panoramic views of the Royal NP in the south, the city skyline to the north and the Blue Mountains to the west. Ph: (02) 9895 7440

Parks and gardens

Mt Annan Botanic Garden Map 22

The largest botanic garden in Australia, Mt Annan is the native plant garden of the Royal Botanic Gardens in Sydney, and its plantings will eventually include most of the country's known 25 000 plant species. Plantings are mainly arranged in theme gardens and there are ironbark and local woodland conservation areas.

The Gardens Shop and Nursery sells a variety of Australian plants, books, gifts and more. The visitor centre is also in the shop. There are walking tracks, picnic facilities, a cycling track, maze, gas BBQs and the award-winning Gardens Restaurant, bookings essential (02 4647 1363). The Gardens are open daily, 10am–4pm, Apr–Sept, 10am–6pm, Oct–Mar. Ph: (02) 4648 2477. The gardens are accessible by public transport: buses between Campbelltown Stn and Camden run right past the entrance. Ph: (02) 4655 7501 for a timetable. The M5 East motorway has greatly improved access from Sydney. www.rbgsyd.gov.au/mount_annan_garden

Other attractions

Army Engineers' Museum and Heritage Park Map 20 C3

In Moorebank Ave, **Moorebank**, the Army Engineers' Museum and Heritage Park traces the history of the Australian Army Engineers with displays of historical documents, weapons, uniforms and a library. The Army Engineers' Memorial Chapel was built in the 1960s from salvaged convict-cut sandstone. Open Sun–Wed 10am–4pm and some public holidays, Ph: (02) 9600 4443, www.aamme.com.au

Australian Koi Farm Map 20 C3

This unusual attraction on Jersey Rd, **Bringelly** (near Hwy 69) allows visitors to observe thousands of Japanese koi fish in various stages of growth, both on show and in breeding ponds. Open daily, 9am–5pm. Ph: (02) 4774 8180, www.auskoi.com.au

BURRAGORANG LOOKOUT VIEWS

GLEDSWOOD

Avon Dam Map 22

Avon Dam, completed in 1927, is the 3rd and largest dam in Sydney's water supply system. Along with its nearby sister dam, Nepean, it has BBQ and picnic facilities which are open daily 10am–4.30pm. Nearby is the Dingo Sanctuary and the township of Bargo (p.121). The picturesque drive to Avon Dam is one of its most attractive features.

Australian Aviation Museum
Map 20 D3

Located in Starkie Dr, **Bankstown Airport**, the museum is housed in the relocated hangar of Australia's pioneering aviator Sir Charles Kingsford Smith. It has historic planes, static displays and flying exhibits from around the world. Open Sat–Sun and Wed 10am–4pm. Ph: (02) 9791 3088, www.aamb.com.au

Burragorang Lookout Map 22

The Burragorang Lookout at Burragorang Rd, Nattai, offers sweeping views of the Nattai Wilderness and the Burragorang Valley, which is now Lake Burragorang, flooded after Warragamba Dam was built. There are picnic sites, BBQs and bush trails. Open 10am–5pm, Mon–Fri and 10am–7pm weekends.

Cordeaux Dam Map 22

The Cordeaux Dam at Picton Rd, **Wilton**, has picnic and BBQ facilities and is open

daily 10am–5.30pm. A 1.5km walking track gives a panoramic view of the dam and surrounds, Ph: (02) 4640 1200

Gledswood Map 22

On Camden Valley Way, **Catherine Field**, Gledswood is a unique collection of Georgian colonial buildings dating from the early 1800s. A whole day can easily be spent here. There are tours of the historic homestead (1827), as well as sheep shearing, sheepdog mustering demonstrations, wine tastings in the old sandstone winery, tours of the award-winning gardens, and a restaurant. BBQ and picnic facilities are provided. Open Wed–Sun, 10.30am–4pm, Tues group bookings only. Ph: (02) 9606 5111. Accessible by the Busways Service from Campbelltown Stn.

Maldon Suspension Bridge
Map 20 B4

The Maldon Suspension Bridge is reached by turning right off the Picton–Wollongong Rd, 5km south of **Picton**. Its main cables are anchored at road level, continuing upwards from the bridge towers and are bolted into the cliff face high above the bridge. This construction makes it unique.

Mamre Homestead

This delightful 1820s Georgian homestead off Mamre Rd, **St Marys**, was originally Reverend Samuel Marsden's

STRUGGLETOWN FINE
ARTS COMPLEX

home. Now restored, Mamre offers tearooms and conference facilities. Open Wed–Fri, 10.30am–2.30pm, Sun, 9am–4.30pm. Ph: (02) 9670 6178

Struggletown Fine Arts Complex
Map 20 C3

This complex in Sharman Cl, **Narellan**, has a number of galleries and a restaurant. Open Wed–Sun, 10am–5pm. Ph: (02) 4648 2424

Thirlmere Railway Museum
Map 22

At Thirlmere Railway Museum, Barbour Rd, Thirlmere, exhibits represent the development of NSW railways from the late 1800s to the present day. A covered exhibition area has mock railway platforms enabling visitors to see inside railway engine cabs and carriages.

Return Steam train rides from Thirlmere to Picton are available three times a day on the 1st and 3rd Sun of the month except during summer fire restrictions. The Thirlmere Flyer departs on a return trip from Central Stn to Thirlmere via Campbelltown, bookings essential. Open Mon–Fri 10am–3pm, weekends 9am–5pm. Ph: (02) 9379 1110. Museum Ph: (02) 4681 8001. See p.118 for the Festival of Steam.

Wineries

Vicary's Winery, Sydney's oldest continuously operating winery, is on the Northern Rd at Luddenham, south of Penrith. Attractions include a monthly craft market (2nd Sat of each month, 9am–3pm), a Woolshed Dance with free wine tasting (Fri and Sat nights) and a kid's corner featuring Thomas the Tank Engine, with free picnic and BBQ facilities (Sat, Sun and public and school holidays, 10am–5pm). Vicary's also offers group lunches, wine tasting and sales, Ph: (02) 4773 4161

Kirkham Estate, Argyle St, Camden is open Mon–Sat 9am–5pm, Sun 10am–4pm Ph: (02) 4655 7722

Tastings are available Sun, 11am–3pm at **Camden Estate Wines**, cnr Springs and Macarthur Rds, Elderslie. There are BBQs and picnic areas. Ph: 0411 855 180

TO MARKET

Buxton Markets, held on the 3rd Sun of each month, sell a great range of crafts. They are accessible to people taking the steam train ride from Thirlmere.

Wine has been made for five generations at the **Cognos Bros Winery**, Cobbitty Rd, Cobbitty. The cellar door is open daily for tastings. Picnic and BBQ facilities are provided. Ph: (02) 4651 2281

Belgenny Farm, Elizabeth Macarthur Drive, Camden is open by appt, Ph: (02) 4655 9651

Recreational activities
Canoeing

Some locations for access to flat water paddling include **Douglas Park Causeway**, **Menangle Bridge**, **Cobbitty Bridge**, **Nepean River** at Mulgoa, **Bents Basin** and **Thirlmere Lakes**.

Cycling

Sydney's SW offers a variety of cycleways. The longest and possibly most scenic is from Camden to Warragamba Dam via The Oaks. Mirambeena RP at Chipping Norton contains the **Lansdowne Cycling Circuit**, while there is also a cycleway along the southern shore of the Georges River through Chipping Norton and on through Liverpool to Lurnea. A shorter ride exists along the reserves of Orphan School and Clear Paddock Creeks at Wakeley. Info and maps are available from the RTA. Freecall: 1800 060 607

BALLOONING WITH BALLOON ALOFT

MACARTHUR AIR EXPERIENCES

TOP SPOT

Little River is a beautiful swimming hole near Buxton, accessible by walking 1km from the carpark at the quarry at the end of Boundary Park Rd. Cross the river and follow the old farm road to the right.

Horse racing

Canterbury Park Racecourse is one of Sydney's major racecourses, located 30min SW of the city. Accessible by road or rail with ample free parking, it has race meetings most Wed, to check Ph: (02) 9930 4000. **Warwick Farm** racecourse is located on the Hume Hwy at Warwick Farm. Ph: (02) 9602 6199

Horseriding

Horseriding is available at **Mowbray Park**, Bakers Lodge Rd, Mowbray Park, NW of Picton, bookings essential, Ph: (02) 4680 9243. **Scenic Hills Riding Ranch**, Campbelltown Rd, Ingleburn, is located on part of an original land grant made in 1810 and its remaining historic buildings date from the 1820s. The property offers overnight camp-outs and a variety of riding adventures among bushland hills. Ph: (02) 9605 7410, www.scenichills.com.au For other venues contact local tourist offices.

In the air

Macarthur Air Experiences, at Camden Aerodrome, Macquarie Grove Rd, Camden, is the base for a variety of scenic flights over a number of locations in Sydney including **Warragamba Dam**, **Lake Burragorang** and **Yerranderie**, a thoughtfully restored silver mining ghost town in the Blue Mountains. Also available are gliding, skydiving, aerobatics, trial instructional flights and rides in the open cockpit of a vintage biplane. Ph: (02) 4655 8844

Also at Camden Aerodrome is **Global Ballooning** Ph: 1800 627 661, **Cloud 9 Balloon Flight** Ph: 1300 555 711 and **Balloon Aloft**, who operate a sunrise hot air balloon flight over Camden followed by a champagne celebration, weather permitting. Ph: (02) 4653 1562, Freecall: 1800 028 568, www.balloonaloft.com. The **Sydney Ultralight Flying Club** operates from The Oaks Airport, The Oaks. Ph: 0425 251 939

Fun for the young

★ Australian Aviation Museum (p.127)
★ Cycleways — information available from councils or the RTA (p.128)
★ Fairfield City Farm (p.120)
★ Gledswood (p.127)
★ Skateboard ramp — Fairfield City Leisure Centre, Vine St, Fairfield. Ph: (02) 9754 2078
★ Thirlmere Railway Museum (p.128)

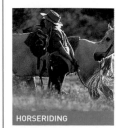
HORSERIDING

**Places of interest
(Warragamba
and beyond)**
❶ Mulgoa (p.123)
❷ Wallacia (p.124)
❸ Bents Basin SCA
   (p.124)
❹ Warragamba Dam
   (p.124)
❺ Burragorang
   Lookout (p.127)
❻ Camden (p.121)
❼ Cobbitty (p.123)

**Places of interest
(Family fun tour)**
❶ Fairfield City
   Museum and
   Gallery (Fairfield
   Regional Heritage
   Centre) (p.120)
❷ Fairfield City
   Farm, Abbotsbury
   (p.120)
❸ Gledswood (p.127)
❹ Picton (p.124)
❺ Thirlmere Railway
   Museum (p.128)
❻ Wirrimbirra
   Sanctuary (p.121)
❼ Dingo Sanctuary
   (p.121)
❽ Avon Dam (p.127)

BELGENNY FARM, CAMDEN

Suggested tours – Map 22

Warragamba and beyond tour

Approximate distance

270km return from Sydney CBD
(CBD to Penrith is 60km)

About this tour

This tour begins at the picturesque
village of Mulgoa. Travel on to Wallacia,
where the Nepean River offers great
canoeing opportunities, before exploring
Sydney's major water storage,
Warragamba Dam. Bents Basin SCA,
is a perfect place for a bushwalk or
summer swim. Take in the sweeping
views of the Nattai Wilderness from
Burragorang Lookout before meandering
back to the city via the historic villages
of Camden and Cobbitty.

Family fun tour

Approximate distance

240km return from Sydney CBD
(CBD to Parramatta is 35km)

About this tour

This tour focuses on family-based
activities in and around SW Sydney.
Visit a working city farm; enjoy historic,
charming Gledswood; ride a steam train
at Thirlmere. Drop in at the dingo and
wildlife sanctuaries before taking
advantage of the picnic facilities,
views and walks at scenic Avon Dam.

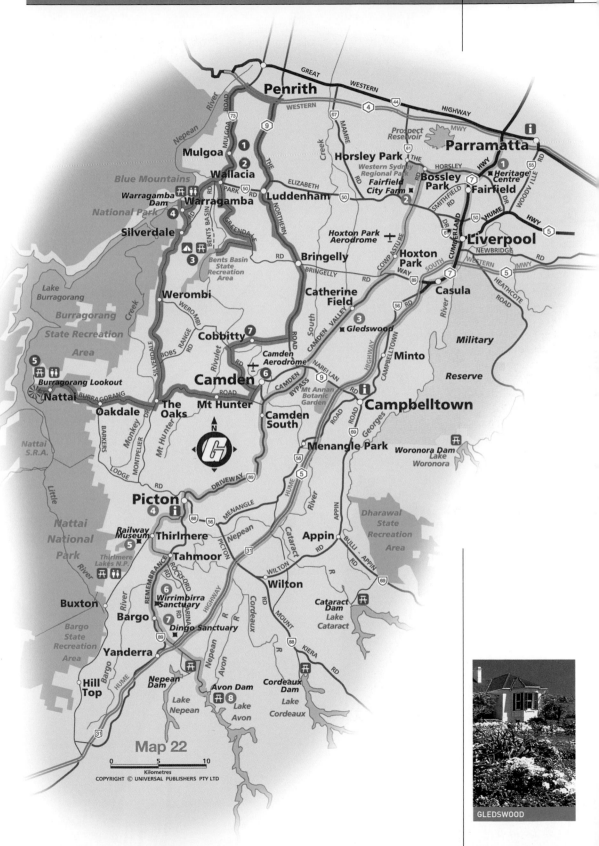

Penrith

Mulgoa

Wallacia

Warragamba Dam
National Park

Warragamba

Silverdale

Blue Mountains

Bents Basin
State
Recreation
Area

Werombi

Cobbitty

Camden
Aerodrome

Camden

The
Oaks

Mt Hunter

Camden
South

Oakdale

Lake
Burragorang

Burragorang
State Recreation
Area

Burragorang Lookout

Nattai

Nattai
S.R.A.

Little

Nattai
National
Park

River

Picton

Railway
Museum

Thirlmere

Tahmoor

Thirlmere
Lakes N.P.

Buxton

Bargo

Wirrimbirra
Sanctuary

Dingo Sanctuary

Yanderra

Bargo
State
Recreation
Area

Hill
Top

Nepean
Dam

Lake
Nepean

Avon Dam

Lake
Avon

Cordeaux
Dam
Lake
Cordeaux

Wilton

Appin

Dharawal
State
Recreation
Area

Cataract
Dam
Lake
Cataract

Menangle Park

Woronora Dam
Lake
Woronora

Campbelltown

Minto

Military

Reserve

Georges River

Casula

Liverpool

NEWBRIDGE

Hoxton
Park

Catherine
Field

Gledswood

Bringelly

Hoxton Park
Aerodrome

Luddenham

Horsley Park

Western Sydney
Regional Park

Fairfield
City Farm

Bossley
Park

Fairfield

Heritage
Centre

Parramatta

Prospect
Reservoir

GREAT WESTERN HIGHWAY

WESTERN

Nepean River

Map 22

0   5   10
Kilometres
COPYRIGHT © UNIVERSAL PUBLISHERS PTY LTD

GLEDSWOOD

Must see, must do
★ Australian Rainforest Sanctuary (p.144)
★ Australian Reptile Park (p.144)
★ Cruising on Brisbane Water (p.146)
★ The Entrance (p.137)

Radio stations
SeaFM: FM 101.3
2GO: FM 107.7
Radio Five-O-Plus: FM 95.3 (weekends only)

Tourist information

Central Coast Tourism
Rotary Park, Terrigal Drive,
Terrigal 2260;
200 Mann St, Gosford 2250;
Marine Parade,
The Entrance 2261;
18–22 The Boulevard,
Woy Woy 2256
Ph: (02) 4385 4430
www.visitcentralcoast.com.au

National Parks and Wildlife Service
Central Coast District
207 Albany Ave
Gosford 2250
Ph: (02) 4320 4280
www.nationalparks.nsw.gov.au

LEFT: PELICANS

the central coast

WHILE SCARCELY AN HOUR NORTH of Sydney, the NSW Central Coast is a total contrast to the bustle of the State capital. The area is richly endowed with sandy beaches, quiet waterways and lush forest and has long been a playground for Sydneysiders. The sleepy, relaxed hamlets and coastal villages were traditionally characterised by modest retirement cottages and weekenders, but the atmosphere and style of housing is gradually changing.

Reminders of thousands of years of Aboriginal habitation of the area can be explored in the national parks, while the early history of European settlement in the region has been secured through the conservation of historic buildings.

There is no shortage of excellent restaurants, many in superb waterfront locations. A visit to the Central Coast can be as busy or relaxed as one chooses, and may include a horseback ride through unspoilt forests, cruising the Brisbane Water, fossicking through an antique dealer's store or the simple pleasures of fishing from a jetty or surfing.

The area is also a paradise for children of all ages, who revel in its natural attractions as well as others like the Australian Reptile Park.

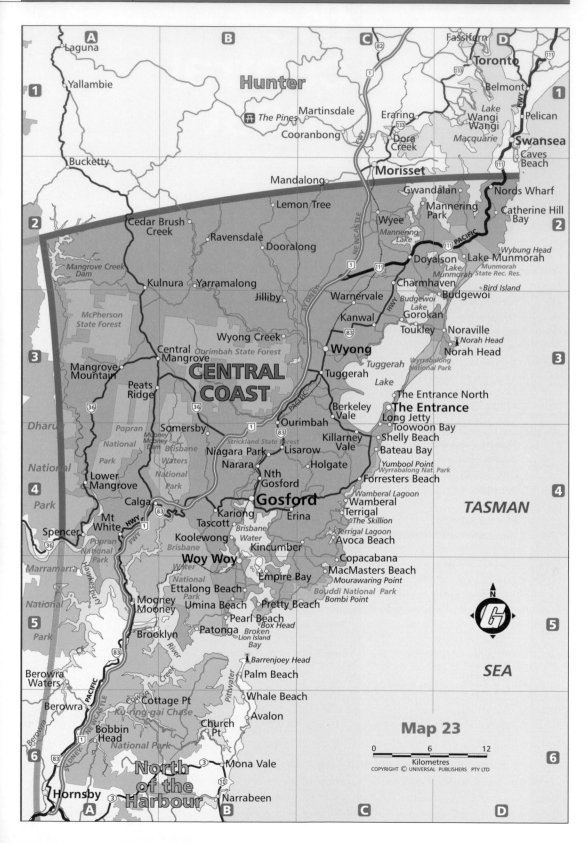

Map 23

Kilometres

COPYRIGHT © UNIVERSAL PUBLISHERS PTY LTD

Natural features

From the south, the gateway to this region is the bridge over the Hawkesbury River at Brooklyn. This river forms the divide between the Central Coast and the area north of the harbour. To the north of the Central Coast, Lake Macquarie provides a natural barrier between the Central Coast and the southern suburbs of Newcastle. An inland boundary is provided by rugged hills and dissected plateaus which eventually become the Great Dividing Range to the west.

The Central Coast can be divided into three narrow strips, running parallel to the Tasman Sea. The 1st strip is the coast itself, at the northern end little more than sandy spits between the ocean and the lakes, with wonderful beaches separated by rocky headlands. To the south, the coast becomes more rugged and by the time it gets to Broken Bay, there are high sandstone cliffs. Gosford sandstone is of such quality that it is to be found in buildings and walls all over Sydney.

Behind the coast, the 2nd strip is made up of many lakes and inlets with mainly flat land between them. Lake Macquarie in the north is the largest; there are numerous small lakes between it and Tuggerah Lake, which dominates the middle part of the Central Coast. Brisbane Water to the south is an arm of Broken Bay and its rugged shores can be explored by boat from Gosford.

Further inland, much of the hilly 3rd strip is either national park or state forest, making it a quiet bush retreat from the busy lakes and beaches. Locals claim that on hot summer days temperatures in the hills can be 10°C

TERRIGAL BEACH (BACKGROUND)

lower than on the coast. Vegetation varies from dry scrub on the ridges to a few stands of almost undisturbed rainforest.

Native animals such as kangaroos, bandicoots and wallabies are plentiful and there are occasional koala colonies. The extensive birdlife includes lyrebirds, bell-miners (the bellbirds of Henry Kendall's poem) and scrub turkeys. In the spring, wildflowers are a major attraction.

History

The Central Coast once provided a rich environment for its Aboriginal in-habitants, the Awabakal and Darkinjang people. They had an extensive knowledge of edible plants in the surrounding area and fish were plentiful in the lakes and the ocean.

For the European settlers in the 1820s, the attractions of the Brisbane Water area were its proximity to Sydney and its wealth of timber resources. The shores

What's in a name?

The Aboriginal communities who lived along the Central Coast have contributed many of the colourful names of the towns and villages in the area. Here are the meanings of a few of them: Budgewoi — young grass; Dooralong — timber for making spears; Ettalong — place for drinking; Narara — black snake; Patonga — oysters; Toukley — most brambles; Woy Woy — big lagoon; Kariong — a meeting place; Tumbi Umbi — plenty of water there; Umina — repose; Terrigal — place of little birds.

CENTRAL COAST SURFER

PELICAN FEEDING AT
THE ENTRANCE

of the waterways were occupied by small groups of settlers (including many ex-convicts) while the timbered country on Erina and Narara creeks was dominated by the gentry. Farming land was progressively taken up along the fertile creek valleys, but the growth of the area was restricted by transport problems until the railway arrived in 1887. Tiny settlements then grew into towns.

Citrus orchards began to dominate farming in the area and are still significant to the region's economy. More recently, this part of the coast has virtually become part of Sydney's metropolitan area, bringing with it a marked increase in service industries.

Getting there

By road

It is easy to reach the Central Coast by car. The F3 Sydney–Newcastle Fwy from Wahroonga, in Sydney's northern suburbs, has exits to all parts of the Central Coast. For a more leisurely trip, take the old Pacific Hwy (Hwy 83). Instead of turning on to the F3 at Wahroonga, continue along the Pacific Hwy through Hornsby, Mt Colah and Berowra. The Hwy from here is a scenic route which connects many of the small communities of the Central Coast. It parallels the freeway to Somersby, where it diverts to

Gosford and then runs north, on a slightly more easterly route, to Newcastle.

Bennett's Airport Shuttle operates daily services between the Central Coast and Sydney Airport terminals. They also provide transport services for winery tours. Bookings essential.
Ph: 1300 130 557. www.ben-air.com.au

By rail

The public transport system is excellent and many people living on the Central Coast commute to Sydney daily. Trains run from Central Stn to Hornsby (via the north shore or northern lines) and Gosford and beyond. Local bus services connect with the railway stns. State Rail Infoline 131 500

By ferry

A ferry service operates from **Palm Beach to Patonga** daily, Ph: (02) 9974 2159

Central Coast Fast Ferries operates a service from Woy Woy to Empire Bay via Saratoga and Davistown. Ph: (02) 4363 1311 or 0418 631 313 www.centralcoastferries.com.au

Palm Beach Ferry Services run from Palm Beach to Ettalong via Wagstaff. Ph: (02) 9918 2747 or 0414 555 522 www.palmbeachferry.com.au

Getting around

The MV *Lady Kendall II* cruises the Brisbane Waters on Sat–Wed and daily during school holidays. Take the morning cruise, stop off for lunch at a waterfront restaurant at Woy Woy and return on the afternoon cruise. Cruises depart from Gosford and Woy Woy. Contact **Starship Cruises**, Ph: (02) 4323 2974 www.starshipcruises.com.au

On a Central Coast Explorer Tour, horseriding, abseiling and bushwalking are among the variety of activities offered by **Sydney Day Tours** for visitors to the Central Coast.Tours available Sun–Mon, Wed and Fri. Bookings essential Ph: (02) 9251 6101. www.sdtours.com

Blunsdon Day Tours and Charters run regular day tours throughout the year, including the Beach & Bush Tour and Dolphin Watch Tour. Tours also cover the Blue Mountains, Hunter Valley,

ABORIGINAL ENGRAVING, BRISBANE WATER NP

Southern Highlands and Canberra Floriade. Ph: (02) 4328 1317

Festivals and events

Gosford Country Show

This traditional country show is held at the **Gosford Showground** in early May and features livestock and handicrafts from the region, and a wood chopping competition. Ph: (02) 4323 6895

Terrigal Beach Food and Wine Festival

The festival in Jul brings together many of the area's leading restaurateurs to present their signature dishes. There are also tastings of the wines of the region. Ph: (02) 4385 4430

Australian Springtime Flora Festival

The diversity of the Central Coast flora is celebrated each Sept with the Australian Springtime Flora Festival at **Mt Penang**, Kariong. Ph: (02) 4385 4074 or tollfree: 1800 806 258

Gosford Arts Bazaar

Pick up interesting Christmas presents or just browse at Gosford Arts Bazaar, held in Nov at the Gosford City Arts Centre at **East Gosford**. Ph: (02) 4325 0056

Firefly Magic Festival

Take a twilight stroll in the **Australian Rainforest Sanctuary** at Ourimbah and see the enchanting display of fireflies in the forest. Firefly Magic (p.144) is offered Wed–Sun 6–9.30pm in Nov only. A **Sound and Light Show** is included in the evening. This superb show is set in a lovely natural amphitheatre and is viewed from undercover.Ph: (02) 4362 1855 www.australianrainforest.com

Tuggerah Lakes Festival

This family oriented community celebration takes place in Dec. Ph: (02) 4333 5377

Main localities and towns

The area is fairly densely settled with many small holiday towns and villages spread along the coastal strip near the beaches and larger centres further inland following the railway line.

The Central Coast offers plenty of accommodation ranging from modest caravan or camping sites to 5-star deluxe living of a style equal to anywhere in Australia. A call to any of the local estate agents will uncover various homes available for weekend or holiday rental at reasonable cost.

Avoca Map 23 C4

This relaxed beach village is a favourite weekend and holiday getaway spot for Sydneysiders and locals. The beach, with a sheltered rockpool area at the southern end, is popular with families. Several cafes and restaurants offer a range of dining options. The old-fashioned **Avoca Beach Theatre**, opened in 1952, has retained its original atmosphere, and shows an assortment of films.

The Entrance Map 23 C3

The Entrance is located at the point where the ocean meets the Tuggerah

BATEAU BAY

Lakes (encompassing Tuggerah, Budgewoi and Munmorah). A $15 million redevelopment of public areas at The Entrance has revitalised the town, with **Vera's Watergarden**, a children's playground, and **Pelican Plaza** a magnet for families. The town centre has been extensively planted and a number of giant palm trees guard the entry and crossing points along Main St.

Stretching along the foreshores of The Entrance Channel up to the town's surf club, **The Boardwalk** starts from **Memorial Park**, where entertainment is provided on weekends and during school holidays. The deep shade cast by spreading trees makes this an ideal picnicking spot at any time of the year.

The pelican is the main tourist symbol of the Central Coast, and **pelican feeding** occurs at 3.30pm each day at Pelican Plaza in Memorial Park. An informative commentary accompanies the hand-feeding of these interesting creatures.

North of the town lies the natural bushland of **Red Gum Forest Nature Reserve** which covers most of the low spit of land leading up to Toukley. There are several marked walking trails in the reserve.

At Dunleith Caravan Park, North Entrance, the **Shell Museum** displays an extensive collection of shells as

BOOGIE BOARDING AT AVOCA BEACH

well as interesting old photographs of the area.

Visit The Entrance's **Lions Markets**, which are held at the carpark behind the picture theatre every Sun 8am–noon. Ph: (02) 4332 2172 www.theentrance.org

Gosford Map 23 B4

A scenic town on Brisbane Water, Gosford is the Central Coast's main centre. Many of its residents commute to Sydney, a fast train ride away.

Local attractions include **Henry Kendall's Cottage and Historical Museum**, Henry Kendall St, West Gosford, once the home of the poet and

VERA'S WATERGARDEN, THE ENTRANCE

FISHING IN TRANQUIL WATERS NEAR GOSFORD

STARLIGHT CINEMA

During the summer months, the **Avoca Beach Theatre** (pictured) also runs the **Alfresco Cinema**, presenting films such as *Il Postino*, *Casablanca* and *Romeo and Juliet*. Take along a picnic and enjoy cinema under the stars. Ph: (02) 4381 1488

now a museum. The cottage is set in parkland with picnic and BBQ facilities. Open Wed, Sat, Sun, school and public holidays, 10am–3pm. Ph: (02) 4325 2270

On Brisbane Water, set in parkland at Caroline Bay, East Gosford, is the **Gosford Edogawa Commemorative Garden** incorporating **Gosford Regional Gallery**. The garden was a gift from Gosford's Japanese sister city, Edogawa. Take an audio tour of this traditional Japanese garden, which includes small bridges, a teahouse and a koi pavilion where the fish may be fed. The Gallery showcases a range of works by Central Coast artists. A cafe serves lunch and light refreshments. The garden is open daily, 9am–5pm, admission free. Ph: (02) 4325 0056

Noraville and Toukley
Map 23 D3 & C3

Edward Hargraves, the man whose discovery of gold triggered Australia's gold rush, fell in love with the rugged coast at **Noraville** and built his home there in 1856. The house, in Elizabeth Dr, is not open to the public but may be seen from the road.

For spectacular views of the area, park at the Bush St Reserve and take a walk to **Norah Head Lighthouse,** built in 1903 (see Map 24). Landcare has been involved in the regeneration of a small section of rainforest, and the con-struction of a nature trail and viewing

platforms. Walk through the reserve up to the historic lighthouse, down the steps to Lighthouse Beach, and along the beach to the swimming pool.

On the other side of the peninsula, on the spit of land separating Tuggerah Lake from Budgewoi Lake, is Toukley, a good place for sailing, canoeing, windsurfing and fishing. There is also a scenic golf course bordering the lake. South of these two towns on the North Entrance Peninsula is Wyrrabalong NP (see p.144).

Pearl Beach Map 23 B5

A weekend refuge for Sydneysiders on the Central Coast, Pearl Beach offers a

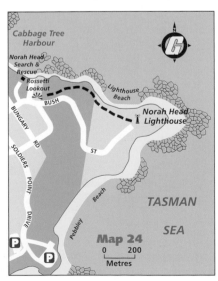

Cabbage Tree Harbour

Norah Head Search & Rescue

Rossetti Lookout

BUSH

Lighthouse Beach

Norah Head Lighthouse

BUNGARY RD

SOLDIERS POINT DRIVE

ST

Beach

Pebbley Beach

TASMAN SEA

Map 24
0   200
Metres

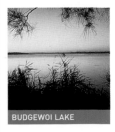

BUDGEWOI LAKE

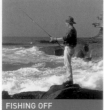

FISHING OFF
THE SKILLION

PEARL BEACH

as a top surfing spot and its beautiful location on Broken Head have drawn visitors here for many years. Visitors can enjoy a barefoot cappuccino at one of the popular cafes or an excellent meal at a local restaurant. The beach, fringed with towering Norfolk pines, provides the quintessential Australian summer experience, under the watchful gaze of the local lifesavers.

An easy walk up to **The Skillion Lookout** on Broken Head at Terrigal provides outstanding views of the coast.

North of town at **Forresters Beach** is the Swingers Golf Complex offering putt putt (mini) golf, a driving range and a 9-hole course. Ph: (02) 4384 3321

A variety of inviting towns with ocean beaches line the coast north and south of Terrigal, including **MacMasters**, **North Avoca** and **Wamberal**, all patrolled by local surf lifesaving clubs and each attracting a different kind of crowd.

Woy Woy Map 23 B5

On the southern shore of Brisbane Water, surrounded by holiday villages, Brisbane Water and Bouddi NPs and the Hawkesbury River, Woy Woy is a convenient base for exploring this part of the Central Coast. Boating, fishing and swimming are popular pursuits on the various waterways, and the national parks provide some splendid bushwalking (see p.142). When the town

beautiful sweep of beach cradled by cliffs and bushland, with some appealing dining venues on the water. For a delightful forest walk on easy terrain, **Crommelin Native Arboretum** is 4.5ha of native, mainly open forest with small areas of rainforest species along the creeks. Located in Crystal Ave, Pearl Beach, it is open at all times.

South of Pearl Beach, nestled in Brisbane Water NP, the tiny town of **Patonga**, which can be reached by ferry from Palm Beach (see p.58). The wharf here is a favourite spot for fishing.

Terrigal Map 25

Terrigal is now a fashionable Central Coast beachside town, but its reputation

B&B

Fairbanks Lodge B&B at Terrigal has its own deer park situated on 10ha with unspoilt views down to Avoca Lake and the ocean. Ph: (02) 4384 1752 www.fairbankslodge. com.au

THE SKILLION, TERRIGAL

was connected to Sydney by rail, it became a resort for city visitors. Now, as in the case of Gosford, many Sydneysiders have moved here and choose to commute.

South of town is **Mt Ettalong Lookout**, which offers a sweeping coastal panorama. On weekends at **Ettalong Beach**, dozens of colourful stalls attract crowds who enjoy browsing through these undercover markets, 9am–4pm.

Wyong Map 23 C3

The administrative centre of the Tuggerah Lakes district, Wyong was formerly a logging town and is now surrounded by the state forests of Watagan, Olney and Ourimbah.

The **Wyong Shire Heritage Centre** at Alison Homestead, Cape Rd off Alison Rd, has changing displays on local history and artefacts reflecting the labour and leisure of Wyong pioneers. It also houses a comprehensive body of research material on the settlement and history of Wyong Shire from 1822 to the present. The homestead sits in 2ha of lawns and gardens with picnic facilities. Open Sat, Sun, noon–4pm, Ph: (02) 4352 1886/(02) 4351 2886 www.alisonhomestead.org.au

Wyong is situated on the Wyong River near the shores of Tuggerah Lake, and has a number of recreation opportunities, including boating, sailing and

WOY WOY

fishing and two attractive golf courses. **Wyong Farmers and Craft Market** is held in the Town Park, Alison Rd, on the 2nd Sun of each month, 8am–1pm.

Yarramalong Map 23 B2

One of the gems of the Central Coast hinterland, Yarramalong's **St Barnabas Church** is the oldest in the Wyong Shire, built in 1895. The caretakers open the church for visitors and the cemetery is well worth a visit. In Yarramalong township, **Yarramalong Manor** is open daily for lunch and dinner. Ph: (02) 4356 1066. Also along

CROMMELIN NATIVE ARBORETUM

EXPLORING THE
ROCKPOOLS

Yarramalong Rd is the **Yarramalong Macadamia Nut Farm**, situated on a picturesque property where visitors are welcome. In the centre of the plantation is a coffee shop which sells a range of macadamia products.

Further west at **Kulnura**, the **Bumble Hill Studio** specialises in painting, pottery and glass from all over Australia and is regarded as one of the leading galleries in NSW. Open Fri–Sun, 10.30am–5pm, or by appt, Ph: (02) 4376 1253

National Parks, State Recreation Areas and State Forests

Much of the Central Coast coastline is dedicated parkland and there are many smaller reserves and state forests inland. Three national parks cover a significant proportion of the northern shores of Broken Bay and the Hawkesbury River.

More info about the parks can be obtained from the NPWS's Hawkesbury district office, Albany St, Gosford.

PUTTY BEACH, BOUDDI NP

Open Mon–Fri 8.30am–4.30pm
Ph: (02) 4320 4280

Bouddi NP Map 25

Bouddi NP covers the northerly entrance to Broken Bay and preserves a variety of habitats. Blackbutts, coachwoods, bangalow palms and coastal tea tree are all common.

Animal life includes northern brown bandicoots, brown antechinus (marsupial mouse), sugar gliders, wallabies and echidnas. Birds are prolific and include white-breasted sea eagles, known to nest in the park, while lyrebirds, bell-miners, bowerbirds and scrub turkeys are often seen.

A unique feature of Bouddi NP is the marine extension covering 300ha between Gerrin and Bombi Pts. Fishing is prohibited in this area which includes Maitland Bay and the remains of the *Maitland*. An extensive **walkway**, including a raised boardwalk, runs along the coast at **Killcare**, providing spectacular views south to Pittwater, Barrenjoey Lighthouse (see p.58) and the coastal fringe of Sydney.

There are numerous lookouts and picnic sites in Bouddi NP, and bushwalking and swimming are popular. The highest point is Mt Bouddi, 152m above sea level. Visitor facilities are limited but backpack camping is allowed at Little Beach and Tallow Beach. Car-based camping (not campervans or caravans) is available at Putty Beach. Volunteers staff the Maitland Bay Info Centre in the park on weekends. Camping permission essential. Ph: (02) 4320 4280

Brisbane Water NP Map 23 B4

This park comprises 11 458ha of bushland south and west of Gosford. The main entrance is at **Girrakool**. Facilities include picnic areas with shelters, amenities, gas BBQs, and there are many small waterholes to swim in. The **Mooney Nature Walk**, a 6.5km round trip, starts here. Magnificent views of the Hawkesbury River, Brisbane Water and Broken Bay are a feature of the park, which is also famous for its waratahs in spring and Christmas bells and Christmas bush in summer.

There are a number of **Aboriginal art sites** in the park, mostly rock engravings. Two Aboriginal groups, the Dharruk and Darkinjung, are known to have occupied parts of the area for at least 11 000 years. Nevertheless, the age of the carvings has been difficult to determine. Some are probably less than 200yr old as they depict such European objects as sailing ships. The most accessible can be seen at **Bulgandry**, off Woy Woy Rd, 3km south of the Pacific Hwy, with a walk of around 250m from the carpark to the rock carvings. Ph: (02) 4320 4280 (general enquiries) and (02) 4320 4203 (camping enquiries).

Dharug NP Map 23 A4

On the western outskirts of the Central Coast region, between Mangrove Creek and Macdonald River, the 14 850ha Dharug NP was dedicated in 1967 and named after an Aboriginal group. It contains a wealth of Aboriginal carvings, some of which are thought to be more than 8000yr old. Aboriginal archaeological sites can be visited only through the NPWS **Discovery Program** on weekends and school holidays.

A good way to explore the area is by canoe from the junction of the Hawkesbury and Macdonald Rivers. Over 700 plant species have been recorded within the park, including more than 20 different eucalypts. Reptiles such as gecko and brown tree snakes are commonly sighted. Tree-dwelling marsupials include yellow-bellied gliders and sugar gliders. Wombats are common near Mill Creek.

The most impressive remnants of the Great North Rd to the Hunter Valley are situated within the park, 1km upstream from Wisemans Ferry. Access to the convict-built stonework, with sandstone blocks forming culverts, embankments, buttresses and bridges, is by foot, horseback or mountain bike only. Picnic areas and fireplaces are at Mill Creek and Hazell Dell and camping is permitted at Mill Creek and on the Great North Rd

WOMBAT

at Ten Mile Hollow. Bookings advised. Ph: (02) 4320 4280

Munmorah SCA Map 23 D2

This conservation area stretches 12km along the coast from Catherine Hill Bay to Budgewoi. The ranger station is off Elizabeth Bay Dr, Lake Munmorah.

The terrain includes wooded heath, wetlands and pockets of rainforest, as well as superb beaches and spectacular lookouts and campgrounds. Camping is allowed at Freemans Park near Birdie Beach and Frazer Park. Toilets, cold showers, picnic tables and BBQs are available at both sites. Bookings essential, Ph: (02) 4358 0400

Popran NP Map 23 A4

Popran NP, north of the Hawkesbury River and 25km west of Gosford, covers 3970ha and contains a wide range of vegetation types as well as many endangered flora and fauna species. The area is rich in **Aboriginal engravings**, paintings, shell middens and axe grinding grooves, left by the Dharruk and Guringai people who lived here for thousands of years.

The Central Coast District Discovery program offers guided walks, canoe trips, mountain biking, spotlighting walks and other activities Ph: (02) 4320 4280

WARATAH

WATAGAN STATE FOREST

while the north is sandy. Whales are often seen off the Central Coast during winter and the high cliffs make a good spotting position. There is a wide variety of fauna and flora on both sections. The park also includes **Terilbah** and **Pelican Islands** on Tuggerah Lake.

North Wyrrabalong encloses some 480ha of the sand barrier separating Tuggerah Lake from the Pacific Ocean. There are no formal picnic areas or amenities and the only road access is via Wilfred Barrett Dr. Walking tracks include the 4.6km **Lillypilly Loop Trail**.

South Wyrrabalong is a 130ha thin strip of coastline from Blue Lagoon to Forresters Beach. The park is reached at The Entrance Rd, Bateau Bay. The **Coast Walking Track** is 3.5km long and links Blue Lagoon with **Wyrrabalong Lookout**. It is a day-use only area and camping is not permitted. Ph: (02) 4358 0400

Parks and gardens

The Australian Rainforest Sanctuary
Map 25

This pristine rainforest has been pre-served at Ourimbah Creek Rd, near Ourimbah. Well laid out and maintained tracks lead visitors through the forest, allowing for all-weather exploration. There are 126 native bird species, native animals and 200 species of rainforest flora in the park. Wallabies and birds are hand-fed daily. The park also contains an art gallery featuring local artists, and in Sept **Jazz in the Forest** is staged.

Picnic areas with token-operated gas BBQs overlook a landscaped valley, and native plants are for sale at the kiosk. Open Wed–Sun, 10am–5pm and on school and public holidays. Open 6–9.30pm in Nov only for **Firefly Magic** (p.137). Ph: (02) 4362 1855. www.australianrainforest.com.au

Other attractions

Australian Reptile Park Map 25

A giant frill neck lizard welcomes visitors to the multi-award winning Australian Reptile Park, where they can see a wide range of reptiles, take a stroll through the nature trail and have a photograph taken with a huge snuggly python or, for

Watagan & Heaton State Forests
Map 23 B2

In the range of hills north of the Yarramalong Valley, Watagan and Heaton State Forests have yielded much timber in the past 150 years, including giant cedars and turpentines, useful because of their resistance to marine borers.

Timber is still harvested but the forest is also used for recreation. Camping, bushwalking, sightseeing and 4WD trips are all popular pastimes. BBQs also available. Although they are only 600m high at most, the Watagans are very rugged. There are many waterfalls and lookouts, as well as marked walking trails — from Heaton Lookout three tracks lead to different environments.

At Gap Creek, there is a track to a 40m waterfall that is quite impressive after heavy rain. The main access road to the forest is from Mt Faulk Rd, off Freemans Dr. Ph: (02) 4358 0400

Wyrrabalong NP Map 25

Divided into two sections by The Entrance, Wyrrabalong NP conserves the last littoral rainforest on the Central Coast. The southern part has high headlands, cliffs and rock platforms,

WHALE SPOTTING

In **Wyrrabalong NP**, head towards Crackneck Lookout or Wyrrabalong Trig (on the northern end of Forresters Beach) to observe migrating humpback and southern right whales. Whales head north at the beginning of winter, and south to the Antarctic at the end of winter.

FANS WATCH AS ERIC THE CROCODILE GETS A FEED

SPIDER WORLD

Become acquainted with spiders at the Australian Reptile Park's Spider World. In Funnel-web Corner see these deadly spiders milked for their venom. Spider World is an interactive and fun exhibition

the less daring, a cuddly koala. The park also is home to warm-blooded Australian animals such as kangaroos, wombats, Tasmanian devils and echidnas

Hands-on shows starring reptiles are held twice daily. This is where visitors can pat tame alligators, lizards and pythons. The park's largest and most famous resident is Eric, a 5m saltwater crocodile who lives in his own heated pool. Eric is fed in front of an audience on Sundays at 1pm and more frequently during school holidays. Reminiscent of an *Indiana Jones* movie scene the exhibit Lost World of Reptiles takes visitors on a journey back in time, with the opportunity to view some very large, cute and deadly reptiles at close range. The park also has the largest display of exotic tarantulas anywhere in Australia.

Facilities include the **Hard Croc Cafe**, BBQs and picnic areas and a children's adventure playground. Open daily, 9am–5pm. Ph: (02) 4340 1022, www.reptilepark.com.au

Kims Beachside Retreat Map 23 C4

At Toowoon Bay, a 2hr drive north of Sydney, Kims offers a sophisticated escape. With a reputation for fine food and wine, this historic retreat provides unique beachhouse accommodation. Ph: (02) 4332 1566

Mangrove Creek Dam Map 23 A2

Drive through the lovely **Yarramalong Valley** and up **Bumble Hill** to find this huge rock-lined dam which holds one-third the volume of water in Sydney Harbour. The Public Works Department has provided visitor facilities including BBQs, shelter sheds and an unstaffed

TARANTULA, SPIDER WORLD, AUSTRALIAN REPTILE PARK

SCUBA DIVING

visitors centre which includes an audiovisual presentation. Access is signposted from George Downs Dr, Kulnura.

Sara Lee Factory and Shop Map 23 B4

At **Lisarow**, 8km north of Gosford, the kitchens of Sara Lee produce in excess of 800 000 cakes weekly. The company has a separate factory shop in Niagara Park Shopping Centre, Washington Ave which is open Mon–Fri, 9am–5.30pm, Sat, 8.30am–3pm and Sun 10am–2pm The company's lingerie division, Sara Lee Intimate, also has an outlet nearby. Ph: (02) 4329 8444

Somersby Falls Map 25

At Somersby, near the Australian Reptile Park, is Somersby Falls with the **Falls Walking Track** which descends to two stages of the falls. Allow 90min for the walk which provides excellent photographic opportunities. This is also an ideal picnic spot.

Recreational activities

Action

Central Coast Bushworks offers group abseiling and corporate team and school activities. Activities are wide ranging, including low and high ropes, wall climbing, archery, canoeing and orienteering. Open daily, bookings

essential Ph: (02) 4363 2028 or 0419 254 906.

Cycling

Cycleways are being developed throughout the Central Coast, with an extensive network completed around Tuggerah Lake linking Berkley Vale, Killarney Vale, Long Jetty, Bateau Bay and The Entrance. Also in Wyong Shire, a cycleway is in place linking Buff Point and Budgewoi.

In Gosford, a scenic cycle route along Fagans Bay, the Broadwater and Caroline Bay links many of the city's natural and historic attractions. Central Coast Tourism provides a handy map.

On the water

Free lessons are provided by **Long Jetty Catamaran Hire** when their catamarans and sailboards are hired. Canoes and pedal boats are also available. Open 9am–5pm Fri–Mon and school holidays; other days by arrangement. Ph: (02) 4332 9362

Explore Brisbane Water using the small boats for hire from **Anderson's Boatshed** at Booker Bay. Open daily. Ph: (02) 4341 3219

A little further north at Wyong, get out onto the water with **Wandering the Lakes Cruises**, which tour both the lakes

KAYAKING ON STILL MORNING WATERS, CENTRAL COAST

Saddle up and explore

The Central Coast is much more than beaches and waterways and there are few better ways of discovering its hidden treasures than on horseback. Explore 1000ha of coastal hinterland, starting just 15min from the centre of Gosford. Billed as Australia's largest horseriding centre, **Glenworth Valley Horseriding** has more than 200 horses and provides free range or guided rides through some of the State's most pristine forests and rolling countryside. Riverfront camping is available. Riding lessons are provided for beginners. Ph: (02) 4375 1222, www.glenworth.com.au

and the river. Ph: (02) 4393 6246 or 0417 374 443. www.wanderingcruises.com.au

Aquabikes, boats, fishing tackle and diving gear can be hired from **The Entrance Boathouse**. Ph: (02) 4332 3399

Cruise the Hawkesbury with the **riverboat postman** (see p.67).

On the Central Coast, **houseboats** are available for hire on Lake Macquarie. Houseboats on the Hawkesbury River are rented from boat yards on the river's southern side at Brooklyn and Wisemans Ferry (see pp.66, 110).

On Lake Macquarie, **Luxury Afloat Houseboats** at Marmong Point has boats with up to 10 berths. No licence or prior skills necessary, chart and instructions provided. Lake Macquarie is about four times the size of Sydney Harbour, providing a wonderful environment for a relaxing holiday. Open Thur–Tues, bookings essential. Ph: (02) 4958 3044, www.luxuryafloat.net.au

Southern Adventures Kayak Tours offer self-guided or guided tours of the Central Coast's waterways. Open daily, Ph: 0429 856 231, www.southernadventures.com.au

Ocean Planet offers kayaking adventure tours and training to suit all levels of fitness. An easy, relaxing paddle in a backwater accompanied by the sounds of nature is an excellent introduction to the sport. For a more challenging and adventurous trip there is sea kayaking, or catching waves created by the ships. Ocean Planet can tailor tuition or trips to fulfil the desire for challenge or relaxation. Bookings essential Ph: (02) 4342 2222

ABSEILING

or 0412 534 458. www.oceanplanet.com.au

Scuba diving

The crystal waters of the Central Coast offer good visibility and a variety of dives for experienced and novice divers. **Pro Dive** at **The Entrance** provides diver training and supplies. Open Mon–Fri 9.30am–5pm , weekends 9am–4pm . Ph: (02) 4334 1559. www.prodivecentralcoast.com.au

Terrigal Diving School has a diver training school and supplies, as well as organising deep sea fishing and diving trips. Ph: (02) 4384 1219. www.terrigaldive.com.au

Fun for the young

★ Abseiling, bushwalking, Central Coast Bushworks (p.146)
★ Cycleways (p.146)
★ Horseriding (p.147)
★ Kayaking (p.147)
★ Pelican feeding, The Entrance (p.138)
★ Firefly Magic (p. 144)

Places of interest (Hinterland and heritage tour)

❶ Glenworth Valley horseriding (p.147)
❷ Bumble Hill Studio, Kulnura (p.142)
❸ Yarramalong Manor (p.141)
❹ Australian Rainforest Sanctuary (The Forest of Tranquility) (p.144)
❺ Somersby Falls (p.146)

Places of interest (Family fun tour)

❶ Henry Kendall's Cottage (p.138)
❷ President's Hill Lookout, Gosford
❸ Starship Cruises (MV *Lady Kendall II*) (p.136)
❹ Old Killcare Store
❺ Walkway at Bouddi NP (p.142)
❻ Terrigal Beach (p.140)
❼ Fragrant Garden
❽ Pelican feeding, The Entrance (p.138)
❾ Norah Head Lighthouse (p.139)

Suggested tours – Map 25

Hinterland and heritage tour

Approximate distance

70km from Sydney CBD to the Gosford Interchange; round trip tour from the Gosford Interchange (via Peats Ridge) — 85km

About the tour

This tour captures many natural and historic attractions that belong to the hinterland of the Central Coast. Meander through some of the region's most beautiful forests and valleys, and enjoy a picnic at the Rainforest Sanctuary. Visit scenic Glenworth Valley and Somersby Falls for some wonderful photographs.

Family fun tour

Approximate distance

70km from Sydney CBD to the Gosford Interchange; round trip tour from Gosford Interchange (via Terrigal) — 135km

About the tour

Quiet lakes, pounding surf beaches and pristine forests can be savoured, along with lunch, at the water's edge, in cheerful restaurants or at the many picnic sites along the Central Coast. For a panoramic view of the area, visit the Norah Head Lighthouse. This tour takes in some of best beaches and views of the coast as well as some of its main attractions.

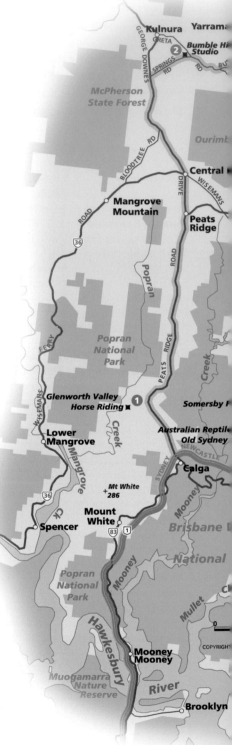

Yarramalong Manor

Wyong State Forest

Jilliby

Wyong Creek

Warnervale Airport
Warnervale
Gorokan

Budgewoi Lake
Budgewoi

Toukley
Noraville

Norah Head
Soldiers Pt

Wyong
Tuggerawong

Ourimbah State Forest

Tuggerah

Wyong Creek

Tuggerah Lake

Wyrrabalong National Park

Forest Of Tranquillity

The Entrance North
Pelican Feeding
The Entrance
Long Jetty

Ourimbah

Berkeley Vale

Tumbi Umbi

Killarney Vale

Strickland State Forest
Lisarow

TASMAN

Narara

Bateau Bay

Wyrrabalong National Park

Map 25

Presidents Hill Lookout

Wamberal

Forresters Beach

SEA

Gosford
Henry Kendall Cottage
Lady Kendall Cruise

Erina

Fragrant Garden
Terrigal
The Skillion

Brisbane Water

Kincumba Mountain Reserve

Avoca Beach

Kincumber

Copacabana

Woy Woy

MacMasters Beach

Ettalong Beach

Killcare
Old Killcare Store

Bouddi National Park

Umina Beach

Box Head

Lion I.
Broken Bay

PUBLISHERS PTY LTD

Must see, must do

★ Barrington Tops (p.171)

★ Dolphin Watch cruise,
Port Stephens (p.167)

★ Hunter Valley wineries (p.172)

★ Morpeth Heritage
Walk (p.162)

Radio stations

2NC: AM 1233

2NM: AM 981

ABC Upper Hunter: AM 1044

2HD: AM 1143

New FM: FM 105.3

2NUR: FM 103.7

Tourist information

**Lake Macquarie Visitor
Information Centre**

72 Pacific Hwy, Blacksmiths 2281

Ph: (02) 4972 1172

Freecall: 1800 802 044

www.lakemac.com.au

**Hunter River Visitor
Information Centre**

cnr New England Hwy and
High St, Maitland 2320

Ph: (02) 4931 2800

www.hunterrivercountry.com.au

**Muswellbrook Visitor
Information Centre**

87 Hill St, Muswellbrook 2333

Ph: (02) 6541 4050

www.muswellbrook.org.au

**Newcastle Visitor
Information Centre**

363 Hunter St, Newcastle 2300

Ph: (02) 4974 2999

Freecall: 1800 654 558

www.visitnewcastle.com.au

**Port Stephens Visitor
Information Centre**

Victoria Pde, Nelson Bay 2315

Ph: (02) 4980 6900

Freecall: 1800 808 900

www.portstephens.org.au

**Hunter Valley Wine
Country Tourism**

455 Wine Country Drive
Pokolbin 2325

Ph: (02) 4990 0900 or 4990 4477

www.winecountry.com.au

the hunter region

SO MUCH, SO CLOSE ... A SCENIC 90min drive from Sydney, the Hunter region presents visitors with a range of very different travel experiences, from meticulously restored reminders of Australia's colonial past to unspoilt surf beaches and tranquil lake shores. Not far from dynamic regional centres lie sleepy rural hamlets like Wollombi and relaxed holiday spots such as Port Stephens.

The Hunter is best known, however, as a wine-growing region — and with good reason. Home to some of Australia's most respected wineries, the region caters to the needs of wine lovers with cellar door sales, winery tours, restaurants, picnic areas and a diverse range of accommodation. While many initially come to the Hunter to sample the fruits of the vine, it is not just wine that encourages their return.

Lake Macquarie, Newcastle, Port Stephens and the Myall Coast offer magical beaches and waterways. Nelson Bay is a centre for recreational and professional fishing fleets, with year-round dolphin spotting. The region also provides innumerable glimpses into Australia's rich colonial heritage. From the smallest towns to the centre of Newcastle, fine examples of pre-Federation architecture abound, many restored and open to the public.

Wine, surf and a strong sense of history await visitors to the Hunter region.

LEFT: HISTORIC BUILDINGS, MAITLAND

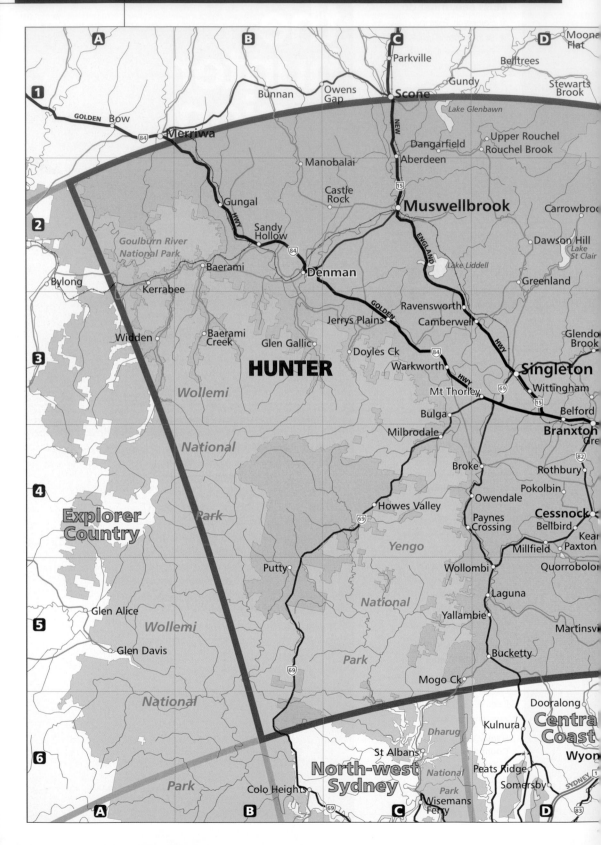

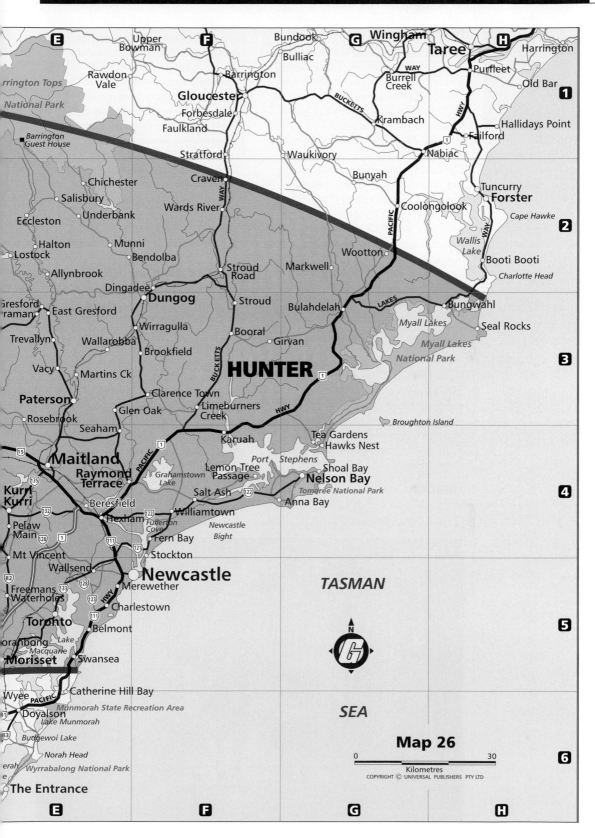

Map 26

0   30
Kilometres
COPYRIGHT © UNIVERSAL PUBLISHERS PTY LTD

MAGICAL FORESTS

The lush forests of the **Watagan Ranges** offer a magical escape to nature for families and serious bushwalkers alike. The area is renowned for its wildflowers, ferns, palms, native fauna, waterfalls and tranquillity.

Natural features

As the name suggests, the Hunter region is the valley of the Hunter River where it nears the sea. The heartland of the region is fertile, gently rolling pastoral country, ideal for winegrowing, and horse and cattle grazing.

To the south lie the Watagan Ranges. Although small by international standards at only 600m, these steep, rugged outcrops provide excellent vistas of Lake Macquarie. To the west, the Broken Back Range protects the vineyards, while the Hunter River and its tributaries and overflow lakes lie to the north, with the Pacific Ocean stretching out to the east. The Myall Lakes system, on the coast abutting the northern edge of the region, is the largest fresh-brackish lake system on the NSW coast, an important breeding ground for fish and prawns.

While the region is endowed with natural beauty, huge seams of high quality coal are found throughout the valley, and coal mining is still a pillar of the local economy. Mining activity, however, is localised to specific areas and does not impose on the serendipity of the valley.

History

While the Hunter region is now a centre for colonial architecture, archaeological exploration has revealed evidence of widespread Aboriginal settlement in the valley. It is believed the Hunter's original inhabitants were the Awabakal people.

The first non-Aboriginal people to arrive in the Newcastle region in 1791 were a group of convicts on the run. They soon discovered coal in their new hideout. In 1797, their pursuer, Lt John Shortland, also realised the valley's subterranean wealth, ensuring the establishment of the city of Newcastle.

Nevertheless, the initial growth of the Newcastle region was relatively slow. Morpeth and Maitland at the head of the Hunter River attracted the first settlers, offering better access to the valley's rich agricultural lands. From 1858, when the railway from Newcastle to Maitland was completed, Newcastle grew rapidly and became the region's port and industrial centre.

The Hunter wine industry began with James Busby, a Scottish civil engineer who arrived in Sydney in 1824 to supervise coalmining at Newcastle and construction of Sydney's first water supply (the famous Busby's bore which provided the city's water until 1858).

During the 1830s, Mr Busby visited Spain and France, collecting hundreds of vine cuttings. Some were planted in the Sydney Botanic Gardens, others at Busby's estate at Kirkton in the Hunter.

HUNTER VALLEY VINEYARD

The estate vines flourished, proving the region's wine producing potential.

The fledgling industry encountered some problems, however, experiencing a cycle of prosperity and depression by the end of the 19th century. With Federation in 1901, the removal of state trade barriers allowed cheap wine from SA to swamp the NSW market. The 1930s Great Depression only made matters worse, and by 1947 a mere 445ha remained under cultivation.

It was not until the 1970s that the Hunter began to re-emerge as a major winegrowing region. The wine boom of this period revitalised the industry, which continues to thrive and is now a major player in many international markets.

Getting there

By road

For Sydneysiders, the Hunter region is easily accessible, with many alternative routes available. The most direct is to take the F3 Sydney–Newcastle Fwy, which begins at Wahroonga in Sydney's northern suburbs.

If heading for Newcastle, take the exit ramp and follow the Newcastle Link Rd into the city.

To access the lake and beach side of Lake Macquarie, take the East Lake Macquarie exit; for the lake and mountains side, take the Morisset exit.

For Port Stephens and Nelson Bay, continue along the F3 Fwy, until you come to the roundabout where you can turn right onto John Renshaw Dr. Continue along John Renshaw Dr and veer right onto the overpass that takes you onto the New England Hwy; take the Taree exit, cross the bridge at Hexham and follow Route 122.

For Bulahdelah and the Myall Coast, from Raymond Terrace continue along the Pacific Hwy, where turnoffs lead to Tea Gardens, Hawks Nest, Myall Lakes NP and, north of Bulahdelah, Seal Rocks.

To get to the wineries of the Lower Hunter, turn left off the hwy at Freemans Interchange and follow Route 82 to Cessnock. Pokolbin, the centre of the winegrowing region, is just 13km NW of Cessnock. For the Upper Hunter region,

continue along the New England Hwy through Maitland and Singleton to Muswellbrook and Scone.

An alternative to the fwy is the old Pacific Hwy. It more or less parallels the fwy from Wahroonga to Wyong, where it turns east and becomes Route 111 at Doyalson, following the coast to Newcastle. The fwy has dramatically decreased the traffic on this road, making it an unhurried alternative.

A longer route to Cessnock leaves the fwy at Calga and continues north to Peats Ridge. The road to Wollombi turns left here, continuing north through scenic bush and forest country via Bucketty and Laguna. A short section of the road is unsealed, but in fair condition.

Another unsealed back road from Wisemans Ferry, on the Hawkesbury River, joins the Wollombi road at Bucketty after passing through the historic hamlet of St Albans.

The main alternative route north is the Putty Rd (Route 69), joining Windsor and Singleton via the plateau above the Macdonald and Colo River valleys.

A number of private interstate and intrastate coach lines service the area.

SCOTLAND DOWNUNDER

More than a quarter of the Hunter Valley's original free settlers came from Scotland during the early 1820s. Various place names throughout the valley reflect this early Scottish influence.

PEPPERS CREEK WINERY, POKOLBIN

PUB CRAWL WITH ALTITUDE

Sydney Helicopters has a flight that covers Sydney, northern beaches and on to the pub at Wollombi, then the Hunter Country Estate for a fabulous lunch with selection of wines and finishing at the historic village of St Albans and a drink at the 1836 Settlers Arms Inn. Ph: (02) 9637 4455

By rail

Two fast train services cover the Maitland area: the Sydney–Murwillumbah and the Northern Tablelands XPTs. The XPT also stops at Muswellbrook and Scone. There are daily train connections to Newcastle, and the State Rail Sydney–Armidale coaches stop in Singleton on the northern edge of the Hunter Valley.

By ferry

A ferry service operates daily between Newcastle's Queen's Wharf and Stockton across the mouth of the Hunter River. Ph: (02) 4929 2106. Another daily ferry service operates between Nelson Bay and Tea Gardens across Port Stephens. Ph: (02) 4997 1084

QUEEN'S WHARF, NEWCASTLE

Getting around

Hunter Valley Day Tours offer full and half day tours around the wineries, which includes wine and cheese tastings. Operates daily with pickups from Hunter region hotels. Bookings essential. Ph: (02) 4938 5031. www.huntertourism.com/daytours

Wine Country Tours operate from Sydney with a max of eight customers. Morning tea is taken at Peppers Guest House, Pokolbin, followed by guided tastings at some of the leading wineries. Lunch at Robert's Pepper Tree Restaurant before continuing the exploration of the vineyards and wineries. Bookings essential. Ph: (02) 9484 0477

Hunter Valley Wine Tours has a range of tours from Sydney to the region, including Port Stephens, the Hawkesbury River and national parks, with lunches and overnight accommodation optional. Ph: (02) 9498 8888. www.sydneytours.com.au

Great Sights have full day Hunter Valley and Dolphin Watch tours to Port Stephens departing from Sydney. Ph: (02) 9241 2294. www.greatsights.com.au

Upper Hunter Tours offer trips to horse studs, mines, wineries and various other attractions. Available by appt only. Ph: 0417 439 776 or (02) 6547 2442, www.upperhuntertours.com.au

Port Stephens 4WD Tours offer one, two and three hour tours of Stockton Bight sand dunes. Ph: (02) 4984 4760

Port Stephens Coaches offer tours of the Tomaree Peninsula, Port Stephens and the vineyards. Bookings essential, Ph: (02) 4982 2940. A Bay Explorer ticket can be purchased from the bus driver and allows unlimited bus trips on any one day on the Tomaree Peninsula.

Festivals and events

Hunter Valley Steamfest

The annual celebration in Apr of Maitland's long association with steam locomotives and the railway journeys to Muswellbrook, Singleton and Paterson. Events centre around **Maitland**

SAND DUNES, STOCKTON BEACH

HUNTER VALLEY STEAMFEST

CHOPPER TOURS
See the Hunter from above and access its remote places. **Thunderbolt Helicopters** operate scenic and charter flights, as well as winery lunches and horse stud tours. Ph: (02) 6547 4589

(pp.160-61) and the **Richmond Vale Railway and Mining Museum** (p.159).

National Trust Heritage Festival

Maitland and **Morpeth** celebrate their rich cultural heritage in Apr with many private historic homes and gardens being opened as well as concerts, lectures and exhibitions.

Tocal Field Days

Special exhibits and demonstrations for those interested in the land and country living. Held annually on the 1st weekend in May at **Tocal Agricultural College**, Paterson. Ph: (02) 4939 8820. www.tocal.com

Scone Horse Festival

For 12 days in early May, Scone celebrates its status as the 2nd largest horse breeding centre in the world, with a parade, rodeo, horse show and the feature event, the Scone Cup. Ph: (02) 6545 1526

Hunter Valley Caravan, Camping, 4WD and Outdoor Show

This is the complete outdoor event where you can investigate it, see it and buy it! Held annually in May at Maitland Showground, Blomfield St, Maitland.

Maitland Garden Ramble

In Sept, many of Maitland's outstanding historic homesteads and beautiful gardens are open to the public. A detailed leaflet is available from the Maitland Visitor Info Centre. The beautifully restored Georgian grandeur of **Tocal House** in nearby Paterson can also be inspected.

Steamfest

While the city of Maitland might not have the high profile of Newcastle, to train buffs everywhere it is a premier destination. Maitland is home to the annual **Hunter Valley Steamfest**, which is held every Apr as part of the National Trust Heritage Festival celebrations. Carefully restored locomotives, rare steam traction engines and vintage farm machinery, as well as vintage and hot rod cars, are all on display. Train enthusiasts have a chance to step back in time by taking a ride on an authentic 3801 locomotive restored to its former glory by local tradesmen. Those yearning for the smell of soot and squeal of brakes should contact the Maitland Visitors Centre. Ph: (02) 4931 800, www.steamfest.com.au

SCONE THOROUGHBREDS

DON BURROWS ON CLARINET, JAZZ IN THE VINEYARDS

HUNTER VALLEY GARDENS

Mattara

In early Oct Mattara (the Festival of Newcastle) celebrates the city's past and present. Civic Park is the epicentre of festivities, which feature an outdoor art exhibition and a variety of live concerts.

King St Fair

The usual traffic noise along King St, Newcastle is silenced late Nov–early Dec for the King St Fair. The street is closed to all traffic as crowds on foot check out the street stalls, shops and a variety of entertainment.

There are many annual events in the region including: **Blessing of the Fleet,** Nelson Bay (Jan); **Newcastle and Maitland Shows, Wyndham Estate Signature Concert** (Feb); **Muswellbrook Show and Rodeo, Surfest** (Mar); **Hunter Valley Harvest Festival** (Mar–Apr); **Beaumont St Wine Food & Music Festival, Vintage Jazz at the Rothbury Estate** (Apr); **Dobell Art Festival, Morpeth Jazz Festival** (May); **Festival of the Whales,** Nelson Bay, **Hunter Wine Country ArtsScrawl** (June); **Morpeth Craft Crawl/Vintage Farm Machinery Rally** (Jun/Jul); **Newcastle Jazz Festival, Morpeth Crazy Teapot Exhibition** (Aug); **This is Not Art,** Newcastle (Sept–Oct), **Speed Boat Spectacular,** Port Stephens, **Myall Spring Festival,** Hawks Nest, **Feast of the Olive** (Sept); **Blue Heeler Country Spring Festival,** Muswellbrook Shire (Sept–Nov); **Opera in the**

Vineyards, Jazz in the Vineyards, **Lake Glenbawn Fishing Classic** (Oct); **Bulahdelah Music Festival** (Nov); **Carols in the Vineyards by Candlelight.**

Main towns and localities

Branxton Map 26 D4

Wine and history create this little town's appeal. Nestled on the northern edge of the valley, Branxton is home to historic **Dalwood House** on the Wyndham Estate Winery. Classified by the National Trust, the property includes the remains of one of Australia's first and finest Greek Revival buildings (1828). There is a small museum section. Bookings essential.

Recognised for fusing soul enriching elements, award-winning wine, great food and spectacular cultural events, **Wyndham Estate,** situated on the banks of the Hunter River, was established in 1828 and is Australia's oldest continuously operating winery. Wine tasting tours begin at 11am where the traditional open vat fermentation and basket press can be seen. Restaurant and wine tasting daily 10am–4.30pm, Ph: (02) 4938 3444

Bulahdelah Map 27 B1

On the Pacific Hwy 70km north of Raymond Terrace, Bulahdelah is the gateway to the Myall Lakes. Surrounded by waterways and state forests, the town is a good base for exploring the area. A boat ramp provides access to

ON THE HOP

On the Hop in the Hunter is a handy quarterly calendar of events for the region. Available from visitor centres and wineries.

the **Myall River** which flows through the town, and houseboats and cruisers are available to hire. **Bulahdelah Markets** are held on the1st Sat of each month in Crawford St next to the Visitor Centre.

North, at Bulahdelah State Forest, is the **Grandis**, the tallest tree in NSW. Another pleasant spot close by is **Alum Mountain**, known for its rare rock orchids (there are a total of 89 varieties of rock orchids in the area). A walk to the summit through tall forest is rewarded by views of the Myall River and Lakes system, and at the mountain's base is an attractive picnic and BBQ area. Bulahdelah Visitor Info Centre, Ph: (02) 4997 4981

Cessnock Map 29 C6

Reflecting the valley's historical links with Scotland, Cessnock was named by settler John Campbell after Cessnock Castle in Scotland. Although the township's initial prosperity was due to the discovery of the rich Greta coal seam, today it is better known for its proximity to the wineries of Pokolbin. Touring info and a variety of good local wines for tasting are available at the **Hunter Valley Wine Country Visitor Info Centre**, 455 Wine Country Dr, Pokolbin. This is a great starting place for first-time visitors to the wine district. Open daily, 9am–5pm. Ph: (02) 4990 0900

On the northern outskirts of Cessnock at Lomas La, Nulkaba, **Rusa Park Zoo** is set in 9ha of natural bushland. The native and introduced species on display include kangaroos, koalas, snakes, monkeys, parrots, deer and antelope; a Reptile Show features crocodiles. A major attraction is the mob of rare albino euro kangaroos. Picnic area and gas BBQ facilities are provided. Open daily, 9.30am–4.30pm. Ph: (02) 4990 7714. www. crocodileencounters.com.au/rusaparkzoo

Nestled in the heart of the Hunter is **Hunter Valley Gardens**, a superb property featuring spectacular international display gardens, boutique hotel, Tallawanta Lodge, Harrigans' Irish Pub and Accommodation, Roche Wines and a boutique shopping village with an array of specialty shops and attractions. Ph: (02) 4998 7600. www.hvg.com.au

Nearby is **the Hunter Valley Cheese Factory** in the McGuigan Complex, McDonalds Rd. A talk about cheese is held daily at 11am and the cheesemaking process can be seen through viewing windows. Tastings and takeaway supplies are available. Open daily 9am–5.30pm, Ph: (02) 4998 7602

The **Richmond Vale Railway and Mining Museum** on Main Rd, 4km south of **Kurri Kurri**, brings the era of steam locomotives alive on the 1st two Suns of each month. The last steam-hauled train ran here in 1987 after almost 100 years of continuous operation. Today, heritage trains depart every hour 10.30am–3.30pm, subject to change without notice.

The museum is located within the **Richmond Main Colliery Historic Park**. Special events include Steamfest (Apr), Model Railway Exhibition (May), Coalfields Steam (Jun), Friends of Thomas (Sep) and Santa's Steam Special (Nov). The park provides mining exhibits, a museum, restaurant and kiosk, souvenir shop, picnic areas, wood-fired BBQs and guided tours. Ph: (02) 4937 5344

Denman Map 30 B2

Around 25km SW of Muswellbrook, Denman was traditionally known for its **horse and cattle studs** in the nearby Widden Valley. These days, although the horses and cattle remain a feature, wine

HUNTER VALLEY RED

BROKENBACK TRAIL

The Brokenback trail loops around the foot of Brokenback Mountain, and takes in many of the area's wineries, restaurants, accommodation, tours and activities. Local visitor centres have lists of the trail's main attractions.

THOROUGHBRED STUDS

It is possible to gain an inside perspective on the Upper Hunter's horse breeding industry with a **Horse Stud Tour**, visiting two thoroughbred studs, Woodlands and Coolmore. Ph: (02) 6547 2442 or 0417 439 776, www.upperhuntertours. com.au

HIGH ST HERITAGE MALL
Developed in 1988 as a Bicentennial project, Maitland's Heritage Mall has closed off High St, providing a focus for the CBD and the city's heritage image.

making has also come into focus, with a number of major vineyards in the area. The town itself is an attractive rural centre, with many old buildings still standing along the main street. Goulburn River NP is 50km to the west (see p.171).

Dungog Map 26 F3

Surrounded by velvety hills, Dungog began as a farming community and timber district in the 1820s. Farming is still important to the area, and state forests surround the town, but Dungog's main attraction is its proximity to Barrington Tops NP (see p.171).

Other activities nearby include horseriding, canoeing and fishing; details available from the Visitor Info Centre. Also available is a brochure, *Welcome to Dungog*, documenting Dungog's history with a heritage walk and town drive. Visit the **Dungog Historical Museum**, and nearby charming old towns including **Clarence Town**, **Paterson**, **Gresford**, **Vacy** and **Stroud**.

Nearby, **Chichester** and **Lostock dams** provide excellent recreational opportunities, both with pleasant picnic and BBQ areas, and fishing, boating and windsurfing at Lostock. For more info contact Dungog Visitor Info Centre Ph: (02) 4992 2212, www.visitdungog.com

Lake Macquarie Map 26 E5

South of Newcastle, the largest seaboard lake in Australia, with a 174km foreshore and four times the size of Sydney Harbour, Lake Macquarie is a magnet for watersports enthusiasts. The Pacific Hwy along the eastern border provides great water views and passes through such towns as **Swansea** and **Belmont**. Other towns, including **Speers Pt**, **Wangi Wangi** and **Toronto** provide quiet, out of the way retreats. Despite marked population increases in recent years, Lake Macquarie retains much of its sedate holiday atmosphere.

The 1922 National Heritage listed home and studio of artist **Sir William Dobell** at 47 Dobell Dr, Wangi Wangi has been retained as he lived in it. Open weekends, public holidays, and each Wed in Jan, 1–4pm. Ph: (02) 4975 4115

CRICKETING LEGEND
Raised on a dairy farm just outside Dungog, **Doug Walters**, first-class Australian cricketer, is the town's most famous son.

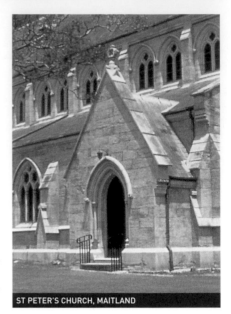

ST PETER'S CHURCH, MAITLAND

Lake Macquarie Cruises has a series of cruises which explore the shoreline with a detailed commentary on the history of the area. Coffee, luncheon and twilight dinner cruises are available Wed and Sun, groups any day by arrangement. Bookings essential. Ph: (02) 4973 2513

Squids Ink Boat Hire & Restaurant in Belmont have tinnies and canoes that can be hired to explore the beauty of the Lake Macquarie waterways Ph: (02) 4947 7223

Maitland Map 26 E4

The flavour of 19th century Australia is nowhere more evident than at Maitland in the Hunter. The New England Hwy sweeps past the city 35km west of Newcastle, but it is well worth the effort to turn in and explore. Maitland today still reflects the prosperity of the area in the mid-1800s when it served as the regional centre of the Hunter Valley.

East Maitland in particular offers beautiful heritage buildings and churches. One way to appreciate the city's historic architecture is to follow the **East Maitland Heritage Walk** or the **Maitland Heritage Walk**. Maitland Visitor Info Centre has walking maps, including an *Eastern Precinct Children's Heritage Walk* pamphlet which encourage interaction in their walks.

WALKA WATER WORKS, MAITLAND

The Maitland skyline is dominated by the Gothic spires of **St Peter's Church**. This elegant Victorian building was designed by Edmund Blacket in 1875 and completed by his son Cyril in 1885. Of particular interest is the marble and alabaster pulpit, imported from Italy.

Maitland Gaol in John St, East Maitland was built in 1844 by colonial architect Mortimer Lewis and was modelled on London's Pentonville prison. Sleepovers and evening tours on the weekend are available by arrangement; self-guided visits daily 11am–3pm, guided tours Thur–Sun at 11am also 2pm Sun, Ph: (02) 4936 6610

Church St is home to two of the city's finest Victorian homes. **Grossmann House** (1862) and **Brough House** (1870) are 'mirror image' 2-storey townhouses. Grossmann House has been restored by the National Trust and is now a Victorian folk museum. Open Thur–Sun 1.30–4.30pm. Ph: 4933 6452. Housed in a superb, classic Federation Gothic building, the **Maitland Regional Gallery** has a significant collection of contemporary Australian art as well as hosting touring exhibitions. Exhibition details Ph: (02) 4934 9859

Walka Water Works Reserve, 1.5km north of Maitland, is a Heritage listed building, the most fully intact water works complex remaining in NSW. BBQs, a children's playground and walking trail make it a pleasant recreational facility for lovers of both history and nature. Open dawn to dusk, a daily tour of the building and reserve is available, Ph: (02) 4932 0533

The Glebe Burial Ground and **Hiland Crescent Cemetery**, both dating from the early 1800s, offer a fascinating insight into the families that helped shape the Maitland region.

In keeping with its heritage feel, **antiques** are big business in Maitland; allow some time to browse the stores in **Melbourne St** and **High St.**

Maitland Park in the heart of the city provides a pleasant area for picnics beneath its shady trees. **Maitland Fair Markets** are held on the 1st Sun of each

Les Darcy — Maitland hero

One of Australia's greatest boxers, Les Darcy, was born at Woodville near Maitland in 1895. His talents in the ring were noticed early and at 13 he was already a schoolboy champion. Darcy's first professional fight was at 16 in the Maitland Town Hall. He went on to be undefeated in his first 17 bouts, and rapidly became a wealthy young man.

But in 1916, when the country was embroiled in a bitter debate over conscription for the Great War, Darcy was criticised for not enlisting. He left for America shortly before his 21st birthday, saying he would enlist in Canada or England once he had made enough money to support his family in Australia. Sadly though, he never realised his full potential and died in Memphis in 1917 of pneumonia. His funeral in East Maitland was the largest ever in the city. A section of the New England Hwy at Maitland is named after him.

SPOONBILLS IN FLIGHT, TEA GARDENS

BLUEY

month (except Jan), also the 3rd Sun of the month Oct–Dec at the Maitland Showground, Bloomfield St. Ph: (02) 4962 5522

Morpeth Map 31

On the banks of the Hunter River NE of Maitland is Morpeth, the river port town of the Hunter Valley in the 19th century and one of the most unspoilt heritage towns in NSW. The entire village has been classified by the National Trust and is the subject of a permanent conservation order by the Heritage Council of NSW.

Morpeth in its day was one of the busiest river ports in the country, with the first steamship arriving from Sydney as far back as 1831. Some people of vision from Morpeth include William Arnott (Arnott's Biscuits), Caleb Soul (WH Soul Pattinson) and Walter Bramble (Brambles Transport).

A **Heritage Walk** brochure is available from the Hunter River Country Visitor Info Centre in Maitland. **Swan St**, the town's main street, parallels the Hunter River and is a good place to start a walking tour. The original sandstone kerbing laid by convicts is still in evidence throughout the town and many of the heritage buildings are used today as antique stores, coffee shops and restaurants. There are BBQs on the town common and by the river.

At 164 Swan St, **Teddy Bears Downstairs** is home to more than 4000 teddies and gollies from as far afield as USA, UK and NZ. Open daily, 10.30am–4pm. Ph: (02) 4933 9794. Next door is **Grandma's Feather Bed**, which is full of hand-crafted goods and collectable dolls. Open Wed–Sun, 11am–4pm. Ph: (02) 4933 1224

At 175 Swan St, **Campbell's Store Craft Centre**, taste traditional ginger beer and stock up on hand-made lollies and sweet treats.

The **Court House** (1864) is now a local history museum. Open Tues–Fri, 10am–4pm.

Muswellbrook Map 30 D1

Muswellbrook Shire is known as 'Blue Heeler Country', because the first Australian cattle dog was bred by Thomas Hall, a local pastoralist, at his property 'Dartbrook', 12km north of Muswellbrook. Today, the town is still surrounded by pastoral activity and **Bengalla**, a large open-cut coal mine. Explore the town's past with the **Muswellbrook Heritage Walk** brochure, which describes around 30 places of interest, available from the Visitor Info Centre.

Located in the Town Hall (1871), **Muswellbrook Regional Gallery's**

BROOM MAKER, MORPETH

BAYSWATER POWER STATION

Located south of Muswellbrook, Bayswater Power Station is the largest thermal power station of its type in Australia.

Hunter wines in the one location. Open daily, 10am–5pm. Ph: (02) 6541 4211. www.hunterwine.com.au

Myall Coast Map 27

North of Port Stephens is the Myall Coast, incorporating Myall Lakes NP (see p.177), a number of coastal and inland holiday towns, long beaches and a host of thing to see and do. On the northern edge of Port Stephens are the twin towns of **Tea Gardens** and **Hawks Nest**, connected by the 'singing bridge'.

Tea Gardens/Hawks Nest is surrounded by the Pacific Ocean, Port Stephens and the Myall River and Lakes. Hawks Nest surf beach stretches 40km north and is accessible to 4WD. The area is a blue water paradise, offering fishing, swimming, sailing, surfing and diving. Wild dolphins, koalas, kangaroos, abundant birdlife and wildflowers in spring attract many visitors. Other activities include many walking tracks, bike hire, golf, bowls and tennis.

Visitors can holiday afloat by hiring a houseboat. Several companies operate from Tea Gardens, details available from the Visitor Centre. Also based at Tea Gardens is **Simba Luxury Cruises** who conduct dolphin watching and adventure cruises. Ph: (02) 4997 1084

At the northern end of Myall Lakes NP is **Seal Rocks**, a small coastal town with excellent surfing and beach fishing. Also

program covers a range of national and local art and changing exhibitions. The Gallery boasts the largest art prize in NSW. Open Tues–Fri, 10am–5pm. Ph: (02) 6543 3984. Markets are held on the 2nd Sun of the month starting at 9am at Muswellbrook Showground. Ph: (02) 6541 4050

Muswellbrook is surrounded by a number of wineries which welcome visitors and provide a convenient excuse to tour the countryside. An alternative is the **Upper Hunter Wine Centre**, 87 Hill St, which offers tastings and sales of Upper

SEAL ROCKS, TREACHERY HEAD AND SUGARLOAF PT

TOP VIEWS AND SEAFOOD

One of the best places in Newcastle to enjoy seafood and ocean views is the award-winning **Scratchley's** restaurant at Wharf Rd, Newcastle. Scratchley's was named Best BYO in NSW at the 1997 Restaurant and Catering Awards. Ph: (02) 4929 1111

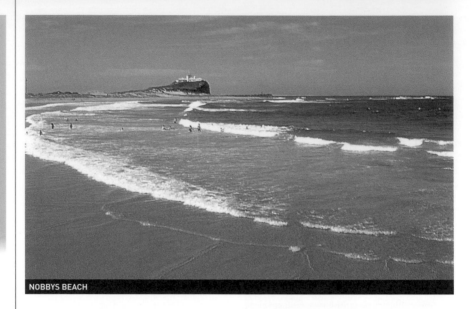

NOBBYS BEACH

of interest is Seal Rocks Lighthouse, built in 1875 and offering sweeping views with access to Lighthouse Beach. Seal Rocks also has a blowhole, and was the site of a dramatic whale rescue in 1992.

Newcastle Map 26 F5

Newcastle is Australia's 6th largest city, a leading port which has been a major centre of heavy industry for much of its life, though this is rapidly declining. With a strong heritage and a flourishing cultural life, Newcastle is emerging as an important educational centre with evident tourist potential.

The city was founded in 1804 as a penal settlement for the purposes of coal mining, lime burning, cedar cutting and salt making. From the mid-19th century, coal, and later steel, were the mainstays of the city's economy.

This early prosperity provided Newcastle with its many substantial public buildings. The **Newcastle East Heritage Walk** pamphlet, available from the Visitor Info Centre, lists sites of heritage value to the city, including **Rose Cottage**, Newcastle's oldest building (1828) and site of the Convict Barrack, and the **Boatman's Row Terraces** (1892). **Newcastle Railway Station** (I878) is one of the State's finest remaining pieces of Victorian railway architectures, while

Newcastle Post Office retains much of its original Edwardian glory. The **Customs House**, designed by colonial architect James Barnet around 1876, is particularly graceful.

The **Police Station Museum**, built in 1861, is well worth a visit. For opening times Ph: (02) 4925 2265. The venue also houses the **John Paynter Gallery** which hosts regular exhibitions. Open Fri–Sun, noon–6pm. Ph: (02) 4925 2265

Designed by Horary Hunt in 1883, **Christ Church Anglican Cathedral**, Church St, is a Newcastle landmark and has been splendidly restored following the 1989 earthquake. The nearby Roman Catholic **St Mary's Star of the Sea** (1866) is also well worth visiting.

The **Newcastle Regional Museum** is housed in the former Castlemaine Brewery cnr Wood and Hunter Sts, Newcastle West. The Museum showcases the industrial, technological and social history of the area, and features a walk-through coal mine. Within the museum is **Supernova**, a hands-on, interactive science centre. Open Tues–Sun, Mon during school and public holidays 10am–5pm. Ph: (02) 4974 1400

The **Newcastle Region Art Gallery**, Laman St, the largest provincial art gallery in Australia, displays works drawn from its vast permanent Australian collection. The Gallery often hosts major travelling exhibitions. Open Tues–Sun, 10am–5pm. Ph: (02) 4974 5100, www.newcastle.nsw.gov.au/go/artgallery

Fort Scratchley occupies a prime position on the Newcastle foreshore. Built in 1882 because of fears of a Russian invasion, the fort was not used in combat until World War II when a Japanese submarine shelled the city. The army maintained continuous occupancy of the position for 129 years — view from the outside. The **Maritime Centre**, on the waterfront at Honeysuckle Dr, will house the **Newcastle Region Maritime Museum** from late 2005.

One of the city's major attractions is **Newcastle's Famous Tram**, which leaves Newcastle Railway Station in Watt St Mon–Fri 10am–1.45pm, weekends and school holidays 10am–2pm. The tour includes an expert commentary from the driver guide. Ph: (02) 4963 7954

For those wishing to explore the modern face of Newcastle, **Queen's Wharf** is an excellent starting point. Along **Beaumont St** in Hamilton, cafes, restaurants, delis, bookshops and pubs express the city's cosmopolitan character.

Popular for picnics and BBQs is **Blackbutt Reserve**, a 182ha of parkland

and natural bushland oasis on Lookout Rd, New Lambton. The Reserve features native animals, koala encounters, a wombat exhibit, an aviary, an old miner's cottage and children's playground. Open daily, sunrise–sunset (see also p.177).

Yamuloong Bush Tucker Tours give adults and children the opportunity to learn about Aboriginal culture, lifestyle, and which fruits and berries are edible, cooking methods and more. Children can experience a variety of activities such as didgeridoo playing, Dreamtime stories, dot painting, and dance workshops. Traditional bush tucker and conventional lunches are available. Yamuloong is on the land of the Awabakal people near Charlestown. Open Mon–Fri 8.30am–4.30pm, Ph: 4943 6877. www.yamuloong.com.au

More than 200 bird species have been spotted at **The Wetlands Centre** in Sandgate Rd, Shortland, at the southern end of Hexham Swamp. Hire a canoe and paddle Ironbark Creek (7km) or follow the walking paths to see a wide variety of waterbirds, including egret colonies. In recent years, magpie geese have been successfully reintroduced to the wetlands. Once a month, a 'Breakfast with the Birds' is held (bookings

SHIPWRECK WALK

Markers along the northern breakwater of **Newcastle Harbour** at Stockton point to the graveyards of ships that foundered off Newcastle over the years.

NEWCASTLE FORESHORE

COASTAL SPLENDOURS

Newcastle's **King Edward Park** provides picnic space with delightful terraced gardens and spectacular coastal views. The bandstand is often used for concerts.

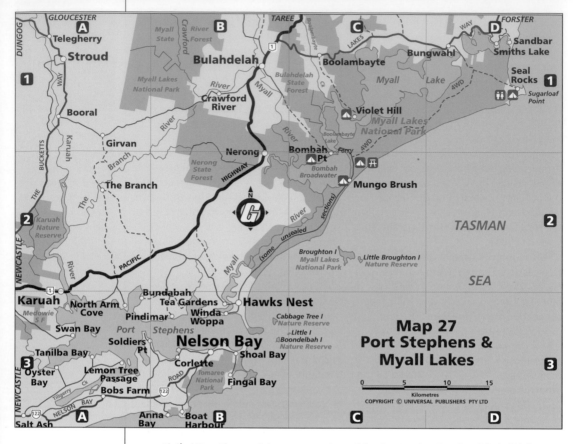

Map 27
Port Stephens &
Myall Lakes

COPYRIGHT © UNIVERSAL PUBLISHERS PTY LTD

essential). Attractive sculptures around the walking paths provide info on a wide variety of wetland habitats. The centre is an important research facility and displays relating to wetlands are located in the Visitor Centre. There is also a cafe. Open daily, 9am–5pm (extended during daylight saving). Ph: (02) 4951 6466. www.wetlands.org.au

Newcastle boasts a number of fine beaches, including **Nobbys Beach** (ideal for families) and **Newcastle Beach** with its famous Bogey Hole. Other popular Newcastle beaches are **Bar**, **Merewether** and **Dixon Park**. An interesting way to explore the coastline is by taking the **Bathers Way**, a 5km scenic walk stretching from Nobbys Headland to Glenrock Reserve.

Pokolbin Map 29 B4

The heart of the wine industry in the Hunter Valley, this small village is also well known as a centre for arts and crafts. (See the other entries in this chapter for details of Pokolbin's various attractions.)

Port Stephens Map 27

Described as 'Blue Water Paradise', Port Stephens is an expansive waterway twice the size of Sydney Harbour, whose sandy beaches and bays have proved a magnet to generations of holiday-makers.

The main town on the Tomaree Peninsula is **Nelson Bay** (towards the northern tip), with the nearby townships of **Shoal Bay**, **Fingal Bay**, **Anna Bay**, **Salamander Bay** and **Soldiers Pt** providing a wide range of accommodation and activities year round.

While much of the action happens on the waters of Port Stephens, the area has many land-based activities, including 4WD tours, golf courses, beach and bush horseriding, cycleways, tennis, and exploration of Tomaree NP (p.177). The area is also noted for its koala colonies.

Game fishing is popular and boats of all sizes are available for charter. Port

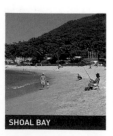

SHOAL BAY

GALAHS, FINGAL BAY

HISTORIC HOME

Tanilba House at Caswell Cres, Tanilba Bay, is a graceful old home built by convicts in 1831. Teas and lunches served. Open Wed, Sun 10.30am–4.30pm. Ph: (02) 4982 4866

Stephens hosts the largest game fishing tournament in the world each year and Nelson Bay hosts several game fishing competitions during the year. The free guide supplied by the Visitor Info Centre has full details on the various charter boats available.

The wild dolphins in Port Stephens are a major attraction and a fleet of **Dolphin Watch** cruise craft ensure visitors have ample opportunity to enjoy close encounters with the numerous bottlenose dolphins living permanently in the area. In winter and spring,

SUNSET, PORT STEPHENS

migrating whales are often sighted from lookouts around **Tomaree Head**.

Port Stephens has approx 12 cruise operators offering a great variety of cruises including dolphin watch, whale watch, Broughton Island, sunset, Myall River and Lakes, Tea Gardens, western harbour, and more. For enquiries and bookings, contact Port Stephens Visitor Info Centre.

The **Nelson Head Inner Lighthouse Reserve** is a National Trust listed complex at Little Beach, Nelson Bay which has heritage displays and a maritime museum, and shows historical films daily. Alfresco dining with great views. Wheelchair accessible. Open daily, 10am–4pm. Ph: (02) 4984 1944 and (02) 4984 2505 (cafe), www.coastalpatrol.nelsonbay.com

Tamboi Queen Cruises conduct daily dolphin watching cruises at Port Stephens. Both vessels have large boom nets that can be used in summer, and underwater hydrophones to hear the dolphins communicating with each other. A Myall River luncheon cruise is also offered. Bookings required. Ph: (02) 4981 1959

Award-winning **Moonshadow Cruises** run tours to see dolphins and whales (in season), and Broughton Island NP. Dinner cruises are also available. Ph: (02) 4984 9388. www.moonshadow.com.au

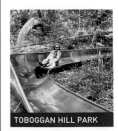

TOBOGGAN HILL PARK

WILD DOLPHINS

Imagine Cruises offer four quality ecotours on a 20m sailing catamaran equipped with boom and bow nets, hydrophone and snorkelling gear. Ph: (02) 4984 9000. www.portstephens.org.au/imagine

The **Tilligerry Habitat Information Centre**, Shop 14, Tilligerry Plaza, Tanilba Bay, runs Koala Walks twice daily 10.30am and 2.00pm along the waterfront of the Tilligerry Peninsula. Learn about and see koalas in their natural habitat. Aboriginal and settler bush culture is explained with a chance to try boomerang throwing. Bookings appreciated. Open Mon-Sat 9.30am-4pm. Sun 10am-2pm. Ph: (02) 4982 4441

The scenery and mild climate make cycling a great way of exploring the Nelson Bay area. An excellent network of cycle paths links the various communities of Port Stephens and bicycles can be hired at Nelson Bay and other locations.

The **Native Flora Garden Walk** at Fly Point meanders through forest, stopping at 15 vantage points to enjoy the wildflowers and views along the way.

At **Toboggan Hill Park**, Salamander Way, Nelson Bay, toboggans are towed up the hillside then released for a 700m downhill dash through natural bushland. Other activities include mini golf, Krazy Cars, canoe rides and indoor rock climbing. Open daily, 10am-5pm winter, 9am-6pm summer. Ph: (02) 4984 1022

At the **Oakvale Farm and Fauna World**, Salt Ash, farm and native animals roam freely about the park and baby animals are nursed and bottle-fed daily at 11am and 2pm. The park has several aviaries; activities include train rides. A kiosk and BBQ facilities are provided. Open daily, 10am-5pm. Ph: (02) 4982 6222. www.oakvalefarm.com.au

On the road to Nelson Bay from Newcastle at the RAAF's Williamtown base is **Fighter World**, a display centre for military fighter aircraft. The exhibit traces the history of the RAAF's fighter squadrons. Open daily, 10am-4pm. Ph: (02) 4965 1717

Horse Paradise at Nelson Bay Rd, Williamtown, offers a 'beach and bush'

canter along the 32km Stockton Beach. Open daily by appt. Ph: (02) 4965 1877, www.users.bigpond.com/horseparadise

Raymond Terrace Map 26 E4

Straddling the Pacific Hwy north of Newcastle, Raymond Terrace is located at the junction of the Hunter and Williams Rivers. In the 19th century it was a major river port used by woolgrowers and an access point for travel to the New England Tablelands.

A number of fine old sandstone buildings from the town's most prosperous era still remain and a walking guide is available from the Raymond Terrace Public Library.

Sketchley Cottage, a timber slab colonial homestead built in the late 1850s, was originally located near the Williams River. In the 1970s the house was moved to a site near the Pacific Hwy at Raymond Terrace and restored by the historical society. A separate museum was added in 1988. Open Sun, 10am-4pm.

St John's Church was designed by Edmund Blacket in Gothic style and built of Muree sandstone. It was consecrated in 1862 and its bell is from the ship *Ceres*, wrecked off Norah Head in 1835.

Off Tomago Rd, north of Hexham, lies **Tomago House**, a National Trust property built in 1843 for Sydney barrister Richard Windeyer's agricultural holdings in the area. The house is built of

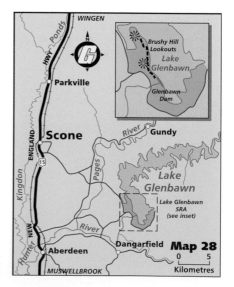

Map 28

SEGENHOE STUD FARM, SCONE

fine Muree sandstone with superb cedar joinery that has been fully restored. The family chapel dates from 1861. Light refreshments available. Open Sun, 11am–3pm. Ph: (02) 4964 8123

Scone Map 26 C1

Set in the rolling upper Hunter countryside, Scone calls itself the 'Horse Capital of Australia' because of the outstanding thoroughbred and stock horse studs in the area, second only to Kentucky, USA. There is a bronze mare and foal statue in **Elizabeth Park**, and regular race meetings are held at the **Scone Equine Complex**. For those interested in working horses, the **Australian Stock Horse Museum** in Kelly St is the national headquarters for the Australian Stock Horse Society (open Mon–Fri).

Scone's **Historical Society Museum**, originally the town lock-up and with two of the old prison cells still out the back, documents the history of the Scone district. Open Sun 2.30–4.30pm and Wed 9.30am–3pm. Ph: (02) 6545 1598

Scone's heritage can also be appreciated on an historic walk — leaflet available from Scone Visitor Info Centre. Plane buffs will enjoy **Pay's Flying Museum**, with a private collection of rare war planes including an early model Spitfire. By appt only, Ph: (02) 6545 1166

Lake Glenbawn SP is on the shores of Lake Glenbawn, 12km east of Scone and is the largest waterway of the Upper Hunter. The lake area provides watersports, bushwalking (see Map 28), golf, tennis courts, fishing (catfish, bass, golden perch, trout), kiosk, picnic and BBQ facilities, camping areas and cabins. Ph: (02) 6543 7193

Scone also has two designated tourist drives, one to Singleton via Merriwa taking in the Upper Hunter wineries, and the other to Gloucester via Moonan Flat and into the Barringtons. For details on

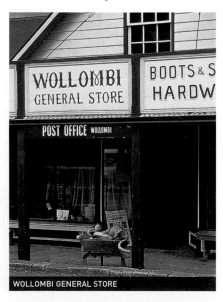
WOLLOMBI GENERAL STORE

WINEMAKING
EQUIPMENT

these and shorter drives, contact Scone Visitor Info Centre. Ph: (02) 6545 1526

Singleton Map 26 D3

At the geographic heart of the Hunter Valley, Singleton is on the Hunter River, surrounded by fertile land. Coal mining has joined the traditional local pastoral industry and the town provides a service centre for both. The town's architectural development can be enjoyed on the **Town Walk** that begins at the Singleton **Historical Museum**; leaflet available from the Visitor Info Centre. The town boasts an enormous sundial, one of the largest in the southern hemisphere.

Other interesting in Singleton attractions include the **Royal Australian Infantry Corps Museum of Small Arms** at the Singleton Military area, open Wed–Sun 9am–4pm Ph: (02) 6570 3257. About 30km north, **Lake St Clair** provides many recreational opportunities. For more info contact Hunter Heartland Visitor Info Centre Ph: (02) 6571 5888. www.hunterheartland.com.au

Wollombi Map 26 C5

Once a thriving town with four inns and two schools, Wollombi was first settled by Europeans in the 1830s after the completion of the Great North Rd by convict labour. For the scenic route to Wollombi, take the Peats Ridge turnoff from the F3 Fwy and follow the road to this gateway to the Hunter wine country.

Sandstone buildings dominate this pretty village's main street in much the same way they would have in the 1800s. The quaint **General Store**, built in the late 1800s, has information about local attractions and activities as well as accommodation details. Open Mon–Fri 8am–6pm weekends 8am–7pm, Ph: (02) 4998 3230

The **Endeavour Museum** is the centrepiece of Wollombi and showcases the town's strong links with the past. It is housed in the former Wollombi Court House which dates from 1866. Open daily, 10am–1pm.

Wollombi Cottage occupies an 1840s slab-style building in the main street and sells antiques, handcrafts and gifts. Open daily 10am–4pm. Ph: (02) 4998 3340

Stapleton Station offers morning and afternoon horse trail rides on the station's 120ha of rolling countryside. Gentle and obedient horses and small rides make this an enjoyable experience. Catering to both beginners and experienced riders. Ph: (02) 4998 8408. www.stapletonstation.com.au

There are a number of guesthouses and cottages, all of which are listed in the *Hunter Valley Wine Country Visitors Guide*, available from the Cessnock Visitor Info Centre.

VINEYARDS, HUNTER VALLEY

MYALL LAKES

The **Koolang Observatory** at Bucketty, 23km south of Wollombi, is a user-friendly astronomical observatory. Nestled in bushland, it features telescopes, binoculars, space science displays and guided tours of the night skies. Open daily and nightly. Bookings essential. Ph: (02) 4998 8216

National Parks, State Recreation Areas and Reserves

Barrington Tops NP Map 26 E1

Ranging from almost sea level to 1568m, the Barrington Tops NP landscape varies widely. The Park lies to the north of the Hunter region, and is accessed from towns such as **Dungog**, **Gloucester** and **Scone**. Covering 74 000ha, much of the Park is protected wilderness and all of it has a World Heritage Area listing. It contains part of a mountain range separating the Upper Hunter River valley from the Manning River valley. The rugged landscape encompasses wild rivers, swamps, tall open forests and rainforest, part of the World Heritage-listed rainforests of eastern Australia.

A number of threatened animal species find refuge in the park, which provides excellent bushwalking, trout fishing, swimming, liloing, 4WD trails and camping in designated areas. The state forests bordering the park add to the recreational opportunities. Ph: (02) 4984 8200

Goulburn River NP Map 26 A2

Located between **Mudgee** and **Sandy Hollow**, Goulburn River NP conserves 70 000ha of dissected sandstone country bordering a 90km stretch of the Goulburn River. The park's sandstone country provides shelter from the heavily cultivated surrounding areas, harbouring a unique and varied mixture of plants and animals.

The main feature of the park is the river, meandering through a valley surrounded by a sandstone plateau, with many caves along its length. Another outstanding feature is the number of **Aboriginal sites** within the park, such as stencils, paintings and axe-grinding grooves. Activities and facilities in the park include bushwalking, picnic sites, camping, photography, swimming and liloing in the river. There is plenty of opportunity to spot the abundant wildlife, including kangaroos, wallabies, wallaroos, emus, wedge-tailed eagles and lyrebirds Ph: (02) 6543 3533 (Muswellbrook) or (02) 6372 7199 (Mudgee).

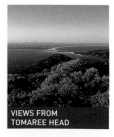

VIEWS FROM TOMAREE HEAD

Lower Hunter wineries

Wineries of the Hunter

Centred on the **Pokolbin** region, the wineries range in size from small family operations to very large complexes with outstanding tourist facilities. Check at the **Hunter Valley Wine Country Visitor Centre** (p.159) on (02) 4990 0900 for any changes to this list.

NAME	MAP 29	ADDRESS	PHONE	OPEN
Allandale Winery	D4	Lovedale Rd, Lovedale	(02) 4990 4526	9am–5pm Mon–Sat, 10am–5pm, Sun
Allanmere Wines	B3	@ First Creek Wine Centre cnr McDonalds & Gillards Rds	(02) 4998 7293	9am–5pm Mon–Fri, 9.30am–5pm weekends
Apthorpe Estate	D3	Lot 1073 Lovedale Rd, Lovedale	(02) 4930 9177	10am–5pm weekends, Mon and Fri 10am–4pm
Audrey Wilkinson Vineyard	A4	DeBeyers Rd, Pokolbin	(02) 4998 7411	9am–5pm Mon–Fri, 9.30am–5pm, weekends
Bellona Estate	B2	Lot 1 Old North Rd, North Rothbury	(02) 4938 3484	10am–5pm weekends and public holidays
Bimbadgen Estate	B3	Lot 21, McDonalds Rd, Pokolbin	(02) 4998 7585	10am–5pm daily
Blueberry Hill Vineyard	B2	cnr McDonalds & Coulson Rds, Pokolbin	(02) 4998 7295	10am–5pm daily
Briar Ridge Vineyard	B6	Mt View Rd, Mt View	(02) 4990 3670	10am–5pm daily
Brokenwood Wines	B4	McDonalds Rd, Pokolbin	(02) 4998 7559	10am–5pm daily
Calais Estate	C3	Palmers La, Pokolbin	(02) 4998 7654	9am–5pm daily
Capercaillie Wine Co.	D4	Londons Rd, Lovedale	(02) 4990 2904	9am–5pm Mon-Sat, 10am–5pm, Sun
Carindale Wines	C3	Palmers La, Pokolbin	(02) 4998 7665	10am–5pm Wed–Mon
Constable & Hershon Vineyards	B3	1 Gillards Rd, Pokolbin	(02) 4998 7887	10am–5pm daily
Cooper Wines	D3	Lovedale Rd, Lovedale	(02) 4930 7387	10am–5pm daily
De Bortoli Wines	C4	Branxton Rd, Pokolbin	(02) 4993 8800	10am–5pm daily
De Luliius Wines	A3	Lot 21 Broke Rd, Pokolbin	(02) 4993 8000	10am–5pm daily
Drayton's Family Wines	B5	Oakey Creek Rd, Pokolbin	(02) 4998 7513	8am–5pm Mon–Fri, 10am–5pm weekends
Emma's Cottage Vineyard	C3	Wilderness Rd, Lovedale	(02) 4998 7734	10am–5pm Fri–Mon, other times by appt
Evans Family Wines & Antiques	B4	Broke Rd, Pokolbin	(02) 4998 7237	10am–5pm daily
Farrells Limestone Creek Vineyard	B6	Mt View Rd, Mt View	(02) 4991 2808	10am–5pm daily
Gabriel's Paddocks Vineyard	B2	Deasys Rd, Pokolbin	(02) 4998 7650	10am–5pm Fri–Mon and Wed
Gartelmann Hunter Estate	D3	Lovedale Rd, Lovedale	(02) 4930 7113	10am–5pm daily
Golden Grape Estate	B5	Oakey Creek Rd, Pokolbin	(02) 4998 7588	10am–5pm, daily
Hardys Hunter Ridge	A2	Hermitage Rd, Pokolbin	(02) 4998 7500	9.30am–5pm daily
Hermitage Hunter Estate Winery	A2	Hermitage Rd, Pokolbin	(02) 4998 7521	10am–5pm daily
Hermitage Road Cellars	A2	@ Hunter Resort Country Estate, Hermitage Rd, Pokolbin	(02) 4998 7777	9am–5pm daily
Honeytree Estate Wines	B3	16 Gillards Rd, Pokolbin	(02) 4998 7693	10am–5pm weekends, Wed–Thur 11am–4pm, other times by appt

Lower Hunter wineries (cont.)

NAME	MAP 29	ADDRESS	PHONE	OPEN
Hungerford Hill Wines	A5	1 Broke Rd, Pokolbin	(02) 4998 7666	9am–5pm Mon–Fri, 10am–5pm weekends and public holidays
Hunter Valley Wine Society	C4	Cnr Broke and Branxton Rds, Pokolbin	1300 303 307	8.30am–8.30pm Mon–Fri, 10am–2.30pm weekends
Iron Gate Estate	B5	Oakey Creek Road, Pokolbin	(02) 4998 6570	10am–4pm daily
Ivanhoe Wines	A5	Marrowbone Rd, Pokolbin	(02) 4998 7325	10am–5pm daily
Jackson's Hill Vineyard	B5	Mt View Rd, Mt View	(02) 4990 1273	10am–5pm Thurs–Mon and public holidays
J.Y.T. Wine Co	A4	DeBeyers Rd, Pokolbin	(02) 4998 7528	10am–5pm Thur–Tues
Kelman Vineyard	C5	cnr Marrowbone, Oakey Creek & Mount View Rds, Pokolbin	(02) 4991 5456	10am–5pm Thur–Mon other times by appt
Kevin Sobels Wines	B4	Broke Rd, Pokolbin	(02) 4998 7766	9am–5pm daily
Kulkunbulla's Brokenback Estate	A3	1595 Broke Rd, Pokolbin	(02) 4998 7140	9am–5pm daily
Lakes Folly Vineyard	C4	Broke Rd, Pokolbin	(02) 4998 7507	10am–4pm Mon–Sat when wine available
Lindemans Wines	A4	McDonalds Rd, Pokolbin	(02) 4998 7501	9am–4.30pm Mon–Fri, 10am–4.30pm weekends
Little's Winery	B3	Lot 3, Palmers La, Pokolbin	(02) 4998 7626	10am–4.30pm daily
Lowe Family Wine Company	A4	cnr Broke & Ekerts Rds, Pokolbin	(02) 4998 7121	10am–5pm Wed–Mon
McGuigan Cellars	B4	McDonalds Rd, Pokolbin	(02) 4998 7402	10am–5pm daily
McLeish Estate	B4	Lot 3, DeBeyers Rd, Pokolbin	(02) 4998 7754	10am–5pm Fri–Mon
McWilliams Mt Pleasant	B5	Marrowbone Rd, Pokolbin	(02) 4998 7505	10am–4.30pm daily
Madigan Vineyard	C2	Lot 1 Wilderness Rd, Rothbury	(02) 4998 7815	11am–5pm weekends,
Margan Family Winegrowers	A1	266 Hermitage Rd, Pokolbin	(02) 6574 7004	10am–5pm daily
Marsh Estate	A2	95 Deasys Rd, Pokolbin	(02) 4998 7587	10am–5pm daily
Mistletoe Wines, Pokolbin Gallery, Mistletoe Sculpture Garden	A2	771 Hermitage Rd, Pokolbin	(02) 4998 7770	10am–6pm daily
Molly Morgan Vineyard	C2	Talga Rd, Rothbury	(02) 4930 7695	10am–4pm weekends
Moorebank Private Vineyard	C3	Palmers La, Pokolbin	(02) 4998 7610	10am–5pm Fri–Tues, or by appt
Mount View Estate	B5	Mt View Rd, Mt View	(02) 4990 3307	9am–5pm daily
Oakvale Winery	A3	Broke Rd, Pokolbin	(02) 4998 7520	10am–5pm daily
Peacock Hill Vineyard	C3	Palmers La, Pokolbin	(02) 4998 7661	10am–5pm Fri–Mon, plus public & school holidays
Pendarves Estate	A1	110 Old North Rd, Belford	(02) 6674 7222	11am–5pm weekends
Peppers Creek	A3	Broke Rd, Pokolbin	(02) 4998 7532	10am–5pm daily
Pepper Tree Wines	B4	Halls Rd, Pokolbin	(02) 4998 7539	9am–5pm Mon–Fri, 9.30am–5pm weekends
Peterson's Champagne House	C4	Broke Rd, Pokolbin	(02) 4998 7881	9am–5pm daily
Peterson Wines	B6	Mt View Rd, Mt View	(02) 4990 1704	9am–5pm Mon–Sat, 10am–5pm, Sun

Lower Hunter wineries

NAME	MAP 29	ADDRESS	PHONE	OPEN
Piggs Peake Winery	A2	697 Hermitage Rd, Pokolbin	(02) 6574 7000	10am–5pm daily (and 6pm during summer)
Pokolbin Estate Vineyard	B4	McDonalds Rd, Pokolbin	(02) 4998 7524	10am–6pm daily
Reg Drayton Wines	A5	Cnr McDonalds and Pokolbin Mountain Rd, Pokolbin	(02) 4998 7523	10am–5pm daily
Roche Wines	B4	@ Tempus Two , cnr Broke & McDonalds Rds, Pokolbin	(02) 4993 3999	10am–5pm daily
Rothbury Estate	B3	Broke Rd, Pokolbin	(02) 4998 7555	9.30am–4.30pm daily
Rothbury Ridge Wines	D2	171 Talga Rd, Rothbury	(02) 4930 7122	10am–5pm daily
Rothvale Vineyard & Winery	B2	Deasys Rd, Pokolbin	(02) 4998 7290	10am–5pm daily
Saddlers Creek Winery	B5	Marrowbone Rd, Pokolbin	(02) 4991 1770	10am–5pm daily
Sandalyn Estate	D2	Wilderness Rd, Rothbury	(02) 4930 7611	10am–5pm daily
Scarborough Wine Company	B3	Gillards Rd, Pokolbin	(02) 4998 7563	9am–5pm daily
Serenella Estate	A3	Hermitage Rd, Pokolbin	(02) 4998 7992	10am–5pm Mon–Fri, 10am–4pm, weekends
Small Winemakers Centre	B4	McDonalds Rd, Pokolbin	(02) 4998 7668	10am–5pm daily
Sovereign Hill Vineyard	C2	370 Talga Rd, Lovedale	(02) 4930 7755	10am–5pm daily
Tallavera Grove	B6	Mount View Rd, Mount View	(02) 4990 7535	10am–5pm Fri–Mon, other times by appt
Tamburlaine	B4	McDonalds Rd, Pokolbin	(02) 4998 7570	9.30am–5pm daily
Tatler Wines	D3	477 Lovedale Rd, Lovedale	(02) 4930 9139	10am–6pm daily
Tempus Two	B4	cnr Broke & McDonalds Rds, Pokolbin	(02) 4993 3999	10am–5pm daily
Terrace Vale Wines	A2	Deaseys Rd, Pokolbin	(02) 4998 7517	10am–4pm daily
Thalgara Estate	B4	DeBeyers Rd, Pokolbin	(02) 4998 7717	10am–4.30pm daily
Tinklers Vineyard	A5	Pokolbin Mountains Rd, Pokolbin	(02) 4998 7435	9am–5pm daily
Tintilla Estate Vineyard & Olive Grove	A2	725 Hermitage Rd, Pokolbin	(02) 6574 7093	10.30–5.30 daily
Tower Estate Wines	B4	cnr Halls & Broke Rds, Pokolbin	(02) 4998 7989	10am–5pm Mon–Sun
Tulloch Wines	B4	DeBeyers Rd, Pokolbin	(02) 4998 7580	9.30am–5pm daily
Tyrrells Vineyards	A3	Broke Rd, Pokolbin	(02) 4993 7000	9am–5pm Mon–Sat
Van De Scheur Wines	B5	O'Connor Lane, Pokolbin	(02) 4998 7789	10am–5pm daily
Vinden Estate Wines	B3	17 Gillards Rd, Pokolbin	(02) 4998 7410	10am–5pm daily
Wandin Valley Estate	D2	Wilderness Rd, Lovedale	(02) 4930 7317	10am–5pm daily
Warraroong Estate and Vineyard	D3	Wilderness Rd, Rothbury	(02) 4930 7594	10am–5pm Thur–Mon, other times by appt
Wilderness Estate	C4	Branxton Rd, Pokolbin	(02) 4998 7755	9am–5pm daily
Windarra Winery & Pottery	B4	DeBeyers Rd, Pokolbin	(02) 4998 7648	10am–4pm Tues–Sun and public holidays
Windsor's Edge Wines	B2	McDonalds Rd, Pokolbin	(02) 4998 7341	10am–5pm weekends, Mon–Fri by appt
Wright Family Wines	B2	Deasys Rd, Pokolbin	(02) 4998 7781	10am–5pm daily
Wyndham Estate (off map)		700 Dalwood Rd, Dalwood via Branxton	(02) 4938 3444	10am–4.30pm daily

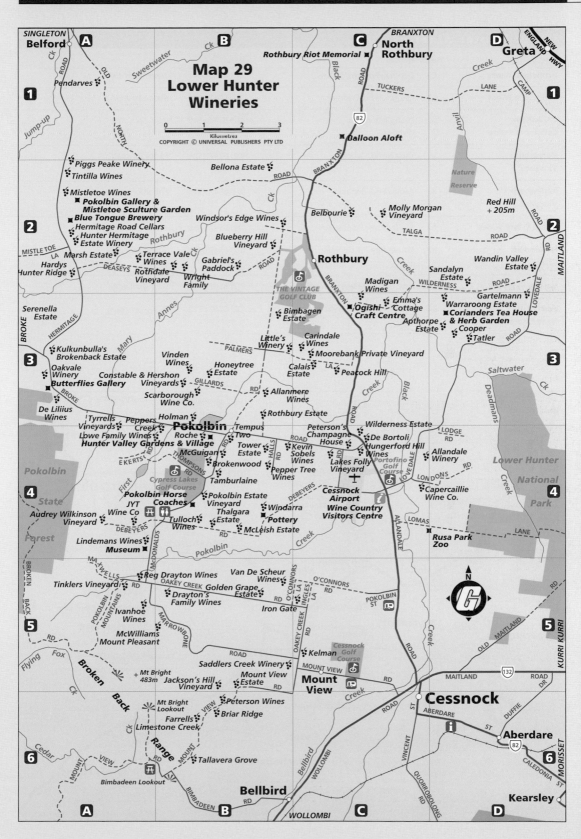

Map 29
Lower Hunter
Wineries

0   1   2   3
Kilometres
COPYRIGHT © UNIVERSAL PUBLISHERS PTY LTD

SINGLETON
Belford
Pendarves
Piggs Peake Winery
Tintilla Wines
Mistletoe Wines
Pokolbin Gallery &
Mistletoe Sculture Garden
Blue Tongue Brewery
Hermitage Road Cellars
Hunter Hermitage
Estate Winery
Marsh Estate
Hardys
Hunter Ridge
Terrace Vale
Wines
Rothdale
Vineyard
Wright
Family
Gabriel's
Paddock
Windsor's Edge Wines
Blueberry Hill
Vineyard
Bellona Estate
Rothbury Riot Memorial

BRANXTON
North
Rothbury
Greta
NEW ENGLAND HWY

Dalloon Aloft
Belbourie
Molly Morgan
Vineyard
Red Hill
+ 205m
Nature
Reserve
Wandin Valley
Estate
Sandalyn
Estate
Gartelmann
Warraroong Estate
Corianders Tea House
& Herb Garden
Cooper
Tatler
Apthorpe
Estate
Emma's
Cottage
Madigan
Wines
Ogishi
Craft Centre
Rothbury
THE VINTAGE
GOLF CLUB
Bimbagen
Estate
Little's
Winery
Carindale
Wines
Moorebank Private Vineyard
Peacock Hill
Calais
Estate
Serenella
Estate
Kulkunbulla's
Brokenback Estate
Oakvale
Winery
Butterflies Gallery
De Liliius
Wines
Vinden
Wines
Constable & Hershon
Vineyards
Scarborough
Wine Co.
Honeytree
Estate
Allanmere
Wines
Rothbury Estate
Wilderness Estate
Peterson's
Champagne
House
Tyrrells
Vineyards
Peppers
Creek
Holman
Lowe Family Wines
Hunter Valley Gardens & Village
Pokolbin
Tempus
Two
Roche
Tower
Estate
Brokenwood
McGuigan
Tamburlaine
Kevin
Sobels
Wines
Pepper Tree
Wines
Lakes Folly
Vineyard
De Bortoli
Hungerford Hill
Wines
Allandale
Winery
Cypress Lakes
Golf Course
Pokolbin Horse
Coaches
JYT
Wine Co
Pokolbin Estate
Vineyard
Thalgara
Estate
Tulloch
Wines
McLeish Estate
Windarra
Pottery
Capercaillie
Wine Co.
Audrey Wilkinson
Vineyard
Lindemans Wines
Museum
Cessnock
Airport
Wine Country
Visitors Centre
Portofino
Golf Course
Rusa Park
Zoo
Reg Drayton Wines
Tinklers Vineyard
Golden Grape
Estate
Van De Scheur
Wines
Drayton's
Family Wines
Iron Gate
Ivanhoe
Wines
McWilliams
Mount Pleasant
Kelman
Cessnock
Golf
Course
Saddlers Creek Winery
Mt Bright
483m
Jackson's Hill
Vineyard
Mount View
Estate
Mount
View
Cessnock
Mt Bright
Lookout
Peterson Wines
Briar Ridge
Aberdare
Farrells
Limestone Creek
Tallavera Grove
Bimbadeen Lookout
Bellbird
Kearsley
WOLLOMBI

Lower Hunter
National
Park
Pokolbin
State
Forest
Broken
Back
Range

Pokolbin
Mountains

Upper Hunter wineries

NAME	MAP 30	ADDRESS	PHONE	OPEN
Arrowfield Wines	C3	Denman Rd, Jerry's Plains	(02) 6576 4041	10am–5pm daily
Bell's Lane Wines	C2	Mangoola Rd, Denman	(02) 6547 1191	Phone for appt
Cruikshank Callatoota Estate	B1	2656 Wybong Rd, Wybong	(02) 6547 8149	9am–5pm daily
Horseshoe Vineyard	B3	Yarrawa Rd, Denman	(02) 6547 3528	Phone for appt
Inglewood Vineyard	B2	Yarrawa Rd, Denman	(02) 6547 2556	Phone for appt
James Estate Wines	A2	951 Rylstone Rd, Baerami	(02) 6547 5168	10am–4pm daily
Rosemount Estate	B2	Rosemount Rd, Denman	(02) 6549 6400	10am–4pm daily
Verona Vineyard	D1	New England Hwy, Muswellbrook	(02) 6541 4777	9am–5pm daily
Yarraman Road Estate	B1	700 Yarraman Rd, Wybong	(02) 6547 8118	10am–5pm daily

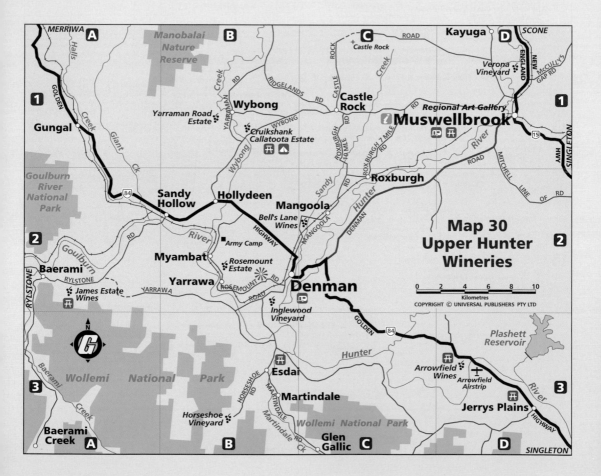

Thanksgiving Festival

While drinking wine might be one of life's little pleasures, harvesting the grapes that produce it is definitely a serious business. Throughout the Hunter Valley, the harvest season usually concludes in mid-Apr each year. As the weary workers reach the end of the crop, their thoughts turn to celebration.

Visitors to the valley can join in the end of harvest fun by participating in the Hunter Valley Thanksgiving Festival. Leading wineries toast a (hopefully) bumper crop with a variety of banquets, lunches and dinners as well as more traditional activities like barrel tastings, art exhibition and live music. The festival is a perfect opportunity to experience wine country culture, tradition and bounty.

Hunter Region Tourism, Ph: (02) 4990 4477

Lake Macquarie SCA Map 31

This 667ha conservation area on Lake Macquarie features coastal and lake shore forests. It offers magnificent views of the lake, Watagan Ranges and the Pacific Ocean. There are walking, fishing and boating opportunities. At Wangi Point Tourist Park car-based and caravan camping is available and there are on-site cabins. Tourist Park open daily, bookings essential, Ph: (02) 4972 1172

Myall Lakes NP Map 27 C1

This large (47 493ha) park is dominated by Myall Lakes, one of the state's largest network of coastal lakes. Also protected here is **Broughton Island**, 40km of beaches and a range of native flora and fauna. Much of the recreation at Myall Lakes NP is water-based, embracing windsurfing, fishing, boating and canoeing in the calm lakes, with surfing and beach fishing across the dunes. Scuba diving is also popular around Seal Rocks, Broughton Island and Little Gibber.

On land, walks criss-cross the park, ranging from the 30min Mungo Brush Rainforest Walking Track, to the 21km Mungo Track from Mungo Brush to Hawks Nest. There are also beach access routes for 4WD vehicles, and car-based camping areas. Ph: (02) 4984 8200 (Nelson Bay), (02) 6591 0300 (Pacific Palms).

Pulbah Island
Nature Reserve Map 31

The 70ha reserve is situated in the southern section of Lake Macquarie.

Sugar gliders and goannas thrive in the dry eucalypt forest which makes up most of the island's vegetation. Access by charter or hire boat. Ph: (02) 4972 1172

Tomaree NP Map 27 B3

Tomaree NP's 2347ha offers golden beaches, forests and heathlands full of wildflowers. Surfing, swimming and sunbathing are all popular in this park; and a nudist beach at Samurai allows visitors to get an all-over tan. There are several walking tracks, including a pretty one through forest and heathland to Tomaree headland which provides panoramic views of Port Stephens. Ph: (02) 4981 1579

Yengo NP and Parr SRA Map 26

Linking the Hawkesbury River with the Hunter Valley, Yengo NP and Parr SRA cover over 190 000ha of rugged sandstone country, rainforest, tall open forest, open woodlands and swampland.

The terrain in Yengo NP is often rugged, but camping, birdwatching, bushwalking, canoeing and cycling are all possible. Ph: (02) 4320 4280

Parks and gardens
Blackbutt Flora and Fauna Reserve

This 182ha bushland reserve is Newcastle's most popular recreational park. Visitors can picnic with native Australian animals and birds and take walking trails through natural bushland ranging from native eucalypts to ferns and rainforest trees.

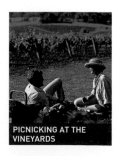
PICNICKING AT THE VINEYARDS

Gardens of the Hunter

At **Constable & Hershon Vineyards** in Gillards Rd, **Pokolbin** this series of beautifully maintained gardens include a sculpture garden, traditional English rose garden, knot and herb garden, secret garden and wisteria walk. Visitors are welcome to stroll around the gardens or take an organised tour which begins 10.30am Mon–Fri. Ph: (02) 4998 7887

Historic garden tours

Many historic houses in **Maitland** and **Morpeth** boast well restored period gardens. The Maitland Visitor Info Centre organises weekend garden rambles. Enquire at other tourist centres in the region about public access to their historic gardens.

Hunter Region Botanic Gardens

The Hunter Region Botanic Gardens are located on the Pacific Hwy 4km north of the Hexham Bridge. They have the region's largest dedicated flora display, and garden lovers, particularly those with an interest in cottage or heritage gardens, are well catered for. There are theme areas, including acacias, proteas, banksias, grevilleas, bush tucker plants and more. Easy walking trails lead through natural bushland. The grounds house a Visitor Centre and reference library, cafe, gift shop and several pleasant picnic areas. Open daily,

QUAD BIKES, STOCKTON BEACH

10am–4pm. Ph: (02) 4987 1655. www.huntergardens.org.au

Other attractions

Butterflies Gallery Map 29 B4

At **Pokolbin**, the Butterflies Gallery on Broke Rd has changing exhibitions of contemporary and traditional Australian art, as well as affordable hand-crafted gifts and lovely garden cafe. The gallery is an interesting diversion when touring the local wineries. Open daily, 10am–5pm. Ph: (02) 4998 7724

Hunter Valley Horse Coach Tours Map 29 B4

Hunter Valley Wine and Dine Carriages, 48 Pokolbin St, Kearsley, take visitors on leisurely horse-drawn carriage tours to sample the best food and wine the Hunter Valley has to offer. Bookings Ph: 0410 515 358. This company also offers **Pokolbin Trail Rides**, suitable for experienced and novice riders, bookings Ph: 0411 110 126. www.huntervalleycarriages.com.au **Pokolbin Horse Coach Tours** leads wine appreciation tours around some of the best Hunter Valley countryside, with frequent stops at wineries for tastings and explanations of the winemaking process. Ph: (02) 4998 7305

Recreational activities

Action

Sand Safaris, an award-winning tourism company, offers several thrilling adventure tours of the largest moving

---

Fun for the young

★ Quad bike riding and sandboarding on Stockton Dunes, (p.178–79)

★ Eastern Precinct Childrens Heritage Walk, Maitland (p.160)

★ Fishing at Myall Lakes (p.163) or Lake Macquarie (p.160)

★ Newcastle's Famous Tram (p.165)

★ Rusa Park Zoo (p.159)

★ The Wetlands Centre (p.165)

★ Teddy Bears Downstairs, Morpeth (p.162)

★ Toboggan Hill Park, Nelson Bay (p.168)

sand mass in the southern hemisphere. Ride a quad bike or sandboard down the dunes at Stockton Dunes, go beach fishing or join a 4WD safari for an unforgettable experience. Ph: (02) 4965 0215, www.sandsafaris.com.au

Cycling

An extensive network of well maintained cycle paths are a feature of the **Newcastle** and **Port Stephens** areas. One of the most pleasant ways of taking in the sights of Newcastle is to take advantage of the city's cycle paths.

The Newcastle Network runs for 30km and takes in the Newcastle City Centre and surrounds. It begins at **Newcastle Beach**, and depending on the route chosen, takes the rider past **Newcastle University**, the **International Sports Centre** and both the **Newcastle** and **Merewether Golf Links**.

The Hunter Region is a fantastic destination for cycling; contact local Visitor Info Centre for more info and detailed ride maps. www.huntertourism.com/cycle

Golfing

Pokolbin's superbly located **Cypress Lakes Resort** offers an international standard golf course, as well as stunning views of the Hunter's vineyards and the magnificent Brokenback Ranges. With its dual fairway, the course caters for novices as well as experienced golfers.

After the game, golfers can enjoy the relaxing atmosphere of the restaurant and lounge, with log fires in winter and decks, terraces and gardens for outside dining in summer. Ph: (02) 4993 1555. www.cypresslakes.com.au

In the air

Take a tandem hang glider flight or a course to learn it by yourself with **Air Sports** Ph: 0412 607 815. www.air-sports.com.au

Action Aerobatics offers a unique opportunity to ride in a classic open cockpit biplane, taking in superb wine country views. Gentle scenic flights or thrilling aerobatics are available. Take-off is at Maitland Airport. Ph: 0408 474 307. www.aerobatics.com.au

For a birdseye view of the wine country, **Balloon Aloft** are located just south of Branxton in Main Rd, North Rothbury. They operate a series of hot air balloon flights including popular sunrise flights followed by a champagne celebration, weather permitting. Ph: (02) 4938 1955. www.balloonaloft.com

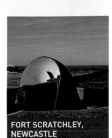
FORT SCRATCHLEY, NEWCASTLE

TEA GARDENS, MYALL LAKES NP

Places of interest
(Family fun tour)

❶ Fighter World, Williamtown (p.168)

❷ Tanilba House (p.181)

❸ Oakvale Farm and Fauna World, Salt Ash (p.168)

❹ Toboggan Hill Park (p.168)

❺ Dolphin Watch Cruise, Nelson Bay (p.167)

❻ Inner Lighthouse (p.167)

❼ Tomaree NP (p.177)

❽ Anna Bay (p.166)

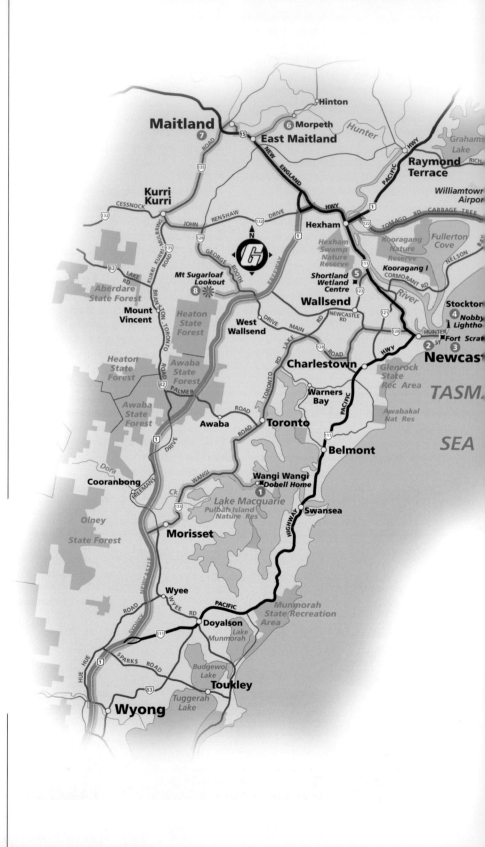

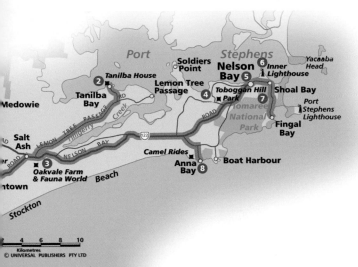

Port Stephens

Soldiers Point
Tanilba House ❷
Nelson Bay ❺
❻ Inner Lighthouse
Yacaaba Head
Lemon Tree Passage
Tanilba Bay
Medowie
Toboggan Hill Park ❹
Shoal Bay
Tomaree National Park
Port Stephens Lighthouse
Fingal Bay
Salt Ash
Camel Rides
Oakvale Farm & Fauna World ❸
Anna Bay ❽
Boat Harbour
Beach
ntown
Stockton

2 4 6 8 10
Kilometres
© UNIVERSAL PUBLISHERS PTY LTD

Map 31

Places of interest (Heritage and views)

❶ Dobell Home, Wangi Wangi (p.160)
❷ Newcastle East Heritage Walk (p.164)
❸ Fort Scratchley (p.165)
❹ Nobbys Lighthouse (p.164)
❺ The Wetlands Centre (Shortland) (p.165)
❻ Morpeth (p.162)
❼ Maitland (p.160)
❽ Mt Sugarloaf Lookout

Suggested tours – Map 31

Heritage and views tour

Approximate distance

110km from Sydney CBD to Morisset Interchange; round trip tour from Morisset Interchange — 160km

About the tour

Begin your tour on the shores of Lake Macquarie before exploring some of the historic and natural highlights of Newcastle. At The Wetlands Centre in Shortland you can venture out in a canoe, then drive further inland to enjoy the heritage and crafts on offer at Maitland and Morpeth. On the scenic return trip to Sydney, stop off at Mt Sugarloaf for breathtaking views.

Family fun tour

Approximate distance

170km from Sydney CBD to Hexham; round trip tour from Hexham — 160km

About the tour

There is something for all the family in this tour which explores the Port Stephens area of the Hunter region. From the high-speed jets of Fighter World, travel back in time at historic Tanilba House, then drop in at Oakvale on the way to Nelson Bay. Top off your action-packed visit with a ride on a quad bike, 4WD or sandboard on the dunes at Stockton Beach.

HISTORIC BUILDINGS, MORPETH

Must see, must do

★ Echo Pt, Katoomba (p.196)
★ Great Zig Zag Railway, Lithgow (pp.191–92)
★ Jenolan Caves (p.191)
★ Leura (p.198)
★ Megalong Valley (p.192)
★ Norman Lindsay Gallery, Faulconbridge (p.194)

Radio stations

Lithgow
2LT: AM 900
KISS FM: FM 95.3
Blue Mountains
2WS: FM 101.7
1 FM: FM 96.1
2BLU FM: FM 89.1
Tourist Radio: FM 87.7

Tourist information

**Blue Mountains
Tourism Authority
Echo Pt Visitor
Information Centre**
Echo Pt Rd, Katoomba 2780

**Glenbrook Visitor
Information Centre**
Great Western Hwy,
Glenbrook 2773
Ph: 1300 653 408

**Lithgow Visitor
Information Centre**
Great Western Hwy, Lithgow 2790
Ph: (02) 6353 1859

**National Parks and Wildlife
Heritage Centre**
Govetts Leap Rd, Blackheath 2785
Ph: (02) 4787 8877

Websites
www.visitnsw.com.au
www.bluemountainstourism.org.au
www.bluemts.com.au
www.nationalparks.nsw.gov.au

Wonderland Information Centre
157 Lurline St, Katoomba 2780
Ph: (02) 6355 6200

LEFT: BLUE MOUNTAINS

the blue mountains

FOR THE EARLY EUROPEAN colonists, the Blue Mountains represented a barrier to the Australian inland. A crossing was eventually found, then a road built, and the splendour of these ancient landforms began to draw people from the city. These days, the Mountains continue to attract visitors keen to enjoy the fresh air, inspiring scenery and warm hospitality.

The Blue Mountains district has a longstanding tradition of hotels and guest houses to accommodate the many visitors who come here, often to escape the pressures of city life. The 26 mountain towns and villages lining the Great Western Hwy offer a range of diversions, including shopping, galleries and a host of excellent restaurants, hotels and cafes.

Further west in the region, the awe-inspiring Jenolan Caves, and Lithgow with its famous Zig Zag Railway, are not to be missed.

A profusion of inviting bushwalking tracks lace the magnificent Blue Mountains NP. They provide the ideal way to experience and appreciate the breathtaking landscape, and the diverse range of plant life and native animals. The sheer diversity and grandeur of the whole area contributed to it being appointed the Greater Blue Mountains World Heritage Area.

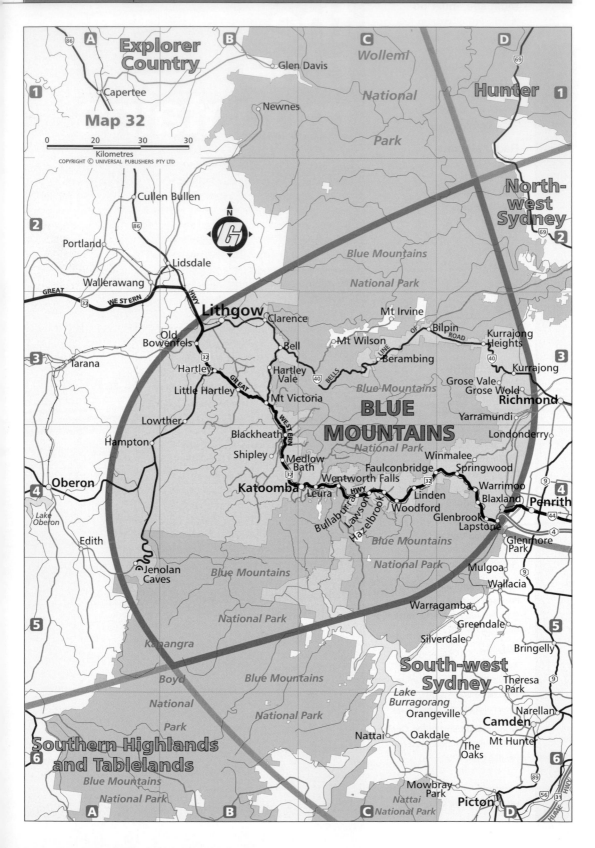

Natural features

The Blue Mountains are the result of a series of ancient geological events. Some 300 million years ago the rocks that now make up the mountains and the Sydney Basin were being laid down. About 170 million years ago, underground pressures forced the rock strata to rise, creating a fault in the layers of rock, which allowed the land on each side of the strata to move independently. The eastern side moved down, forming the Sydney Plain, and the western side rose to form the Blue Mountains and expose a sheer escarpment, which can be seen today, just west of Penrith and the Nepean River.

The process was slow, allowing streams and rivers to cut their way down as the land rose, and leaving the mountains as a plateau dissected by watercourses. The layers of rock exposed by water and wind vary enormously in their hardness and resistance to erosion. Nature has carved these forms in many different ways and created such diverse landforms as Mt Banks (1059m) towering over the plateau, and Narrow Neck, a thin line of high country separating the Megalong and Jamison Valleys.

The rise from the coastal plain begins in earnest at Glenbrook, 65km west of Sydney, and continues to Blackheath, the highest town in the Blue Mountains, more than 1065m above sea level.

History

Long before Europeans arrived, Dharruk and Gundungura Aboriginal people occupied the valleys of the Blue Mountains. Some Aboriginal culture survives in the Mountains, including original rock engravings and hand stencils, and there are several places where visitors can view examples of Aboriginal art and craft.

Governor Arthur Phillip recorded sighting the Mountains while exploring the northern shores of Port Jackson in 1788. It was clear that in order for the colony to expand, the barrier of the Blue Mountains had to be crossed.

History has it that in 1813 Gregory Blaxland, William Lawson and William Wentworth were the first Europeans to successfully cross the Mountains. According to recent research, however, the Mountains were penetrated by white people well before this. Aboriginal people had long established trade routes through the region, and their knowledge and assistance played a large part in European exploration. It now appears that several expeditions into the Mountains preceded the three explorers who received the credit; but it was not in

JAMISON VALLEY

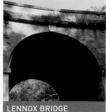

LENNOX BRIDGE

FURTHER READING

For a more wide ranging look at the Blue Mountains read *Artificial Horizons* by Martin Thomas, University of NSW Press.

the early colonial government's interest to publicise this. They did not want convicts to think that there might be an easy escape route to the west.

In 1814, a road was built with the aid of convict labour. By 1816, 160km of mountain road led to Bathurst. However, it was only with the building of the Great Western Railway, completed between 1867 and 1868, that a significant population arrived to inhabit the Mountains.

The Bells Line of Road, built by convicts in 1841, also opened up an alternative access route a little further to the north.

For more than a century the Blue Mountains region has been a favourite holiday resort for Sydneysiders. In the late 1870s, many well-to-do Sydney folk discovered the area's charms and built fine houses here, escaping the humid summer heat of the city.

Grand hotels such as the Carrington at Katoomba and the Ritz at Leura were built in the 1880s, and the Grand Mercure Hydro Majestic at Medlow Bath opened at the turn of the 20th century.

The original boom ended after WWII; as more families owned cars, they came to the Mountains for the day and sought other areas for holidays. In the affluent 1980s, however, another boom began and the Blue Mountains again became popular for weekends away.

Just west of the Mountains, Lithgow started as a tiny European settlement and progressed very slowly until 1869, when at last trains could cross the Mountains, allowing the city and its huge coal reserves to attract industry. Since WWII, an effort has been made to maintain local industries and establish new ones, including education, de-centralised government departments and tourism.

Getting there

By road

Two major roads serve the Mountains from Sydney. The M4 Mwy connects with the Great Western Hwy (Hwy 32) through Penrith to Katoomba, while farther north, Bells Line of Rd parallels the highway from Richmond to Lithgow.

The Darling Causeway from Bell to Mt Victoria connects these two routes at the western end of the Mountains, and creates an excellent loop drive which takes in practically all the area's attractions. The longer route continues on to Lithgow.

Buses link up with rail services at many stations and a number of coach companies offer day trips to the Mountains. Overnight accommodation can also be arranged. For bookings and further info contact Tourism NSW on 132 077 or contact Blue Mountains Tourism, Ph: 1300 653 408.

By rail

Trains leave Sydney's Central Stn for the Mountains every 30min during peak times and hourly in quieter times. The trip from Central to **Lapstone** takes an hour, to **Springwood** another 30min and the total time to **Katoomba** is about 2hrs.

Lithgow is connected to Sydney with a daily Countrylink XPT service, and is also serviced by Sydney's regular electric train system on the Blue Mountains Line. Timetables available from State Rail. Ph: 131 500

Getting around

Fantastic Aussie Tours' Explorer Bus service — a London-style double-decker bus — departs from the railway steps at Katoomba and makes 30 stops on an hour-long round trip. Passengers may disembark at any of the stops and board a later bus to continue their tour. The

TOURING THE BLUE MOUNTAINS IN A VINTAGE MG

bus operates, 9.30am–5.15pm. **Blue Mountains Trolley Tours** offer a similar service with 29 stops on the tour. Both companies also run tours and transfers to Jenolan Caves; their offices are conveniently located at Katoomba Stn Ph: 1300 300 915 or (02) 4782 1866 (Fantastic Aussie Tours); and 1800 801 577 (Trolley Bus Tours). www.trolleytours.com.au

Festivals and events

Task Force 72 Model Shop Regatta
On the last weekend in Feb, **Wentworth Falls Lake** becomes a popular venue for its races, novelty events and variety of watercraft. For info, Ph: (02) 9614 0927

Blue Mountains Music Festival
This Blue Mountains music festival featuring local and international artists, is held in **Katoomba** over three days in Mar. Concerts, workshops, arts and craft fair, stalls and more are offered. Ph: 1800 651 322. www.bmff.org.au

Twilight Jazz Picnic in the Gardens
This annual jazz concert under the stars celebrates Norman Lindsay's birthday (Feb). Held in the grounds of the Norman Lindsay Gallery, 14 Norman Lindsay Cres, Faulconbridge. Bookings essential, Ph: (02) 4751 1067

Six Foot Track Marathon
Held in Mar, this is one of the world's toughest off-road foot-races. It begins at the Explorers Marked Tree on the Great Western Hwy near Katoomba, traverses the **Megalong Valley** and Black Range, and ends at **Jenolan Caves**. Ph: 1300 653 408. www.coolrunning.com.au

Lithgow Ironfest
A festival celebrating Lithgow's industrial heritage. Events include 'open city' weekend, a procession, displays and a highland festival featuring pipe bands, dancing and games. Held last week in Mar. Ph: (02) 6353 1859

Celebrate Lithgow
A week-long festival celebrating **Lithgow's** pride is held in Nov. Festivities culminate in a street party held in Lithgow's main shopping precinct with entertainment, amusements, stalls and more—it's fun for the whole family.

Kowmung Music Festival
A wonderful series of concerts in Mar by international chamber musicians; held

SCENIC WENTWORTH FALLS

AUTUMN COLOUR, MT WILSON

LOOPING THE MOUNTAINS

For a comprehensive self-guided scenic driving tour, pick up a copy of the *Grand Circular Tourist Drive* brochure from the Blue Mountains Visitor Info Centres. Visitor Centres also offer free accommodation booking service, itinerary planning, bushwalking info and maps to assist the visitor.

APPLE ORCHARD, BILPIN

3km SW of Oberon. Ph: (02) 6336 0239. www.bluemts.com.au/kowmung

Food and Wine with Altitude Fair
A celebration of food and wine held in Blackheath on the 1st weekend in May. www.bluemts.com.au/foodfestival

Mt Wilson Autumn Colour
From mid Apr to mid-May many of the gardens of this picturesque little community are open to the public. The many deciduous trees and shrubs produce magnificent colour.

Yulefest in the Blue Mountains
Over two decades ago a group of Irish tourists reminiscing about a **winter Christmas** asked at their hotel for dinner with all the trimmings. Now the Mountains re-create the romance of a northern hemisphere winter every year, June–Aug. Ph: 1300 653 408

Winter Magic Festival
Parades, art, culture and stalls are a feature of this winter solstice celebration in Jun. www.wintermagicfestival.com

Leura Gardens Spring Festival
This big event runs for nine days in mid-Oct and attracts thousands to celebrate spring. Many superb private gardens are opened and a village fair, **Floralia**, takes place during the open garden period.

www.hermes.net.au/leuragardens/ and www.leuravillage.com

Open Garden Spring Festivals
The **Hazelbrook/Woodford Garden Festival** and **Oberon Daffodil Festival** are other major events featuring open gardens in the springtime. For more info on garden festivals Ph: 1300 653 408

Blackheath Rhododendron Festival
In early Nov, Blackheath celebrates the beauty of its rhododendron plantings with a two-week festival. Events include a street fair, procession, art exhibition, competitions, games, guided bushwalks, woodchopping and gymkhana. www.bluemts.com.au/rhododendron/garden

Carols by Candlelight
Carols are held at various locations throughout the Blue Mountains prior to Christmas, including at **Glenbrook** Ph: (02) 4739 2233 and **Jenolan Caves**. Ph: 1300 763 311

Other events include: **One Van Puppet Festival** (Jan); **Springwood Foundation Day** (Apr); **Winmalee Autumn Artfest** (May); **Songlines Festival** (Oct); and **Glenbrook Village Art & Craft Fair** (Nov).

Main localities and towns
The major Blue Mountains towns are grouped in three areas: the Bells Line of Rd; the towns just to the west of Katoomba; and along the railway line on the Great Western Hwy.

WOLLONGAMBE RIVER
Behind Mt Wilson Fire Brigade is the **trail** to the Wollongambe River. For info on self-guided and guided **tours** including liloing trips, contact the Hawkesbury Visitor Centre. Ph: (02) 4588 5895

RHODODENDRON SPECIES IN FULL BLOOM

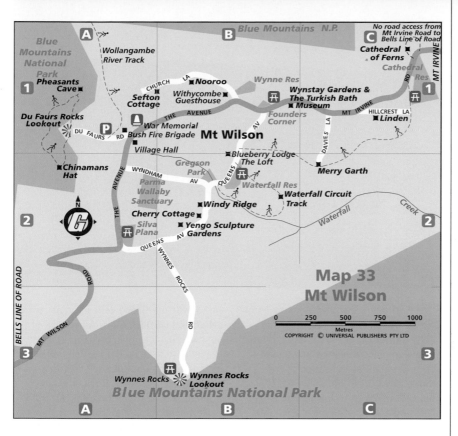

Map 33
Mt Wilson

Bells Line of Rd

This is a far more spectacular route from the city than the Great Western Hwy. Named after Archibald Bell who discovered the crossing in 1823, the original road was built by convicts in 1841, and evidence of their stonework is still visible along the way.

Lookouts at **Pierces Pass** and **Mt Banks** provide panoramas over the Blue Mountains NP, with picnic areas and walking tracks.

Bilpin Map 32 C3

This pretty little village is famous for the apples grown in surrounding orchards. Roadside stalls in the area sell fresh local fruit and vegetables. Nearby, **Waratah Native Gardens** is a perfect picnic spot, with the added attraction of a short walk along the Gorge Track.

Kurrajong Map 32 D3

The historic village of Kurrajong nestles at the bottom of **Bellbird Hill** where the steep ascent of Bells Line of Rd begins.

On a quiet day, visitors can hear the liquid sounds of the birds which give the hill its name.

Kurrajong Hts Map 35

Stop at Kurrajong Hts, the historic village at the top of Bellbird Hill. Relax over a cuppa at the **Heavenly Bell Cafe**, or take in the fabulous views over the plains back to Sydney.

Mt Wilson Map 33

Off the Bells Line of Rd beyond the Grose Valley, along an 8km scenic winding route, is the attractive hamlet of Mt Wilson. For many years this area has provided a secluded retreat for wealthier Sydney citizens. Its rich volcanic soil and the cooler climate allow many northern hemisphere plants to flourish. Spectacular private gardens open to the public in autumn and spring, including **Nooroo**, **Wynstay**, **Windy Ridge**, **Merry Garth**, **Yengo**, **Koonawarra** and **Sefton Cottage**, which is open year round. The lovely old **Turkish Bath Museum** is part of the

GOVETTS LEAP LEGENDS

Two legends surround Govetts Leap (lookout pictured): one of a **bushranger**, Govett who, when trapped by troopers, leapt over the cliff on his horse; and the more plausible story of **Government Surveyor** William Govett, who discovered the 'Leap', an old Scottish word for waterfall.

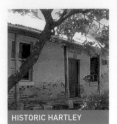

HISTORIC HARTLEY

HANGING ROCK, BLACKHEATH

State Heritage registered Wynstay estate (see Gardens, p.202).

The **Cathedral of Ferns**, a magnificent enclave of giant treeferns and towering gums, provides an indication of the diverse plant life found in the Blue Mountains. There is a picnic and BBQ area here and others near the village.

Beyond Katoomba
Blackheath Map 32 B4

Blackheath, named by Governor Lachlan Macquarie after its 'black, wild appearance', was the location of a large stockade housing convicts and soldiers in the 1840s. Now this quiet town is a weekend haven, and an excellent point from which to enjoy the **Grose Valley** area of the Blue Mountains NP.

At the end of Govetts Leap Rd is the **Blue Mountains Heritage Centre**, the NPWS's main info office for the region, with a good selection of books, souvenirs, walking track brochures, cold drinks and snacks. An exhibition details the geology, history and culture of the Mountains, while a theatrette shows nature videos. Open daily, 9am–5pm. Ph: (02) 4787 8877

Next to the Centre is the **Fairfax Heritage Track**, a 1.8km wheelchair-accessible trail, with markers along the way explaining different aspects of the natural surroundings. The path ends up at **Govetts Leap Lookout**, with fabulous views over the Grose Valley and attractive picnic and BBQ facilities. A network of bushwalks is easily accessible in the Blackheath area, and other lookouts include **Evans Lookout** down Evans Lookout Rd, and **Anvil Rock**, a wind-eroded cave, at the end of Hat Hill Rd.

Memorial Park and Pool on Gardiners Cr boasts one of the many rhododendron gardens in Blackheath. **The Campbell Rhododendron Gardens** in Bacchante St are run by the Blue Mountains Rhododendron Society of NSW Inc (see p.201).

The **Blackheath Craft Markets** are held on the 3rd Sun of each month at Blackheath Community Centre.

Hartley Map 32 B3

Relive the charms of yesteryear at **Hartley Historic Site**. The village of Hartley nestles at the base of **Victoria Pass**, just before the turnoff to Jenolan Caves on the Great Western Hwy. The **Hartley Court House** was built in 1837 and over the next 50 years a bustling village developed. The beautiful sandstone building is now a museum where visitors can inspect the convict cells and watch a mock trial. Open daily, 10am–1pm, 2pm–4.30pm. Other beautifully preserved buildings include inns and churches. The **Farmers Inn** houses the Visitor Info Centre, run by the NPWS who also conduct guided tours of the site. Ph: (02) 6355 2117

GUEST HOUSE DINING

Dine casually without staying overnight at: **Where Waters Meet**, Leura; **Lilianfels**, **Mountain Heritage** and **Balmoral House**, Katoomba; **The Chalet**, Medlow Bath; . Bookings essential.

Jenolan Caves Map 32 A5

Among Australia's oldest and best known tourist attractions, the spectacular limestone caverns of Jenolan Caves have been open for public inspection for well over 100 years. The surrounding 2430ha nature reserve also has a number of walking tracks. The tracks lead from Caves House to Carlotta Arch, the Devils Coach House, McKeowns Valley, the Blue Lake and the weir. Jenolan Caves are also one end of the famous **Six Foot Track** (see pp.196 and 198).

Guided tours (9am–5pm) to five caves run throughout the day on weekdays, and to nine caves at weekends. A **ghost tour** runs most Sat night at 8pm (bookings essential). There are also adventure tours which must be booked well in advance. A series of classical concerts are performed in the caves, usually once a month. Contact the Guides Office. Ph: (02) 6359 3911. www.jenolancaves.com.org

The roads leading down to the caves are challenging and must be negotiated with care, but the beauty of the mountain scenery makes the trip worthwhile.

Lithgow Map 32 B3

In 1827 the explorer Hamilton Hume named the Lithgow valley in honour of Governor Brisbane's private secretary, William Lithgow. Set amidst mountain splendour, Lithgow is a town rich in culture. Immerse yourself in Aboriginal tradition, step back in time to an era where steam dominated transport and where industry was the town's backbone.

One of Lithgow's most famous attractions, the **Great Zig Zag Railway**, features a beautiful steam powered engine, whistling to life as she moves off from Clarence station, for the ride down the escarpment. The series of zig zags were constructed in 1869 to transport the valley's vast quantities of coal reserves. Today the tourist attraction is open daily, following the original rail route, with trains departing at 11am, 1pm and 3pm. Steam trains operate on weekends, Wed and school holidays. All other times a diesel locomotive makes the 90min return trip. Ph: (02) 6355 2955. www.zigzagrailway.com.au

Discover the wonders of World Heritage Listed **Wollemi** and **Gardens of Stone** NPs, both of which are easily accessed from Lithgow.

Lithgow boasts numerous scenic waterways and rivers to experience water sports and fishing. For a guaranteed catch, visit **Archvale Trout Farm**. Ph: (02) 6352 1341.

CAVES SURPRISES

The extensive Jenolan Caves system has revealed Aboriginal skeletal remains, an underground river, cave pearls, cave-adapted shrimp and a skeleton of the extinct Tasmanian Tiger.

RELICS OF INDUSTRY, ESKBANK HOUSE

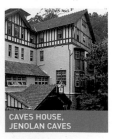

CAVES HOUSE, JENOLAN CAVES

SCENIC DRIVE

Tourist Drive 1 starts from Lithgow St, Lithgow and leads to Hassans Wall Reserve. A dirt road winds up to **Hassans Wall Lookout**, with fantastic views over Hartley Vale and the Blue Mountains.

ZIG ZAG RAILWAY, LITHGOW

Eskbank House Museum is fine sandstone structure that is set amidst manicured grounds with cottage gardens and displays depicting Lithgow's early history. Ph: (02) 6351 3557

Lithgow's manufacturing heritage provides the opportunity to absorb yourself in our working culture. The **Delta Energy Expo**, with interactive and educational displays, takes you into the world of power. A guided tour of the station will answer all those questions you've ever had about the flick of a switch. Open daily 9am–4pm, tours 11am. Ph: (02) 6354 8155. The **Small Arms Factory Museum** provides a visual journey through one of the most important factories of the war years. The museum contains one of the largest examples of military weapons and small arms in Australia. Open weekends and public holidays. Ph: (02) 6351 4452. The poppet head towers over **State Mine Heritage Park & Railway**, signifying the struggle to bring black gold to the earth's surface. The museum's collection of memorabilia and artefacts depict tough working life in the area's coal mines. Open weekends and public holidays. Groups can also arrange tours at other times during the week. Ph: (02) 6353 1513. www.statemine.org.au

Special events held in Lithgow include **Portland Art Show** (Mar), **Ironfest** (Apr), **Yulefest** (held throughout winter), and **Celebrate Lithgow**, a week-long festival held in Nov. Festivities culminate in a street party held in Lithgow's main shopping precinct with entertainment, amusements, stalls and more — it's fun for the whole family. The **Great Zig Zag Railway** also runs specialty trains including Friends of Thomas and Wizard's Express throughout the year. **Daffodils at Rydal** features wonderful displays of daffodils in the heritage village and nearby properties (Sep).

The Lithgow Visitor Information Centre, located in the big Miners Lamp on the Great Western Hwy, provides info, brochures and bookings for all local attractions, tour operators, accommodation, health retreats and the region's bushwalks and 4WD tracks. Ph: (02) 6353 1859. www.tourism.lithgow.com

Megalong Valley Map 35

Accessible by road from Blackheath, this secluded valley has become the horseriding centre of the Mountains, as animals are not allowed into the NP. However, there are other enjoyable discoveries to make here.

At the top of Megalong Rd overlooking the valley is **Shipley Plateau**, known for its apple orchards. The plateau has two impressive lookouts, **Hargraves**, with views over the Megalong Valley, and **Mt Blackheath**, looking back towards the Kanimbla Valley.

On the way down into the valley, Megalong Rd passes a track leading to **Mermaids Cave**, and further down, the **Coachwood Glen** walk is a short round walk through rainforest, with a treefern dell and pretty creek.

The **Megalong Australian Heritage Centre** on Megalong Rd offers a huge range of attractions, including displays of sheep shearing, cow milking, whip cracking and working dogs — shows are for groups of 20 or more and must be booked in advance. There's horseriding, pony rides for children, quad bikes for big children, as well as a picnic and BBQ area and farmstay accommodation.

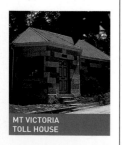

MT VICTORIA TOLL HOUSE

MT VICTORIA MUSEUM EXHIBIT

NORMAN LINDSAY GALLERY AND MUSEUM

Open weekends and public holidays, 10am–4pm, Ph: (02) 4787 8688. www.megalong.cc

Other options for horseriding in the valley include **Werriberri Trail Rides**, Ph: (02) 4787 9171

Devonshire teas and light lunches are available at the **Megalong Tearooms and Kiosk**, and **Old Ford Reserve** is popular for picnics, swimming and bushwalking.

Mt Victoria Map 32 B3

Initially the Pass of Victoria, the name was changed to Mt Victoria when the railway opened in 1868. This charming village is classified by the **National Trust**. The railway stn, old post office, toll house and cemetery are of particular interest.

Mt Victoria and District Historic Museum of Australiana occupies the old refreshment rooms at the railway stn in Station St. Open weekends, public and school holidays, 2pm–5pm or by appt. Ph: (02) 4787 1210

Bric-a-brac and antique shopping along Mt Victoria's main street provide a pleasant diversion, and there are several lovely walks in the area (see p.205).

The **Victoria Falls** track, Victoria Falls Rd, is an example of the spectacular walking tracks of the northern section of the Blue Mountains NP; there are also good walks and lookouts at **Mt Piddington** and **Pulpit Rock Reserve** to the south. Excellent views, picnic facilities, and monuments to the explorers, as well as Governor Macquarie and early pioneers, are all found at **Mt York Historic Site**. Walks along historic road routes from Mt York include **Lawsons Long Alley, Lockyers Rd Loop, Cox's Rd** and **Berghofers Pass**.

NORMAN LINDSAY'S GARDEN STUDIO

MT VIC FLICKS

The old hall at Harley Ave, Mt Victoria, is a rare example of the traditional community picture theatre. Screenings Thurs–Sun, and daily during school and public holidays. Ph: (02) 4787 1577

SCENIC DETOUR

Take the Explorers Rd off the Great Western Hwy through **Lapstone**. At the end of Emu Rd, **Bluff Reserve** has shaded picnic tables and three lookouts, back to the city and across Glenbrook Gorge.

LAPSTONE ZIG ZAG

At the end of Knapsack St, the **Lapstone Zig Zag** walk follows a railway route built in 1867, the first engineering feat of its kind in NSW. The walk ends up at **Elizabeth Lookout**, with views over the plains.

Great Western Hwy
Faulconbridge Map 32 C4

Faulconbridge is named after the country house of one of its most famous residents, **Sir Henry Parkes**, the 'father of Federation'. He died here in 1896, five years before Australia was declared a Federation. His grave is in the cemetery on Sir Henrys Pde. Also on Sir Henrys Pde is the **Prime Ministers' Corridor of Oaks**, where every Prime Minister of Australia, or a relative, has planted a tree.

Norman Lindsay Gallery and Museum, at 14 Norman Lindsay Cr, Faulconbridge, was the home of the famous and often controversial artist, cartoonist and writer (1879–1969) and contains some of his most significant works: oils, watercolours, etchings, sculptures, ship models, and *Magic Pudding* puppets and illustrations. The landscaped gardens are decorated with his fountains and statues. His garden studio, which includes an unfinished painting, is as he left it. Open daily, 10am–4pm. Ph: (02) 4751 1067 www.hermes.net.au/nlg

Glenbrook Map 32 D4

The 1st main town of the Blue Mountains on the Great Western Hwy from Penrith, Glenbrook was once a railway siding and today is a thriving lower mountain village. Nearby **Blaxland** is also rapidly expanding, with many people choosing to live here and commute to the city. **Warrimoo** is a quiet village enhanced by beautiful flowering trees and shrubs.

Glenbrook Native Plant Reserve and Nursery displays Blue Mountains native flora. Run by the Society for Growing Native Plants, the reserve has an info centre selling plants, seeds and books. Open Wed, Sat, Sun, noon–4pm. Ph: (02) 4758 6637

Along Mitchells Pass is **Lennox Bridge**, the oldest stone bridge on the Australian mainland, built in 1832 by stonemason David Lennox and 20 convicts. On the way to the bridge is **Glenbrook Lagoon** which, thanks to the conservation work of the Lagoon Society, has become a peaceful haven for native wildlife.

On Hare St, the **Centre Gallery** is the outlet for the Blue Mountains Creative Arts Centre, displaying all kinds of arts and craft work produced by members for sale. Open Fri–Sun, 10am–4pm. Ph: (02) 4739 2587

From Feb–Dec, the **Glenbrook Craft Markets** are held on the 1st Sun of every month in Glenbrook Cinema Complex next to the Tourist Info Centre. Ph: (02) 4739 3137

Wascoe Siding Miniature Railway on Grahame St, Blaxland, steams up at 10.30am on the 1st Sun of each month except Jan. There is also a BBQ area and kiosk. Ph: (02) 4735 2301

RED HANDS CAVE, GLENBROOK

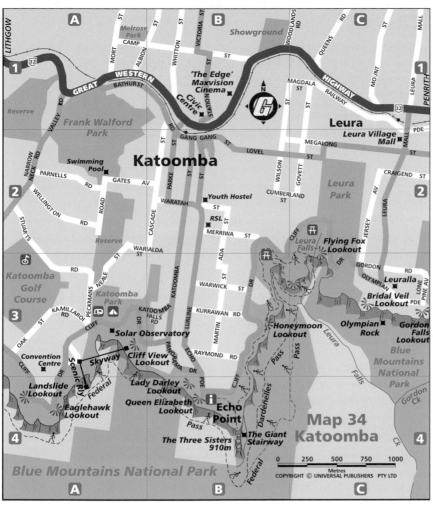

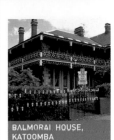

BALMORAL HOUSE, KATOOMBA

For the Glenbrook entrance to the **Blue Mountains NP**, follow Burfitt Pde to Bruce Rd. This is a particularly popular section of the park, with swimming at **Jellybean Pool** and **Blue Pool**, camping, BBQ and picnics at **Euroka Clearing** and lots of walks to features such as **Glenbrook Gorge** and **Red Hands Cave**. The cave was discovered in 1913 during a search for a lost child, and contains Aboriginal hand stencils on the walls. Cycling is also popular here, particularly on **The Oaks Fire Trail**. Open daily, 8.30am–6pm (7pm in summer).

Hazelbrook Map 35
On Railway Pde, National Trust listed **Selwood Science and Puzzles** is a unique Mountains attraction, particularly for children. Children gravitate straight to the hands-on displays of puzzles, mazes, science gallery, magic section and educational books. Many items are also for sale. Open Thur–Mon 9am–5pm . Ph: (02) 4758 6235

Just up the road is **Lawson** which offers some good walks, including a short round-trip walk to Fairy Falls and Dantes Glen, and longer walks to Echo Bluff and along the Empire Pass track to Frederica Falls (see p.204).

On the 3rd Sun of each month, the **Lawson Magpie Markets** are held at Lawson Public School on the Hwy.

Katoomba Map 32 B4
Early in the 1870s Katoomba was the site of a quarry known as The Crushers. In 1887 the name was changed to Katoomba, a corruption of an Aboriginal

THE SCENIC SKYWAY

The sisters' legend

The story goes like this ...

When leaving his daughters Meehni, Wimlah and Gunnedoo, the witchdoctor, Tyawan, would place them on a high cliff in the mountains to protect them from the bunyip. One day, Meehni, frightened by a large centipede, threw a stone at it. The stone rolled over the cliff, causing the rock behind to split open, and leaving the girls isolated on a thin ledge. The bunyip, angry at being awoken from his sleep by all the commotion, lurched at the sisters. When Tyawan saw this, he pointed his magic bone to turn his daughters to stone and keep them safe until the bunyip left. Then the witchdoctor, himself trying to escape from the bunyip, became trapped by a rock, so changed himself into a lyrebird. Everyone was safe — but Tyawan had lost his magic bone. He is still searching for it today, while the three sisters stand silently watching.

word meaning 'shiny, falling waters'. The town is the main Mountains centre, generally busier than the other villages but with pleasant arcades, neat streetside cafes and leafy walkways.

The **Three Sisters**, out on their rocky promontory, are the most famous of all the Blue Mountains attractions. They are best seen from **Echo Pt**, where the wonderful view also takes in the Ruined Castle, Mt Solitary and the Jamison Valley. It is worth seeing in the evening, as the Sisters are floodlit at night, an ethereal spectacle. A walkway leads to the Sisters from behind the Visitor Centre which provides info, souvenirs,

refreshments, walking track brochures, maps and film. Visitors can also visit the **World Heritage Plaza** at Echo Point.

Near the Three Sisters, the **Giant Stairway's** 841 steps descend to the beautiful **Jamison Valley**, but it is not necessary to climb back up. A track through the rainforest around the base of the cliffs leads to the **Scenic Railway** which takes walkers back to the top, from where they can return along **Prince Henry Cliff Walk**. The full trip takes about 3.5hr and is fairly strenuous (see p.205).

The Scenic Railway, Sceniscender, Scenic Skyway and Scenic Cinema are

SIX FOOT TRACK

To walk the entire **Six Foot Track** from Katoomba to Jenolan Caves usually takes three days, but shorter sections can be walked. Brochures are available from the NPWS and BMTA Visitor Info Centres. Ph: 1300 653 408. www.coolrunning.com. au/sixfoot

KATOOMBA

LEURALLA

CLIFF DRIVE

This scenic 8km **Tourist Drive 5** starts from Narrow Neck Rd off the Great Western Hwy just west of Katoomba, or in Leura (pictured). It follows the clifftops and includes several lookouts and **Katoomba Falls Reserve**, a pretty, grassy picnic area.

all part of **Scenic World** in Violet St, off Cliff Dr. The railway began life in 1878 as transport to the coal mines in the valley below and now provides visitors with a thrilling, almost vertical ride, the steepest incline railway in the world, with grades of up to 52°. At the bottom, passengers can wander the **Rainforest Boardwalk**, either to see the old coal mines, or to the base of Katoomba Falls, past the 500 year-old **Turpentine Tree**.

The new **Scenic Skyway's** cable car gives the impression of walking on air over the Jamison Valley giving spectacular views of the Three Sisters, Katoomba Falls and Mt Solitary. The **Sceniscender** is Australia's steepest aerial cable car ride, travelling 545m into the Jamison Valley. If an armchair view is preferred, then visit the **Katoomba Scenic Cinema**, which screens a film of the magnificent views and activities on offer in the area. Scenic World opens 9am–5pm daily. Ph: (02) 4782 2699

Back in town, the restored **Carrington Hotel** (Katoomba St) was built in the town's heyday, in 1880. It is a splendid example of Art Nouveau style, with a stained glass dome. Tours of this landmark building — allegedly haunted by a snooker-playing ghost — can be organised in advance. Ph: (02) 4754 5726. Another landmark is the **Paragon Cafe** at 65 Katoomba St, with its classic Art Deco interior and irresistible chocolates.

For an alternative Blue Mountains experience, try Maxvision Cinema, known as **The Edge**, on the Great Western Hwy near the Katoomba Civic Centre. View the wonders of the surrounding wilderness on a giant screen six storeys high. This film screens at sessions throughout the day from 10am, and in the evenings the latest feature movies are shown. Ph: (02) 4782 8928

Katoomba Community Markets are held at the Civic Centre in Katoomba on the 1st and 3rd Sat of each month.

The remains of the tree blazed by Blaxland, Lawson and Wentworth during their successful crossing of the Blue Mountains is named the **Explorers Marked Tree**. It stands 2km west of Katoomba on the Great Western Hwy.

KATOOMBA FALLS AND CASCADES

SCENIC RAILWAY

LEURA GOLF COURSE OVERLOOKING THE JAMISON VALLEY

Across the road is a remarkable sandstone amphitheatre with glorious views over the Jamison Valley.

The beautifully landscaped **Everglades Gardens** are also a popular feature of Leura (see p.201). **Leura 1st Sunday Markets** occur on the 1st Sun of the month at Leura Public School.

Gordon Falls Park in Olympian Pde provides outstanding views of the Jamison Valley, and is ideal for picnics, BBQs and walks to the **Pool of Siloam**, **Lyrebird Dell** and **Leura Cascades** (see p.204). Keen walkers can hike around to Katoomba on the Prince Henry Cliff Walk.

Further along Cliff Dr on Scenic Drive 5, Leura Cascades is an irresistible place to stop, with lots of parking, grassy lawns perfect for picnics, and BBQs. An easy walk heads down to the waterfalls through a shady gully full of treeferns. The walk can be extended to Gordon Falls or Echo Pt. **Prince Henry Cliff Walk** can be followed all the way to Echo Pt, or to Katoomba Falls and Scenic World — a total of 7km of breathtaking clifftop scenery.

Springwood Map 32 D4

When travelling on the new road to Bathurst in 1815, Governor Macquarie named Springwood for its water and woodland. Springwood is now a major Mountains centre, the halfway point between the lower mountain areas and the upper regions. Three buildings are National Trust classified: the **railway station**, the elegant **Frazer Memorial Presbyterian Church** and **Braemar**, a Federation home which now houses the local history centre and art gallery.

Fairy Dell in Springwood Ave is reached from behind Springwood Stn. Stone steps built last century lead down to this fern-clad gully which picks up a bushwalk to **Sassafras Gully**. This walk starts at **Picnic Pt Reserve** off Valley Rd.

Hawkesbury Lookout is a popular BBQ and picnic spot on the northern side of the Great Western Hwy at Hawkesbury Hts with views over the Cumberland Plain towards Sydney.

The **Community Ivy Markets** take place on the 2nd Sat of the month, Feb–Dec at

This is the start of the famous 42km **Six Foot Track**, which follows the original 1884 horse route from Katoomba to Jenolan Caves.

At **Medlow Bath** on the Great Western Hwy is the **Grand Mercure Hydro Majestic Hotel**. Opened in 1904, it attracted Sydney's high society and has now been refurbished in the 1920s Art Deco style it displayed at the height of its popularity. Non-guests are welcome to visit the coffee shop, where breakfast, light lunches and Devonshire teas are available with spectacular views over the Megalong Valley. Open 9am–8pm (9pm in summer). Ph: (02) 4788 1002

Leura Map 32 C4

Perhaps the prettiest of all the Mountain townships, Leura is a National Trust-classified village with a leafy mall lined by many stylish shops, galleries, restaurants, cafes and boutiques.

Leuralla, at 36 Olympian Pde, is a grand house of the 1920s, set in 5ha of classical English garden. It now houses the **NSW Toy and Railway Museum** and displays Australia's best collection of toys and model trains. One room of the house is a memorial to Dr H V 'Doc' Evatt, the famed Australian statesman instrumental in setting up the United Nations. Open daily, 10am–5pm. Ph: (02) 4784 1169

DARWIN WALK

Leading down to Wentworth Falls from Wilson Park, the **Charles Darwin Walk** commemorates the famous naturalist's 1836 visit to the area. Accessible from Wentworth Falls Stn.

RAINBOW LORIKEET

GARDEN SCULPTURES, WENTWORTH FALLS

the Springwood Civic Centre; and on the 4th Sat of the month, Springwood Public School hosts the Blue Gum Market.

Wentworth Falls Map 32 C4

Originally Weatherboard, after the wooden inn on the Western Rd which served travellers, the town's name was later changed to honour William Charles Wentworth, a Blue Mountains explorer.

Wentworth Falls Lake off Sinclair Cr is a pleasant picnic spot with BBQ facilities, swimming, fishing, boating, playground equipment and ducks to feed.

The **Conservation Hut** on Fletcher St boasts fantastic views of the Jamison Valley and is a popular place to eat. It is also handy for picking up books and info on walks and the Blue Mountains Conservation Society, formed in 1963.

At the start of Falls Rd is **Wilson Park**, a shady stretch of grass ideal for picnics, with a playground, benches, picnic tables and sheltered huts.

Further down Falls Rd is the **Falls Gallery**, a beautifully restored turn-of-the-century weatherboard house with exhibits of new and established artists. Free tea and coffee are provided on the verandah, where visitors can enjoy the tranquil old garden scattered with some original pottery.

Falls Rd eventually leads to **Wentworth Falls Picnic Area**, providing picnic tables,

toilets, and great views from the carpark. A 200m walk along the road leads to Wentworth Falls Lookout.

A number of popular walks start from here (see p.204). A good option is the 4hr circuit which takes the **National Pass** track through the **Valley of the Waters** and then back via the Overcliff Track, or stop at the Conservation Hut for a break and take the shortcut track back to the carpark.

GEMA'S GARDEN, LEURA

GROSE VALLEY

BUSHWALKING

For shorter strolls, **Fletchers Lookout** is 30min return and **Princes Rock Lookout** is 20min return.

Back down the Great Western Hwy towards Lawson is Tableland Rd. A track off Queen Elizabeth Dr leads to **Ingar** picnic ground and camping site. Back on Tableland Rd, a 15min drive leads to **McMahons Lookout**, with views over Lake Burragorang backwaters.

Kings Tableland Observatory at 55 Hordern Rd, off Tableland Rd, takes advantage of the darkest skies near Sydney to show visitors the stars, planets, moon, constellations and deep sky objects, using a dome and telescopes. The observatory is open to the general public Fri–Sun evenings at 7pm (8pm during daylight saving). Phone first to check the weather. Ph: (02) 4757 2954

Woodford Map 32 C4

A picturesque sandstone complex on the Great Western Hwy, the **Woodford Academy** is the oldest group of buildings in the Blue Mountains, and is owned by the National Trust. Part of the original 1830s inn built by ex-convict Thomas Pembroke remains, and the buildings are mostly as they were in the 1880s. Open 10am–4pm, 3rd Sat of every month. Guided tours can be provided, and special

inspections by appt arranged for parties of 20 or more. Ph: (02) 4758 8743

On the other side of the Hwy, 5km down Bedford Rd (mainly unsealed), **Murphys Glen** is a wooded area with walks, camping and a picnic area.

National parks
The Greater Blue Mountains World Heritage Area

This Area conserves over one million hectares of diverse eucalypt dominated eco-systems with an enormous range of bio-diversity. Included in this territory are the Blue Mountains, Wollemi and Kanangra NPs as well as other areas.

Reserves to protect the scenic and natural values of the area began in the 1890s and Blue Mountains NP was declared in 1959. It is the most accessible of the three parks that cover most of the Blue Mountains. Detailed information on all aspects of the park is available from the Visitor Info Centres.

Blue Mountains NP Map 32 C4

River-eroded gorges and huge eucalypt forests are the principal features of this 266 942ha NP, which is divided into northern, central and southern sections.

A wealth of recreational opportunities range from car-based sightseeing to bushwalking — there are over 140km of walking tracks of all grades. The region contains unique flora and a wonderful variety of birds and animals, including the swamp wallaby, eastern water dragon, peregrine falcon, brush-tailed rock wallaby, tiger quoll and koala. Flora and fauna of the Mountains is on display at the **Blue Mountains Heritage Centre**, Blackheath (see p.190).

The **Grose Valley** (northern section) extends north from the Great Western Hwy (which provides access to most of the attractions) to Bells Line of Rd. This area has picnic facilities at **Evans Lookout** and **Govetts Leap**.

The **Glenbrook** (central) section lies south of the Great Western Hwy, from the Nepean River in the east to Lake Burragorang in the south. Euroka Clearing, Red Hands Cave and The Ironbarks have BBQ and picnic facilities.

DISCOVER THE MOUNTAINS

The NPWS runs a **Discovery Program** on weekends and school holidays, with Aboriginal bush tucker walks, 4WD trips and wildlife spotting at night. Ranger guided activities are for all ages and levels of fitness including toddlers. Ph: (02) 4787 8877

South of Katoomba to the Wombeyan Caves and east to Lake Burragorang, is the **Greater Southern** section, which is essentially a wilderness area with no facilities.

Attractions, lookouts and walks in the NP are briefly described in this section under the towns from which they are most readily accessible. For camping in the NP, see p.203.

Kanangra-Boyd NP Map 32 B5

Lying to the south and west of the Mountains, this park covers 68 000ha of very steep and remote country, incorporating the spectacular cliffs of **Kanangra Walls Lookout** and several scenic bushwalking tracks (see p.225).

Wollemi NP Map 32 C1

North of Bells Line of Rd, stretching north of Katoomba to Bulga, Wollemi NP contains the largest wilderness area left in NSW. Although general access is limited, activities include canoeing, horseriding along the National Horse-riding Trail and camping (see also p.226).

Gardens

The Campbell Rhododendron Gardens Map 35

These unique gardens in Bacchante St, **Blackheath**, feature an amazing display of rhododendrons, azaleas, a conifer garden, deciduous trees, as well as fern glades by the lakeside — all of the gardens are set in natural bushland, so the effect is superb. Best visited in Apr when the autumn colours are at their height, and in Sep–Nov, when the rhododendrons are blooming, Oct–Nov is the most colourful period. The kiosk sells souvenirs, teas and great scones. Open daily, 9am–4pm (gold coin donation).

Everglades Gardens Map 35

At 37 Everglades Ave, these are among **Leura's** most spectacular gardens. Designed in the 1930s, they are classified by the National Trust. The gardens contain magnificent azaleas and rhododendrons, sandstone terraces, a grotto pool and lovely views. An exhibition of the work of Danish master gardener, Paul Sorensen, who created this and other famous Blue Mountain gardens, can be viewed. A gift shop, coffee shop, art gallery and tearooms are also available. Open daily Sept–Feb, 10am–5pm, Mar–Aug, 10am–4pm. Ph: (02) 4784 1938

Mt Tomah Botanic Gardens Map 35

The superbly landscaped Mt Tomah Botanic Gardens, on **Bells Line of Rd** via **Bilpin**, combine panoramic views over

KANANGRA-BOYD NP

MT TOMAH BOTANIC GARDENS

TOP DEVONSHIRE TEAS

★ **Bay Tree Tea House**, Mt Victoria

★ **Bygone Beautys Tearoom**, Katoomba

★ **The Carrington Hotel**, Katoomba

★ **Conservation Hut**, Wentworth Falls

★ **Grand Mercure Hydro Majestic**, Medlow Bath

★ **Norman Lindsay Cafe**, Faulconbridge

the Grose Valley with waterfalls, rock pools, native rainforest and cool climate plants from all over the world. The visitor centre has a shop, exhibition area, picnic area with BBQs and an acclaimed restaurant. Open Mar–Sept, 10am–4pm, Oct–Feb, 10am–5pm. Ph: (02) 4567 2154,

Nooroo Map 33 B1

Another beautiful **Mt Wilson garden** is Nooroo, Church Lane, renowned for its maples, rhododendrons and wisteria, spacious lawns and century-old trees. Open daily, Apr–May and Sept to mid-Nov, 10am–4pm. Ph: (02) 4756 2018

Wynstay Gardens Map 33 B1

Wynstay Gardens, The Avenue, Mt Wilson, are open for a month in autumn and spring (generally Apr and Oct) and contain the unique **Turkish Bath Museum**. Built as a Turkish Bath in the 1880s, this building is being restored to function as a museum and study centre focusing on the history of **Mt Wilson**. Ph: (02) 4756 2006

Yengo Sculpture Gardens Map 33 B2

At Queens Ave, **Mt Wilson**, Yengo Sculpture Gardens were designed in the 1870s with the assistance of Charles Moore, the first director of Sydney's Royal Botanic Gardens. It features an exquisite walled garden and one of the oldest private fauna reserves in

Fun for the young

★ BMX and mountain bike riding (p.203)

★ Bushwalking (pp.204–205)

★ Grass Karting, Kurrajong Heights (p.203)

★ Horseriding in the Megalong Valley (pp.192–93)

★ Jellybean Swimming Hole, Blue Mountains NP, Glenbrook (p.195)

★ Kings Tableland Observatory, Wentworth Falls (p.200)

★ Leuralla, NSW Toy and Railway Museum, Leura (p.198)

★ Nighttime ghost tours, Jenolan Caves (p.191)

★ Scenic World, Katoomba (p.197)

★ Selwood Science and Puzzles, Hazelbrook (p.195)

★ Skateboard ramp, Goldsmith Pl, Katoomba (near railway stn)

★ The Edge Maxvision Cinema, Katoomba (p.197)

★ Wentworth Falls Lake (p.199)

★ Wascoe Siding Miniature Railway (p.194)

Australia. Open 10am–5pm Sat and Sun, Apr–May and Sept–Nov, other times by appt. Ph: (02) 4756 2002

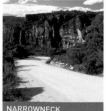
NARROWNECK

HORSERIDING AT THE BLUE MOUNTAINS

Recreational activities

Action

Many thrill seekers are lured to the Blue Mountains, looking for more than a walk and a picnic. A number of **adventure tours** operate in the region, offering activities including abseiling, canyoning, 4WD tours, rockclimbing, mountain biking, horseriding treks, canoeing and camping. Another option is either a Hot Heritage Harley Tour on a motorbike or a chauffeured Mountain Top Trike Tour. For details, contact the Blue Mountains Visitor Info Centres at Glenbrook or Katoomba. Ph: 1300 653 408

Kurrajong Heights
Grass Karting Map 35

At Kurrajong Heights Grass Karting, enjoy the adrenalin rush of zooming down groomed slopes of various grades on specially designed karts. Minimum height of participants 130cm. Picnic areas and BBQ facilities offer superb views over the Hawkesbury valley and Sydney Basin. Open weekends, 9am–5pm, school holidays, 11am–4pm (pre-book any daylight hrs). Ph: (02) 4567 7260

Camping

Camping overnight in the Blue Mountains NP is an excellent way to appreciate the glorious natural surroundings. There are several places to camp in different areas of the Mountains, including **Euroka** at Glenbrook; **Murphys Glen**, along the Bedford Rd from Woodford; **Ingar**, along Queen Elizabeth Dr off Tableland Rd at Boddington Hill, east of Wentworth Falls; and **Perrys Lookdown** at the end of Hat Hill Rd at Blackheath. Bring your own water and fuel stove.

Contact the NPWS for a detailed leaflet and info about permits, fire restrictions and availability. Ph: (02) 4787 8877

Council **caravan parks** are located at **Katoomba** and **Blackheath**. Try to avoid crowded peak times. Katoomba Falls Caravan Park, Ph: (02) 4782 1835; Blackheath Caravan Park, Ph: (02) 4787 8101

Cycling

The Blue Mountains area is popular with cyclists, particularly mountain biking enthusiasts. In general, mountain bikes are allowed to ride in the NPs as long as they keep to existing fire trails or service roads — it is prohibited to ride any kind of bicycle on walking tracks. Some of the best rides include the **Blue Gum Swamp** track at Winmalee; the track out to **Faulconbridge Pt** at Faulconbridge; the **Oaks Fire Trail** from Woodford to Glenbrook; the **Mt Hay Rd** at Leura; and the **Narrowneck** track at Katoomba.

Cyclists need to be well prepared for these rides — there is no access to water along the ridgetop rides. The **Visitor Info Centre** at **Glenbrook** sells cycling guides and can provide details on bicycle routes.

MEGALONG VALLEY HORSES

Bushwalking in the Blue Mountains

The Blue Mountains offer an unrivalled range of walks, but please note that it is important to check the status of a walk before starting out — some areas occasionally have to be closed.

Walkers on longer treks are advised to keep a few basic precautions in mind:

★ Tell someone where you propose to walk and when you expect to return

★ Take enough food and water

★ Do not walk alone, and keep your party together

★ Wear suitable footwear and clothing as it can get cold in the Blue Mountains, especially at night, even in summer

★ Take first aid equipment. If someone is injured, do not leave them alone. Send the fittest person in the party for help

★ If you become lost, stay in one place and light a fire. Don't be careless with fire

★ Boil all water collected for drinking

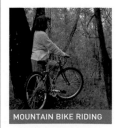
MOUNTAIN BIKE RIDING

Blue Mountains walking tracks

Walking track guides and maps are available from the Heritage Centre at Blackheath and the info centres at Glenbrook and Echo Point. The list of walks has been graded EASY (all ages, but take great care must be taken with children) MED (average fitness) HARD (lots of steps).

GLENBROOK/LAPSTONE/WARRIMOO

Jellybean Pool or Blue Pool	Return	1hr	MED	Start at NP entrance, Glenbrook. Popular picnic area, summer swimming spot.
Red Hands Cave	Circuit	4hr	MED	Start at NP entrance, Glenbrook. Round walk from Causeway, return along Campfire Creek. Aboriginal hand stencils, axe grinding site.
Euroka Creek/Nepean River	Return	1hr	EASY	Start at Euroka Clearing in park. Views, birds.
Jack Evans Track	Return	4hr	HARD	Start Jack Evans parking area in park. Follow Erskine Creek. Views, rainforest, birds.
Florabella Pass	One way	3hr	MED	Start Florabella St, Warrimoo finish Blaxland, return by train. Views, rainforest, birds.
Lapstone Zig Zag/Knapsack Gully Viaduct	Return	2hr	EASY	Start Knapsack St. Original rail line, abandoned station, views Cumberland Plain.

SPRINGWOOD/FAULCONBRIDGE

Wiggins Track/Sassafras/ Glenbrook/Magdala Creek	Circuit	5hr	MED	Start Yondell Ave, Springwood. Views, waterfalls, rainforest, birds.
Springwood/Sassafras Gulley/ Victory Track/Faulconbridge	One way	4hr	EASY	Start Sassafras Gully Rd, Springwood. Views, waterfalls, rainforest, birds. Return by train.

LAWSON

Dante's Glen/Empire Pass	Circuit	2.5hr	MED	Start at camping area end of Park Rd, Lawson. Waterfalls, ferny glades, steep steps to Dante's Glen.
South Lawson Waterfall Circuit	Circuit	2.5hr	MED	Start at Honour Ave. Picturesque waterfall walk through quiet gullies.

WENTWORTH FALLS

Rocket Point	Return	1.5hr	MED	Start Falls Reserve end of Falls Rd. Cross Jamison Creek. Walk to lookout. Excellent view Wentworth Falls and Jamison Valley.
Princes Rock/Undercliff Walk	Circuit	2hr	MED	Start Falls Reserve. Views, waterfalls, birds.
Den Fenella	Return	1.5hr	MED	Start Falls Reserve. Views, rainforest, waterfalls, birds.
Overcliff/Undercliff/National Pass/Valley of the Waters	Circuit	4.5hr	HARD (VERY)	Start Conservation Hut, Fletcher St. Waterfalls, views, rainforest. One of the best walks in the area. Experienced walkers only.
Valley of the Waters/ Wentworth Pass/National Pass	Circuit	5hr	HARD	As above but deeper descent into valley.
Valley of the Waters Nature Track	Circuit	3hr	MED	Start Valley of the Waters Picnic Area to Edinburgh Castle Bluff. Views, waterfalls, rainforest, birds.

LEURA

Lyrebird Dell/Pool of Siloam	Circuit	2hr	MED	Start Gordon Falls Picnic Area. Ferny glades along Gordon Falls Creek. Waterfalls, pool, cave. Return via road.
Leura Cascades to Bridal Veil Falls	Return	1hr	EASY	Leura Cascades Picnic Area. Pockets of rainforest, ferns, open woodland and views.
Gordon Falls to Leura Falls	One way	1hr	EASY	Start Gordon Falls Picnic Area. Lookout over falls and Jamison Valley views, birds.
Leura Cascades/Leura Forest/ Fernbower Circuit	Return	3hr	HARD	Leura Falls Picnic Area. Views, waterfalls, rainforest, birds.

KATOOMBA

Three Sisters/Echo Point	Return	30min	EASY	Echo Point Info Centre. Walk to Three Sisters.
Prince Henry Cliff Walk/ Katoomba Falls	Return	2hr	EASY	Start Echo Point. Jamison Valley views, Katoomba Cascades and waterfall.
Giant Stairway/Federal Pass/ Scenic Railway/Prince Henry Cliff Walk	Circuit	2.5hr	HARD	Start Echo Point. Descend valley by Giant Stairway (841 steps). Federal Pass, up on Scenic Railway then Prince Henry Cliff Walk.
Echo Point/Prince Henry Cliff Walk/Katoomba Falls	Return	1.5hr	EASY	Start Echo Point. Superb views of Jamison Valley.
Giant Stairway/Dardanelles Pass/Prince Henry Cliff Walk	Circuit	4.5hr	HARD (VERY)	Start Echo Point. Views, rainforest, birds. Experienced walkers only.
Rainforest Walk/Furber Steps/ Scenic Railway	Circuit	1.5hr	MED	Start Katoomba Falls Kiosk, Cliff Dr. Walk in shaded gullies, views Katoomba Falls. Some steep sections. Return Scenic Railway.
Scenic Railway/Ruined Castle	Return	7hr	MED	Down Scenic Railway, walk to Ruined Castle, rock formation with 360° views. Shorter walk (5hr) from Golden Stairs off Glenraphael Dr.
Furber Steps/Ruined Castle/ Golden Stairs	Circuit	8hr	HARD (VERY)	Start Katoomba Falls Kiosk. Difficult but rewarding walk. Experienced walkers only.
Katoomba Falls Round Walk	Circuit	1hr	MED	Start Katoomba Falls Kiosk. Views, rainforest.
Boars Head Rock/Cahills Lookout	Return	30min	MED	Start Cahill's Picnic Ground, Cliff Dr. Views Boars Head Rock and Megalong Valley.

BLACKHEATH

Fairfax Heritage Track	One way	1hr	EASY	Start Heritage Centre, finish Govetts Leap. Suitable wheelchairs and strollers. Views of Grose Valley and Bridal Veil Falls.
Govetts Leap/Evans Lookout	One way	1.5hr	MED	Start Govetts Leap. Open woodland and heath. Grose Valley views.
Govetts Leap/Pulpit Rock	Return	3hr	MED	Start Govetts Leap. Views of Grose Valley, Bridal Veil and Horseshoe Falls, hanging swamps, abundant birdlife.
Braeside Walk/Govetts Leap	Return	1.5hr	MED	Start Braeside St., Blackheath. Open woodland, views Horseshoe and Bridal Veil Falls.
Neates Glen/Grand Canyon/ Evans Lookout	Circuit	4hr	MED	Start picnic area, Evans Lookout Rd. Ferny glen, natural tunnel to canyon, sandstone formations. Side track to Beauchamp Falls. Return from Evans Lookout by road.
Perrys Lookdown/Blue Gum Forest	Return	5.5hr	HARD (VERY)	Start end Hat Hill Rd, Blackheath. Views, some rainforest and birds. Experienced walkers only.
Centennial Glen/Porters Pass	Circuit	3hr	MED	Start Bundarra St, near Blackheath Stn. Ferns and waterfalls, views Megalong Valley. Finish Ada St and back to stn (or reverse).

MT VICTORIA

Reinitz Pass/Bushrangers Cave	Circuit	3hr	MED	Start Kanimbla St. Zig Zag track to beautiful Reinitz Pass, Bushrangers Cave, Wilsons Glen and Ross Cave.
Fairy Bower/Cox's Cave/ Mt Piddington	Return	2.5hr	MED	Start Fairy Bower, views, waterfall, rainforest and birds.
Victoria Falls Lookout/ Burra Korain Flat	Return	5hr	HARD	Good views, waterfalls, rainforest and birds.
Berghofers Pass	Return	1hr	MED	Good views and birds.

MT WILSON/BELLS LINE OF ROAD

Cathedral of Ferns	Circuit	30min	EASY	Short walk through treeferns, rainforest.
Mount Banks Walk	Return	2hr	MED	Start Mt Banks Picnic Area. Views, birds.

Suggested tours – Map 35

Weekend escape tour

Approximate distance

70km from Richmond to Sydney CBD; tour route (Glenbrook to Richmond) — 360km

About the tour

Take advantage of the region's guest house tradition and book a weekend package to stay overnight somewhere along this route. Drive along the M4 Mwy to the foot of the Mountains, then follow the Great Western Hwy, detouring to Jenolan Caves, and completing the loop along the Bells Line of Rd with a stop at Mt Wilson.

Gardens tour

Approximate distance

80km from Sydney CBD to Glenbrook; tour route (Richmond to Glenbrook) — 180km

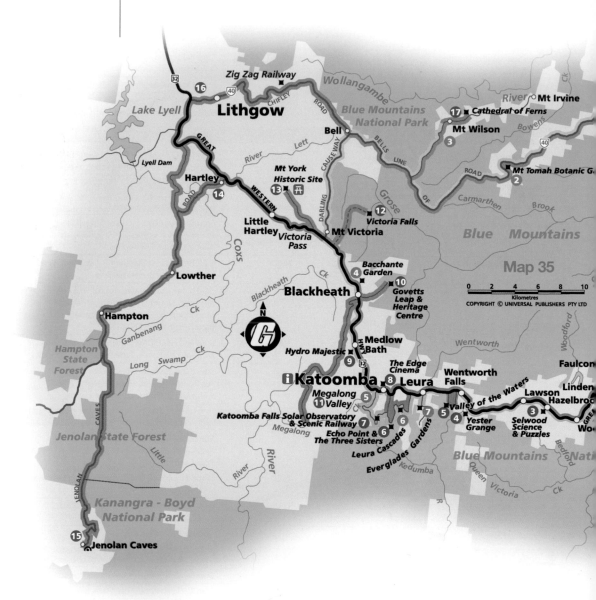

About the trip

Because of the cooler climate and its rich soil, the Blue Mountains have produced many spectacular gardens, some with impressive views. Spring and autumn are often the best times for garden lovers to tour, particularly at Mt Wilson, where many gardens are open seasonally. Enjoy the magnificent surroundings, while climbing into the Mountains, via the scenic Bells Line of Rd, and winding back down to Sydney through the Blue Mountain villages on the Great Western Hwy.

Places of interest (Weekend escape)

1. Visitor Info Centre, Glenbrook (p.194)
2. Lennox Bridge (p.194)
3. Selwood Science and Puzzles, Hazelbrook (p.195)
4. Yester Grange (outside)
5. Valley of the Waters and Conservation Hut, Wentworth Falls (p.199)
6. Echo Pt and The Three Sisters (p.196)
7. Scenic World (p.197)
8. The Edge Cinema, Katoomba (p.197)
9. Grand Mercure Hydro Majestic Hotel, Medlow Bath (p.198)
10. Blue Mountains Heritage Centre, Govetts Leap, Blackheath (p.190)
11. Megalong Valley (p.192)
12. Victoria Falls (p.193)
13. Mt York Historic Site (p.193)
14. Hartley (p.190)
15. Jenolan Caves (p.191)
16. Lithgow (p.191)
17. Cathedral of Ferns, Mt Wilson (p.190)

Places of interest (Gardens)

1. Kurrajong Heights, for breathtaking views back to Sydney (p.189)
2. Mt Tomah Botanic Gardens (p.201)
3. Mt Wilson (p.189)
4. The Campbell Rhododendron Gardens, Bacchante St (p.201)
5. Narrow Neck Rd to Cliff Drive — wonderful scenic route along the escarpment (see map 34)
6. Leura Cascades (p.198)
7. Everglades Gardens, Leura (p.201)
8. Norman Lindsay Gallery, Faulconbridge (p.194)
9. Glenbrook Native Plant Reserve, Glenbrook (p.194)

Must see, must do

★ Abercrombie Caves (p.214)

★ Food and wine of
    Mudgee (p.220)
    and Orange (p.222)

★ Mt Panorama Racing Circuit,
    Bathurst (pp.215)

★ Sofala (p.223) and
    Hill End (p.219)

★ Wollemi NP (p.226)

Radio stations

Bathurst
2BS: AM 1503
B-Rock FM: FM 99.3
Mudgee
2MG: AM 1449
REAL FM: FM 93.1
Orange
2CR: AM 549

Tourist information

Bathurst Visitor Information Centre
1 Kendall Ave, Bathurst 2795
Ph: (02) 6332 1444
www.bathurstcity.com

**Hill End Historic Site Visitor
Centre & Museum**
High St, Hill End 2850
Ph: (02) 6337 8206

Mudgee Visitor Information Centre
84 Market St, Mudgee 2850
Ph: (02) 6372 1020
www.mudgee-gulgong.org

Gulgong Visitor Information Centre
109 Herbert St, Gulgong 2852
Ph: (02) 6374 1202

National Parks and Wildlife Service
203-209 Russell St, Bathurst 2795
Ph: (02) 6332 9488
1/160 Church St, Mudgee 2850
Ph: (02) 6372 7199
Ross St, Oberon 2787
Ph: (02) 6336 1972
www.nationalparks.nsw.gov.au

Oberon Tourist Information
48 Ross St, Oberon 2787
Ph: (02) 6336 0666
www.oberonaustralia.com.au

Orange Visitor Centre
Civic Sq, Byng St, Orange 2800
Ph: (02) 6393 8226
www.orange.nsw.gov.au

explorer country

THERE ARE MANY GOOD REASONS
to visit Explorer Country which is
centred on Bathurst, just west of the
majestic Blue Mountains. The first port
of call for early explorers on their way
to discover the great inland of Australia,
the area has a long and fascinating
history. Other diverse attractions include
natural wonders such as limestone
caves and trout-stocked waterways, Mt
Panorama Raceway, and the fine wines
and produce of Mudgee and Orange.
This winning combination results in
a prime holiday destination.

Bathurst is the oldest inland
settlement in Australia, and this area
on the western slopes of the Great
Dividing Range recalls a significant
historical period. It was here that gold
was first discovered in Australia — an
event that played a pivotal role in the
region's development.

Bathurst offers many reminders of
the prosperity brought by gold, as well
as being an attractive modern city, while
small towns like Sofala, Hill End and
Ophir are authentic relics of the
goldrush era. On the outskirts of the
area, Orange and Mudgee are two fine
regional centres surrounded by fertile
countryside and historic villages. This
part of the country supports a thriving
food and wine industry and provides a
real taste of rural Australia only a couple
of hours from Sydney.

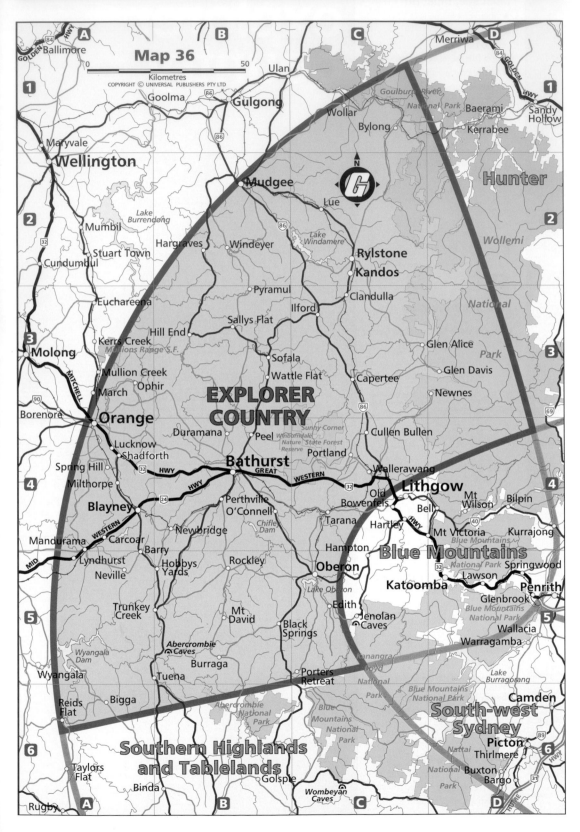

Natural features

This region lies west of the Great Dividing Range, which separates the rivers flowing east to the Pacific Ocean from those running south and west to the Southern Ocean. Like the Blue Mountains, much of the Range is made up of sandstone but there are also shale and limestone outcrops. The countryside is hilly, with pretty valleys sheltering willow-lined streams, and ridges affording panoramic views. There are also many state forests, mainly pine plantations.

The geology of the country around Bathurst has had an enormous influence on the development of the region. The fertile soil brought the early pastoralists; and the many small streams of the region yielded gold, triggering the goldrushes of the 1850s that brought prosperity to the area. Shale oil brought extensive industrial development at Newnes and Glen Davis, while the vast coal reserves of Lithgow Valley led to the development of Lithgow. Natural limestone deposits formed the extensive cave system at Abercrombie, which is now a very popular local attraction.

Ancient volcanic activity, centred on Mt Canobolas near Orange, has resulted in rich volcanic soils which provide perfect conditions for the impressive local food and wine industry.

History

For at least 40 000 years — possibly nearer 60 000 years — before white settlement occurred, the Wiradjuri Aborigines lived in the region now known as the Macquarie Valley.

Surveyor George Evans was sent to explore the region after Europeans crossed the Blue Mountains (see p.185). He named the Macquarie River and also the Bathurst Plains, returning with favourable accounts of both areas. Governor Macquarie decided that a road should be built over the mountains.

Completed in January 1815, the road was built by William Cox. He and William Lawson were the first private pastoralists, making Bathurst the first European settlement west of the Great Dividing Range. Not surprisingly, however, the white settlers met with resistance from the Wiradjuris and there was a long period of war for the land.

To begin with, Bathurst was predominantly a convict and military settlement and the earliest free settlers, who named their town Kelso, were restricted to the east side of the river.

Eventually the land was opened up and Bathurst became the centre of a large pastoral area. The town boomed in the 1850s and 1860s with the discovery of gold and in 1862, the world famous Cobb & Co Coach Company established

LAKE CANOBOLAS

LAVENDER FARM NEAR ORANGE

east, the M4 Mwy leads out of Sydney to the Great Western Hwy (Hwy 32) which climbs the Blue Mountains escarpment, crossing the mountains via Katoomba before reaching the Western Slopes at Victoria Pass, 127km from Sydney.

Further north is Bells Line of Rd (Route 40). It begins where Richmond Bridge crosses the Hawkesbury River and climbs the escarpment to Kurrajong Hts, running through orchards and natural bushland to Lithgow, where it reaches the Western Slopes, some 136km from Sydney.

The two roads join in Lithgow, an easy 2hr drive from Sydney, and divide again into the extensive road network covering the area. To get to Mudgee, take the turnoff near Lithgow. For Orange, continue on the Mitchell Hwy from Bathurst. State Rail coaches as well as private coach companies service the area.

By rail

Bathurst and Lithgow enjoy an excellent rail connection with Sydney, with a daily service provided by the Countrylink XPT. Lithgow is also serviced by Sydney's regular electric train system on the Blue Mountains Line. To get to Mudgee, a coach from Lithgow Stn connects with the trains. Orange is linked to Sydney with a daily Countylink XPT service.

Getting around
By taxi

If you arrive in Bathurst without a car, you can take a taxi tour around the city to attractions such as Mt Panorama and stately homes. Drivers generally have good local knowledge. Contact Bathurst Visitor Info Centre, Ph: (02) 6332 1444

Cycling

Bathurst has several routes for bicycles including a short circuit along the Macquarie River and a longer route around town. Keen cyclists can even ride around the Mt Panorama Racing Circuit (anti-clockwise is the recommended direction). Other popular peddling trips in the area are out to Perthville, Georges Plains, Rockley and Newbridge. The surrounding state forests and nature

its headquarters here. Rail arrived in 1876, and in 1885 Bathurst was declared a city.

Once Bathurst had been established, settlers were attracted west to farm and graze the fertile land. Orange was first settled by Europeans in the late 1820s and the district boomed with the goldrush, spurred on by the discovery of Australia's first payable goldfields at nearby Ophir in 1851.

The towns that remained when the gold ran out were those with other riches, and Orange was certainly one of these. Now a city, Orange and the surrounding districts benefited from the rich soils, reliable rainfall and distinct seasons to become one of Australia's top agricultural areas.

Similarly, Mudgee's history began when William Lawson found good grazing country on the banks of the Cudgegong River in 1821. It was proclaimed a municipality in 1860, making it the 2nd oldest town west of the Great Divide. Although the goldrush of the 1850s and 1860s arrived in the area, Mudgee (like Orange) never depended on gold alone for its prosperity, profiting instead from the rich land which supported cattle, sheep and grape vines. Whereas many of the surrounding towns died when the gold ran out, Mudgee survived and continues to thrive.

Getting there
By road

There are two major roads connecting Sydney to the Bathurst area. From the

HISTORIC DETAIL

An original **Cobb & Co coach** is on display at Bathurst Visitors Centre on William St.

reserves also provide exciting trails for mountain biking.

In **Mudgee**, a popular way to tour the vineyards is by bicycle, with bike hire available from the Riverside Caravan Park. Ph: (02) 6372 2531

By air

Take to the air with **Bathurst Vintage Joyflights** in a beautifully restored Tiger Moth for views of the area from the open cockpit. Ph: 0409 455 084. For those with a desire for speed, jet fighter flights can be arranged (Ph: 1800 880 501), or slow right down in a glider with the **Bathurst Soaring Club**. Ph: (02) 6337 1180

Festivals and events

Wattle Flat Bronze Thong and Family Fun Day

A classic bush race meeting held in Jan at **Wattle Flat**, north of Bathurst on the way to Sofala, set in a paddock with horse races, music and craft stalls.

Rockley Rodeo

This typical country rodeo is held in Feb each year with loads of fun for spectators and competitors.

Orange Winefest

Orange producers showcase their wines during the annual Winefest, held in Oct. www.orangewines.com.au

Sofala Show

An enjoyable rural show, with exhibitions, stalls and animals, held in Feb.

Rylstone and District Show

Held on the last Sat in Feb. There are competitions for horses, cattle, sheep, dogs and wood chopping, as well as stalls and a range of entertainment for the whole family.

Banjo Paterson Festival

The birthplace of Banjo Paterson, **Orange** celebrates its literary heritage and culture every year in Feb/Mar.

Bathurst Gold Crown

The southern hemisphere's richest country 2-year-old harness racing event is held at the Bathurst Showground, Kendall Ave in Mar each year incorporating lead-up races and other festivities.

Mudgee Show

A two-day agricultural show held in early Mar.

Bathurst and Villages Autumn Heritage Festival

A celebration of the heritage of Bathurst and surrounding villages, this festival coincides with the **Autumn Colours Program** from Mar to May.

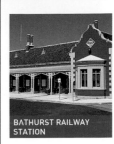
BATHURST RAILWAY STATION

TIGER MOTH, BATHURST VINTAGE JOYFLIGHTS

ABERCROMBIE HOUSE, BATHURST

FOOD WEEK

Royal Bathurst Show

On the 2nd weekend after Easter, Bathurst hosts one of the largest agricultural shows in country NSW, with animals, crafts, rides and food, at the Showgrounds, Kendall Ave.

FOOD (Food of Orange District) Week

Every year in Apr, **Orange** celebrates the agricultural abundance of the region, with local food and wine in the spotlight.

Bylong Mouse Races

Held in Apr at Bylong, 50km north of Rylstone.

Henry Lawson Heritage Festival

Every Jun long weekend, a three-day celebration of Henry Lawson's literary traditions is held in **Gulgong** with writing, poetry reading, street theatre, buskers and street markets.

Mudgee Small Farms Field Days

One of Australia's premier rural educational events, drawing huge crowds from well beyond the district. Held over two days (Fri–Sat) in Jul.

Mudgee Wine Festival

Since 1979, the winemakers and people of Mudgee have marked the start of the new growing season with this month-long festival in Sept.

Oberon Daffodil Festival

Late in Sept, when the daffodils are at their best, the town celebrates the arrival of spring with a weekend of garden competitions and other festivities.

Bathurst 1000 Touring Car Race

The Bathurst 1000 motor race held on the 2nd weekend in Oct has become a major national sporting event, with many festivities taking place in the preceding week. The **Mt Panorama** racing circuit is a demanding one for drivers, but offers spectacular viewing for motor racing fans, especially from the top of the mountain.

Australian National Field Days

In Oct/Nov, **Orange** is home to the biggest rural expo in the country, attracting huge crowds each year.

Carols by Candlelight

Carols are held in Dec in at **Machattie Park** in Bathurst and also at **Abercrombie Caves**.

Main localities and towns

Abercrombie Caves Map 39

Situated just south of Trunkey Creek on the Goulburn Rd are Abercrombie Caves, one of the region's most appealing spots.

The main cavern, the imposing **Archway**, swept by subterranean Grove Creek, is the largest natural limestone arch in the southern hemisphere. Solid masses of limestone decorate the cave walls, highlighted by the soft natural light from each end. Miners built a platform for dancing during the goldrush, and it is sometimes used today for underground concerts and weddings. Just before Christmas it may be the setting for 'Carols in the Caves'.

The caves are surrounded by natural bushland with swimming holes and at the southern end the 70m **Grove Creek Falls**. The reserve has some good bushwalks, including tracks to the Falls and **Mt Gray Goldmine**, where evidence of mining can still be seen. One of the area's pleasures is the abundant wildlife: colourful native birds, kangaroos, wallabies, eastern water dragons, wombats and possums.

The reserve is busy on weekends and holidays; it is worth trying to visit during

ABERCROMBIE CAVES

the week, when things are generally quieter and wildlife more easily spotted.

The caves are open for a self-guided tour daily, 9am–4pm. Special or evening inspections can be arranged with the Caves Superintendent. Ph: (02) 6359 3311

Bathurst Map 37

Bathurst is a thriving city, retaining many of its historic attractions such as mining, agriculture, art galleries, houses and parks. Bathurst is also a centre for car racing enthusiasts, with the **Mt Panorama Motor Racing Circuit** hosting professional races twice a year, and various other motoring events at other times. Experience a taste of the area and something of the excitement and disappointment of motor racing on the mountain at the **National Motor Racing Museum** at Murrays Corner, Mt Panorama. Changing displays feature famous racing cars and bikes, memorabilia and photographs. Open daily, 9am–4.30pm. Ph: (02) 6332 1872

Also at Mt Panorama, at the top of Conrod Straight, the **Bathurst Goldfields** provide an authentic reconstruction of gold mining operations as they were at Hill End, Sofala and Trunkey Creek during the goldrush era. Although the Goldfields only cater for group tours, individuals are welcome to join in if one is being conducted. Tour times available

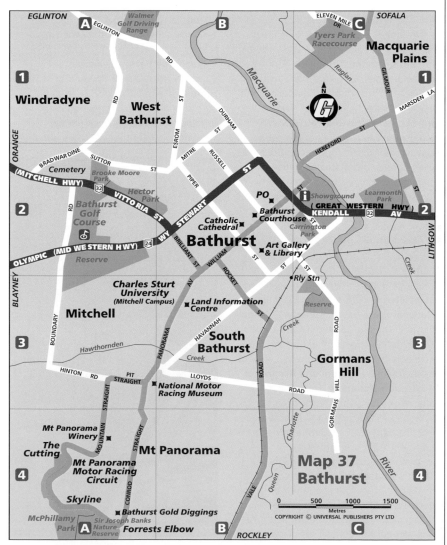

Map 37
Bathurst

0   500   1000   1500
Metres
COPYRIGHT © UNIVERSAL PUBLISHERS PTY LTD

CRIMINAL HISTORY

The notorious Ribbon Gang were believed to have used **Bushranger Cave** at Abercrombie Caves in 1830 as a hideout before they were captured, tried and hanged for murder, bushranging and horse stealing.

from Bathurst Visitor Info Centre.
Ph: (02) 6332 2022

Visit **McPhillamy Park** at the top of Mt Panorama for stunning views over Bathurst and the surrounding farms.

Back in town, the **Regional Art Gallery** in Keppel St displays a fine collection, which includes some outstanding works by Lloyd Rees. Open Tues–Fri 10am–5pm, Sat 10am–5pm (closed 1–2pm), Sun and public holidays 2pm–5pm. Ph: (02) 6331 6066

Check out the **T-Rex** at the **Australian Fossil & Mineral Museum**, the home of the Somerville Collection. This superb collection consists of fossils and minerals from all over the world. Open Mon–Sat 10am-4pm, Sun 10am–2pm Ph: (02) 6331 5511

Designed by Government Architect James Barnet and completed in 1880, the **Bathurst Court House** in Russell St is now the district court. It is a fine example of Victorian architecture and is listed by the National Trust. The west wing contains the **Central Western Music Centre**, a branch of the Sydney Conservatorium of Music, and the east wing houses the **Historical Museum**. The courthouse is open weekdays 10am–4pm (closed 1pm–2pm). The museum is open Tues, Wed and weekends 10am–4pm. Ph: (02) 6332 4755

Abercrombie House in Ophir Rd, Mt Pleasant, is one of the finest stately homes in Australia. Built of local granite, the huge Scottish baronial mansion was completed in 1878 and is a magnificent National Trust-listed property. It is now home to the Morgan family and contains a fascinating collection of objects and artefacts from around the world, as well as the unique **Museum and Archive of Australian Monarchy**. Open most Sun afternoons for public tours, on other days by appt. Closed mid-Jul to late Sept. Ph: (02) 6331 4929 or Bathurst Visitor Info Centre for tour times.

Another historic building is **Miss Traill's House**, at 321 Russell St. Built in 1845, the Georgian cottage has formal gardens and a collection which provides an accurate record of the life and times of a pioneering family. Part of every visit

is a tour explaining the house's history and collections, which Miss Traill bequeathed to the National Trust in the late 1970s. Open for tours 10am–3pm weekends only in winter and Fri–Sun Sep–May. Guided group tours can be arranged outside these days and hours. Ph: (02) 6332 4232

Chifley Home, at 10 Busby St, was the home of Bathurst's most famous citizen, former Prime Minister of Australia (1945-49), Ben Chifley, and his wife Elizabeth. Open Sun–Mon, 11am–3pm, Contact Bathurst Visitor Info Centre.

Old Government Cottage is the remains of the building which housed the town's commandant. It contains a collection of colonial furniture and historic artefacts. Open Sun, 1.30pm–3.30pm, or contact the Bathurst Historical Society. Ph: (02) 6332 4755

Machattie Park, behind the courthouse, was once the site of Bathurst Gaol, but is now a large park featuring a superb begonia house, fountain, fern house, duck ponds, rotunda and beautiful old trees, ideal

BATHURST COURT HOUSE

ROYAL HOTEL,
BATHURST

for a picnic. Another popular picnic spot is **Macquarie River Bicentennial Park** on the banks of the river, with an excellent children's playground, cycleways and a stone weir.

The park opposite the courthouse, **Kings Parade**, is a focal point for the city. It was designed to house the Evans and Boer War Memorial monuments. The Carillon bell tower was built here in 1933 as a memorial to people of the Bathurst region who served in WWI. The bells mark the quarter and half hours and chime on the hour. Musical excerpts are played daily at noon and 1pm.

Live animal shows are conducted at the Bathurst Sheep and Cattle Drome, Limekilns Rd. This 400ha sheep grazing property is also popular for farmstay holidays offering visitors the chance to experience Australian farm life. Horseriding, bushwalking and golf are also available. Ph: (02) 6337 3634.

Bathurst Observatory is situated on the same sheep grazing property and offers spectacular views of the night skies. Open on clear nights with bookings essential. Ph: (02) 6337 3988

Excellent fresh fruit and vegetables from the surrounding areas are for sale at the **Farmers' Markets** held at the Bathurst Showground on the 4th Sat of each month. Local cheeses, jams, pickles, olive oil and other produce are showcased.

OLD GOVERNMENT COTTAGE, BATHURST

Blayney Map 39

The service centre for Blayney Shire, Blayney lies 38km SW of Bathurst. The town's prosperity has been maintained by the surrounding agricultural country and by mining gold, copper and iron. The area still has large gold deposits, currently worked by the large **gold mine** at nearby **Cadia**. With European settlement dating back to the mid 1800s, the town has some historic buildings of note, pleasant parks and the Viv Kable Museum in the Blayney Library. Blayney's wide streets are lined with deciduous trees, particularly attractive in autumn. Ph: (02) 6368 2104

Ben Chifley — the light on the hill

Former Australian Prime Minister Ben Chifley spent much of his childhood with his grandparents on a farm outside Bathurst. His strong Labor convictions grew from his observations of the lives of working class people, including battling farmers. A union representative before entering Parliament in 1928 (after several attempts), he later became Treasurer in Curtin's government and assumed the Prime Ministership on John Curtin's death one month before the end of WWII. Chifley played a leading and inspirational role in Australia's post-war reconstruction. His achievements include the setting up of the Snowy Mountains Hydro Electric Scheme, the Trans Australia Airline (TAA) and the Australian National Shipping Line, nationalising Qantas, and reorganising and enlarging the CSIRO and the Australian National University. He died in 1951. The Bathurst branch of the ALP's annual dinner honours the man for whom 'the light on the hill was forever beckoning'.

VALLEY VIEWS

On the way to Lithgow just up the hill from Capertee, take a short detour up to **Pearsons Lookout** for splendid views over the Capertee Valley.

Burraga Map 36 B5

Approximately 70km south of Bathurst, Burraga was established in the 1880s when a copper mine began operations nearby. The remains of the mine, at its peak the third largest copper producer in Australia, can still be seen from the village, with an enormous chimney stack rising from the ruins.

Wool, cattle and pine plantations are now the area's main industries, while fossicking remains a popular pursuit.

Burraga Dam used to supply the mine's water and now provides a picturesque area for picnicking and camping, as well as some good trout fishing. Burraga Sports and Recreation Club is the town's main social and sporting focus, with an oval, cricket pitch and golfing facilities. Open Wed and Fri evenings, Sat 2–11pm and Sun 1–7.30pm Ph: (02) 6337 0362. The Village Store is the local transaction centre, Ph: (02) 6337 0255 The route to Burraga from Rockley includes 5km of unsealed road.

Carcoar Map 39

Nestled in the Belubula Valley, Carcoar has a fascinating history which is still proudly on display. Many of the town's 19th century buildings are **National Trust classified**, including the courthouse, hospital, churches and Commercial Bank (where Ben Hall's gang staged Australia's first daylight bank hold-up). The best way to appreciate the atmosphere is with a walking tour map and by visiting the local museums, galleries and antique shops. The **Belubula River** is a pleasant spot for picnics, BBQs and swimming. For info on Carcoar, Ph: (02) 6367 3085

Glen Davis Map 39

Glen Davis, at the head of the beautiful **Capertee Valley**, was formerly a shale mining town with a population of 2000. After WWII the government decided the industry was not economically viable and had to be closed. Miners went on strike for 26 days underground, but in 1952 everything was shut down and most of the people left. The present population is about 20.

The Glen Davis Park camping ground offers visitors a place to stay in the village, as well as a pleasant picnic spot. Bushwalkers, birdwatchers and artists visit often, and it is said that sometimes a ghostly figure can be seen wandering among the ruins.

A bushwalking trail in the Wollemi NP leads up to **Newnes** (see p.220), and the valley is renowned for its variety of native birdlife.

MACQUARIE WOODS

West of Bathurst on the Mitchell Hwy, **Macquarie Woods** is a State Forest Recreation Area which explains different aspects of forestry, with an info centre, picnic facilities, lookouts and walking tracks. Leaflet available from Bathurst Visitors Centre.

LOCAL MUSEUM, CARCOAR

HILL END STREET SCENE

4WD FAVOURITE
From Hill End, the 4WD **Bridle Track** follows closely the route of the original bridle track between Bathurst and the Hill End goldfields, along the Macquarie and Turon Rivers. Map available at Bathurst Visitor Info Centre.

Hill End Map 39

After gold was found at Hawkins Hill in the 1870s, Hill End, 84km NW of Bathurst, became one of the largest inland towns in NSW. High on the plateau above the Turon River, the town was home to a boom that lasted two decades, but when the gold ran out the population dwindled as miners moved on to new areas.

Most of Hill End's buildings date back to the early 1870s, and little has changed. With a population of around 150, the township is now an Historic Site. Hill End Visitor Centre & Museum, formerly the district hospital, is open daily and offers a wealth of information about the area. The museum houses many interesting artefacts of the gold-rush era and provides a fascinating look at life in those times.

The **Bald Hill Mine** has been restored by the NPWS who conduct regular tours, contact the Visitor Info Centre for details. The village has a general store, accommodation establishments that include the **Royal Hotel** and **Hosies B&B** (both 1872), and the Village and Glendora camping areas with amenities that include hot showers. Ph: (02) 6337 8206

Kandos Map 39

Situated just off the Lithgow-Mudgee Rd on the western edge of the Great Dividing Range, Kandos was settled in the early 1900s and owes its presence to the production of cement. It provides access to the beautiful **Capertee**, **Cudgegong** and **Bylong Valleys**.

The **Kandos Bicentennial Industrial Museum** at 22 Buchanan St was originally a Methodist Church, built in 1919 when the American cement works manager offered to supply free cement, providing the church was built in the style of those in his home town in the USA. As a result, the architecture is unique in Australia. The museum has an interesting range of exhibits highlighting the district's industrial heritage. Open Fri, 3pm–4.30pm, weekends and public holidays 10.30am–4.30pm, or by appt. Ph: (02) 6379 4057 or (02) 6379 4057

Lucknow Map 36 A4

A small village 8km east of Orange, Lucknow has a colourful history dating back to 1851 when two tenant farmers found a deposit of gold on the hill behind the settlement. Unlike most finds (which were on Crown land), the Lucknow goldfield was on private land and therefore not open to the public. For many years, until mining finally ceased in 1937, the field produced gold of a very rich and distinctive nature.

Lucknow's name became official in 1863 with the opening of the post office. Today, visitors can search for treasure and crafts in the local stores.

Millthorpe Map 39

Halfway between Bathurst and Orange, south of the Mitchell Hwy at Shadforth, Millthorpe calls itself a living museum — the entire village is registered on the National Estate and offers interesting

KANDOS BICENTENNIAL INDUSTRIAL MUSEUM

VINEYARD, MUDGEE

FOOD AND WINE

Mudgee's fertile countryside supports much more than wine and honey. Many other kinds of quality produce can be enjoyed at local restaurants or on the area's **Food and Wine Trails**. Contact Mudgee Visitor Info Centre.

art, craft and antique shops. At the **Golden Memories Museum**, rural Australian life from 1880 is recalled with an extensive collection. Open weekends, 1.30pm–5pm (4pm in winter), public and school holidays, 10am–5pm. Ph: (02) 6366 3079. A brochure, available from local shops and businesses, describes the town in great detail. Ph: (02) 6366 3253

Mudgee Map 39

About 50km NW of Rylstone and Kandos is Mudgee, set in a green and pleasant landscape. The wine industry around Mudgee dates back to the 1850s, when it was started by the German immigrant, Adam Roth. Although wine making survived the 19th century gold rush, the industry declined in later years and only experienced a resurgence in the 1970s. The region now has over 35 wineries and is credited with introducing the chardonnay grape to Australia.

The profusion of flora in the region attracts bees, and several honey companies have taken advantage of this, with different kinds of honey produced at various times of the year by skilled beekeepers. Two local companies offer sales and honey tastings: **Mudgee Honey Haven**, cnr Gulgong and Hargraves Rds, Ph: (02) 6372 4478; and **Honey Hive**, 43 Church St, Ph (02) 6372 4589.

A local interlink coach is available to take visitors around town; or book a tour to see wineries and other attractions.

Mudgee's past is well represented with a number of fine old buildings, many listed by the National Trust, outlined in a **Town Walks'** brochure available from the Visitor Info Centre. Also available is a brochure identifying the town's tree species. Some of the trees are so old that the **Mudgee Town Arboretum** was declared, focusing on the plantings in Robertson Park, with its beautiful gardens and band rotunda, and Lawson Park on the banks of the Cudgegong River.

Mudgee's heritage is preserved at the **Colonial Inn Museum**, situated in the **Old West End Hotel**, restored to re-create the 1870s and with a large collection of old photographs. Open 7 days, Mon to Fri, 10–3pm, Sat and school holidays, 2pm–5pm, Sun and public holidays, 10am–5pm.

Newnes Map 36 D3

A walk through Newnes, on the edge of **Wollemi NP** (see p.226), is a fascinating experience. In its heyday, the town serviced a huge shale oil extraction plant which was operational until 1932. These days, although there is a kiosk open on Sats, Newnes is really a **ghost town**.

The NPWS looks after the ruins, and there is a 2.5km interpretive walk around the ruins. Experienced bushwalkers can walk **The Pipeline Track** to Glen Davis in the next valley, an 18km return walk. The Newnes camping area straddles the Wolgan River. Facilities include pit toilets and BBQs (take your own wood). The Newnes Hotel is open weekends for supplies and information about the area. More info and a walking track guide are available from the NPWS Heritage Centre at Blackheath. Ph: (02) 4787 8877

Oberon Map 36 C5

Oberon is the gateway to **Jenolan Caves** (see p.191) and **Kanangra-Boyd NP** (see p.225). Its main industry is timber, grown predominantly in pine tree plantations. The countryside is popular with fossickers for gold, sapphires and other gemstones. **Fossicking tours** run from Oberon, and there are designated fossicking areas available.

MUDGEE WINERY

At the old Railway Stn on Lowes Mt Rd is the **Oberon and District Museum**, open Sat, 2pm–5pm or by appt. Ph: (02) 6336 1016

Lake Oberon in Jenolan St is stocked with trout and has picnic facilities, a playground and BBQs. While fishing is permitted, boating and swimming are not. **Horseriding** is on offer in the area, and there are a number of **farmstay** opportunities around Oberon.

Also highly prized are the exotic **wood mushrooms** which grow in the pine forests, although pickers must be careful to distinguish between edible and inedible fungi. The best time for mushrooming is from late Jan–end of May. Contact the State Forest (Macquarie Region) for a leaflet, Ph: (02) 6331 2044. Oberon Visitor Info Centre also provides leaflets on mushrooming, fishing and driving tours from Oberon, and much else besides. Ph: (02) 6336 0666. The **Cobweb Craft Shop** in Oberon St, showcases the town's priceless Bicentennial Tapestries. These stunning tapestries took 13 000hrs to make and almost everyone in Oberon took part in the project. Ph: (02) 6336 1895, www.cobwebcraftshop.com

On the way out of town towards Jenolan Caves on Ross St, the **National Parks and Wildlife Service Office** mainly caters for bushwalkers, with maps and info on Kanangra-Boyd, the Southern Blue Mountains and Abercrombie River NPs, and Yerranderie SRA. Open most Mon–Fri, 8.30am–5pm. Ph: (02) 6336 1972

O'Connell Map 36 B4

Located 18km from Bathurst on the Oberon Rd, O'Connell was first settled in the early 1820s when the Sydney Rd passed right through the valley. It is now classified by the **National Trust** and the restored **O'Connell Hotel** is a pleasant place to stop, with its beer garden under the shade of an old elm tree. The hotel also offers hearty counter meals and the publican is happy to answer questions about the local area. Ph: (02) 6337 5745

There are some top fishing spots around O'Connell. **Chifley Dam** is well-stocked with trout and native fish species, and is also popular for waterskiing, sailing and camping.

About 6km from O'Connell along the Tarana Road is **Flat Rock**, a favourite local choice for fishing and swimming, and ideal for picnics under the shady trees. Another good location is just out of Tarana by the river on the O'Connell–Tarana Rd.

Ophir Reserve Map 39

In 1851, Ophir was the site of Australia's first official gold find, precipitating the country's first goldrush. By 1852, that

PLOUGHING, ORANGE

GOLD MINER, OPHIR RESERVE, ORANGE

rush was over, with miners moving on to more promising goldfields, although Ophir was never completely abandoned. In 1866, another phase of reef mining began, and even today, gold can be found.

Ophir is now a **recreation reserve**, focusing on a pretty picnic and camping ground. Visitors can also take a guided tour through **Gunnadoo Goldmine**, a working mine at the reserve. Ophir is 27km north of Orange, with about half the route on unsealed road. A brochure from Orange Visitor Info Centre describes Ophir's history and some interesting walks in the area.

Orange Map 39

A prosperous city servicing a prime agricultural area, Orange is named after the 'Prince of Orange', later King of Holland. In fact, oranges are one of the few things that don't grow in the region. The huge range of delicious local produce can be enjoyed in Orange's cafes and award-winning restaurants, and the area's excellent cool–climate **wineries**—there are over 50—welcome visitors for sales and tastings. www.orangewines.com.au

The city has a surprising number of parks — 130 in all — including **Cook Heritage Park**, **Robertson Park**, the **Botanic Gardens** with themed gardens that showcase the four seasons, and **Banjo Paterson Park**, at the birthplace of the famous Australian poet, marked by the **Banjo Paterson Memorial**. Cook and Robertson Parks are included in the

Orange City Heritage Trail brochure (available from Orange Visitor Info Centre) which describes the many historic buildings and features around the city centre. It also has a number of other brochures describing walks around Orange.

The town is proud of its cultural institutions, such as the **Regional Gallery** (and library) which displays travelling and permanent exhibitions and has excellent research facilities. Ph: (02) 6393 8136. At nearby Canowindra, **The Age of Fishes Museum** is the home of fascinating fossils dating back 360 million yrs. Ph: (02) 6344 1008

Orange is also the home of **Mt Canobolas**, at 1395m above sea level it is the highest point in the central west. The peak is located in Mt Canobolas SRA, which supports an enormous diversity of vegetation as well as being home to a unique range of plants and animals, some of them endangered. The park is popular with birdwatchers and there are seven walking trails. Two of the trails lead to waterfalls (Federal and Hopetoun) that are spectacular after heavy rain; there are sweeping views from the summit. There are several picnic areas and camping at Federal Falls.

Nearby, **Lake Canobolas** offers swimming, walking and non-powered boating.

Portland Map 36 C4

The main attraction of Portland (situated 50km NE of Bathurst) is the **Mt Piper Power Station**. The **Energy Expo** visitor info centre has hands-on displays such as touch-screen computers, wind turbines, solar panels and videos. Open daily, 9am–4pm, power station tours daily 11am. Ph: (02) 6354 8155

Rockley Map 36 B5

Classified by the **National Trust**, Rockley is a beautiful historic village 34km south of Bathurst. In 1829, Governor Darling granted land to Captain Steel who named Rockley after his birthplace in Wiltshire, England. The opening of the Summerhill Copper Mine in 1848 brought a significant increase in population, which grew even further with the goldrushes of the 1850s.

The village is best visited on a Sun when the art and craft shop and museum are open. There are many attractive historic buildings in Hill and Pepper Sts, not far from **Rockley Mill**, which is now a museum open Sun and public holidays 11.30am–4.30pm. Ph: (02) 6337 9624 In nearby Church St, **Stephen's Park** has old shady trees, a river swimming hole, BBQ and a children's playground set against a steep hillside backdrop.

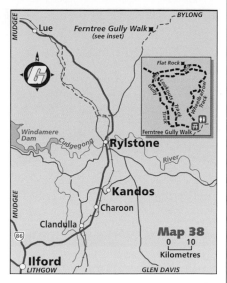

Rylstone Map 39

This picturesque town near Kandos dates back to the 1850s, with a number of original stone and slab structures remaining. Several businesses along the main street occupy the old sandstone buildings. **Rylstone Courthouse** dates from 1872, and on the footpath nearby is the starting point of the **Rylstone Heritage Tour**. A leaflet explains the history of all the main buildings. A number of galleries and craft shops operate in town, and at Rylstone Railway Stn, the **Rylstone Kandos Art and Craft Co-op** is open Thurs–Sun and all public holidays, 10am–4pm.

Rylstone Shire is renowned for its waterways and wilderness areas, with **Goulburn River NP** (p.225) and **Wollemi NP** (p.226) nearby. Scenic Drive 2 heads out to **Dunns Swamp** in Wollemi NP, 25km east of Rylstone, ideal for swimming, canoeing, camping, fishing and bushwalking. An Aboriginal art site can be seen on a short walking track from the picnic area (see Map 38).

To the west on the Cudgegong Rd out to the highway, **Cudgegong Waters Park** on Windemere Dam offers fishing, waterskiing, sailing, a boat launching ramp, BBQs, picnic areas and camping.

Sofala Map 39

Sofala is the oldest surviving **gold town** in Australia. En route to Hill End, 45km north of Bathurst by sealed road, the village dates from the 1851 discovery of gold on the Turon River (shortly after Australia's first gold discovery at the Ophir diggings). During the goldrushes up to 40 000 people, including 10 000 Chinese, lived here. The town is rich in

history, retaining its unique character, and gold can still be found in the region.

At the peak of its population boom, Sofala stretched for 17km along the **Turon River**. A fraction of that size now, the picturesque village is tucked in a valley, backed by the river and rolling hills. Many original buildings still line the narrow winding streets, and it is easy to see why famous artists such as Russell Drysdale, Donald Friend and Brett Whiteley were inspired to paint Sofala and the surrounding countryside.

The town today has a hotel, general store, craft shop, cafe and souvenir shop, and the river provides many pleasant swimming and camping spots. **Cafe Sofala** is open for lunch and dinner

ORCHARDS, ORANGE

SOFALA GENERAL STORE

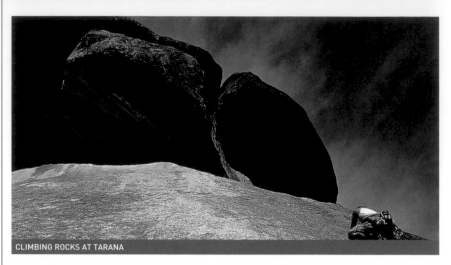

CLIMBING ROCKS AT TARANA

Fri–Sun. Fossicking tours can be arranged at the Souvenir Store and gold pan hire is available. Local gold nuggets and jewellery are on display and are for sale. Ph: (02) 6337 7075

Tarana Map 36 C4

Tarana is a pretty village in a secluded valley halfway between Bathurst and Lithgow. Access is via Brewongle, O'Connell or from the Great Western Hwy at Kirkconnell. It was from the top of the granite outcrop at **Evans Crown Nature Reserve**, not far from Tarana, that Surveyor George Evans first saw the Bathurst Plains. The reserve, with its impressive granite tors and a range of flora and fauna, can be accessed from Honeysuckle Rd. A half-hour walk leads to the top for sweeping views. This is a popular spot among rockclimbers.

Trunkey Creek Map 39

One of the earliest goldfields in Australia, Trunkey Creek is 56km south of Bathurst, on the road to Abercrombie Caves. Reminders of the goldrush include the **Golden Age Hotel**, dating from the 1860s. Some restoration has been done on the building, making it a favourite with photographers.

Although the gold has run out, the area now produces some of Australia's quality merino wool. The village provides refreshments at the **Billabong Tea House** and **The Black Stump** pub. Ph: (02) 6368 8627 or (02) 6368 8604

Yerranderie

Yerranderie is a lovingly restored **ghost town** on the edge of the **Blue Mountains NP** (see p.200). The town lies 100km from both Bathurst and the Sydney CBD. Travelling this relatively short distance, however, takes visitors on a trip back through time.

Yerranderie is yet another old mining town, but its precious metal was silver. Between 1891 and 1930, the town's 16 mines collectively yielded silver worth more than $50 million at today's prices. In the decade from 1900, the town's population grew from 100 to more than 2000, but as the silver ran out, the people left. In 1959, when direct access from Camden was cut by the flooding of the

YERRANDERIE LODGE

TOP SPOT

Bob Taylor of Sofala Souvenirs recommends **Wallaby Rocks**, a beautiful location on the Turon River 4km from Sofala along the unsealed Hill End Rd, with shady trees for picnics and a swimming hole.

Burragorang Valley (part of Warragamba Dam project), the remaining inhabitants departed, leaving Yerranderie with a population of two.

Now the site is run as an historic privately-owned ghost town. The town is an **eco-tourism venture**, catering for tourists seeking a combination of seclusion, wilderness scenery and stimulating history, both European and Aboriginal.

Lodge accommodation and camping facilities are available, and the town is an excellent base for exploring the surrounding country either on foot, bicycle, or by 4WD. Visitors can fly in from Camden or drive in by 4WD. Bookings essential, Ph: (02) 4659 6165 or (02) 9955 8083. www.yerranderie.com

National parks

Three large national parks (**Blue Mountains**, **Kanangra-Boyd** and **Wollemi**) and two smaller ones (**Gardens of Stone** and **Goulburn River**) roughly form the eastern border of Explorer Country. Detailed info about the parks is available from the **Blue Mountains Heritage Centre**, Govetts Leap Rd, Blackheath. Ph: (02) 4787 8877

Blue Mountains NP Map 36 D4

Bordering the eastern edge of the western slopes, the park includes much of the Blue Mountains. The area was nominated for World Heritage Listing in 1998 (see p.200 for main entry).

Gardens of Stone NP Map 39

About 30km north of Lithgow on the way to Mudgee, this park protects 400 million-year-old pagoda formations (sandstone with ironstone plates). A great variety of plants and animals thrive in this area, including koalas, powerful owls and turquoise parrots, however, the rocky landscape is especially suited to reptiles.

Apart from a few fire trails for walking there are limited facilities in the park. Day-use facilities are available at **Baal Bone Gap**, where bushwalks lead to Pantoneys Crown and excellent views.

Goulburn River NP Map 36 C1

East of Mudgee, this park protects the scenic reaches of the Goulburn River. A good range of facilities and activities is available (see p.171).

Kanangra-Boyd NP Map 36 C5

This 68 000ha park lies 5km south of Jenolan Caves, off the Oberon Rd. About 90% of this area is part of the Kanangra-Boyd Wilderness Area and conserves two main areas: elevated Boyd Plateau and the labyrinth of creeks, rivers, gorges and ridges where the plateau falls off.

JOEY AT YERRANDERIE LODGE

GARDENS OF STONE NP

PANTONEYS CROWN, GARDENS OF STONE NP

Access to the park's main attraction, the stunning cliffs of **Kanangra Walls**, is via a 30km gravel road. three short walks start from the Kanangra Walls carpark: the Lookout, Waterfall and Plateau Walks. Other longer walks can be taken in the park, although overnight walks and long treks need to be well planned.

There are also several popular **4WD routes** in the park. Many species of plants and wildlife are found within this wilderness area, and for visitors who wish to stay overnight, a vehicle-based campsite with pit toilets and wood burning BBQs (take firewood) is available at the Boyd River Camping Area. Ph: (02) 6336 1972

Wollemi NP Map 36 D2

Located between the western slopes and the Putty Rd, and covering 492 976ha, this is the largest wilderness area in NSW. Compared with Blue Mountains NP, it offers only limited access. Nevertheless, the Colo and Capertee Rivers are popular with canoeists. Horseriding is permitted on public roads, management trails and the Bicentennial National Trail which passes through the western side of the park. Vehicle-based camping is allowed in three spots: **Dunns Swamp**, **Wheeny Creek** and at the **Newnes** historic ruins. Swimming is possible at Wheeny Creek, and nearby tracks lead to the Colo River. Although some maps show a 4WD track between Mt Coricudgy and Putty, much of it is impassable.

A special feature of Wollemi is the **Glow Worm Tunnel**, formerly a railway tunnel and now the home of millions of glow worms. Take the Great Western Hwy or Bells Line of Road to Lithgow; from there, a 34km gravel road leads through the Newnes Forest to the tunnel's parking areas. There is a carpark at the edge of Wollemi NP (a 5km walk from the tunnel), and another carpark at the vehicle barrier in the NP, which is a 1km walk from the tunnel. Parking here is limited and both walks are difficult in some parts. Strong shoes and a torch are necessary, as the ground is damp and slippery in the tunnel.

RECENT DISCOVERY

In 1994, a new species of tree, the **Wollemi Pine** (pictured), was discovered in Wollemi NP. The species has been described as a living fossil whose closest relatives are ancient fossils from 100 million years ago.

Fun for the young

★ Camping, swimming, canoeing — Dunns Swamp, Wollemi NP (p.226)

★ Energy Expo, Mt Piper (p.222)

★ Glow Worm Tunnel, Wollemi NP (p.226)

★ Horseriding and fossicking tours, Oberon (p.220–21)

★ Self-guided cave tour, Abercrombie Caves (p.214)

★ T-Rex at the Australian Fossil & Mineral Museum, Bathurst (p.216)

Mudgee wineries

NAME	ADDRESS	PHONE	OPEN
Abercorn Winery	Cassilis Rd, Mudgee	(02) 6373 3106	10.30am–4.30pm Mon, Thur–Sat, 10.30am–3pm Sun
Blue Wren Wines	Cassilis Rd, Mudgee	(02) 6373 5320	10am–4pm Sat–Mon
Botobolar	89 Botobolar Rd, Mudgee	(02) 6373 3840	10am–5pm Mon–Sat, 10am–3pm Sun
Brittens	Stoney Creek Rd, Cooyal (off Wollar Rd)	(02) 6373 5320	9.30am–4.30pm Sat 9.30am–3pm Sun and public holidays; other times by appt
Burnbrae	Hargraves Rd, Mudgee	(02) 6373 3504	9am–5pm, every day except Tues
Craigmoor	Craigmoor Rd, Mudgee	(02) 6372 2208	10am–4.30pm Mon–Sat, 10am–4pm Sun and public holidays
Elliot Rocke Estate	Craigmoor Rd, Mudgee	(02) 6372 7722	9am–4pm Mon–Sun
Farmers Daughter Wines	791 Cassilis Rd, Mudgee	(02) 6373 3177	9am–5pm daily
Half Mile Creek	George Campbell Dr, off Cassilis Rd, Mudgee	(02) 6373 3954	10am–4pm daily
Huntington Estate	Cassilis Rd, Mudgee	(02) 6373 3825	9am–5pm Mon–Fri, 10am–5pm Sat, 10am–3pm Sun
Knights Wines	Henry Lawson Dr, Eurunderee (opposite Eurunderee School)	(02) 6373 3954	10am–4pm Sun–Fri, 9am–5pm Sat
Lawson Hill Estate	Henry Lawson Dr, Mudgee (entrance next to Henry Lawson Memorial)	(02) 6373 3953	10am–4.30pm daily
Mansfield Wines	Eurunderee Rd, Mudgee	(02) 6373 3871	9am–5pm Mon–Sat, 11am–5pm Sun
Miramar Wines	Henry Lawson Dr, Mudgee	(02) 6373 3874	9am–5pm daily
Montrose	Henry Lawson Dr, Mudgee	(02) 6373 3883	10am–4.30pm daily
Mount Ilford	2km off the Sydney road at Ilford	(02) 6358 8544	10am–4pm daily
Mt Vincent Mead	2km west along Common Rd, Mudgee (follow signs)	(02) 6372 3184	10am–5pm Mon–Sat, 10am–4pm Sun
Mudgee Wines	280 Henry Lawson Dr, Mudgee	(02) 6372 2258	10am–5pm Thurs–Mon, Tues and Wed by appt
Pieter van Gent	Black Springs Rd, Pipeclay, Mudgee	(02) 6373 3807	9am–5pm Mon–Sat, 11am–4pm Sun
Platts	Cnr Cassilis Rd and Henry Lawson Dr, Mudgee	(02) 6372 7041	from 9am daily
Seldom Seen	1/14 Industrial Ave, Mudgee	(02) 6372 4482	9.30am–5pm daily
Steins Wines	Pipeclay La, Mudgee	(02) 6373 3991	10am–4 pm daily
Thistle Hill	McDonalds Rd, Mudgee	(02) 6373 3546	9am–5pm daily
Two Furlongs	Stoney Creek Road (off Wollar Rd), Cooyal	(02) 6373 5320	10am–4 pm Mon–Fri, 11am–3pm weekends
Vinifera	194 Henry Lawson Dr, Mudgee	(02) 6372 2461	10am–5pm daily

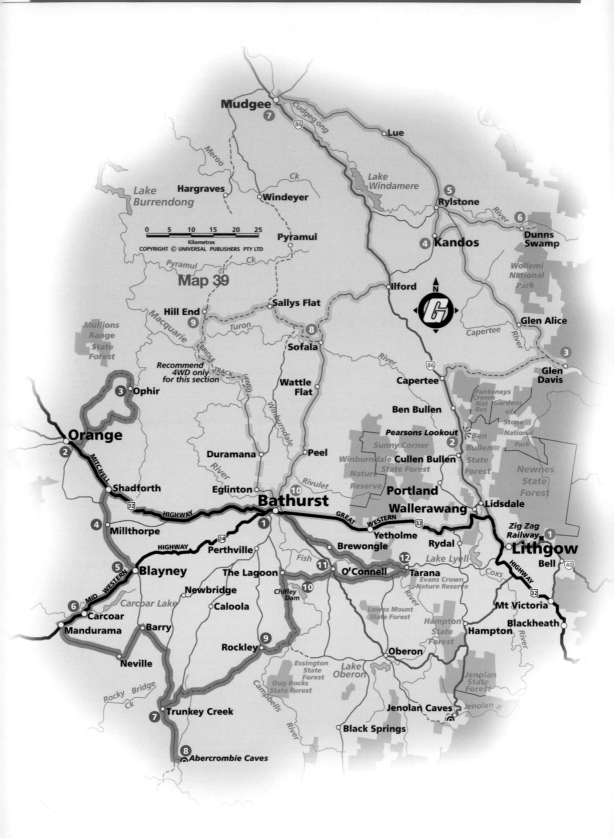

Mudgee 7

Lue

Cudgegong

Meroo

Ck

Lake Windamere

Hargraves

Windeyer

Rylstone 5

River

6

Lake Burrendong

Pyramul

Dunns Swamp

0 5 10 15 20 25
Kilometres
COPYRIGHT © UNIVERSAL PUBLISHERS PTY LTD

Kandos 4

Wollemi National Park

Pyramul Ck

Map 39

Ilford

N
G

Macquarie

Turon

Hill End 9

Sallys Flat

8

Capertee River

Glen Alice

Mullions Range State Forest

BRIDLE TRACK (4WD)

Sofala

River

3

Ophir 3

Recommend 4WD only for this section

Wattle Flat

Capertee

Glen Davis

Winburndale

Ben Bullen

Pantoneys Crown Nat Res

Gardens of Stone National Park

Orange

Duramana

Peel

Pearsons Lookout

Sunny Corner

Ben Bullen 2

Newnes State Forest

2

MITCHELL

River

Rivulet

Winburndale Nature Reserve

Cullen Bullen

Ben Bullen State Forest

Shadforth

Eglinton

32 HIGHWAY

Bathurst 1

GREAT WESTERN

Portland

Wallerawang

Lidsdale

Millthorpe 4

Perthville

24

HIGHWAY

Yetholme

Rydal

Zig Zag Railway

Lithgow 1

Brewongle

Lake Lyell

Bell 40

Blayney 5

The Lagoon

Fish

11

O'Connell

12

Tarana

Coxs

32

HIGHWAY

Newbridge

Chifley Dam

10

Evans Crown Nature Reserve

Mt Victoria

Carcoar Lake

Caloola

Lowes Mount State Forest

River

32

Carcoar 6

Barry

Hampton State Forest

Blackheath

Mandurama

Rockley

9

Hampton

Neville

Essington State Forest

Lake Oberon

Oberon

Jenolan State Forest

Rocky Bridge Ck

Dog Rocks State Forest

Campbells

Trunkey Creek 7

River

Jenolan Caves

Jenolan R

Abercrombie Caves 8

Black Springs

Suggested tours – Map 39

Note: Both these tours include some unsealed road, but a normal vehicle should have no problems.

Scenic tour from Bathurst

Approximate distance

235km from Sydney CBD to Bathurst; round trip tour from Bathurst — 350km

About the tour

The Bathurst region encompasses some marvellous countryside, and it is very easy to spend a pleasant couple of days exploring the area at your leisure.

If you have time, spend a night at Abercrombie Caves — the native wildlife there is more active in the evenings. Tour the caves, go goldpanning at Trunkey Creek, stop for a beer at O'Connell, try a spot of fishing in Chifley dam, or climb to the top of Evans Crown for magnificent views. Or, of course, you can just take in the fresh country air.

Historic tour

Approximate distance

175km from Sydney CBD to Lithgow; round trip tour from Lithgow — 470km

About the tour

Explorer Country is rich with many reminders of Australia's earliest goldrush days, and also bears the marks of localised industries like coal mining at Lithgow and cement production at Kandos.

This tour allows visitors to travel back in time as well as travelling the region. Spend the night at one of the charming old gold towns such as Hill End, Glen Davis or Rylstone. Stroll through Sofala, the oldest surviving gold mining town in the country. Have a bushwalk or camp in Wollemi NP to appreciate the area's rugged beauty.

There are some wonderful wines and honeys to be enjoyed at Mudgee, and there are cafes and restaurants to suit every budget. Explore the diverse attractions offered by the thriving regional centre of Bathurst and perhaps visit the home of former Prime Minister Ben Chifley. Visit the Observatory on a clear night and marvel at the millions of stars. Or simply have a family picnic at one of the many beautiful parks in the area.

Places of interest (Bathurst)

❶ Bathurst (p.215)
❷ Orange (p.222)
❸ Ophir (p.221)
❹ Millthorpe (p.219)
❺ Blayney (p.217)
❻ Carcoar (p.218)
❼ Trunkey Creek (p.224)
❽ Abercrombie Caves Reserve (p.214)
❾ Rockley (p.222)
❿ Chifley Dam (p.221)
⓫ O'Connell (p.221)
⓬ Tarana and Evans Crown (p.224)

Places of interest (Historic)

❶ Great Zig Zag Railway (p.192)
❷ Pearsons Lookout (p.218)
❸ Glen Davis (p.218)
❹ Kandos (p.219)
❺ Rylstone (p.223)
❻ Dunns Swamp, Wollemi NP (p.226)
❼ Mudgee (p.220)
❽ Sofala (p.223)
❾ Hill End (If you have a 4WD, take the Bridle Track from Hill End along the Macquarie River to Bathurst.) (p.219)
❿ Bathurst (p.215)

SOFALA LOCAL

southern highlands and tablelands

WHILE CLOSE TO METROPOLITAN Sydney, the Southern Highlands are distinctly different because of their cooler climate. Comparisons are often made with the countryside of England, and the region is at its most beautiful in autumn and spring, when the open gardens are a major drawcard.

The Highlands are a paradise for lovers of art, craft and antiques with dozens of interesting shops and galleries at pretty centres such as Berrima, Moss Vale and Bundanoon.

Picturesque towns like Bowral, Moss Vale and Joadja reflect the area's rich history, with many lovely old buildings restored and open to the public. Those who prefer outdoor leisure can take advantage of the local national parks or the caves at Wombeyan, or the combined historic and natural charms of Kangaroo Valley.

Further south, the city of Goulburn nestles on the Southern Tablelands, a region of high, relatively flat land used mainly for sheep grazing. Nearby Crookwell is a commercial centre for this rich agricultural area.

The whole region is perfect for a day trip from Sydney or for spending some time away at the many cosy hotels and B&Bs.

Must see, must do

- ★ Berrima (p.235)
- ★ Bundanoon (p.237)
- ★ Fitzroy Falls (p.243)
- ★ Joadja Creek Heritage tour (p.245)
- ★ Kangaroo Valley (p.239)
- ★ Morton NP (p.243)
- ★ Tulip Time Festival, Bowral (p.237)

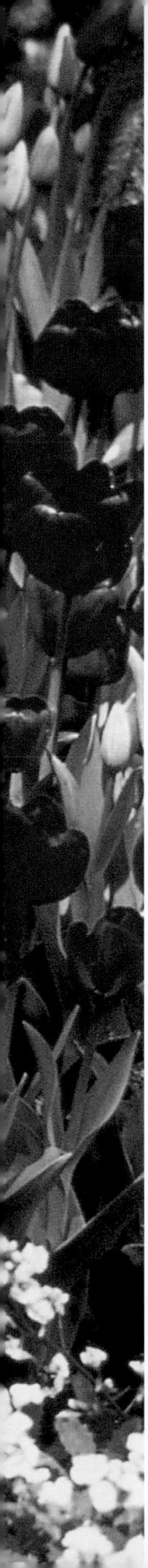

Radio stations

Southern Highlands Tourist Radio: FM 87.6
Eagle FM: FM 93.5, Goulburn
2GN: AM 1368
Community Radio: FM 103.4
2WKT: FM 107.1, Highland Community Radio
Tourist Radio: FM 88

Tourist information

Berrima Court House (Museum Information Centre)
Wilshire St, Berrima 2577
Ph: (02) 4877 1505
www.berrimacourthouse.org.au

Goulburn Visitor Information Centre
201 Sloane St, Goulburn 2580
Ph: (02) 4823 4492
www.igoulburn.com

National Parks and Wildlife Service, Fitzroy Falls Visitors Centre
Nowra Rd, Fitzroy Falls 2577
Ph: (02) 4887 7270
www.nationalparks.nsw.gov.au

Tourism Southern Highlands
Old Hume Hwy, Mittagong 2575
Ph: (02) 4871 2888 or
Freecall: 1300 657 559
www.southern-highlands.com.au
www.highlandsnsw.com.au

LEFT: TULIP TIME FESTIVAL DISPLAY

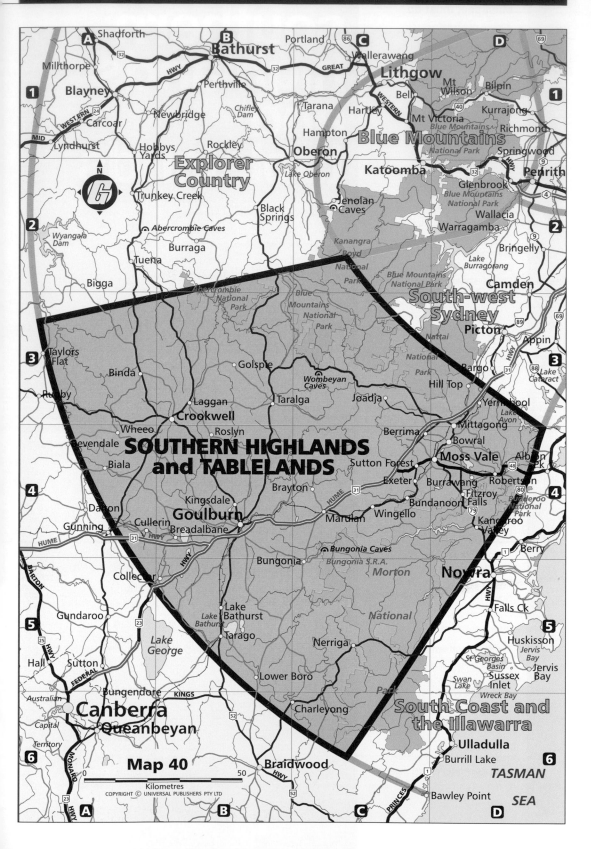

Natural features

Unlike much of Australia, the Highlands enjoys four distinct seasons. Summer temperatures range between 10°C and 30°C, while in winter the thermometer frequently drops to zero and rarely exceeds 15°C. A mild spring and a bracing autumn are reminiscent of those seasons in the northern hemisphere.

The Southern Highlands are generally between 650m and 860m above sea level, and it is this elevation that causes the cooler and more varied climate. They are made up primarily of Hawkesbury sandstone, but volcanic action has also left a legacy of rich red soils in some areas.

The region's interesting geographic variety includes towering sandstone cliffs, waterfalls, deep rainforested valleys and limestone caves.

The early settlers took advantage of the cool climate and planted many deciduous trees on their farms and in their gardens as well as along the roadsides. The changing colours of the autumn leaves and the spectacular arrival of spring blossom accentuate the changing seasons all the more. But not all the Highlands have been Europeanised; pockets of original rain-forest still survive, especially on the edge of the Illawarra Escarpment in the unspoilt expanse of Morton NP.

The Wollondilly River makes its way through the western part of the Southern Highlands, on its way to becoming part of Sydney's water supply. There are also many smaller rivers and two large reservoirs: the Wingecarribee and Fitzroy Falls Dams.

History

The area's Aboriginal heritage is recalled in many places with Aboriginal names such as Wingecarribee, which means 'flight of birds', and Berrima, which means 'black swan'. The Wadi Wadi tribe inhabited the Southern Highlands for at least 40 000 years.

The initial European exploration of the area in 1798 was based on a rumour that had gained currency among the colony's convicts. They believed that China lay no

more than 150 miles (240km) from Sydney, and that in China they would find an easy, comfortable life. More realistic exploration began in 1815 when Surveyor-General John Oxley took his cattle into the region. Other settlers quickly followed and prospered, building large estates.

The first major township, at Bong Bong on the Wingecarribee River, was proposed in 1821. It was not a success; the site flooded very easily, and during drought the river dried up. The site of Berrima was chosen in 1829 and although it was planned as a main town of the district, it was bypassed by the railway during 1867 and never reached the prominence originally planned for it.

By the mid-19th century, wealthy city dwellers had discovered the cooler summer climate and the area became known as the 'sanatorium of the south'. It received the final imprint of society's approval in 1865 when the Government of NSW leased Throsby Park at Moss Vale as a summer residence for the Governor.

Getting there
By road

The most direct route to the Southern Highlands and Goulburn is via the F5

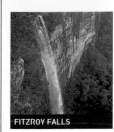

FITZROY FALLS

WOMBEYAN WATERFALLS

IT'S SHOWTIME!

The **Robertson and Moss Vale Shows** in Mar have been operating for over 100 years. Moss Vale Show has the biggest pavilion exhibit after the Royal Easter Show. Contact Tourism Southern Highlands.

Tollfree 1300 657 559

Fwy, accessible via the Hume Hwy (Hwy 31) from Liverpool. The F5 Mwy runs from King Georges Rd, Beverly Hills to the Hume Hwy. There are also roads leading inland from the coast to the Southern Highlands. The Princes Hwy (Hwy 1), is the coastal road south from Sydney. Route 69, a pleasant road to Appin and on to Picton, leaves Hwy 1 before Bulli.

Further south, at Wollongong, Route 88 leads to Picton. It offers both an impressive climb up Mt Keira and access to Cordeaux Reservoir which also has picnic facilities. Further south again, near Albion Park, the Illawarra Hwy (Hwy 48) leaves the Princes Hwy to climb the coastal escarpment via the spectacular Macquarie Pass. At the top is the town of Robertson, right on the edge of the Southern Highlands. Regular coach services run between Sydney, Canberra and the Highlands.

By rail

Train services to Mittagong, Bowral, Moss Vale, Bundanoon and Goulburn depart daily from Sydney's Central Stn.

Getting around

The Illawarra and Southern Highlands Tourist Railway, known as the **Cockatoo** Run (see also p.244), climbs from Port Kembla over the Illawarra Escarpment to the Southern Highlands along one of the most scenic rail routes in NSW. The train ride can be boarded at Sydney, Hurstville, Sutherland, Thirroul and Wollongong. Bookings essential. Freecall: 1300 653 801

Festivals and events

Exeter Olde English Village Fayre

Held on the 3rd Sat in Nov at Exeter Oval, this is a feast of entertainment, a great fun event. There is Morris dancing, a village maypole, hilarious Jack Russell terrier races and Indian runner duck races. Jesters, a Dutch street organ, music, steam train rides and medieval warriors fighting the Battle of Hastings are all part of the fun. Over 65 stalls sell a range of wearable, edible and usable goods, and the Exeter Arms sells Olde English Ale. Parking is free. Ph: (02) 4883 4078. www.exetervillage.com

Goulburn City Rose Festival

Held in Mar, and widely accepted as the best rose display outside the Sydney metropolitan area. Over 8000 named roses are displayed, including the 'City of Goulburn' rose, and the competitive section is strongly contested. Workshops

BOWRAL RAILWAY STATION

TULIP TIME FESTIVAL

celebration with over 100 000 tulips and 26 000 annuals in glorious bloom. Held from late Sept to the end of the Oct long weekend. The displays centre on mass plantings in **Corbett Gardens**, with a number of private gardens also open to the public. Admission charges apply. The festival includes other events such as exhibitions and organ recitals.

Goulburn Lilac City Festival
Held over the long weekend in Oct, the festival features numerous events such as a street carnival, window displays, parade, crowning of the festival queen, country markets, doll and teddy bear shows, live entertainment and fireworks. Many of the local gardens enter in the garden competition and are open for viewing during the festival.

Bong Bong Picnic Races
One of rural NSW's most anticipated race meetings, the Bong Bong Picnic Races are held each year in Nov. Entry is by membership only. Ph: (02) 4862 2155

Main localities and towns
Southern Highlands
Berrima Map 41 A2
The historic town of Berrima was founded in 1831 and several of its buildings are listed on the National Estate. Completed in 1838, the Berrima Court House is an outstanding example of Georgian architecture and houses a museum, the Petty Bookshop and Visitor Info Centre. A 15min video explains the town's history and a tableau and tape recording re-creates the trial of Lucretia Dunkley. Open daily, 10am–4pm. Ph: (02) 4877 1505. www.berrimacourthouse.org.au

Across the road is Berrima Gaol, opened in 1839 and now operating as a medium security prison.

Collect a brochure from the visitor centre and undertake a walking tour of the town, taking in the **Berrima District Historical Society Museum**. Open weekends and public holidays, 10am–4pm.

Harper's Mansion, one of the best examples of an 1830s townhouse in

with a panel of garden experts are part of the festival in a city famous for roses, lavender and lilac.

Bundanoon Highland Gathering (Brigadoon)
According to the Scottish myth, the sleeping village of Brigadoon only comes to life once a century. In **Bundanoon**, Brigadoon is celebrated every year on a Sat in Apr with the largest Scottish Highland gathering in Australia, attracting highland dancers and pipe bands and competitors from all over Australia. Traditional games include haggis hurling, shot put, kilted races and caber tossing. The games begin with a street parade and close with the haunting playing by the lone piper. www.highlandsnsw.com.au/brigadoon

A Winter Christmas
Rescheduling Christmas festivities to late Jun and early Jul, the people of the Highlands celebrate with Christmas fare, roaring log fires and occasionally even some snow. Many hotels and motels offer the mid-year celebrations, or visitors can share in the family atmosphere at one of the many guesthouses.

Tulip Time
The region's best known festival is **Bowral's** Tulip Time, an annual spring

WHITE HORSE INN, BERRIMA

BERRIMA CERAMICS

Berrima is full of shops selling arts, crafts and souvenirs. The **Bell Gallery** in Jellore St has a fine collection of leading contemporary Australian artists. Open Fri–Mon, 11am–4pm. Ph: (02) 4877 1267. For book lovers, **Berkelouw's Book Barn**, on the Old Hume Hwy, stocks 200 000 quality secondhand books and there is an antiquarian book section.

Picnic with an alpaca or browse through the wide range of alpaca products at the **Australian Alpaca Centre**, next to the Wingecarribee River. Ph: (02) 4877 1399

With all these treats available, Berrima is a great place to stay the weekend and has many B&Bs.

Bowral Map 41 C2

Bowral began as part of the estate of explorer John Oxley. Today it is a thriving town—the commercial centre of the Southern Highlands with many fine restaurants, cafes, boutiques and galleries, However, Bowral is best known for its association with the legendary cricketer, Sir Donald Bradman.

The **Bradman Museum**, located in St Jude St, overlooks **Bradman Oval** and Sir Donald's former home in Glebe St. It is regarded as the best cricket museum in the world. It offers a significant collection of cricket memorabilia including a history of The Ashes and Sir Donald. Open daily, 10am–4pm. Ph: (02) 4862 1247. The **Bradman Walk**, a self-guided tour of sites associated with Sir Donald, starts at the museum.

NSW, was built for the first licensee of the **Surveyor-General Inn**, Australia's oldest continually licensed hotel still trading within its original walls. Meals are available daily. Ph: (02) 4877 1226

The **White Horse Inn** was built by convict labour in 1832. It offers a unique dining experience in a range of dining areas, including five private dining rooms furnished with genuine antiques. It also has a teashop, outdoor eating area and accommodation. Ph: (02) 4877 1204. www.whitehorseinn.com.au

Excellent architecture can also be seen in the **Elingrange**, built in 1834 as a Cobb and Co staging house and brewery, now offering quality dining. Ph: (02) 4877 1977

Joadja — the tale of a ghost town

NSW has many ghost towns and one that recalls past industrial glory is the former shale mining town of Joadja (Map 40 C3, p.232). Located in a hidden valley not too distant from Mittagong, Joadja thrived in the late 19th century. Shale oil, from which kerosene, benzine, paraffin oils and other by-products were produced, was the treasured commodity beneath Joadja's valley floor.

Many miners were brought out from Scotland, as they had the necessary experience to mine the shale. At the peak period of production (when 100 000 barrels of kerosene were produced a year), up to 1200 people lived in the village. But electricity soon replaced kerosene as a source of power and by the first decade of the 20th century, the mines at Joadja had closed down.

Although **Corbett Gardens**, with its thousands of springtime tulips and flowers, is the centrepiece of the **Tulip Time Festival**, it is worth seeing any time of the year. Drive or walk along **Bendooley St** to admire the houses. Most are not open to the public. Some 19th century buildings include the **Court House** (1896), **Municipal Chambers** (1890) and **St Jude's Church** (1887).

At Bowral Primary School, the **Bowral Farmers Market** is held on the 2nd Sat of every month 8am–1pm.
Ph: (02) 4862 4910. **Bowral Markets** are held in the grounds of the Rudolph Steiner School on the 3rd Sun of each month. Ph: (02) 8250 2563

Just outside the town, **Mt Gibraltar** provides fine views of the area from four lookouts (see Map 42).

Bundanoon Map 40 C4

Part of Bundanoon's appeal is its proximity to the scenic splendour of **Morton**

BRADMAN OVAL

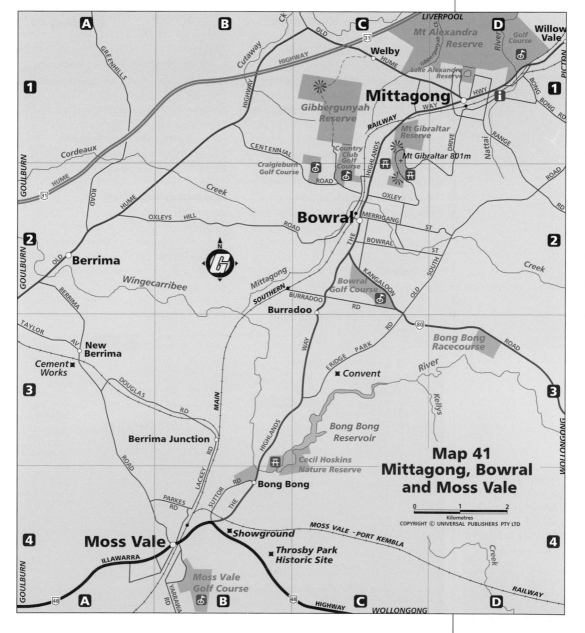

Map 41
Mittagong, Bowral and Moss Vale

0   1   2
Kilometres
COPYRIGHT © UNIVERSAL PUBLISHERS PTY LTD

MAIN STREET, BUNDANOON

NP (see p.243). A quiet, pretty town, Bundanoon was a favourite destination for honeymooners in the 1940s and continues to attract visitors.

The town is renowned for providing excellent accommodation and food, with an array of comfortable guest houses as well as the health resort **Solar Springs** (Ph: 02 4883 6027). Accommodation info is available from Tourism Southern Highlands.

For a weekend with a difference, the **Tree Tops Guesthouse** hosts Murder Mysteries from time to time; or just soak up the old world atmosphere and great food any weekend, Ph: (02) 4883 6372

Many visitors prefer to explore Bundanoon on foot or by bicycle (hired from **Ye Olde Bicycle Shop** in Church St). Ph: (02) 4883 6043. Take a torch and walk for 20min from William St to the **Glow Worm Glen** which becomes a fairyland after dark from Sept–May. The NPWS often conduct school holiday guided walks. To check dates, Ph: (02) 4887 7270

Bundanoon Pottery, Osborne St, specialises in decorative and functional wood-fired and gas-fired stoneware and ceramics. Open daily 10am–5pm Ph: (02) 4883 6453

Bundanoon Markets are held the 1st Sun of the month at the Memorial Hall.

En route to Bundanoon from Moss Vale, stop off at **The Village Pump**

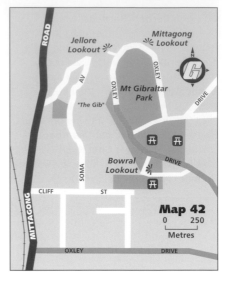

Map 42
0   250
Metres

Antiques at the main intersection in Exeter, packed with fascinating old items. **A Little Piece of Scotland**, Exeter Rd, Sutton Forest, is full of Scottish collectables and quality knits.

Burrawang Map 40 D4

West of Robertson, this quaint, sleepy village has a number of authentic colonial cottages. The **Burrawang Village Hotel** (1926) has been renovated and is popular for weekends away and casual dining in the picturesque open courtyard. Advance booking essential. Ph: (02) 4886 4206

MEDITATE

You can meditate every night at 7pm at Bundanoon's **Buddhist Monastery** which also provides accommodation. Open weekends for lunch. Bookings essential, Ph: (02) 4884 4262

VIEW FROM MT GIBRALTAR

On Easter Saturday each year, Burrawang hosts the biggest market day in the Southern Highlands, with everything from livestock to local produce, displays of specialty crafts, and workshops.

Kangaroo Valley Map 40 D4

Nestled among rolling green pastures backed by the steep, rainforested slopes of the escarpment SE of Moss Vale, this picturesque valley is a popular retreat for city dwellers. A few professional farmers remain in the valley, along with many hobby farmers. The village of Kangaroo Valley is steeped in history, with several national estate-listed buildings more than 100 years old. The quaint sandstone 1889 **Hampden Suspension Bridge** is Australia's oldest suspension bridge.

On the western side of the bridge, the **Pioneer Museum Park** is an excellent place to learn about local history. It features an 1860s homestead, early settler's hut, blacksmith's forge and reconstructed 1880s dairy. The Kangaroo Valley Markets are held here on the 2nd Sat of the month 10am–2pm. Open Fri–Mon 10am–4pm (summer), 11am–3pm (winter), daily during school holidays. Ph: (02) 4465 1306. www.kangaroovalley.net/members/pioneers

The village of Kangaroo Valley has several art, craft and antique shops, eating places and a good pub, the aptly named **Friendly Inn** (1892). To the west of Kangaroo Valley, the road ascends the precipitous **Barrengarry Mountain** with breathtaking vistas of palm-filled valleys opening up at every turn, and a lookout where the spectacular Fitzroy Falls can be viewed. The **Barrengarry Old Store** (1880) is an excellent example of an authentic old general store; it reputedly sells the world's best pies. Ph: (02) 4465 1360

Great picnic sites line the river and a booklet available from local shops, *Walks Guide — Kangaroo Valley and Adjacent NPs*, describes 25 walking tracks in the area, ranging from leisurely strolls to difficult walks,.

Kangaroo Valley Fruit World on Mt Skanzi Rd offers tours of a 15 000-tree orchard on a tractor train, a Friendship Farm, many activities and delicious fruit. Open daily, 10am–4pm, Ph: (02) 4465 1383

At **Upper Kangaroo River**, 13.5km NE of the village, are picnic and BBQ facilities and a remarkable wire suspension footbridge. Another 4.4km takes you to **Flat Rock**, one of the Valley's best swimming holes. There is also an excellent picnic area at **Bendeela**, 8km west of Kangaroo Valley.

More adventurous visitors can explore the valley's magnificent countryside by

KANGAROO VALLEY LANDSCAPE

MOONSHINE

The last of the moonshiners, **Granny Humphries**, used the Kangaroo River's waters to make her legendary drop. She died in 1906 aged 106, after drinking the last bottle!

booking a safari, an adventure canoeing trip or a horseriding tour (see p.245). www.kangaroovalleytourist.asn.au

Mittagong Map 41 C1

From Sydney, Mittagong is the first major town of the Southern Highlands. One of the town's greatest attractions is **Lake Alexandra**, an artificial lake set in a reserve. It is a pleasant picnic spot, and is home to a profusion of friendly birdlife. Access to the **Mt Alexandra Walking Trail** is from Queen St off the Old Hume Hwy.

The **Sturt Craft Centre**, cnr Waverley Pde and Range Rd, features pottery, weaving, glass and textiles workshops, with an exhibition gallery and craft shop. Open daily, 10am–5pm, Ph: (02) 4860 2083. **Mittagong Markets** are held on the 3rd Sat of each month 8am–3pm, Ph: (02) 4871 1354

For a wonderful **scenic drive**, take Range Rd from Mittagong to Glenquarry and then Route 80 back to Bowral.

The **Box Vale Mine Walking Track** follows an historic railway line built in 1888, passing through cuttings, embankments and an 84m long tunnel. The easy 4.4km track starts just off the Hume Hwy, 3.7km south of Mittagong.

North of Mittagong on the Old Hume Hwy is **All Aboard Braemar Model Railways**, with operating model trains, a garden railway, sales and cafe. Open daily 10am–4.30pm. Ph: (02) 4871 2966. www.allaboard.com.au

Moss Vale Map 41 A4

With its typically cooler Southern Highlands climate, Moss Vale became a popular retreat for Sydneysiders when the railway first reached the area. A highlight of the district is **Leighton Gardens**, a splendid park in the middle of Moss Vale. An historic walking tour brochure is available from Tourism Southern Highlands. **Browley**, **Yarrawa**, **Throsby** and **Argyle Sts** contain a variety of early housing styles. Other historic buildings include **Moss Vale Railway Stn** and **Moss Vale Public School** both built in 1867, and **Moss Vale Hotel** which was built in 1850 and where meals are now available. Ph: (02) 4868 1007

RURAL ROBERTSON

The **Southern Highlands Regional Gallery** in the Civic Centre, is an exhibition only gallery displaying local and national art. Open Mon–Fri, 9am–5pm.

Built in the 1830s, a gracious colonial Georgian residence is now contained within the **Throsby Park Historic Site**. It is one of the few homesteads within a day's drive of Sydney with farm buildings that reflect early rural lifestyles. Open by arrangement. Contact Fitzroy Falls Visitor Centre, Ph: (02) 4887 7270

Moss Vale has several antique shops, described in a brochure available from Tourism Southern Highlands. There is also an 18-hole championship **golf course** — one of the state's best.

Robertson Map 40 D4

Robertson's rich, red volcanic soils are ideal for growing vegetables and the town is the centre of the largest potato growing area in NSW. The surrounding rolling green hills provide some of the Highlands' prettiest scenery, as seen in the movie *Babe*. The drive from Robertson to Albion Park along the narrow, winding, rainforested **Macquarie Pass** is inspiring.

The town's main attraction is **Ranelagh House**, an English manor house built in 1924, now a private hotel. With wonderful views down the escarpment to the coast and surrounded by

HAMPDEN SUSPENSION BRIDGE, KANGAROO VALLEY

beautiful cool-climate gardens, Ranelagh is renowned for its Devonshire teas. Ph: (02) 4885 1111

Don't miss the **Robertson Pie Shop**, cnr Illawarra Hwy and Jamberoo Rd. Call in at **The Old Cheese Factory**, which manufactures and sells wonderful wooden toys, including dolls' houses, rocking horses, puzzles and trains, also gifts and crafts—there is something for everyone here. Open Mon–Fri 9am–5pm, Sat–Sun 10am–4pm, Ph: (02) 4885 1133

Just outside town in South St is the 2ha **Robertson Nature Reserve** containing one of the few remnants of Yarrawa Bush, the original rainforest that once covered the region. Its attractive paths provide easy wheelchair access. For rural scenery and the **Wingecarribee Reservoir**, divert off the Illawarra Hwy to the village of **Kangaloon**.

A pamphlet on the **Robertson Guild**, a cooperative of Highlands' arts and crafts people, is available from the Tourism Southern Highlands Office.

Wombeyan Caves Map 40 C3

On the road to Berrima, 5km west of Mittagong, is the turnoff to Wombeyan Caves. The 60km road is winding but the trip is most scenic. Caravanners should seek advice from the NRMA.

The caves are an awe-inspiring sight with stalactites, stalagmites, frozen cascades and waterfalls presenting a magical vista. Five cave tours are available, with the **Fig Tree Cave** self-guided. **Victoria Arch** is the place to spot rock wallabies at dusk.

Tent sites are plentiful but caravan sites are limited, there are also on-site cabins. Bookings essential There is a communal kitchen, BBQs and a kiosk. Ph: (02) 4843 5976

Southern Tablelands
Crookwell Map 40 B3

Situated on the Crookwell River NW of Goulburn, Crookwell is a commercial centre for the rich surrounding pastoral and agricultural area. Some of Australia's best wool, cattle and fat lambs are produced here, and local orchards produce a range of fruits. Crookwell is also home to Australia's first grid-connected wind farm.

The many rivers and creeks, as well as **Grabine SP**, provide wonderful opportunities for fishing, boating and watersports. Crookwell has many beautiful parks and gardens with glorious spring and autumn displays of colour. The town hosts festivals and events throughout the year, including rural shows, rodeos and the Autumn Festival. Several farms in the area offer **farmstays,** where visitors can experience a range of farming activities.

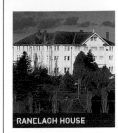

RANELAGH HOUSE

WOMBEYAN CAVES

JEMMY MOSS

Moss Vale is said to be named after Jemmy Moss, a herdsman once employed by the Throsby family who were granted land in the area by Governor Macquarie in 1819.

LOCK-UP

Goulburn's first lock-up was established as early as 1830. Floggings were common at the gallows, built in 1832. The original courthouse (pictured), built in 1849, is still standing today.

Goulburn Map 40 B4

Located in **Capital Country**, Goulburn was Australia's first inland city, proclaimed by Queen Victoria in 1863. The city has had a history in law enforcement since the 1830s, when it was the centre for police operations searching out bushrangers. Today it is the home of **Goulburn Gaol** and the **NSW Police Academy**, which is open for coach tours by appt, contact the Visitor Info Centre for details Ph: (02) 4823 4492.

Dominating the city is **Goulburn War Memorial and Museum** on Rocky Hill, which offers panoramic views of the surrounding countryside. The museum houses military memorabilia, available for viewing weekends and public holidays 11am–3pm. The **Lookout Gallery** at the top of the memorial is open daily 9am–5pm.

The famous explorer **William Hovell** is buried at **St Saviour's Cemetery**. One of the very finest white sandstone cathedrals in the southern hemisphere, **St Saviour's Anglican Cathedral** (1884) has stained glass windows, a magnificent organ and a bell tower. Volunteer guides are available most days to show visitors around the cathedral, or see it as part of the **Heritage Walking Tour**. Maps are available from the visitor centre. **Sts Peter and Paul's Old Cathedral** (1871) is also worth a visit.

Goulburn's many fine old buildings include the **St Clair Museum**, open weekends 1pm–4pm or by appt, Ph: (02) 4821 1156; **Garroorigang Homestead**, formerly a bullockies' inn and now a residence of the Hume family, guided tours by arrangement, Ph: (02) 4822 1931; and **South Hill Homestead and C19th School**, open for tours, an 1880s classroom experience and morning teas. Browse through its antiques, books and the animal art gallery. Bookings essential, Ph: (02) 4821 9591

The **Rail Heritage Centre** houses steam and veteran diesel locomotives, rolling stock and **The Roundhouse**, a heritage rail workshop. Open Tues–Sat, 10am–4pm. The **Old Goulburn Brewery** is Australia's oldest industrial and brewing complex. Tours and tastings available daily, Ph: (02) 4821 6071

The innovative **Goulburn Regional Gallery** presents a program of exhibitions showcasing art in its many forms, open Mon–Fri 10am–5pm, Sat and public holidays 1–4pm. Ph: (02) 4823 4443. For a peaceful day out in lovely surroundings visit **Mt Wayo Station Lavender Farm** Oct–May, Ph: (02) 4848 1255

Belmore Park is situated in the centre of the city on the site of the original marketplace (1843). Mature trees and flowers frame the beautiful Victorian architecture of the band rotunda and various civic monuments. Part of the park's Victorian heritage are six gas lamps remaining from the 1870s. The park's conservatory also houses excellent floral displays, rated equal to those in the botanic gardens of the capital cities.

On the southern outskirts is the **Big Merino Complex**, a giant replica of a ram standing 15m high, built in recognition of Goulburn's wool industry. Visitors can climb to the top for a ram's eye view. Open daily, 8am–8pm, Ph: (02) 4822 8011. At the **Pelican Sheep Station**, Braidwood Rd, tours and accommodation on this working property are available. Bookings essential, Ph: (02) 4821 4668

WORLD'S BIGGEST MERINO

GOULBURN'S HISTORIC COURT HOUSE

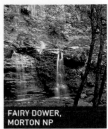

FAIRY DOWER,
MORTON NP

National Parks, State Recreation Areas and Reserves

Budderoo NP Map 40 D4

The NW section of this park contains **Carrington Falls**, a striking waterfall at the head of a sandstone gorge. The falls are accessible from a turnoff on Jamberoo Pass Rd, 8km SE of Robertson. **Thomas' Place** picnic area and eastern rim lookouts are found off the left-hand fork in the road, while **Nellies Glen** picnic area and swimming hole are accessed from the right-hand fork. Budderoo NP also includes **Minnamurra Falls** (see p.264). NPWS Ph: (02) 4236 0469 (Minnamurra) and (02) 4887 7270 (Fitzroy Falls).

Bungonia SRA Map 40 C4

The rugged scenery of Bungonia SRA in the Southern Tablelands offers caving, canyoning, canoeing and walking through the limestone gorge which towers over Bungonia Creek. The deepest **limestone caves** on the Australian mainland are protected here, but cavers must seek permission before venturing out. Booking is advisable for the camping ground which includes hot showers and a communal kitchen, Ph: (02) 4844 4277

Cecil Hoskins Nature Reserve Map 41 C3

Located 2km north of **Moss Vale**, the reserve has wetlands supporting over 90 bird species, about one-third of them waterfowl. The NPWS runs school holiday guided birdwatching walks in the summer months, Ph: (02) 4887 7270

Morton NP Map 40 C5

This park protects part of the Southern Highlands plateau as well as a stretch of the Illawarra Escarpment. Its northern section centres on the **Shoalhaven River** and tributaries, with impressive vertical cliff faces and beautiful, deep river gorges cut into sandstone.

From the Highlands, the park is accessible at Fitzroy Falls and Gambells Rest. About 20km from Moss Vale on the Nowra Rd, **Fitzroy Falls** has an excellent Visitor Centre, picnic huts and fireplaces. The falls plunge 81m over the sandstone cliffs into the rainforest of the Yarrunga Valley. Walks vary from short strolls to longer tracks along the western rim of the escarpment.

Accessible from Robertson or Fitzroy Falls, **Belmore Falls** is another highlight. The lookout on the northern side of the creek crossing provides views of the falls dropping twice into rocky pools, and a walking track leads to **Hindmarsh Lookout** with marvellous views of the **Kangaroo Valley**. Signposted 1km south of the Myra Vale turnoff, **Manning Lookout** has more views of the valley.

Gambells Rest near Bundanoon offers good picnic grounds and a small camping ground (bookings essential). There are excellent views from the lookouts at **Echo Pt**, **Grand Canyon** and **Beauchamps Cliffs**, all accessible by

TOP SPOT
On a hot summer's day, don't miss a swim at **Nellies Glen**, a beautiful shaded swimming hole on the road to **Carrington Falls**, much treasured by locals.

BELMORE FALLS

vehicle. **Badgery's** and **Long Pt Lookouts**, accessible from the Hume Hwy at Marulan, provide superb views of the upper reaches of the Shoalhaven.

Some 16 walking tracks thread the area, described in a NPWS leaflet. Morton NP also offers opportunities for extensive remote area bushwalking from a number of locations; backpack camping is permitted in most of the park. Ph: (02) 4887 7270

Parks and gardens

Open gardens

The Southern Highlands boasts an ever-growing number of beautiful private gardens which open for public inspection at different times of the year, usually during spring and autumn. Further details on open gardens can be obtained by contacting Tourism Southern Highlands.

Other attractions

Antique and art and craft shops

The Highlands boasts an abundance of antique and art and craft shops and galleries of all kinds. Details are provided in a brochure available from Tourism Southern Highlands.

The Cockatoo Run (heritage train)

The Cockatoo Run travels one of the most scenic railway lines in NSW. The train, with its traditional 1930s carriages, can be boarded at Sydney, Hurstville, Sutherland, Thirroul and Wollongong. The line climbs the escarpment (with amazing views of some of the best rainforest on the east coast), runs through tunnels and over a viaduct to Robertson. Stops are made at **Summit Tank** to admire the view and at **Ranelagh House**.

Passengers have time at **Robertson** to explore and have lunch at any one of a number of venues. The train operates Wed and Sun. Bookings essential, Ph: 1300 653 801

Wineries

There are an increasing number of wineries in the Highlands, many open for tastings and sales, including **Eling Forest Vineyard & Winery**, Hume Hwy, Sutton Forest. Open daily, 10am–5pm, Ph: (02) 4878 9499. On the corner of Joadja and Greenhills Rds, **Joadja Vineyard & Winery** is open daily, 10am–5pm, Ph: (02) 4878 5236, www.joadja.com. The **McVitty Grove Vineyard** also has a store selling delicious local produce. Tastings daily 10am–5pm, Ph: (02) 4878 5044. At **Mundrakoona Estate's** added attractions include a blacksmith's demonstration. The wrought-iron work made by the smithy is for sale. Open daily 10am–5pm. Ph: (02) 4872 1311. www.mundrakoona.com.au and www.artemiswine.com.au

FITZROY FALLS

Joadja Creek Heritage Tours
Map 40 C3

Built in the late 1870s to mine kerosene shale, Joadja today is a fascinating collection of ruins in a picturesque valley (see p.236). This sensitive site is National Estate and NSW Heritage listed and accessible to guided tours only and must be pre-booked. Joadja offers insights into the life and workings of an industrial centre of that time, as well as local history. Railway buffs will find info about the old railway particularly interesting. Open Wed–Sun, Ph: (02) 4878 5129

Montrose Berry Farm Map 40 C4

On the cnr of Exeter Rd and Ormond St, **Sutton Forest**, Montrose Berry Farm is a 'pick your own' berry farm. The shop sells jams, vinegars, pickles and chutney made from berries; frozen berries are available throughout the year. Picnics can be held in the gardens. Open 10am–5pm every weekend and Tues–Sun from Oct to Easter. Tours of the beautiful heritage-listed colonial house built in 1861 can be arranged for groups of 20 or more. Ph: (02) 4868 1544

Recreational activities

Water-based activities

A popular trip with canoeists is to launch in the **Kangaroo River** beneath Hampden Bridge at Kangaroo Valley, camp at **Bendeela** and paddle further up the river to **Tallowa Dam** (no camping). Canoes and kayaks and mountain bikes can be hired from the Kangaroo Valley Tourist Park and Kangaroo Valley Escapes, where a range of facilities and 'escapes' are available. Open daily 8am–8pm, Ph: (02) 4465 1310, www.kangaroovalleyescapes.com.au

Over 80km of the Kangaroo River is suitable for canoeing and **Kangaroo Valley Safaris** will plan your trip, hire canoes, tents and organise pickups and transfers. Ph: (02) 4465 1502, www.kangaroovalleycanoes.com.au

Learn the art of fly fishing with **Fly Fishing Southern Highlands NSW** Discover the secrets to mastering the art of fly rod casting and enjoy an introduction to the exciting world of fly

SUTTON FOREST

fishing in some of the Highlands most beautiful waterways. The Briars Country Lodge Lesson & Lunch package begins at 9am and finishes in time for lunch at the historic **Briars Inn**. Other packages on offer include the **Stay & Learn to Fly Fish Weekend Escape**. All equipment is provided, bookings essential, Ph: (02) 4868 3566 or (02) 4883 6324. www.ffshnsw.bigpondhosting.com

Horseriding

Tugalong Station, Tugalong Rd, Canyonleigh, offers supervised trail rides twice daily. Bookings essential, Ph: (02) 4878 9171. The **Man From Kangaroo Valley** offers trail rides weekends, and weekdays by appt only. Weekend getaways also available. Bookings essential, Ph: (02) 4465 1912. www. kangaroovalleyhorseriding.com

Fun for the young

★ All Aboard Braemar
  Model Railways (p.240)

★ Bradman Museum, Bowral (p.236)

★ Cockatoo Run Heritage
  Train Ride (p.244)

★ Cycling at Bundanoon (p.238)

★ Horseriding (p.245)

★ Rollerblade ramp at Loseby Park,
  Ascot Rd (behind Bowral Hospital)

★ Wombeyan Caves (p.241)

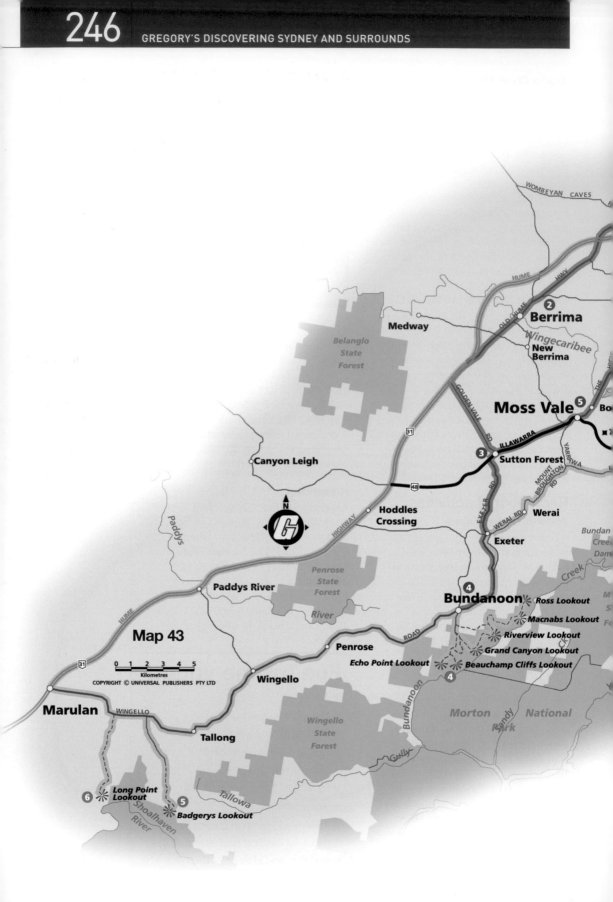

WOMBEYAN CAVES

HUME HWY

2 Berrima

Wingecaribee

New Berrima

Medway

Belanglo State Forest

OLD HUME

GOLDENVALE RD

THE HIGH

Moss Vale **5** Bo

31

ILLAWARRA

3 Sutton Forest

YARRAWA

Canyon Leigh

48

Werai

Bundan Creek Dam

MOUNT BROUGHTON RD

EXETER RD

WERAI RD

Paddys

Hoddles Crossing

HIGHWAY

Exeter

Creek

Penrose State Forest

Paddys River

River

4 Bundanoon

Ross Lookout

Macnabs Lookout

Riverview Lookout

Map 43

HUME

Penrose

Grand Canyon Lookout

Echo Point Lookout

Beauchamp Cliffs Lookout

4

BUNDANOON ROAD

0 1 2 3 4 5
Kilometres
COPYRIGHT © UNIVERSAL PUBLISHERS PTY LTD

31

Wingello

Marulan WINGELLO

Morton National

Randy Park

Wingello State Forest

Tallong

Tallowa

Gully

6 *Long Point Lookout*

5 *Badgerys Lookout*

Shoalhaven River

Suggested tours – Map 43

Waterfalls and lookouts tour

Approximate distance

120km from Sydney CBD to Mittagong; round trip tour from Mittagong (via Marulan) — 180km

About the tour

After the drive from Sydney, Lake Alexandra Reserve provides a great morning tea stop. The rest of this tour focuses on the outstanding natural features of the Southern Highlands, including Fitzroy Falls, the rugged scenery of Morton NP, and a number of excellent lookouts. Take your time, and enjoy the bushwalking, picnicking and photo opportunities.

Antiques tour

Approximate distance

120km from Sydney CBD to Mittagong; round trip tour from Mittagong (via Moss Vale) — 75km

About the tour

This trip offers plenty of opportunities to track down those elusive finds in one of the many antique shops of the Southern Highlands. A brochure outlining details of individual antique shops is available from Tourism Southern Highlands. Shopping and browsing can be combined with exploration of many historical features of interest, especially in Berrima and Moss Vale. If you decide to make a weekend of it, the area has many charming B&Bs and good restaurants to choose from.

RURAL SCENE IN THE SOUTHERN TABLELANDS

Places of interest (Waterfalls and lookouts)

❶ Lake Alexandra Reserve (p.240)
❷ Mt Gibraltar (p.237)
❸ Fitzroy Falls (p.243)
❹ Morton NP Lookouts: Echo Pt, Grand Canyon and Beauchamps Cliffs (p.243)
❺ Badgery's Lookout (p.244)
❻ Long Pt Lookout (p.244)

Places of interest (Antiques)

❶ Mittagong (p.240)
❷ Berrima (p.235)
❸ Sutton Forest (p.245)
❹ Bundanoon (p.238)
❺ Moss Vale (p.240)
❻ Bowral (p.236)

Radio stations

98 IFM: FM 98.1

Power FM: FM 94.9

Wave FM: FM 96.5

ABC Illawarra: FM 97.3

Tourism Radio: FM 88

Tourist information

**Booderee National Park and
Botanic Gardens Visitor Centre**
Jervis Bay Rd, Jervis Bay 2540
Ph: (02) 4443 0977
www.booderee.np.gov.au

**Kiama Visitor
Information Centre**
Blowhole Pt, Kiama 2533
Ph: (02) 4232 3322
Freecall: 1300 654 262
www.kiama.com.au

Shoalhaven Visitor Centre
cnr Princes Hwy and Pleasant Ave,
Nowra 2541
Ph: (02) 4421 0778
www.shoalhaven.nsw.gov.au

Tourism Shellharbour
Lamerton House, Lamerton Cres
Shellharbour City Centre 2529
Ph: (02) 4221 6169

**Tourism Wollongong
Visitors Centre**
93 Crown St, Wollongong 2500
Ph: (02) 4227 5545
Freecall: 1800 240 737
www.tourismwollongong.com

Ulladulla Visitor Centre
Civic Centre, Princes Hwy,
Ulladulla 2539
Ph: (02) 4455 1269
www.shoalhaven.nsw.gov.au

LEFT: ON THE BEACH AT JERVIS BAY

south coast and the illawarra

FROM THE NORTHERN Illawarra's sheer cliffs to the long, sandy beaches of the South Coast and the lush green hinterland, this region is a pleasure to behold and a marvellous place in which to unwind. The region's immaculate shoreline lures many looking for a break, but this is by no means the only reason to visit.

Surfing at Kiama, hang gliding at Stanwell Park, walking Wollongong's harbourfront, touring the Port Kembla Steelworks, fishing in Lake Illawarra, shopping at Berry, diving at Jervis Bay, cruising the Shoalhaven River, bushwalking at Minnamurra Falls, prawning at Burrill Lake, dolphin-spotting at Ulladulla — a vast range of activities and pastimes is on offer. Visitors can immerse themselves here for as little as a day or as long as they choose, because there is always something new to discover.

The Illawarra and the South Coast offer something for everyone. For those wanting to get back to nature, each headland reveals another stunning stretch of coastline, while lush rolling green hills, rainforest and unspoilt bushland offer numerous walking excursions. Visitors whose interests lie more in arts, crafts, history and rural retreats are also in for delightful surprises as they discover quaint village stores, local museums, rustic cafes and charming B&Bs in the many picturesque villages of this region.

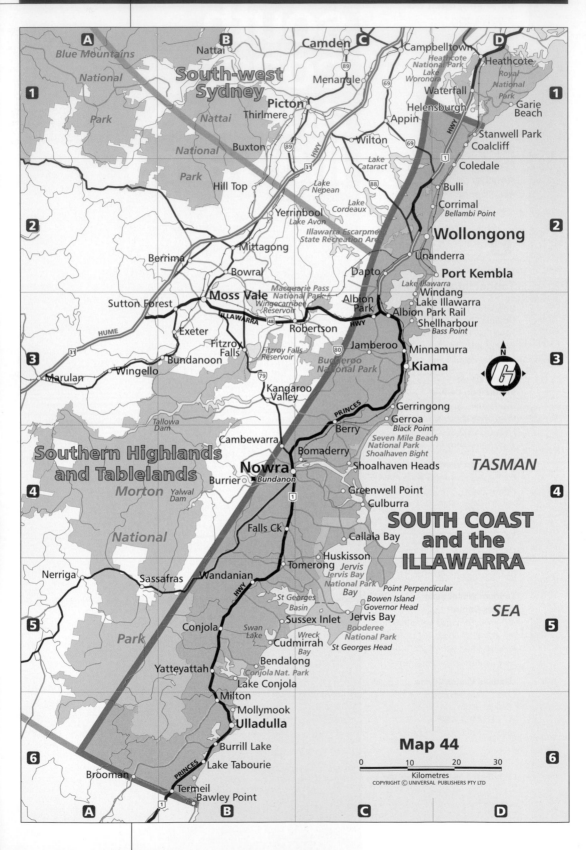

Blue Mountains
National
Park

A **B** Nattai **C** Camden Campbelltown **D** Heathcote

Heathcote National Park
Lake Woronora

South-west Sydney

Menangle

Waterfall

Royal
National
Park

1

Nattai

Picton
Thirlmere

Waterfall

Helensburgh

Garie Beach

Wilton

Appin

National

Buxton

Lake Cataract

Stanwell Park
Coalcliff

Park

Coledale

Hill Top

Lake Nepean

Bulli

Lake Cordeaux

Corrimal
Bellambi Point

2 Berrima

Yerrinbool
Lake Avon

Illawarra Escarpment
State Recreation Area

Wollongong

Mittagong

Bowral

Dapto

Unanderra

Port Kembla

Sutton Forest

Moss Vale

Wingecarribee
Reservoir

Macquarie Pass
National Park

Albion Park

Lake Illawarra

Windang
Lake Illawarra

Albion Park Rail

Shellharbour
Bass Point

3

HUME

Exeter

ILLAWARRA 48

Robertson

Jamberoo

Minnamurra

Fitzroy Falls

Fitzroy Falls
Reservoir

Budderoo
National Park

Kiama

Bundanoon

Marulan

Wingello

Kangaroo Valley

Gerringong

Gerroa
Black Point

PRINCES

Berry

Seven Mile Beach
National Park
Shoalhaven Bight

TASMAN

Tallowa Dam

Cambewarra

Bomaderry

Southern Highlands and Tablelands

Nowra

Burrier

Bundanon

Shoalhaven Heads

Morton

Yalwal Dam

Greenwell Point

Culburra

4

National

Falls Ck

SOUTH COAST

Callala Bay

and the

Nerriga

Sassafras

Wandanian

Huskisson

Tomerong

Jervis Bay
Jervis Bay
National Park
Bay

ILLAWARRA

Point Perpendicular

St Georges Basin

Bowen Island
Governor Head

SEA

Park

Conjola

Swan Lake

Sussex Inlet

Jervis Bay

Booderee
National Park

5

Cudmirrah
Bay

Wreck Bay

St Georges Head

Yatteyattah

Bendalong

Conjola Nat. Park

Lake Conjola

Milton

Mollymook

Ulladulla

Map 44

Burrill Lake

6

Brooman

PRINCES

Lake Tabourie

0   10   20   30

Termeil
Bawley Point

Kilometres
COPYRIGHT © UNIVERSAL PUBLISHERS PTY LTD

A **B** **C** **D**

Natural features

The northern part of this region is known as the Illawarra, corrupted from an Aboriginal word meaning 'between the high place and the sea'. South of Kiama, the South Coast officially begins.

A sandstone escarpment borders the whole coast, touching it north of Bulli and drawing further away in the south. The plateau rim consists of Hawkesbury sandstone, while the much softer Narrabeen shales beneath have been progressively weathered away, creating cliffs. The coastal plain, with its rich alluvial and basaltic soils, was once covered in red cedar forests, but now mainly supplies pasture for dairy herds.

The shoreline is interrupted by rocky headlands which provide spectacular lookouts, sheltered beaches and a great deal of variety to the coast. Some of the most beautiful and easily accessible waterfalls in Australia are found here, mostly in national parks or reserves.

History

A heavy surf pounded off the Five Islands (at today's city of Wollongong) when explorer Captain James Cook approached the coast in 1770. Had this not been the case, he would have landed on the Illawarra coastline; instead he continued to Botany Bay.

Initially, white settlement in the area was patchy, mostly consisting of timber cutters taking red cedar from the forests and whalers working out of Jervis Bay. Eventually, in 1822, Scotsman Alexander Berry established the settlement of Coolangatta on the Shoalhaven River, and things began to change as the area was opened up.

Subsequent development exploited the easily accessible coal seams under the escarpment for an iron and steel industry, and even now Port Kembla is a major steel-producing centre. By the late 1940s, Wollongong was the centre of a major industrial area.

The steelworks were once the lifeblood of Wollongong, but a downturn in steel and coal production has seen the city rebuilt on modern lines, turning to both high-tech industries and tourism. Wollongong is now the third largest city in NSW and the business hub of the Illawarra region.

Getting there

By road

From Sydney, travel south on the Princes Hwy (Hwy 1); Wollongong is 85km from Sydney, about a 1hr drive. The Kiama area is 120km from Sydney, about a 1.5hr drive, while Sydney to Nowra is 163km and takes about 2hr on the Princes Hwy.

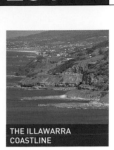
THE ILLAWARRA COASTLINE

WEATHERED SANDSTONE CLIFFS

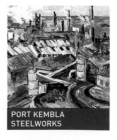
PORT KEMBLA STEELWORKS

ON THE COCKATOO RUN

Ulladulla is another 67km south. This is the most direct route, but there is often heavy fog on the Sydney to Wollongong stretch. For a scenic alternative route to the South Coast, take the Hume Hwy (Hwy 31) through Liverpool to Mittagong; turn off to Bowral and follow the signs to Kangaroo Valley and Nowra.

Another alternative scenic route to the Illawarra is the coast road, Route 68, which takes a left turn off Hwy 1 at Audley, 2km south of Sutherland, and runs through Royal NP to meet the coast at Otford. It then descends the escarpment and hugs the coastal cliffs through a number of picturesque villages to Thirroul, where the coastal plain begins to open out. It joins the road descending from Bulli Pass at Bulli and then continues to Wollongong.

Coaches travelling Hwy 1 between Sydney and Melbourne service the entire Illawarra and South Coast, and local coach lines run along the coast and across to the Southern Highlands.

By rail

Trains to the Illawarra and South Coast leave from Sydney's Central Stn. Most run to Dapto or Kiama or near Wollongong (90min), where they connect with services to Port Kembla or Bomaderry (a village just north of Nowra and the terminus for the South Coast line).

The **Cockatoo Run** rail service (see p.244) connects the coast with Robertson in the Southern Highlands. The route travels through some breathtaking countryside, and the trip from Unanderra to Robertson up the Illawarra Escarpment has been described as the best train trip in NSW.

Getting around

Dinky Di Tours offer personalised guided tours of the Illawarra area for tourists and special interest groups. They specialise in Australia's Industry World tours as well as tours of attractions such as Minnamurra Rainforest, Southern Highland wineries, Nan Tien Temple and Wollongong Harbour. Ph: (02) 4225 9464

Dark Cycle Harley Escorts offer tours of the scenic Illawarra region and surrounding areas on the back of a Harley Davidson motorcycle. For bookings Ph: (02) 4257 1714 or 0414 468 576

Take in **Kiama's** places of interest with a local **Taxi Tour**, Ph: (02) 4237 7505, or via **Kiama Coachlines**, Ph: (02) 4232 3466

In the **Ulladulla** area, **Blue Gum Tours** conduct sightseeing tours to the forest and mountain environments around Milton and Ulladulla, departing from Ulladulla Civic Centre. Ph: (02) 4455 1915

Festivals and events

Australia Day Festival

Held at **Wollongong's** Harbour Precincts on Australia Day, this event features a citizenship ceremony, entertainment, food and wine, stalls, amusement rides and fireworks.

Nowra Show

The Nowra Show, usually held in the 1st week of Feb, is one of the biggest two-day shows in NSW. It includes equestrian events, free entertainment, rodeo, harness racing, exhibits and rides.

Kiama Jazz Festival

On a weekend in Mar, Kiama comes to life with the sound of many different kinds of jazz. The festival has built up an enviable reputation in the jazz world, attracting top overseas artists and the cream of Australian bands.

Illawarra Folk Festival at Jamberoo

The pubs, parks and streets of Jamberoo provide the venue for a wide range of folk entertainment over a weekend in Sep.

Blessing of the Fleet

This annual **Ulladulla** festival held over Easter is based on a religious custom practised by Italian fishermen for many generations, with a parade, fireworks and the blessing of the colourfully decorated local fishing trawlers.

MULTICULTURAL FESTIVAL, WOLLONGONG

The **Ulladulla Festival of Food and Wine By the Sea** is held during Aug.

Milton Settlers Fair

Milton relives its pioneering past every Oct long weekend, with entertainment, exhibitions, markets, competitions and activities for children. Ph: (02) 4455 3056.

The quirky **Milton Scarecrow Festival** is held on the on the Jun long weekend.

Gerringong Street Festival and Parade

Held on the 1st Sat in Dec, this festival is organised by the Gerringong Sunrise Rotary Club.

Main towns and localities

The Illawarra
Bulli Map 44 D2

Bulli is steeped in history and the 1887 railway stn building has been restored to house a local museum. The **Black Diamond District Heritage Centre** features a signal box room, local railway memorabilia and history displays. 'Black Diamond' was the term for coal in the early days of Bulli settlement. Open Sun, 10am–4pm and by appt for groups during the week. Ph: (02) 4267 4312

Gerringong and Gerroa Map 44 C3

South of Kiama, don't miss the **Mt Pleasant Lookout** with its magnificent view of **Gerringong**. In Belinda St, Gerringong, is the 19th century **Old Schoolhouse Wool Workshop**, a unique timber building housing a range of woollen garments, Ph: (02) 4234 0065. The **Gerringong Heritage Centre**, Blackwood St, has some fascinating scale-model displays of buildings, European pioneers and much more. Open weekends, 1pm–4pm, Ph: (02) 4234 1796

On Headland Dr at **Gerroa**, the **Sir Charles Kingsford Smith Memorial and Lookout** commemorates the aviator's take-off from Seven Mile Beach for his first crossing of the Tasman Sea in 1933. It provides panoramic views of **Seven Mile Beach NP** (p.265) and Gerroa.

Both towns offer great beaches and fishing. For a picnic in Gerroa or

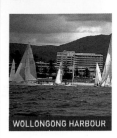
WOLLONGONG HARBOUR

BLACK DIAMOND DISTRICT HERITAGE CENTRE

OLD SCHOOLHOUSE WOOL WORKSHOP, GERRINGONG

Gerringong, try Boat Harbour or Seven Mile Beach NP, both with BBQs, or Crooked River Reserve and the northern end of Werri Beach.

Kiama Map 47

The approach to Kiama by road or rail from either direction offers excellent views, and the town itself is in a winning location with its rugged coast and pristine beaches.

Cathedral Rocks, 3km north of town, is a noted attraction and a photographer's delight. **Storm Bay** is a thrilling sight in stormy weather, and the adjacent pretty harbour provides some great fishing.

A variety of fish can be caught around Kiama's rocky shoreline. Diving and fishing charters are available from **Kiama Charter Service**, Ph: (02) 4237 8496 and **Kiama Harbour Game and Reef Fishing Charters**, Ph: (02) 4232 1725. **Surf**, **Jones** and **Bombo Beaches** are well known surfing spots.

Commenced in 1885, **Kiama Lighthouse** was completed in 1887 and is still a working lighthouse. The town's amazing **Blowhole** at Blowhole Pt sprays water 60m into the air. As it enlarges over time, its display is becoming far less regular than that of the **Little Blowhole** which is well worth a visit. See Map 45 (p.255) for a short walk that takes in the Little Blowhole (off Tingira Cr, hidden in a small reserve among the houses) and

Friars Cave, an enormous sea cave in the cliff face.

Also at Blowhole Pt is the carefully restored **Pilot's Cottage Museum**. Open Fri–Mon 11am–3pm, Ph: (02) 4232 1001. Kiama Visitor Info Centre is located next door and fresh seafood and fish and chips are available down near the harbour.

Known as **The Terrace**, the 1885 quarrymen's terrace houses in Collins St are the only example of weatherboard terraces in NSW. Now restored and containing a variety of art, craft and gift shops, they are Kiama's main shopping attraction.

A fascinating resource for genealogical research is **The Family History Centre** in Railway Pde, with a vast collection of records for public use. Open daily, 9.30am–4.30pm,Ph: (02) 4233 1122. The **Coach House Gallery and Craft Centre**, Farmers St, has local art and craft on display. Open weekends, public holidays and Thur–Fri during school holidays, 3pm–5pm, Ph: (02) 4232 3420

Seaside **markets** are held in Kiama on the 3rd Sun of each month at Black Beach, 9am–3.30pm. Ph: (02) 4237 6111. The **Kiama Produce Markets** are held on the 4th Sat of the month at Black Beach.

Picnic spots in Kiama include Coronation Park, Black Beach, Storm Bay and Hindmarsh Park (all with BBQs); and Blowhole Reserve and, a few km to the west, **Saddleback Mountain**.

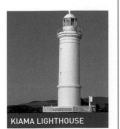

KIAMA LIGHTHOUSE

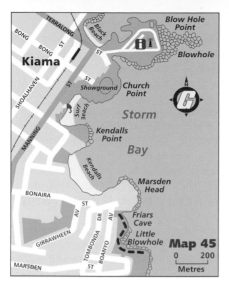

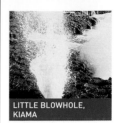

LITTLE BLOWHOLE, KIAMA

Track begins at Saddleback Mountain Lookout and leads up to the escarpment. For more excellent scenery follow Fountaindale Rd to **Jamberoo** (see p.258).

Lake Illawarra Map 44 C2

The lake offers birdwatching, fishing, prawning, sailing, waterskiing, catamaranning and canoeing. At the lovely **Reddall Reserve**, a bicycle track circles the lake and many walks follow its shoreline. A *Lake Illawarra Fishing Guide* pamphlet is available from Tourism Wollongong, and boats can be hired from **Windang Boat Shed**, Ph: (02) 4296 2015

A pamphlet outlining a walk along the cliffs and beaches of Kiama is available from Tourism Kiama. For lush, green hills reminiscent of Ireland, try the **Bushbank Mill Track**. A 2nd pamphlet, *Heritage Walks of Kiama and District*, lists 24 features of interest. Perhaps the best known building is the colourful **Post Office** (1889). Lining **Shoalhaven** and **Bong Bong Sts** is an impressive range of 19th and 20th century architecture.

From Kiama, follow the Jamberoo Rd to **Saddleback Mtn**, 600m above sea level. The views extend 240km along the coast, over the coastline, lush farming land and escarpment. The 1hr **Hoddles**

Shellharbour Map 44 C3

Shellharbour, named for the many local **Aboriginal shell middens**, is recognised as one of NSW's best **diving and snorkelling** locations. Dive shops are located in the main street, and Bass Pt (partly protected by a marine reserve) is a favoured diving spot. Shellharbour's sheltered harbour also offers safe boat launching for fishing enthusiasts, while the beaches attract surfers and beachcombers.

Stanwell Park Map 44 D1

In a beautiful location on the coast, Stanwell Park is a popular holiday spot with a good surf beach. Not far away to the north is **Bald Hill**, where hang

KIAMA BLOWHOLE

WINNING RESTAURANT

The **Ritzy Gritz Mexican Restaurant** at The Terrace in Kiama is a past winner of the 'Best Specialty Restaurant of the Year in NSW'. Ph: (02) 4232 1853

HANG GLIDING FROM
BALD HILL,
STANWELL PARK

gliders soar above the sheer cliffs and some of the most sensational scenery on the NSW coast.

Signposted from Stanwell Park railway stn is the **Wodi-Wodi Track**, a 6.5km round trip scenic walk. It takes in various sites associated with **Lawrence Hargrave**, the famous Australian aeronautical pioneer, as well as rare blackbutt forest, a picnic area and the Bullock Track, the first access route to the Illawarra for early settlers.

The drive south from Stanwell Park is spectacular as the road winds around the coastal cliffs with the towering **Illawarra Escarpment** to the west. Delightful beaches such as **Austinmer**, **Thirroul**, **Bulli** and **Bellambi** are found en route to Wollongong.

Wollongong Map 44 D2

The foreshore of Wollongong's small but busy harbour, **Belmore Basin**, is a pretty place for a stroll. A pamphlet available from Tourism Wollongong, *Wollongong Harbour Heritage Trail*, takes in 13 features including the old iron lighthouse commissioned in 1827. While at the harbour, remember to buy fresh fish from the **Wollongong Fish Markets**.

The **Heritage Harbour Walk** starts in Market Sq behind Wollongong Beach,

taking in the **Courthouse** (1886), **St Michael's Cathedral** (1859) and the Victorian **Post Office** in Crown St as well as the art gallery and museum.

Wollongong City Art Gallery in Burelli St has an absorbing collection of Australian art including Aboriginal works. Open Tues–Fri, 10am–5pm, weekends, noon–4pm, Ph: (02) 4228 7500. The **Wollongong City Mall** has interesting shops and pleasant open air eateries.

The city's first post office at Market St is now the **Illawarra Historical Society Museum**, open Thurs noon–3pm, weekends and public holidays 1pm–4pm, Ph: (02) 4228 7770. For something a little different, the **Science Centre and Planetarium**, Squires Way, Fairy Meadow, is a hands-on scientific museum with over 100 exhibits. Open 10am–4pm daily, weekends and holidays, 1pm–5pm. For group bookings at other times, Ph: (02) 4286 5000, (02) 4286 5022 (Science Centre shop).

The **Port Kembla** industrial area is Australia's most dynamic heavy industrial area. **Australia's Industry World** is the collective name for 15 working industrial sites and info on guided tours is available from Tourism Wollongong. Take the tourist drive around the **Port Kembla Steelworks**. Tours of the steelworks are available Wed and Fri, Ph: (02) 4275 7023.

The **Nan Tien Temple** at Berkeley Rd, **Berkeley** is accessible from the F6 Fwy and is the biggest Buddhist temple in the southern hemisphere. This outstanding temple includes a museum, pagoda, main shrine and meditation hall. Regular extra meditation classes are conducted and vegetarian lunches are available. In addition to the beauty and tranquility found here, the buildings themselves are of great architectural interest. Open Tues–Sun, 9am–5pm. The adjoining Pilgrim Lodge offers accommodation, Ph: (02) 4272 0600

In flowering season, mass plantings bloom at **Rhododendron Park**, Parrish Ave, **Mt Pleasant**. The gardens house a lake, BBQ facilities and several nature walks including a rainforest trail. Open year-round, weekends 10am–4pm, Tues,

COASTLINE FROM STANWELL PARK BEACH

WOLLONGONG BEACH

WOLLONGONG HARBOUR

RHODODENDRON PARK,
MT PLEASANT

8am–noon. With its theme plantings and duck ponds, the **Wollongong City Botanic Gardens** at Murphys Ave, Keiraville, is a wonderful place for a picnic.

The **Illawarra Motoring Museum**, Northcliffe Dr, Kembla Grange, features working exhibits. Devonshire teas and BBQ facilities are available. Open Sun, 10am–5pm, Ph: (02) 4228 7048. The **Illawarra Light Railway Museum** is at Tongarra Rd, Albion Park. Open 2nd Sun of the month Ph: (02) 4256 4637 or (02) 4256 4327

For keen anglers, there are various fishing charters that can be easily organised with local companies including **Delta Blue Fishing Charters**, Ph: (02) 4256 2159; **Access Charters**, Ph: (02) 4267 5262; and **Wollongong Boat Charter**, Ph: (02) 4256 6173

Inland
Berry Map 47

A picturesque village surrounded by rich dairy farming land, Berry is also known as 'Town of Trees' and attracts city people seeking the charms of country life. Many of Berry's buildings are classified by the **National Trust**.

The **Berry Museum** in Queen St traces the area's history from the days of cedar logging. Open weekends, school and public holidays, 10am–3pm. Ph: (02) 4464 3097.

The Post Office (1886) is beautifully restored as the **Postmasters Coffee House**. The CBC bank building (1889) is now the **Bunyip Inn Guesthouse** while the **Berry Hotel** (1883) has won an AHA Award for Excellence.

Berry abounds with art, craft and gift shops, boutiques and eating places. The

NAN TIEN TEMPLE

SURF SPOTS AND BOAT RAMPS

Local tips for the **best surfing beaches** include **Woonona**, **Corrimal** and **Bellambi**, which also has the area's most popular boat ramp. Other boat ramps are located at Austinmer, Wollongong, Berkeley and Windang.

HOLIDAY HOUSES, BAWLEY PT

WINNING RAINFOREST

Minnamurra Rainforest won the 1993, 1994 and 1995 NSW Tourism Award for Excellence in Environmental Tourism and the 1996 Australian Institute of Horticulture National Award of Excellence. More than 80 species of trees have been identified in the rainforest.

Great Southern Hotel has outdoor dining on the verandah. **Berry Stores** (1892) contain some interesting shops and businesses.

The **Berry Country Fair** is held on the 1st Sun of each month (9am–5pm) at Berry Showground, focusing on locally produced art, craft and food.

Jamberoo Map 47

Settled in the 1820s, Jamberoo Valley is one of the State's choicest **dairy areas**. The town itself has many inviting galleries, art and craft shops and seven cemeteries and is a popular weekend destination for Sydneysiders. A heritage walk pamphlet is available from Tourism Kiama, and the award-winning Minnamurra Rainforest (see p.264) is approximately 6km north of the village.

The **Jamberoo Hotel** (1857) is renowned for its Sun afternoon bands, with folk, jazz, blues, rock and more, Ph: (02) 4236 0270. The **Jamberoo Country Markets** are also held here on the last Sun of each month,9am–3.30pm.

Exciting family fun is on offer at **Jamberoo Recreation Park**, off Princes Hwy, with mountain bobsleds, giant waterslides, rock jump and mini-car racing. Also available are a restaurant, picnic and BBQ facilities, all with disabled access. Open weekends, public and school holidays, 10am–5pm, Ph: (02) 4236 0114

South Coast

Bawley Pt Map 44 B6

A quiet town 6km east of **Termeil** on the Princes Hwy, Bawley Pt is an appealing holiday spot with pleasant scenery, rocky headlands, coastal walks and empty beaches where warm currents extend the swimming season. Fishing, surfing, swimming and bushwalking are popular activities, and, in season, the nearby **lakes** of **Termeil**, **Meroo** and **Willinga** are full of prawns. On Bawley Pt Rd, just out of Termeil, is **Mimosa Hill Wildflower Farm**, with displays of both Australian and South African wildflowers.

Burrill Lake Map 44 B6

Just 5km south of **Ulladulla**, Burrill Lake is fringed with natural bushland and offers a large range of water-based pastimes including boating, sailing, windsurfing, waterskiing, swimming and prawning. Boats, sailboards, canoes, surf skis and kayaks can be hired on the lake which has three boat launching ramps, and **Burrill Lake Cruises** provide various cruises and fishing charters, Ph: (02) 4454 0657

Huskisson Map 46 B4

On the crystal clear waters of Currambene Creek and Jervis Bay, Huskisson is ideal for diving, beaches, fishing and bushwalking. **Prodive** organises snorkelling and scuba diving at the bay's most spectacular locations, Ph: (02) 4441 5255. **Jervis Bay Charters** has a comfortable cruiser, Ph: (02) 4441 7107

Dolphins, seals, fairy penguins and seasonally migrating whales frequent the area. **Dolphin Watch Cruises** organise a variety of trips in Jervis Bay. The two decks virtually guarantee a view of a dolphin pod, Ph: (02) 4441 6311. **Jervis Bay Kayak Co**, Huskisson, offers sea kayaking to various locations around Jervis Bay, ranging from half-day to week-long tours, Ph: (02) 4141 7157

Inspired by the return of the retired *Lady Denman*, a Sydney Harbour ferry built in Huskisson in 1911/1912, the *Lady Denman* **Heritage Complex** is a NSW Tourism award winner and includes a fish feeding harbour, maritime museum, mangrove boardwalk and bushwalk, and a gift shop. Open daily 10am–4pm, Ph: (02) 4441 5675

Jervis Bay Map 46 C4

Pronounced as it is spelt, the beaches of Jervis Bay are reputed to have the whitest sand in the world and is certainly a captivating spot for diving and watersports, with pristine beaches including **Cave**, **Murrays**, **Green Patch** and **Callala Beach** which offers excellent still-water swimming along its long white stretch. The gem of the area is **Currarong**, with a host of beaches, rockpools and secluded rocky coves, all delightful swimming places with crystal clear water. The surf at **Abraham's Bosom Beach** is small but the beach is extremely pretty. Divers' air is available from **Currarong Tourist Park**, Ph: 1300 555 515

Several walks crisscross the **Beecroft Headland** from **Abraham's Bosom Reserve**, including the track leading to **Whale Pt**, the site of the SS *Merimbula* wrecked in 1928, and on to **Honeysuckle Pt**. Superb views can be found on any of the tracks leading to the coast, especially at **Mermaid Inlet**, **Old Man's Hat** and **Beecroft Head**, but for one of the most dramatic views of the NSW coastline, follow the track to the cliffs from the Currarong water tower. Walk south about 50m from the end point of the

track along the clifftops to marvel at the towering sandstone cliffs, reputedly the highest on the east coast.

South of Currarong is a turnoff to **Pt Perpendicular**. As part of the RAN Weapons Range, this section of Beecroft Headland is often closed. Nevertheless, the **Pt Perpendicular Lighthouse** is well worth a visit, particularly for the stunning views. There are also several beautiful beaches and bays in this area, such as **Honeymoon Bay**, an ideal spot for snorkelling and swimming. Camping is only allowed at weekends and in school holidays. To book camping and check access to the headland ring the ranger, Ph: (02) 4448 3411

Lake Conjola Map 44 B5

A deep coastal lake flushed continually by the sea, lovely Lake Conjola is surrounded by small holiday villages with access to wonderful beaches, fishing, boating, surfing and walking. To the north, east off the Princes Hwy, is **Bendalong**. Perched around the lake are **Fishermans Paradise**, **Conjola Park** and **Lake Conjola**. **Green Island**, off **Cunjirong Pt**, is ideal for diving and surfing. Also on the lake is **Conjola NP** (see p.264).

JERVIS BAY SUNSET

A SAFE HAVEN

Abraham's Bosom Beach was the site where the shipwrecked passengers of the SS *Merimbula* (pictured) found safety. It is named after the Bosom of Abraham described in the Old Testament, where children found shelter and safety.

FOR THE THIRSTY

While in Huskisson don't miss a drink at the **Huskisson Pub**, known fondly by locals as 'The Husky'.

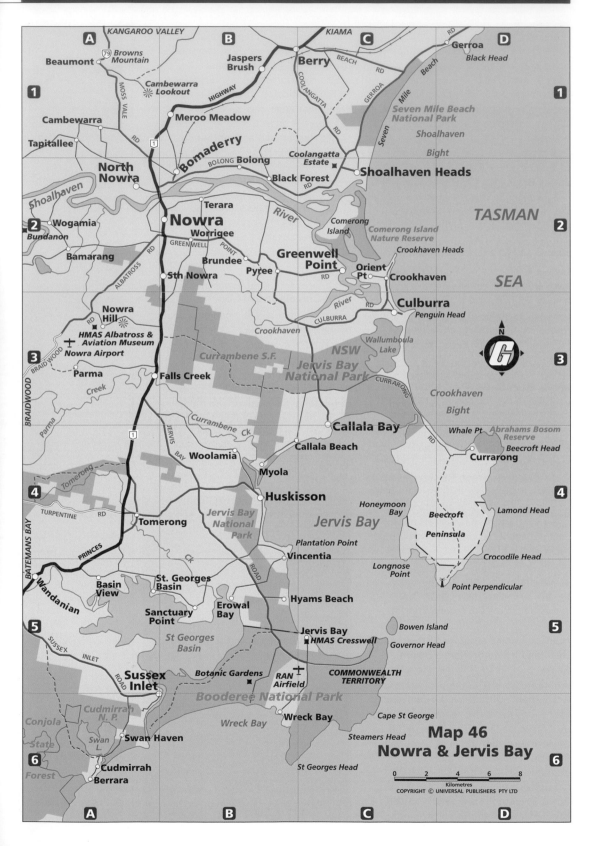

Map 46
Nowra & Jervis Bay

PT PERPENDICULAR LIGHTHOUSE

Lake Tabourie Map 44 B6

Like **Burrill Lake** to the north, Lake Tabourie is bordered by unspoilt bush and provides an important haven for native birdlife. Fish are plentiful and some inviting beaches line the coast nearby. The small town of **Tabourie Lake** has a boat ramp and is a good base for fishing and prawning. On the Princes Hwy, the **Lake Tabourie Museum** displays a diverse collection including Aboriginal artefacts, fossils and pioneering memorabilia. Open weekends, public and school holidays 10am–4pm Ph: (02) 4429 8915

Milton Map 44 B6

The historic town of Milton on the Princes Hwy has been classified by the **National Trust**. Milton was originally established as the centre of a rich farming area, and magnificent homesteads were built as the result of the area's prosperity. Some are still standing and can be visited today. The town's free visitors guide includes *A Stroll Around Milton*, describing places of interest.

Milton is also well-known for its art, crafts, antique shops and cafes, always worth a browse, particularly when the lively **Milton Flea Markets** are held, on the 1st Sat of each month.

Nowra Map 46 B2

Nowra is the **commercial centre** of the Shoalhaven region. Its many fine buildings include the sandstone **Presbyterian Church** built in the 1870s. On the corner of West and Worrigee Sts, **Meroogal Historic House** (1885) gives an insight into the family life of four generations of women who lived in the house. The house contains a fine collection of furniture and many interesting personal objects. Open Sat 1–5pm, Sun 10am–5pm; during Jan Thur–Sun 10am–5pm; groups by appt. Bookings essential, Ph: (02) 4421 8150

Nowra Wildlife Park, on the Shoalhaven's banks, with over 100 species of animals, birds and reptiles, is the largest native animal park on the south coast. Some of these animals can be patted and hand-fed. BBQ facilities, a picnic area and cafe are available. Open daily, 9am–5pm, Ph: (02) 4421 3949

Australia's Museum of Flight is owned and operated by the Australian Naval Aviation Museum Foundation. The museum is the country's premier aviation heritage institution, housing one of Australia's finest collections of historic military aircraft and memorabilia as well as a growing collection of civil aviation aircraft. A research centre is also available to the public. Located in Albatross Rd, overlooking **HMAS *Albatross***, 8km from Nowra. Open daily 10am–4pm.

LAKE CONJOLA

SAILBOARDING AT BURRILL LAKE

AUSTRALIA'S MUSEUM OF FLIGHT, NOWRA

Ph: (02) 4424 1920.
www.museum-of-flight.org.au
   Shoalhaven River Cruises run 2.5hr cruises of the Shoalhaven departing from Nowra Wharf. Food and drink available on board, bookings recommended. Ph: 0429 981 007. The adventurous can contact **Skydive Nowra**, Ph: 0419 446 904.

St Georges Basin and Swan Lake
Map 46 B5 & A6
St Georges Basin and Sanctuary Pt are small settlements located on **St Georges Basin**, a favourite spot for waterskiing, fishing, prawning, sailing and swimming. At the southern end of the inlet to the basin is **Sussex Inlet**, with wonderful beaches, fishing and boating. South of Sussex Inlet, the beaches at **Cudmirrah** and **Berrara** provide some great surfing. Behind the beaches, **Swan Lake** offers sheltered waters for swimming, waterskiing, windsurfing and fishing.

The Shoalhaven Coastal area
Map 46 C2
At the southern end of **Seven Mile Beach**, 15km east of Nowra, **Shoalhaven Heads** offers swimming, boating, bushwalking, and estuarine and beach fishing.
   Nearby **Coolangatta** was the first European settlement on the South Coast. The original convict-built village (1822) is

now the 130ha **Coolangatta Estate**, a winner of a NSW Tourism Award for Excellence. It features bushwalks, golf, restaurants and accommodation. Wine-tasting is available at **Coolangatta Estate Wines**. Open daily, 10am–5pm, Ph: (02) 4448 7131
   Also east of Nowra on the southern side of the Shoalhaven River are several small coastal towns famous for their oysters and fishing. **Crookhaven Heads** fronts onto the Shoalhaven as it flows into the ocean and has the area's largest boat ramp. **Greenwell Pt** is a top fishing spot also known for prawning and boating. On Lake Wollumboola, **Culburra Beach** offers fishing and prawning and a long strip of surfing beach.

Ulladulla and Mollymook Map 44 B6
The neighbouring towns of Ulladulla and Mollymook form a major coastal holiday destination with a large range of recreational activities, beaches and accommodation. **Mollymook Beach** is known for its excellent surf, with surf lifesaving championships frequently held here, and dolphins sometimes surf the waves. Mollymook also has two spectacular golf courses with ocean views.
   Ulladulla is the area's main commercial centre with an important fishing industry. The daily catch can be sampled at local restaurants, or bought

INDIGENOUS CULTURE

Coomee Nulunga
Cultural Tours can be
arranged by the
Budamura Aboriginal
Corporation at
Ulladulla. Boomerang
throwing, bush tucker
and dreaming stories
are offered.
Ph: (02) 4455 5883

ON THE COOMEE NULUNGA CULTURAL TRAIL

COOLANGATTA ESTATE

from the **Fishermen's Co-op** on the harbour, which houses the local fishing fleet. The town's natural assets can be appreciated by strolls in the **Ulladulla Wildflower Reserve**, at **South Pacific Heathland Reserve** or on the **Warden Head Lighthouse** and **Rock Platform** walks. For some Aboriginal history, walk the **Coomee Nulunga Cultural Trail**.

Located on the northern headland, **One Track for All** illustrates Aboriginal and non-Aboriginal history of the area through paintings and carvings. The trail is wheelchair accessible.

For those who want to get onto or into the water, **Ulladulla Boat Charters**, Princes Hwy, can organise boat charters for diving, fishing or pleasure, as well as scuba courses for beginners, Ph: (02) 4455 7255

National Parks, State Recreation Areas and Nature Reserves

Barren Grounds
Nature Reserve Map 47

On Jamberoo Pass Rd, this **heathland reserve** is a mass of **wildflowers** in spring and is renowned for its **birdlife** — the Reserve was created to protect the eastern bristlebird and ground parrot. There are good views of the coastline and countryside, Ph: (02) 4887 7270

Bass Pt Reserve and Killalea SP
Map 47

Near Shellharbour, **Bass Pt Reserve** with its rocky coves, sandy beaches and coastal rainforest is perfect for picnics, diving, snorkelling and fishing. **Bushrangers Bay** at Bass Pt is a well-known NSW location for scuba diving. A little further west of Bass Pt lies **Killalea SP** which is popular for surfing, fishing and diving; camp sites available, for info, Ph: (02) 4237 8589

Booderee NP and Botanic Gardens
Map 46 B6 & B5

Formerly Jervis Bay NP and Jervis Bay Botanic Gardens, these areas were handed back to the Wreck Bay Aboriginal community, who now jointly manage the park with the Federal Government. Booderee is a Dharga word for 'plenty of fish' or 'bay of plenty'.

The park encompasses most of Bherwerre Peninsula, the southern peninsula of Jervis Bay, a mecca for diving, snorkelling, swimming and bushwalking. **Cave Beach** has very good surfing conditions while **Murrays Beach** and **Green Patch** offer quieter waters, as do many other beaches. Camping is available at Bristol Pt, Cave Beach and Green Patch; bookings essential, Ph: (02) 4443 0977.

SOUTH COAST MARINE LIFE

Walking trails and fire trails are described in the pamphlet *Booderee NP Walking Trails*, available from the Visitor Centre. The walks encompass heath, tall eucalypt forest, pockets of rainforest, creeks, swamps, sandstone cliffs and secluded beaches.

Listed on the National Estate register, the **Cape St George Lighthouse**, also known as the Ruined Lighthouse, can be seen from a platform at the end of a short trail. At the turn of the century, explosive charges were used to reduce the tower of the ill-sited lighthouse. Sweeping coastal views encompass Bowen Island and Pt Perpendicular on the northern peninsula of Jervis Bay.

The main focus of Booderee Botanic Gardens is the coastal flora of SE Australia and Koori interpretation of the use of plants. The garden's facilities include nature walks and picnic areas. Open Mon–Fri, 8am–4pm, Sat–Sun and holidays, 10am–5pm (closed Sat from May–Sept), Ph: (02) 4442 1122 The garden has a public reference **herbarium** for use by those wishing to identify their own plants or for detailed study of the region's flora, for an appt, Ph: (02) 4442 1027.

Budderoo NP Map 47

This park has very good walking tracks across the plateau, including one that is wheelchair accessible. From the plateau

there are excellent views towards **Carrington Falls** and **Minnamurra Rainforest**, which is one of the South Coast's most delightful tourist attractions. An elevated boardwalk starts in the Visitor Info Centre and then winds through subtropical and temperate rainforest. A separate paved walk here leads to **Minnamurra Falls**.

The Visitor Info Centre provides souvenirs, cafe, BBQ and picnic facilities. The park is open daily, 9am–5pm (boardwalk closes 4pm) and entry fees apply, Ph: (02) 4236 0469. www.nationalparks.nsw.gov.au

Comerong Island Nature Reserve Map 46 C2

Access to this outstanding **wetlands reserve** (home to a variety of waterfowl and shore birds) is by car ferry across Berry's Canal, 10km east of Nowra. Swimming, fishing and walking are popular activities here. The reserve has a small grassed area for picnicking with access to ocean and estuary areas. Ph: (02) 4423 2170

Conjola NP Map 44 B5

The main method of access to this park, located on the shores of Lake Conjola, is by boat. The park protects important lake foreshore communities, including several threatened wildlife species. Some attractive picnic spots are located along the edge of the lake. Ph: (02) 4423 2170

Cudmirrah NP Map 46 A6

Just south of Sussex Inlet, Cudmirrah NP has extensive forest adjacent to beautiful coastal lakes and estuaries, ideal for picnics, walking, fishing and watersports. Ph: (02) 4423 2170

Illawarra Escarpment SRA Map 47

This SRA is accessible from Mt Keira Rd, 10km from Wollongong. It offers magnificent views from **Robertsons Lookout** at Mt Keira and rainforested escarpment walks. Ranger-led **Discovery Walks** are available. For program details or bookings, Ph: (02) 9542 0649. For further info, Ph: (02) 4225 1455

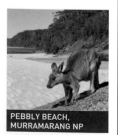

PEBBLY BEACH, MURRAMARANG NP

Macquarie Pass NP Map 47

Macquarie Pass NP preserves some of Australia's most southern subtropical rainforests, found growing on the rugged sandstone escarpment. Picnic areas are located at the foot of **Macquarie Pass** and at the end of Clover Hill Rd.

The park has three waterfalls. **The Cascades** is reached along a 2km return trail starting at the northern-most picnic area at the foot of the Pass. To view **Macquarie Falls**, take the Clover Hill picnic area turnoff from the Pass. A short but quite difficult walk upstream leads to **Balancing Rock** and **Rainbow Falls**. Backpack camping is permitted 1km or more from public access roads. Ph: (02) 4887 7270

Murramarang NP Map 44 B6

The main expanse of this park lies along the coast south of Kioloa, with quiet beaches, undisturbed coastline, native wildlife, offshore islands and beautiful **Lake Durras**. Also included in the park, just south of Bawley Pt, is **Murramarang Resort**, an important site for local Aboriginal people which protects a large midden containing diverse cultural remains. A self-guided walking track displays informative signs. Ph: (02) 4423 2170

Jervis Bay NP Map 46 C3

Near Booderee NP, this park also encompasses white, sandy beaches with safe swimming in crystal clear water at **Hyams Beach** (said to have the whitest sand in the world) and **Greenfields Beach**, linked by the **White Sands Walk** along the coast. The park contains a wide variety of vegetation and threatened species and is rich in Aboriginal heritage. Ph: (02) 4423 2170 weekdays, (02) 4887 7270 weekends.

Seven Mile Beach NP Map 46 C1

This park protects a long, sandy beach flanked by sand dunes between **Gerroa** and **Shoalhaven Heads**. There are excellent opportunities for swimming, fishing and picnicking in this park. Service trails allow exploration of the forest behind the dunes.

Parks and gardens

Bulli Pass Scenic Reserve Map 47

This reserve centres on **Sublime Pt**, **Hopetoun Park** and **Golden View Lookouts** on the Illawarra escarpment. Each lookout is accessible and signposted from the Princes Hwy. A number of tracks connect the lookouts and continue north along the escarpment from Sublime Pt. Info available from Tourism Wollongong.

Other attractions

Bundanon Map 46 A2

One of Shoalhaven's most treasured attractions is Bundanon. Arthur and Yvonne Boyd gifted this National Estate listed 1860s homestead on the Shoalhaven River to the nation. Arthur Boyd, who died in 1999, is one of Australia's most respected artists.

Guided tours of the homestead, artworks and Boyd's studio are available. The house contains antique furniture, letters, photographs, drawings and ceramics by four generations of the Boyd family and works by other artists such as Brett Whiteley and Charles Blackman. Visitors can take self-guided bush and river walks. For info regarding open days or mid-week bookings, Ph: (02) 4423 0433

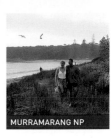

MURRAMARANG NP

ARTHUR BOYD (1920–1999) IN HIS STUDIO AT BUNDANON

Cambewarra Mountain Map 46 A1

Heading NW from Nowra, the scenic, rainforest-edged Moss Vale Rd ascends to Cambewarra Mountain. Soak up the glorious view from the **Cambewarra Mt Lookout** while enjoying a cuppa at the teahouse, open Fri–Sat 9am–9pm, Sun–Thur, 9am–5pm. Ph: (02) 4465 1321

Symbio Wildlife Gardens Map 47

On Lawrence Hargrave Dr at **Stanwell Tops**, the gardens feature 100 species of native and exotic animals. A great place to pat a koala, with BBQ facilities, kiosk, cafe and swimming pools. Open daily, 9.30am–5pm. Ph: (02) 4294 1244

Wineries Map 46 B1

There are a number of wineries in the Shoalhaven area, nearly all of them located in beautiful surroundings. Most wineries offer tastings and sales and provide facilities ranging from picnic areas to award-winning restaurants and accommodation. For more information contact Shoalhaven Visitor Centre Ph: (02) 4421 0778. www.shoalhaven.nsw.gov.au

Berry Wine Tours takes visitors on a tour of Jasper Valley Winery, Silos Estate, Cambewarra Estate and Coolangatta Estate. The tour departs from the Berry Hotel on Sat at 11am, for bookings Ph: (02) 4464 1011 or (02) 4448 3106.

Recreational activities

Bushwalking

Some of the Illawarra escarpment is developed specifically for bushwalking.

Fun for the young

★ Feeding the lorikeets at Bungalow Park, Burrill Lake, Ph: (02) 4455 1621

★ Funland Ulladulla, 93 Princes Hwy, Ulladulla, Ph: (02) 4455 3053

★ Hangdog Indoor Rock Climbing, Wollongong, Ph: (02) 4225 8369

★ Jamberoo Recreation Park (p.258)

★ Nowra Wildlife Park (p.261)

★ Shoalhaven Skateway, Narang Ave, Bomaderry, Ph: (02) 4423 0083

★ Symbio Wildlife Gardens (p.266)

★ The Science Centre, Wollongong (p.256)

★ Ulladulla Leisure Centre, cnr Green and Warden Sts, Ulladulla Ph: (02) 4455 3132

★ Ulladulla Skate Park, right at the end of Camden St, Ulladulla

Mt Kembla has a summit track and round track, while **Mt Keira** has a round track and the more strenuous and challenging **Dave Walsh's Track** leading to the **Five Islands Lookout**.

In the Kiama area, coastal and escarpment trails have been developed. Further details are available from the Kiama Visitors Centre, Ph: (02) 4232 3322

An excellent *Shoalhaven Bushwalks* booklet containing the most popular bushwalks in the area is available

CAMBEWARRA ESTATE

Cycling the 'Gong

A brochure outlining six cycling routes, their distances and a map is available from Tourism Wollongong.

The two most popular rides are along the coast. One commences alongside the beach at **Bulli** and ends at **Wollongong Harbour**, easily accessed from Bulli and Wollongong Railway Stns. It is a scenic, easy ride past beaches, saltwater pools at Towradgi, Woonona and North Wollongong and the Belmore Basin Lighthouse built in 1872. The other starts at Olympic Boulevard, **Port Kembla** and can be accessed from the railway stn. It follows the Lake Illawarra shoreline ending at The Esplanade, Warilla, but you can continue to Oak Flats Railway Stn.

The **MS** (Multiple Sclerosis) **Sydney to the 'Gong Ride** is usually held on the 1st Sun in Nov, Ph: (02) 9413 4166

SKYDIVE THE BEACH

from the Shoalhaven Visitor Centres at Nowra or Ulladulla.

Hang gliding
Bald Hill, near Stanwell Park, is regarded as one of Australia's safest hang gliding sites. For the experience of a lifetime and spectacular views of the coast and national park, fly tandem with **Sydney Hang Gliding Centre**, Ph: (02) 4294 4294

Horseriding
Kimberley Park Stud, Princes Hwy, Foxground, offers instructed trail rides, lessons and horse management, excellent for learners and children. Ph: (02) 4234 1134

Horseriding is also available at **Jamberoo Recreation Park** (see p.258) and **Timbertops** at Termeil, Ph: (02) 4457 1008.

Skydiving
Skydive the Beach offers the experience of a lifetime with NSW's only beach skydive. Operates daily sunrise to sunset, weather permitting. Ph: (02) 4225 8444, www.skydivethebeach.com

Watersports
Experience the fun of an aqua bike or canoe, contact Seven Mile Beach Holiday Park in Gerroa. Ph: 4234 1340

HANG GLIDING AT BALD HILL

Helensburg

Lawrence Hargrave
Memorial Lookout
Stanwell Park

Scarborough

Austinmer

Bulli Lookout
Bulli

Bellambi Point

TASMAN

Rhododendron Park

Botanic Gardens

Flagstaff Point
Figtree
Wollongong

Port Kembla Steelworks
Nan Tien Temple
Kembla
Grange
Port Kembla
Port Kembla Lookout

Dapto

Map 47

Lake
Illawarra

Windang

SEA

0   2   4   6   8   10
Kilometres
COPYRIGHT © UNIVERSAL PUBLISHERS PTY LTD

Blackbutt

Macquarie Pass
Macquarie Pass
National Park
Macquarie
ILLAWARRA   HWY
Albion
Park
Shellharbour

Bass Point

Killalea
State Recreation Area

Carrington
Falls
Minnamurra
Rainforest

Minamurra

Jamberoo

Blowhole
Kiama
Little Blowhole

Saddleback Mountain
Lookout

Mt Pleasant
Lookout

Gerringong

Gerroa
Black Head

PRINCES

Berry

Dharawal
State Recreation
Area

Lake
Cataract

Lake
Cordeaux

Lake
Avon

Kembla
State
Forest

Illawarra
Escarpment
State
Recreation
Area

Budderoo
National
Park

Barren
Grounds
Nature
Reserve

Rodway
Nature Reserve

Seven
Mile
Beach
Nat Park

Suggested tours – Map 47

Northern Illawarra and Wollongong tour

Approximate distance

50km from Sydney CBD to Helensburg; round trip tour from Helensburg — 90km

About this tour

The Northern Illawarra is a spectacular stretch of coastline with a number of excellent surfing beaches as well as some breathtaking views. The approach to it through Royal NP is also scenic with the lookout at Bald Hill providing some of the best coastal views in NSW.

The adventurous can enjoy a day of hang gliding at Bald Hill, Stanwell Tops. Further south, Wollongong and the surrounding areas offer a range of attractions from historical walks and beautiful gardens to the bustling fish markets. Make sure to take the time to stop at the biggest Buddhist temple in the southern hemisphere — you can even stay the night.

Wherever you go, there are arts, crafts and restaurants to be acquainted with.

Kiama, Gerringong and Jamberoo scenic tour

Approximate distance

60km from Helensburg to Albion Park; round trip tour from Albion Park — 110km

About this tour

This tour, which explores the South Coast, will reward the visitor with some of NSW's most stunning coastal and rural scenery. Nature lovers will especially appreciate the lush rainforests, sandy beaches, dramatic blowholes and outstanding views from lookouts such as Saddleback Mountain and Mt Pleasant.

Kiama, Berry and Jamberoo are picturesque towns with many points of historical interest and a variety of art, craft and gift shops and galleries. Jamberoo's recreation park is popular with families, and there are plenty of places to go prawning and fishing. There are also some fine walks in the area. The town of Gerringong is located on a magnificent stretch of beach, great for swimming, surfing and snorkelling.

Places of interest (Illawarra and Wollongong)

❶ Lawrence Hargrave Memorial Lookout, Bald Hill (p.256)
❷ Stanwell Park (p.255)
❸ Bulli (p.253)
❹ Wollongong Harbour Heritage Trail and Belmore Basin Historic Walk (p.256)
❺ Port Kembla Industrial Area Tourist Drive
❻ Nan Tien Temple (p.256)
❼ Wollongong Botanic Gardens (take turnoff to University and Botanic Gardens) (p.257)
❽ Rhododendron Park, Mt Pleasant (p.256)

Places of interest (Kiama, Gerringong and Jamberoo)

❶ The Terrace, Kiama (p.254)
❷ Blowhole Pt, Kiama (p.254)
❸ Little Blowhole, Tingira Cr, Kiama (p.254)
❹ Mt Pleasant Lookout (p.253)
❺ Gerringong (p.253)
❻ Berry (p.257)
❼ Saddleback Mountain Lookout (p.254)
❽ Jamberoo (p.258)
❾ Minnamurra Rainforest (p.264)

BLENHEIM BEACH, JERVIS BAY

Index and Gazetteer

Map Index

A

N

ACKNOWLEDGMENTS

The Publisher would like to gratefully acknowledge the following organisations and individuals for their generosity in supplying photographs and images, and for their permission to reproduce photographic material used in this book.

PO Box 228
Leura NSW 2780
Ph: 61 2 4782 4111
PO Box 19
Lithgow 2790
Ph: 61 2 6353 1859
www.bluemountainstourism.org.au

Tourism House
55 Harrington Street
The Rocks
NSW 2000
Ph: 61 2 9931 1111
Fax: 61 2 9931 1490
www.tourism.nsw.gov.au

Tourism New South Wales

Australian Aviation Museum Inc: p.126 top; Australia's Museum of Flight: p.262 top; Australian Reptile Park: p.145 top; Avoca Beach Theatre and Peter Hindemarsh: p.139 top right; Baha'i House of Worship and David Messent: p.65 bottom; Balloon Aloft Australia Pty Ltd: p.128 bottom; Barry Smith Photography: p.252 top; Bathurst Vintage Joyflights: p.213 bottom left; Bathurst Visitors Centre: p.212 bottom; Baulkham Hills Council: p.97 top right; Bicentennial Park Trust: p.108 bottom; Black Diamond District Heritage Centre (Inc) and Fay Haines, Honorary President: p.253 bottom right; Blair Egarr: p.60 top; p.82; p.83 bottom, top; p.203 bottom; BridgeClimb Sydney: p.48 top; Budamurra Aboriginal Corporation: p.262 bottom; Bundanon Trust: p.265 bottom; Cambewarra Estate: p.266 bottom; Camden Council and Camden Visitors Centre: p.121 bottom, top; p.123 bottom right; p.130; Campbelltown City Council and Quondong Visitor Information Centre: p.121 top; p.123 bottom left; p.125 bottom; Carisbrook Historic Homestead and Lane Cove Library: p.60 bottom; Central Coast Tourism Inc: p.136 bottom; p.138 top left; p.142 top; Clydesdales Restaurant: p.106 bottom left; City of Sydney: p.23 top left; p.28 top; Coolangatta Estate: p.263; Discover the Wonders of Greater Sydney, Graeme and Vivian Dubé Publishers: p.96 top; p.129 top; Fairfield City Council: p.118 bottom; p.120 top left; Fairfield City Council and Fairfield City Farm: p.120 top right; Featherdale Wildlife Park: p.110 bottom; Gledswood: p.127; p.131; Grant Nichol: p.46 bottom; p.53 bottom; p.58 bottom; p.63 top; p.64; p.70 top left; p.150; p.185 bottom right; p.188 top; p.191 bottom left; p.192 bottom; p.193 bottom, top left; p.194; p.198 bottom; p.199 top right; International Buddhist Association of Australia Incorporated: p.257 bottom; Hunter Valley Gardens: front cover top centre, p.158 top right; Jenni Carter, Art Gallery of New South Wales: p.81 bottom; Kandos Bicentennial Industrial Museum: p.219 bottom; Lithgow Visitor Information Centre: p.18, back cover top right; Liverpool Council: p.119 bottom;Local Images Pty Ltd, Craig Hempstead: p.73 bottom, top; p.86 top; p.90; Maitland Tourism: p.157 top; p.160 top left; top right; p161 top left; Manly Visitor Information Centre: p.47 top right; Mike Faulkner: p.76; National Parks and Wildlife Service: p.88 bottom left; p.136 bottom; National Parks and Wildlife Service, Blue Mountains District: p.226 top; Nutcote House: p.65 top; Ocean Planet: p.146 bottom; Oliver Strewe: p.165; Orange Visitors Centre: p.211 bottom; Parramatta City Council: p.95 top; p.96 bottom; p.100; p.101 bottom left, top left, top right; p.109 bottom; Penrith Whitewater: p.104; Roads and Traffic Authority, New South Wales: p.35; p.41 top; Robyn Egarr: p.251 bottom right; Royal Botanic Gardens Sydney: p.226 bottom; Sand Safaris: p.178; Shoalhaven City Council: p.261 bottom, top right; Skydive the Beach: p.267 top; State Theatre: p.31; Struggletown Fine Arts Complex and Malcolm Boyd: p.128 top; Sue Baker: p.251 bottom left; p.255 top; p.259 top; p.261 top left; p.269; Sydney Aboriginal Discoveries: p.53 top; Sydney Convention & Visitors Bureau: p.20 bottom; p.21 bottom; p.25 bottom; p.38 bottom; p.75 bottom right; Sydney Dance Company: p.24 bottom; Sydney Olympic Park: p.108 bottom, p.110 bottom, p.112 top; Sydney Tramway Museum: p.10 bottom; p.74 bottom; The Hawkesbury Gateway: p.55 top left; p.61 bottom; p.62 top right; p.98 bottom, top; p.107 bottom left; Tizzana Winery: p.107; Toboggan Hill Park: p.167 bottom right; Tobruk Merino Sheep Station: p.111; Tourism Kiama: p.254 top; True Blue Cruises: p.38 top;

Tourism New South Wales: front cover all except top centre; p.3; pp.6–7; p.9; p.10 top left, top right; p.11; p.12 bottom; p.13 top left; p.14; p.15 bottom, top; p.16; p.17 bottom, top; p.19 bottom, top; p.20 top; p.21 top; p. 24 top; p.25 top right; p.26; p.27 bottom, top; p.28 bottom; p.29; p.30; p.31; pp. 32-33; p.37; p.40; p.41 bottom; p.42 bottom, top; p.43; p.44 bottom, top; p.45 bottom, top; p.46 top, bottom left; p.47 top left; p.48 bottom; pp.51–52; p.54; p.55 bottom, top right; p.56; p.58 top; p.61; p.62 top left; p.63 bottom; p.66; p.69; p.68 top right; pp.70–71; p.73 bottom; p.74 top; p.75 bottom left; pp.77–78; p.79; p.80; p.81 bottom left, bottom right; p.84; p.85; p.86 bottom; p.87; p.88 top; p.89; pp.92–93; p.95; p.97 top left; p.99; p.101 bottom right; p.102; p.103; p.105; p.106 top; p.108 top; p.110 middle; p.112 bottom; pp.114–115; p.117; p.122; p.124 bottom; p.129 bottom; pp.132-34; p.137; p.138 top; p.139 left, bottom; p.140; p.141; p.142 bottom; p.143; p.144; p.149; p.151; p.154; p.155; p.156; 157 bottom; p.158; 159; p.162; p.163; p.164; p.165 top; p.166; p.167 bottom left, top; p.168; p.169; p.170; p.171; p.177; p.179; p.181; pp.182–83; p.185 bottom left, top; p.187 bottom, top; p.188 bottom; p.189; p.190 top left, top right; p.191 bottom right, top; p.192 top; p.193 right; p.195; p.196; p.197; p.198 top; p.199 top left, bottom; p.199 top left; p.200; p.201 bottom left, bottom right; p.202 bottom left, bottom right; p.203 top; p.208; p.212 top; p.213 bottom right, top; p.214 bottom, top; p.216 bottom; p.217 top left, top right; p.218; p.219 top; p.220 bottom, top; p.221 top; p.222; p.223; p.224 bottom, top left, top right; p.225 bottom, top; pp.229–30; p.233 bottom, top; p.234; p.235 top left, top right; p.236 top left, top right; p.237; p.238 bottom, top; p.239; p.240 bottom, top; p.241 bottom, top; p.242 bottom, top; 243; p.244 bottom, top; p.245; p.247; p.248; p.251 top; p.253 bottom left; p.254 bottom; p.255 bottom; p.256 bottom left, bottom right, top; p.257 top left, top right; p.258; p.259 bottom; p.264; p.265 top; p.267; p.269; back cover top left;

Wollondilly Visitor Information Centre: p.118 top; p.124 top; p.125 top; p.126 bottom;